RELIGION AND PUBLIC DOCTRINE IN MODERN ENGLAND

Cambridge Studies in the History and Theory of Politics

EDITORS
Maurice Cowling   G. R. Elton
J. R. Pole

RELIGION AND PUBLIC DOCTRINE IN MODERN ENGLAND

Volume II: Assaults

MAURICE COWLING
Fellow of Peterhouse, Cambridge

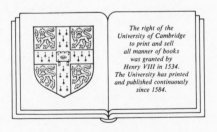

The right of the
University of Cambridge
to print and sell
all manner of books
was granted by
Henry VIII in 1534.
The University has printed
and published continuously
since 1584.

CAMBRIDGE UNIVERSITY PRESS

Cambridge

London   New York   New Rochelle

Melbourne   Sydney

Published by the Press Syndicate of the University of Cambridge
The Pitt Building, Trumpington Street, Cambridge CB2 1RP
32 East 57th Street, New York, NY 10022,USA
10 Stamford Road, Oakleigh, Melbourne 3166, Australia

First published 1985

Printed in Great Britain at the University Press, Cambridge

British Library cataloguing in publication data
Cowling, Maurice.
Religion and public doctrine in modern England.
–(Cambridge studies in the history and theory of politics)
Vol. 2 : Assaults
1. Sociology, Christian–England–History.
2. Conservatism–England–History–20th century
I. Title
301'.0942   BT738

Library of Congress cataloguing in publication data

(Revised for volume 2)

Cowling, Maurice.
Religion and public doctrine in modern England.
(Cambridge studies in the history and theory of politics)
Bibliography: v. 1, p. 469.
Includes index.
1. Sociology, Christian–England–History.
2. Conservatism–England–History.   3. England–Church history.
I. Title.   II. Series.
BR759.C67   274.2'08   80-40614

ISBN 0 521 23289 9 (vol. 1)
ISBN 0 521 25959 2 (vol. 2)

Foreword

As in Volume I, footnotes have been kept to a minimum, being normally biographies of thinkers mentioned in the text and being designed to illustrate the length and range of their literary lives rather than to provide bibliographical comprehensiveness. Where necessary, in order to keep tenses consistent or sentences in shape but without alteration of the meaning, alterations have been made in quotations which appear in the body of the text. The endnotes indicate the locations of all quotations as well as the sources from which the book has been constructed. There is no other bibliography since Volume III will include a bibliographical discussion of the subjects discussed in all three volumes.

For help in tracing articles and books or in checking references and proof-reading, the author is indebted to Mr Alun Vaughan and to librarians in the Cambridge University Library (especially Mr Nigel Hancock and Miss J. Fairholm). He is indebted to Mrs J. G. W. Davies and Mrs Pamela Stockham for typing, and to the Cambridge History Faculty and the British Academy for grants from their funds. Mr W. J. Davies, Mr Richard Fisher and Ms Linda Randall of the Cambridge University Press have helped in preparing the book for publication. The index has been prepared by Mrs I. K. McLean. Mrs H. M. Dunn, the Fellows' Secretary at Peterhouse, has given invaluable and unstinted help throughout.

For reading and commenting on parts of the typescript or for conversation or information relevant to it, the author is grateful to Mr Renford Bambrough, Dr John Beer, Dr Michael Bentley, Mr Michael Black, Dr Richard Brent, Mr A. Carr, Dr J. C. D. Clark, Mr David Cooper, Professor Timothy Fuller, Mr Peter Fuller, Mr John Gale, Mr Martin Golding, Dr J. H. Grainger, Professor Richard Griffiths, Dr Boyd Hilton, Dr Paul Hopkins, Dr Harold James, Mr Colin Kleanthous, Dr Roger Lovatt, Mr J. McGeachie, Dr Roderick Munday, the Rev. Dr E. R. Norman, Dr Roger Scruton, Mr Stephen Taylor, Professor and Mrs J. R. Vincent, Dr John Walsh, Dr David Watkin, Mr Hywel Williams, Mr Ian Willison and Mr B. H. G. Wormald. For

v

747 58

reading and commenting on the type script as a whole the author is grateful to Mr Charles Covell, Mr Ian Harris, Professor E. Kedourie and Dr Jonathan Parry. The Master and Fellows of Peterhouse have continued to provide conditions in which work can be done, the Master, Lord Dacre, in particular, by reason of the brilliance of his enmities, the Enlightened nature of his sympathies and the chronologically locatable character of his distaste for intellectual Toryism and ecclesiastical Christianity, providing goads and spurs of the impact of which he has almost certainly been unaware.

November 1984   MAURICE COWLING

Contents

Projected contents of Volume III
(for publication c. 1988–90)

INTRODUCTION

I THE CHRISTIAN INTELLECT AND MODERN THOUGHT IN MODERN ENGLAND

II THE POST-CHRISTIAN CONSENSUS

CONCLUSION: RELIGION AND PUBLIC DOCTRINE IN MODERN ENGLAND

'A great man does not sit down to work, out of some intellectual notion of advancing his science or department ... The great books of any time are those which are called forth by the consciousness that there is some great work to be done.' Rev. E. B. Pusey *Collegiate and Professorial Lectures and Discipline* 1854 p. 43.

'To hasten this slow process of disintegration, to dissolve the old associations of ideas, and bring about their crystallisation round a new framework of theory, is a task to be performed slowly and tentatively even by the acutest intellects. Even when the reason has performed its part, the imagination lags behind. We may be convinced of the truth of every separate step in a scientific demonstration ... and yet the concrete picture which habitually rises before our mind's eye may express the crude old theories which we have ostensibly abandoned ... It is no wonder, then, if the belief, even of cultivated minds, is often a heterogeneous mixture of elements representing various stages of thought; whilst in different social strata we may find specimens of opinions derived from every age of mankind. When opinion has passed into this heterogeneous state, the first step has been taken towards a complete transformation.' Leslie Stephen *History of English Thought in the Eighteenth Century* 1876 vol. i p. 5.

'I am speaking of evils which in their intensity and breadth are peculiar to these times. But I have not yet spoken of the root of all these falsehoods – the root as it ever has been, but hidden; but in this age exposed to view and unblushingly avowed ... I mean the spirit of infidelity ... You will find, certainly in the future, nay more, *even now*, ... that the writers and thinkers of the day do not even believe there is a God. They do not believe ... the *object* – a God personal, a Providence, and a moral Governor; and ... what they *do* believe, viz., that there is some first cause or other, they do not believe with faith, absolutely, but as a probability.

You will say that their theories have been in the world and are no new thing. No. Individuals have put them forth, but they have not been current and popular ideas. Christianity has never yet had experience of a world simply irreligious.' Rev. J. H. Newman *The Infidelity of the Future, Sermon at the Opening of St Bernard's Seminary, Olton, October 2 1873*, in C. S. Dessain (ed.) *Collected Sermons of Cardinal Newman* 1957 pp. 122–3.

INTRODUCTION

Introduction

I

In *Religion and Public Doctrine* Volume I the author presented himself as the creation, or victim, of an intellectual experience. Volume I was not, however, an autobiography. What it did was extract from the experience it described prescriptive guidance about the ways in which England and the history of English thought should be understood.

From now on the author will evaporate. The rest of the work will display the assumptions that were displayed in Volume I but with a detachment which was absent there. In Volumes II and III the author will neither breathe down his own neck nor breathe down the reader's; here, so far as he can, he will deal with the past-as-it-was.

The past-as-it-was is an artifice, an irrecoverable entity which has little value except as illusion. The past-as-it-was is so intimately connected with the historian's mentality and reflects so much what the historian means that it ought theoretically to be avoided. In practice, of course, it cannot be avoided and nor is it avoided here. Pasts have to be displayed, and the past that is displayed here is a past whose leading feature is the erosion of English Christianity.

In England the erosion of Christianity has been irregular and has been closely connected with the revival of religion, beginning with the revivals of Christianity which were effected by Methodism, Evangelicalism and Tractarianism, continuing through the revivals of religion which were effected by Christianity's assailants, and being halted only when higher education, culture, science and respectability established an institutionalized neutrality between four conflicting attitudes in the twentieth century. Each of these attitudes has been an attitude to Christianity. Each has embodied an intellectual interest and each has produced a voluminous literature dedicated to its propagation. The aim in these volumes will be to unearth the assumptions in which these interests have been embedded, to examine examples of the literatures by which they have been upheld and to sketch the tensions through which they have been related to one another.

The four attitudes are as follows. First, there has been a demand that the enmity towards Christianity which had begun in the eighteenth century should be put through an intellectual mangle and destroyed. Second, there has been an attitude of hostility to Christianity issuing in systematic demands for its supersession. Third, there have been attempts to protect Christianity by showing that it can cohere with non-Christian or anti-Christian thought, or can survive on sufferance alongside them. Finally, there has been an attitude which has assumed that both Christian and anti-Christian thought can be bypassed or absorbed so long as religion is interpreted as normality, sincerity, decency, science, scholarship, discrimination, or whatever secular value is held up for admiration.

These attitudes form the subjects of the six Parts which will make up this volume and the next. They will be presented in the forms they have taken in the writings of about eighty thinkers. Many other thinkers were available for consideration; those who have been considered combined explicitness of argument, comprehensiveness of range and that capacity to exemplify which permits an historical statement to be made through the intellectual biographies of representative individuals.

The idea of exemplification by representative individuals is fundamental. Almost all the thinkers discussed here commanded extensive attention among the educated classes and were able to do so as much because they were receptive to prevailing ideas as because they gave new twists to them. Few of their ideas were new. Some of them had been discussed continuously since the Reformation and many more since the French Revolution; they came to appear original only in so far as the thinkers concerned altered relations between them, stamped them with their own minds and styles, and sent them off into the future with a transformed significance.

The achievement of the thinkers who are to be discussed in Part I was to lay the foundations for the only powerful assaults on the enemies of Christianity that have been made in England since the early nineteenth century. These assaults were varied in range and content. But they were all set off by hostility to the eighteenth century and by the bitter belief that something wicked had been done to Christianity since 1688. It was this that supplied the stimulus to counter-revolution, the animus against Victorian Infidelity and the impetus to belligerence which the Roman Catholic thinkers discussed in Part IV were to renew in face of the indifference they were to intuit once Infidelity had been turned from an argument into an assumption.

Parts II and III will discuss the assaults on Christianity which have been made since 1840. There had been assaults before 1840, and many of the writers who wrote after 1840 assumed that their own assaults were continuations of them. The eighteenth-century assaults, however, had been elbowed aside by Romanticism, evolutionary or historical science and the reconstruction that was implicit in the French Revolution. It is because thought had been complicated in these ways that 'The Assault on Christianity' begins with Mill, whose intellectual development summarized the transition, and goes on to Buckle, Lewes, George Eliot, Spencer, Huxley, Tyndall, Stephen, Harrison, Morley and Reade in one direction and to Tylor, Frazer, Murray, Wells, Shaw, Ellis, Maugham, Russell and D. H. Lawrence in another.

Alongside the Tractarian and Roman Catholic counter-revolutions discussed in Parts I and IV, there have in the period covered by this book been many types of apology for Anglicanism, Roman Catholicism and Nonconformity and innumerable statements of the claim that Christianity is capable of accommodating itself to any power that modern thought might establish – astronomy, geology, history, anthropology, philosophy, psychology and sociology in one mode, Rationalism, Liberalism, Socialism, Feminism, Marxism, Conservatism, sexual permissiveness, even Infidelity, in another. Evangelical and ritualistic mindlessness, the more central apologies for Anglicanism, Roman Catholicism and Nonconformity, and the sometimes painful combination of solemnity, patience, timidity, earnestness, long-suffering, scholarship and virtue embodied in the accommodating type of Christianity, will supply the subject for 'The Christian Intellect and Modern Thought in Modern England' in the first Part of Volume III.

The attempt to reconcile it to modern thought and to proclaim modern thought's powerlessness to harm it have been leading features of twentieth-century English Christianity, but in spite of a visibly continuous presence in English life, there has been a fundamental deterioration in Christianity's power and influence. The concluding Part of Volume III – 'The Post-Christian Consensus' – will reflect this deterioration. It will assume that twentieth-century indifference is more fundamental than Victorian Infidelity and that its depth and pervasiveness are to be measured not so much by external observance as by an internal transformation resulting from the successful propagation and unselfconscious acceptance of simplified variants of the arguments and assumptions that were the stock-in-trade of the thinkers discussed in 'The Assault on Christianity' and 'The Assault on Christianity in the Twentieth Century'.

These arguments and assumptions were the outcome of a discussion in which Jewish, Greek, Latin and Christian thinkers, and Western European thinkers from Alcuin to Goethe and Goethe to Freud, have been as important as the Empiricism, Romanticism, Darwinianism and lapsed-Protestant virtue of the English. In each generation in England the discussion has been anglicized; in the last half-century it has been freed from animus and assault and has contributed to the entrenchment of a body of prejudices which is not very different from that described in 'The Christian Intellect and Modern Thought in Modern England'. These prejudices constitute the most influential of contemporary mentalities. In 'The Post-Christian Consensus' they will be considered both as post-Christian analogues to the types of accommodating Christianity and as heirs to the types of normal thought which the English would have projected upon the world if they had not lost the will to do so.

There is, therefore, a fundamental difference between the present volume and Volume III. In Volume III the subject will be the accommodations which have been effected as the anti-Christian and Christian armies have moved towards common positions. In this volume the subject is the tension which has arisen as the anti-Christian and Christian armies have met in battle – on the anti-Christian side through the line of thinkers which runs from Mill to Morley and Murray to Russell, on the Christian side through the line which runs from Keble to Manning and Patmore to Greene. This has been the critical tension, and the reason for devoting a separate volume to it is that, if a strenuous battle had not been fought by the thinkers discussed here, the blander accommodators of Volume III would have had nothing to be bland about.

A work of this sort ignores the subtleties and coerces the intentions of the thinkers it discusses. It puts a straitjacket on literature and refuses to linger over its complications. It insists on its own interpretation and depends for its power on the plausibility of imposing it on the thinkers whose significance it is designed to illuminate.

In this connection a problem arises about the relationship between what thinkers thought or said they were doing and what interpretation represents them as doing. Most thinkers discussed in this volume, whether Christian or anti-Christian, can be represented as earning a living, pursuing a vocation or relieving their minds by imposing them on the printed page. They can also be represented as claiming for themselves the attention which the clergy had claimed in the Middle Ages and as displaying moral concern or social anxiety about the philistine, democratic or proletarian threats which they believed were threatening literacy, civility and intelligentsia- and bourgeois-security.

Statements to this effect can be found in the writings of most thinkers in both groups. In neither group, however, were literacy, civility and security the predominant preoccupations which, as both groups understood it, were religion and the arguments that would need to be established in order to effect a religious reconstruction. All the thinkers concerned, whatever attitude they took to Christianity, took religion seriously, declined to explain it away in terms of something else, and assumed that the search for a right religion was a matter of the gravest consequence. And this is the point at which in this volume the argument stops. It assumes that religion is ultimate and ubiquitous and cannot be explained away in terms of something else, and that an essential preliminary to a comprehensive account of its rôle in contemporary English life is to describe the views which the English intelligentsia has taken of it during the century and a half which began when the religious structure of the ancien régime which had survived Pitt and the Jacobins was undermined by Wellington and Peel.

The régime whose destruction began in 1828 was the Anglican régime which had been created at the Reformation, consolidated during the reign of Elizabeth, destroyed in 1649, given new teeth in 1662 and made central by Sancroft in 1688. This régime was not as the Tractarians came to imagine it once they had turned against it; in some respects it came closer to the ideal they held up for admiration than any régime they could have expected to replace it with. But they were right to point out that, whatever intellectual influence had been acquired by Anglicanism's enemies previously or was to be retained by the Anglican Establishment thereafter, 1828/9 put the writing on the wall for Anglican pre-eminence in a confessional state. They were right to add that the repeal of the Test Act and the removal of Roman Catholic disabilities announced a future in which the Church of England would be competing on equal terms with Catholicism, Dissent, Judaism and Infidelity at the same time as the ancien régime was replaced by the more mobile régime symbolized by the railways, the Municipal Corporations Act, the provincial press, the extension of the Industrial Revolution beyond the iron and cotton and the expanded constituencies that were created by Reform Acts of 1832, 1867, 1884, 1918 and 1928.

The supersession of the ancien régime was a gradual process masking a general crisis in which social and ideological continuities were less significant than the chronological simultaneity between the death of Anglican pre-eminence and the death of gentry and aristocratic pre-eminence. Between these two deaths the connections were complicated since many of the defenders of the ancien régime had been willing to soften, or abandon, its Anglicanism in order to protect it, and the Church of England, once deprived of pre-eminence, began slowly and disingenuously to make a virtue of detachment from unreconstructed political establishments. In this volume, nevertheless, the two deaths are inseparable. The thinkers it discusses were as much seized of the need for reconstruction in politics as of the need for reconstruction in religion; they all thought of themselves as engaged in a conflict of which the outcome would be provision not only of a new polity but also of a new religion for the English people.

In this volume and the next, the subject will be this new religion which will be discussed through those fundamental predispositions from which all public statement begins – in Volume III in the forms taken by the desire to avoid conflict, in this volume in the forms taken by the pursuit of conflict and the demand for argument as an instrument of conflict.

II

In reviewing Volume I of this work, the Provost of King's College, Cambridge, Mr Bernard Williams, wrote that it used Christianity as an 'instrument of sarcasm' and had 'dark associations' with that 'scepticism and distrust of all merely secular improvement' which was to be found amongst the more 'unreconstructed sort of cardinal' in the 'unliberated heartland of the Church of Rome'. These were flattering accusations – wounds which anyone should be pleased to bear; they showed that Provost Williams had understood that Volume I was designed to put question-marks against the assault on Christianity.

Since Volume I was subjective, it was easy to include thinkers whose attitude to Christianity was ambiguous, while excluding thinkers who were hostile. To that extent its strategy was blurred. In this volume the strategy will be less blurred. 'Secular improvement' will be examined – not all 'secular improvement' and not from an 'unreconstructed' standpoint, but secular improvement as a way of destroying Christianity and from a reconstructed standpoint which will respond as willingly to the conception of the 'unliberated' in the Church of Rome as Volume I responded to the conception of the 'unliberated' in the Church of England.

The conception of the 'unliberated' is important, not because the author is connected with the 'Roman ... heartland', assuming that such a thing exists, or has ever existed in the sense in which the Provost means it, outside the demonology of the Liberal mind, but because of the criticism it implies of the mentalities through which the assault on Christianity has been conducted in England. The conception of the unliberated is central, and the Tractarian and Roman Catholic mentalities of Parts I and IV are to be distinguished from the mentalities described in Parts II and III by reason of their resistance to liberation and the assumption that Christian freedom has to end in obedience.

The idea of obedience has been present in the assault on Christianity, as the Spencerian and Huxleyite emphases on obedience to Nature have shown. So has the prospect of liberation – from Liberalism, Rationalism and Respectability – in Tractarian and Roman Catholic apologetic. It remains true, nevertheless, that 'liberation' has been more intimately connected with the assault on Christianity than with Christian apologetic, and has been central to the assault as we shall be describing it.

One of the criticisms that the Provost of King's made of Volume I was that, in implying preferences among the opinions that it dealt with, it failed to provide arguments to justify them. The author is as sceptical about the use of argument in establishing preferences between religions as Mr Williams appears to be trusting. But Mr Williams was right to perceive that Volume I showed sympathy, as MacNeile Dixon had shown 'sympathy' in his Gifford Lectures of 1935, for the 'men of religion' as against the 'ethical idealists'; he would have been even more perceptive if he had understood that it aimed to challenge the imperviousness to argument which in contemporary England is to be found pre-eminently among Christianity's enemies.

As elsewhere, so in religion, argument is a way of proceeding, but it is not the only way. Minds find themselves saddled with beliefs as much as they choose them, and the most interesting thing to do with beliefs having found that one has them is not necessarily to argue them but to explore and enjoy them, or to affront other minds into considering them. This is why Volume I took the form it took – because it *used* opinions in order to manifest resentment. This is why Volume II will take the form that it will take – because it will use the Tractarian and

Roman Catholic thinkers it discusses in order to point accusingly both at the aggressive secularity of the thinkers who master-minded 'The Assault on Christianity' and at the assumed secularity of the thinkers who have created 'The Post-Christian Consensus'.

In this work Tractarianism and Roman Catholicism are historical phenomena which give significance to a history that would be insignificant without them. They indicate, in ways which would be difficult for more compliant versions of Christianity, that Christianity has been under threat in England for a hundred and fifty years and that an important aid to judging the threat is to be found in that 'Jacobitism' or 'dandyism of the mind' to which reference was made at the end of Volume I.

In the preface to the second edition of *Oxford Apostles* in 1936 Sir Geoffrey Faber remarked that 'ordinary people' in the 1930s were reluctant to believe that Tractarianism could have any interest for them, and that the best way of establishing its interest was to investigate the Tractarians' sexuality, including their homosexuality. 'Taking off ... their surplices and cassocks' as he put it 'and presenting the Tractarians as ... men rather than priests' was illuminating so far as it went, and went a long way towards explaining the introverted intensity of Tractarian life. What it did not explain was the conspiracy element in Tractarianism – the assumption which most of the Tractarians made that they were at odds with the society of which they were a part.

This assumption was central to the Tractarian mentality which assumed that three centuries of Protestantism had not only subverted and parochialized English Christianity but had also made the English incapable of recognizing that anything was wrong. The Tractarians believed that there was an English disease, that Tractarianism was destined to cure it and that the cure was to be re-Christianization. What they did not see was how parochiality was to be destroyed, how protest was to be turned into a plan of action, and how re-Christianization was to occur.

Like the Tractarians, the Roman Catholics discussed in Part IV aimed to distance themselves from the modern mind, both by criticizing it and by offering it the possibility of conversion. Conversion can be a form of dandyism, religious conversion no less than any other, and this has been so in some of the cases discussed here even when it has arisen from the judgments that Infidelity has to be resisted and that Roman Catholicism is the only form of Christianity that is capable of resisting it.

Like the defenders, most of the assailants of Christianity who appear in these pages underwent a conversion arising in their cases from the belief that rejection of Christianity was a form of manifest destiny in an historic crisis. The crisis was not the same in Spencer as in Newman; nor was it the same in Russell as in Manning. But there was a common thread – a belief that the present age demanded the special reactions which were indicated by the history of Europe since the conversion of Constantine and a conspiratorial understanding of the function of thought in relation to it.

In this volume, in addition to the Tractarian conspiracy, three conspiracies are central – Naturalism, Positivism and the Socialistic conspiracy of Shaw, Ellis, Wells and Russell. All three were total philosophies. All three demanded total reconstruction, and all three assumed that reconstruction in practice would depend on reconstruction in theory. All three aimed to bring practice closer to theory. All three were rebarbatively negative, all three were insistently constructive, and all three failed to establish themselves as the English religion which includes decency, respectability, mistrust of enthusiasm, an aversion to theory and an even greater aversion to the dogmatic expression of belief, and has slid towards humanism rather than Tractarianism only because it dislikes Tractarianism more.

The Tractarians were reactionaries who, whatever they said to the contrary, did not expect to prevail. For them the reality was suffering in face of evil and the impossibility of halting evil decisively. Nowhere in English thought in the last century and a half, except intermittently among Roman Catholics and insensitively among Evangelicals and dissenters, has there been any real belief that the negative tension which Tractarian talent demanded would be operating in a world to which Christianity had been restored, and it is in this sense that the Tractarians – and particularly the Anglican Tractarians – must be said to have felt the negative melancholy about Christianity's prospects which many humanist thinkers have felt about humanism's prospects in relation to Democracy.

In this volume Democracy appears as an opportunity, but it also appears as a threat – an opportunity because 'the masses' could be called into play to destroy the respectability of 'the classes', a threat because the mobilization of the masses could turn out to be as destructive of humanism as of Christianity. Among all three groups of humanists fear was restrained only by the conviction that History was on their side.

In anti-Christian apologetic during the last century and a half, History has sustained two aggressive opinions – that historical consideration of the Bible has replaced a divine Jesus by a human one, and that historical consideration of the modern world has disclosed the liberation from authoritarian religion which has been affected by the Renaissance and Reformation, the Enlightenment and Romanticism, the American, French and Russian Revolutions, and the sexual and psychological revolutions of the twentieth century. In Christian apologetic on the other hand History has sustained three defensive opinions – that, since God entered Time in Christ, Christianity is an historical religion to which historical scholarship brings decisive testimony, that the Middle Ages established Christianity's compatibility with both Nature and Reason and that since all past civilizations have been religious, a civilization like contemporary civilization, when it claims not to be, must be reinterpreted to show that it is.

These defensive tactics, however persuasive polemically, are indecisive for assent. As little as scientific investigation do critical exegesis and historical reconstruction resolve problems of assent unless there is a predisposition to resolve them. It is religion which resolves them, and it is with religion's rôle in doing this that this book is concerned – with those directions of the mind and will which precede and transcend all activities and subjects of study.

One of the most important achievements of a century and a half of biblical exegesis has been to confirm far more of a supernatural understanding of the Bible than it seemed likely to do in the 1840s. Rediscovery of a supernatural Bible, however, says nothing about the Bible's truth and objectivity and does nothing to resolve the question of belief, which is more problematical than in 1840 and has been made more problematical still by the establishment of a 'scientific' attitude.

During the last century and a half Science has played a fourfold rôle in English life. It has made possible an understanding and command of nature which was still a dream in 1840; it has supplied an instrument of education which was also a dream in 1840. Through governmental science it has created an Erastianism more effective than Anglican Erastianism; in company with History, for those who have wished to build on them, it has laid the foundations for a post-Christian religion.

The post-Christian religion as it had emerged by 1880 had three features which distinguished it from historic Christianity. It gave a geologically and astronomically validated chronology for the history of the universe, and excluded the biblical chronology; it gave a biologically validated account of organic life, and excluded the biblical account of organic life; and it gave new twists to the doctrine of the regularity of nature and the inconceivability of divine intervention. It concluded that miraculous, or supernatural, Christianity was an impossibility, and that only obscurantism and superstition could pretend that it was not. And all this, though stated in the first place negatively, was converted by the minds and wills of its proponents into the positive religion which will be discussed in Parts II and III.

It would be easy to suggest that rejection of Christianity might have been avoided if dissenting and Evangelical thought had been stronger, if Christian imperviousness had not turned a negative criticism of ecclesiastical obscurantism into an intellectual rebellion, and if Lewes, Spencer, Huxley, Tyndall and the rest could have been presented with a revisionist Christianity which took account of what they were accustomed to call the 'criticism and philosophy of the nineteenth century'. Such fatuities are for the feeble-minded. The assumption here is that no one who did not want to create a post-Christian religion need have done so and that the effort which was made to do so between 1840 and 1930 was deliberate and acquired its authority from being deliberate.

Not all their practitioners treated History and Science as religion. But many of the most intelligent did and in order to do so had to turn them into something else – in the short run into literature, in the long run into academic disciplines.

English universities have for a long time been large, rich and significant, and are of first consequence for the understanding of the English mind. They are not now, however, and were not in the nineteenth century, the only channels of English public thought. In the nineteenth century the main channels, apart from the Churches, were parliament and literature, even when politicians and writers looked to reconstructed universities as the main channels of public thought in the future.

Of the thinkers discussed in this volume only Gladstone and Morley were parliamentary politicians, and neither is discussed primarily in that rôle. Both, and also Salisbury from Volume I, could have been discussed in that rôle, though it is likely that, if they had been, all three would have appeared to be less straightforward and categorical, and less anxious to create tension than they appear in their rôle as contributors to High Thought.

High Thought is as firmly embedded as High Politics in the interests, sympathies and aversions of its creators, and can be explained in terms of responses to publishers, audiences and antagonisms between authors in the same way that High Politics can be explained in terms of responses to constituencies, public opinion and antagonisms between politicians. Moreover, the practitioners of English High Thought, however disreputable personally, have displayed a high sense of national duty and consciousness and have done so even when they have confined themselves to long-term ineffabilities, have been free of assignable responsibility for the consequences of their opinions, and have used their freedom as speculatively and heuristically as freedom has been used in English universities since they ceased to be employment-agencies of the Church of England.

Among the thinkers who appear in Volume II only Huxley, Tyndall, Frazer, Russell, Murray and the Tractarians were teachers by profession, and none of these was limited by the specification of that function. Huxley and Tyndall were primarily researching scientists; Frazer thought of himself primarily as an 'educated man'. Russell and Murray inhabited a wider world than the world in which they taught, and even the Tractarians, whose aim was to capture a working university, thought of Oxford as an instrument of national regeneration. Moreover, since the most significant practitioners of High Politics in England in the last hundred years have been blander and more consensual about Christianity than Gladstone and Morley (in his early phase), and since modern universities are pre-eminently institutionalizations of the post-Christian consensus which will be the subject of Volume III, neither political nor university culture will receive systematic treatment here. Here, on the contrary, the principal subject will be literature – as a register of the nation's mind and as doctrine, both displayed and insinuated, about the way in which thought should be conducted and life lived, and the proper attitude to take to politics, morality and religion.

Literature as a register of the nation's mind is a concept which finds little favour among writers and teachers of literary studies in England where with honourable exceptions the norm for more than half a century has been practical criticism and analysis of language rather than elucidation of meaning, and where the concept of the inseparability of meaning from mode of expression and the suggestive ramifications of structuralism have not prevented the degeneration which so easily accompanies the conversion of a norm into an orthodoxy.

A properly entrenched and intelligent orthodoxy is as valuable as any of the skills which produce industrial and commercial revolutions.

But the orthodoxy we are discussing is defective in three respects – because it is limited by its origin in a negative reaction against the blight cast by a degenerate philosophizing over Victorian and Georgian criticism, because it is insufficiently appreciative of the historically determined nature of the ghettoes from which literatures emerge and because in its period of pre-eminence, while seeming to limit itself to judgments of taste and technique, it has insinuated assumptions which are as contentiously substantive as those which were insinuated by the philosophizing it was designed to replace.

Orthodoxies are valuable when they deepen faith or sustain conduct, and are based on a properly conceived understanding of the nature of existence. But there is no reason to believe that the orthodoxy we are criticizing meets either requirement. There is some reason to criticize it for considering literature in isolation from the persuasions it conveys and the conduct it implies. There is even more reason to suggest a disregard of the contradictions which accompany the widespread propagation through university faculties of a sensibility which imputes to literature the need to follow the requirements of argument or feeling, whatever the consequences for conduct.

To say this is not to demand the subjugation of literature to a moral or social purpose, the replacement of practical by philosophical or religious criticism or a revival of literary history in the manner of Saintsbury or A. W. Ward. It is simply a demand for minimum recognition that in present conditions there is much scope for a history of literature considered as doctrine and much need to open literature up to an articulated range of doctrinal considerations. Marxist criticism understands the need but in England has been incapable of meeting it. This book considers factors to which English Marxism is insensitive. It assumes that literature has been a significant register of the English intelligentsia's religion and must be understood not as ideology but as autonomous and self-confirming thought, and a genuine aspect of the intelligentsia's understanding of its public function.

England has had a low literature as well as a high literature, and a comprehensive discussion of our subject will involve discussion of Bradlaugh, Bottomley and Beaverbrook, for example, as well as of Morley, Mallock and Gilbert Murray. In this volume, however, the subject is high literature, with low literature appearing only as a challenge to the control which the intelligentsia has wished to excercise over popular thought and feeling.

High literature has a limited audience and a limited appeal. But it was for three centuries a crucial instrument of public discourse and the means by which secular intelligentsias subverted kings and priests throughout Europe. Evaluation of the influence of secular intelligentsias in the urban and suburban societies of the last two centuries is a problem which lies in wait for the historian of the modern world. Should History despise the fertility with which secular intelligentsias have externalized their fantasies upon the public mind? Or should it admire the resolve and generosity with which they have poured out their hearts and minds in the service of the people? Are their works diseased assertions of subjective opinion, or are they high statements of public doctrine? These alternatives present themselves in discussing the intelligentsias whose conceptions have dominated modern Europe; they present themselves in discussing the intelligentsias whose conceptions have dominated modern England. In neither case are the alternatives simple, however, and nor should the resolution be. In approaching a resolution, it is sufficient for the moment to emphasize the centrality of the literature we shall be discussing and the importance of the self-identifications that it reveals, and to give full weight to the truth and significance of Carlyle's dictum, quoted at the beginning of Volume I and deserving to be quoted again here, that in a 'modern country', it is the writers of 'newspapers, pamphlets, poems and books' who constitute the 'working effective Church'.

Tractarianism was an attempt to bring Carlyle's 'working Church' under the influence of the ecclesiastical Church, to provide new ways of inserting a Christian component into the national life, and to make the nation understand that Christianity's future presented a problem. Whether there *was* a problem, whether it was prudent to draw attention to it, whether it might not have been wiser to drift on as the Tractarians believed that the Church of England had drifted on during the eighteenth century, whether it was not the Tractarians themselves who precipitated the crisis of which Christianity's assailants took advantage, are questions to which these volumes will give uncertain answers. What they will not be uncertain about is that what has happened since the Tractarians has confirmed as prophecy an analysis which was probably false as history, that the Tractarian analysis, however untrue about the world the Tractarians lived in, has become true about the twentieth century, and that the Tractarians were right to suggest that, unless the assault on Christianity was challenged and contested at every turn, it would succeed in institutionalizing the post-Christian consensus with which we live now.

It is one of the established banalities of post-Romantic historiography that historians mirror chiefly themselves and their own times and in this sense create the pasts that they claim to mirror. This book has been written in the shadow of the banality and also of the power of the idea that the past-as-it-was is unknowable. It recognizes that the search for the past of the nation to which an historian belongs is likely to mirror the historian's past rather than the nation's and that mirroring is not only unavoidable but also desirable in so far as it is part of the process by which historians contribute towards conceptualizing the future.

The 'past-as-it-was' imposes a discipline and draws a contrast with the present. But its immensity has become burdensome and the search for it professionalized to a point of imbecility. The reader who looks for it in these pages will deserve to be disappointed and if, notwithstanding, he expects to find it, he should do so in full awareness of the fact that every serious historian ratiocinates the past that he needs.

The past that an historian needs is the past that he wishes to propose in the situation that he is addressing, and a past which might be suitable for one situation might not be suitable for another. In this work, out of all the pasts which might have been proposed, the author has proposed the past that he thinks the situation needs – a textual history of religion which shows the edifice of belief being taken down brick by brick and many Christian bricks being discarded, and the outcome of which has been the tension between Christianity and its assailants which has formed the theme of this introduction. This tension, even when relegated to the recesses of the public mind, is the central feature of the modern English situation. It is also the tension to which all other tensions have to be related.

I

THE ASSAULT ON THE EIGHTEENTH CENTURY

1

Tractarianism as Assault

'People say to me, that it is but a dream to suppose that Christianity should regain the organic power in human society which once it possessed. I cannot help that; I never said it could. I am not a politician; I am proposing no measures, but exposing a fallacy, and resisting a pretence. Let Benthamism reign, if men have no aspirations; but ... do not attempt by philosophy what once was done by religion. The ascendency of Faith may be impracticable, but the reign of Knowledge is incomprehensible. The problem for statesmen of this age is how to educate the masses, and literature and science cannot give the solution.' Rev. J. H. Newman *The Tamworth Reading-Room addressed to the Editor of The Times by Catholicus* February 1841 in C. F. Harrold (ed.) J. H. Newman *Essays and Sketches* 1848 vol. ii p. 203.

'Do you think ... Satan ... is so unskilfull in his craft as to ask you openly and plainly to join him in his warfare against the Truth? No; he offers you baits to tempt you. He promises you civil liberty; he promises you equality; he promises you trade and wealth; he promises you a remission of taxes; he promises you reform. This is the way in which he conceals from you the kind of work to which he is putting you; he tempts you to rail against your rulers and superiors; he does so himself, and induces you to imitate him; or he promises you illumination – he offers you knowledge, science, philosophy, enlargement of mind. He scoffs at times gone by; he scoffs at every institution which reveres them. He prompts you what to say, and then listens to you, and praises you, and encourages you. He bids you mount aloft. He shows you how to become as gods. Then he laughs and jokes with you, and gets intimate with you; he takes your hand, and gets his fingers between yours, and grasps them, and then you are his.' Rev. J. H. Newman *Tract 83* (1838) in *Tracts for the Times* vol. v 1833–41 pp. 13-14.

'Men of cultivated minds consider great divines or great philosophers merely in an intellectual point of view, and think they have a right to be admitted to their familiarity, when they meet them. They have no objection to exclusiveness, when talent and education, or again when wealth and station, are made the tickets of admission; but they are very much disgusted when they find the exclusiveness conducted on quite another principle ... A man, for instance ... may go a great way in Catholic opinions, and will be allowed to say and do what would be considered monstrous in another, if he does but conform himself to the existing state of things, adopt the tone of the world, take his place in the social body, and become an integral member and a breathing and living portion and a contented servant of things which perish. But if he will not put an establishment or a philosophy in the place of the Church, if he will not do homage to talent as such, or wealth as such, or official eminence as such, then he is out of joint with the age, and not only his words, but his look and his air are like a pail of cold water thrown over every man of the world whom he meets.' Rev. J. H. Newman *The Works of the Late J. W. Davison* in *The British Critic* and *Quarterly Theological Review* 1842 p. 369.

In England the assault on Christianity began with the Renaissance. The earliest assault, however, was uncertain and inconsequential, and had no support from the political power. The collapse of the political power in the 1640s supplied an opportunity which could not be taken, and it was not until Deism, Arianism and Socinianism had shown the way that the assault began to gain ground.

In the eighteenth century the assault stimulated an extensive literature of resistance. At the end of the century, and at the beginning of the nineteenth century, resistance was fertilized and confused by transcendentalism, a feudalizing and mediaevalizing reaction, and the Romantic belief that religion and poetry were natural and connected facets of human activity. All of these were of first importance for the formation of the Victorian intelligentsia poetically and aesthetically, and in history, politics and religion, but all of them were affirmative and sentimental and lacked that feel for the jugular which could have turned affirmation into attack, sentiment into negativity and Anglican confidence in a confessional state into an aggressive demand for a Christian restoration once the confessional state had been subverted.

Tractarianism was such a demand. The Tractarians were children of betrayal and defeat, looked back more in anger than with a view to understanding and conducted a vigorous search for scapegoats. Through a tightly knit group of male friends and by mobilizing Oxford's youth, they developed as aggressive a belligerence as Socialism and Marxism were to develop in mobilizing youth in English universities in the 1930s, arousing suspicion not only because of what they were against but also because they spoke to each other and to God in a special way and bore distinctive and objectionable emblems – emblems of secrecy, self-discipline and self-recognition through which the new Samurai dedicated themselves to bringing the nation back to Christianity as surely as Wells's new Samurai were to be dedicated to keeping them apart.

Tractarian thought began from the belief not only that the eigh-

4

teenth century had been a disaster but also that France had been the scene of the disaster. This was the Tractarian view of 1830 as well as of 1789. It was also the view of De Maistre and Chateaubriand and had been Burke's leading assumption in the 1790s.

Burke's writings in the 1790s were an attack, made before they had prevailed, on almost all the assumptions that dominate public discussion in the modern world. The attack was made from mixed motives in a political context but is not for that reason less useful in demonstrating that what has been held up for conservation by even the most Conservative of thinkers since Burke has been the Jacobinism that Burke attacked, and that Burke's importance for present purposes lies not in his counter-revolutionary politics but in the fact that it was he who made the most striking statement of the religious problem which forms the subject of Parts I and IV.

Burke, though a defender of the Anglican Establishment, was Irish and a Whig, and presented Christianity as a European religion. In conceptualizing a crisis, he explained that Christianity's existence had become a political problem, that its survival could not be assumed and that in face of the 'atheism' which the Jacobins wished to establish throughout Europe, the differences between the Churches were insignificant.

Burke remained a Whig even after 1789 and continued to praise Whig liberty and the revolution of 1688; in defending the ancien régime he was led into affirming of Christianity what he had affirmed of religion in writing *A Vindication of Natural Society,* of Roman Catholicism in writing about Ireland and of Islam and Hinduism in writing about India – that it was crucial to it. Having come to demand a British effort to re-establish Christianity in France, he so far transcended Anglican assumptions as to make Pitt's central duty the use of force to ensure its re-establishment in Europe.

Like Burke the Tractarians were enemies of the Jacobins. But they were not defenders of the aristocratic polity. They were critics of 1688 and believed that, though Protestantism had weakened the Church of England, it had been Rationalistic Liberalism which had brought it down. Until the late 1830s their overriding aim was to restore it and in emphasizing its 'Catholic' character and the 'Catholic' content of its formularies, to contrast it with the corruptions of Trent and the threat which Roman Catholicism presented to Christianity.

The central target for attack was not, nevertheless, Rome but the exaggerated respect which 'the present age' felt for the 'powers and capacities of the human mind'. What the Tractarians feared was what

Burke had feared, though they feared it in a Coleridgean or even a Lamennaisian rather than a Burkean fashion – that the popular imagination was being liberated from Christian control and creating an anarchy of religions as the 'reveries of philosophers' became the 'object ... of belief and ... ground of practice ... among the millions'. It was to this problem that the Tractarians addressed their minds and the fears and enmities it involved which were used to justify their counter-revolution.

These fears and enmities were present in all the leading Tractarians. Keble had them along with the tone he achieved in *The Christian Year*. Pusey had them once he had become part of the Tractarian triumvirate; Newman had them throughout. Ward and Froude were temperamentally acerbic, and Ward had a Benthamite component as well as a romantic one. Hugh James Rose was neither a don, nor strictly speaking a Tractarian. But it was Rose who first gave them polemical expression.

I

Rose had a Jacobite ancestry, was six years older than Newman, and died seven years before Newman's conversion. His father was a clergyman and schoolmaster in Sussex, and, since his own health was poor, Rose was educated at his father's school. In 1813 he went to Trinity College, Cambridge, where he failed to get a Fellowship. In 1818 he was ordained and married and in 1821 became Vicar of Horsham. Having moved to Hadleigh in 1830 and to Fairstead in 1834, he remained there until becoming Principal of King's College, London, a couple of years before his death at the age of forty-three in 1838.

Rose preached two series of sermons in Cambridge, where his influence was compared with Simeon's, and was persuaded by van Mildert to spend 1834 as Professor of Divinity at Durham. As first editor of the revived *British Magazine* from 1832 to 1836, he was an effective journalist, and as Vicar of Hadleigh was host at the unsuccessful meeting from which the Tractarian conspiracy derived some of its reputation. Beginning with attacks on Bentham and Cobbett in the 1820s, he kept up a stream of high-quality polemic which included *The State of the Protestant Religion in Germany*, *Brief Remarks on the Disposition Towards Christianity Generated by Prevailing Opinions and Pursuits* and the long criticism of St Simonianism that he printed as a preface to *The Gospel: An Abiding System* in 1832.

Rose had a Tractarian conception of the need for an Anglican divinity, a patristic scholarship and a Christian journalism, and in company with his brother, Henry, laid the foundations for the *Encyclopaedia Metropolitana*. He intuited, however, an ambiguity in Newman's attitude to Rome and a lukewarmness in his attitude to the Church of England. Rose's 'Catholicism' was Anglican and, even at its most polemical, thought of itself, or rather of 'the English', as opposed to 'extremes'.

What Rose attacked was the spread of Infidelity in England and on the Continent, not only outside the Churches but also inside them. Just as the reverse side of Palmer's *Church of Christ* was Palmer's criticism of Thomas Arnold and Liberal Anglicanism, so Rose's positive works were matched by criticism of Milman, the slide from Protestantism through pietism to disbelief and Semler's 'theory of accommodation' which was 'the most formidable weapon ever devised for the destruction of Christianity'.

The State of Protestant Religion in Germany was an attack on German theology. The introduction to *The Gospel: An Abiding System* was an attack on French Sociology.

Rose's discussion of St Simonianism led to two separate conclusions. On the one hand that the movement's conduct and 'some of its opinions' were absurd. On the other, that respectful attention should be given to its 'wide and philosophical views', the 'plausibility' of many of its observations about history and its refusal to 'acquiesce in a state of society that was almost entirely godless'.

Rose agreed that 'gaining power over others' had been the moral and social principle of antiquity, that mediaeval Christianity had made a political reality of the gospel of love and that there was 'very much of truth' in the view that Liberalism had done a good work in knocking down the 'wrecks of old systems' since the Reformation. He argued, however, that the Liberalism of 1789 had degenerated and would have to be destroyed if selfishness and self-interest were to be replaced, that social solidarity required an 'absorbing passion' to 'take men out of themselves' and that the Christian version of 'absorbing passion' was better than the St Simonian version.

As Rose saw it, St Simonianism was a secularized version of Christianity, recognizing in the gospel of love the Christian contribution to human progress and teaching a necessary mistrust of both the profit-motive and the hereditary principle. His criticism was that St Simonianism was merely a higher version of the doctrine of human perfectability and had failed to understand that it was only by looking 'beyond the grave' that men would be able to move towards the requisite cohesion on earth.

Where *The State of the Protestant Religion* gave a view of Germany and *The Gospel: An Abiding System* a view of France, *Brief Remarks* and the *Cambridge Sermons* that Rose published in 1831 gave a view of English thought as a symptom of England's deterioration.

Brief Remarks praised the revival of learning which had preceded the English Reformation and the 'elevating' and 'immortal' literature which had been produced as a consequence. It specified the Restoration as the point at which 'learning' had been 'brought down' and 'coffee-house ... deism' as a symbol of the obsession with material progress and the recession in the 'knowledge of man' which were the leading defects of the modern intellect.

Rose did not disparage the intellect; he argued simply that man's 'intellectual frame' depended on his 'moral frame' and would only develop properly when religion was made the ... paramount object of ... education'. 'The only mark of progress in the species ... was to be found in God's dealings with mankind', and what mattered, therefore, was not the 'results obtainable by intellectual effort' but the 'discipline derived from them' and God's promise that men would know Him when 'the universe should have crumbled into dust and all its knowledge should have ... been forgotten'.

To some extent Rose's polemic was a conventional High-Church polemic, addressing itself to the threats by which Anglicanism was confronted in the 1820s but involving a High-Church identification between learning and ecclesiastical Christianity. By comparison Froude's polemic was bitter.

II

Much of Froude's[1] writing, though written by 1835, remained private until Newman, Keble and Mozley published the four volumes of his *Remains* in 1838/9. When read then and later in the light of *Tracts for the Times* (especially Tracts 80, 87, 89 and 90), it became obvious that there had been a conspiracy, that in Froude the Church of England

[1] Rev. Richard Hurrell Froude (1803–36). Educ. Eton and Oriel College, Oxford. Fellow of Oriel College 1826–30. Author of contributions to *Tracts for the Times* and J. Keble, J. H. Newman and J. B. Morley (ed.) *Remains of the Late Reverend Richard Hurrell Froude* 4 vols. 1838–9; L. I. Guiney (ed.) *Hurrell Froude: Memoranda and Comments* 1904.

had been harbouring a viper, and that the poison he had been spreading consisted of an attack on the Reformation, on historic and contemporary Anglicanism and on the 'Union of Church and State'. Froude had obviously hated the Whigs who 'by degrees' had taken up 'all the filth that had been secreted in the fermentation of human thought'. He had also admired the Nonjurors, had turned against the Noetics whom he might have been expected to admire, and had praised a gallery of heroes from Pole to van Mildert for reasons which looked only dubiously Protestant. In the political changes which had taken place between 1828 and 1832 he had seen an intrusion by the State into the affairs of the Church, a provocation to 'civil war', and the prelude to a future in which 'Independents ... Socinians ... Jews ... Unbelievers ... Latitudinarians and Dissenters' would replace the Church of England in the 'councils of the nation'.

Froude did not necessarily mean everything that he wrote or said. He certainly hated Milton and 'adored' Charles I. He may well have wished to 'explode' the 'Protestant fancy' that 'the priest must be a gentleman' and may even have convinced himself that 'in a Protestant church the parson ... preached the prayers ... and worshipped the congregation'. It is probable that he did not really 'hope' that the 'March of Mind in France' might prove a 'bloody one' or that a 'flogging' might be thought 'the most sensible qualification for the franchise'. He certainly said so, however, and was the author of the historic remark, which gave great offence when printed after his death, that the Reformation had been a 'badly set ... limb' which would have to be 'broken again in order to be righted'.

In many of his essays Froude criticized Rationalism as a method of interpreting the Bible and sketched the Orthodox method that should be used instead. Thomas Arnold was singled out for claiming to distinguish 'essential' from 'inessential' aspects of the Bible, for dismissing Hooker and Jeremy Taylor and for agreeing with 'half the Protestant world before him' that 'honest and sensible men' could never be in doubt about the 'methods' through which God's revelation should be interpreted.

Froude turned Arnold on his head, arguing that Arnold's method could as easily be used, if Pascal and Bishop Butler were to be followed, in defence of orthodoxy as against it, and since there *were* essentials of belief, that the important question was how doctrines which were 'human theories' could be distinguished from doctrines which were not. His answer was that there was a 'middle road' between submission to Trent and Protestantism's insistence on Biblical Infallibility, and that this would be found in the infallibility of the Apostles and the decisions and declarations through which the early Councils had interpreted it.

Froude's central assumption was that supernatural knowledge superseded human knowledge and that an assault would be needed if supernatural knowledge was to be reasserted against the inroads which ·Rationalism had made in the previous quarter of a millennium. Rationalism was an assertion of human traditions and a diminution of divine traditions, and the assault on it was central because it had destroyed the belief that ecclesiastical knowledge and authority were as potent as secular knowledge and authority.

Froude's *Essay on Rationalism* pursued three lines of attack. It attacked the tendency to 'divest Scripture of its apparent meaning' when 'its apparent meaning' was unintelligible to men's 'natural faculties'. It attacked the assumption that man's natural faculties could 'recognise and explain the action of the Holy Spirit' without external assistance in doing so. And it attacked the belief that the efficacy of the Sacraments 'belonged to them through their natural tendency'. These attacks led to a disparagement of the sermon by contrast with the Eucharist and of reasoning by contrast with faith, and to an assertion of the impossibility of achieving knowledge of God without first having acted upon it.

In describing Reason's rôle in relation to revelation, Froude pitched his case low. He was in no doubt that 'faith' had to be protected from Experience, that Reason had to arbitrate between them and that theologians were no more confined to the facts than Newtonian astronomers were confined to what they saw in the sky. It was Reason's business to decide whether a proposed revelation that was 'contrary to Experience' was 'real' and not only was a 'Bible Christian' who 'rejected all sources of instruction but the Bible' an 'absurdity' but Reason's agent was the Church's 'inward and spiritual character' which preserved its continuity with the Apostles and alone protected it against prevailing respectability.

Like Rose, Froude died young and did not develop his positions systematically. Though it is likely, it is not certain that he would have joined the Roman Church if he had been alive at the time of Newman's conversion. What is certain is that he regarded a national Church as likely to be a Church without a discipline, that he regarded a Church without a discipline as the worst of all Churches, and that he would have preferred a Church to be disestablished if establishment made discipline impossible. In *Thomas à Becket* – his longest work – he emphasized the clerical character of the discipline he envisaged and the autonomous character of the authority on which it would be based. If he had survived into the 1840s, these preferences, along with a long-standing preference for 'obedience' over 'enquiry', would have been as influential with Newman as they had been even before the Mediterranean tour which he, Froude, his father, Archdeacon Froude, and Newman made together in order to restore Froude's health in the winter of 1832.

Having started as a pupil of Keble, Froude became one of the most offensive of Newman's allies. He was not, however, Newman's only offensive ally. Ward was at least as offensive; it was Ward's success in drawing lines between 1841 and 1845 that was responsible for the disintegration of Tractarianism and the parting of the ways between Canterbury and Rome.

III

Ward[1] was more than ten years younger than Newman and began adult life as a Broad Church Utilitarian. For some years he was an admirer of Whately and Arnold, and was sceptical about the Tracts until, as a young Fellow of Balliol, he fell under the spell in the mid-1830s. Having turned, he turned sharply, feeding on Froude's *Remains* and writing, before he preceded Newman into the Roman Church, two Romanizing pamphlets, a series of Romanizing articles in *The British Critic,* and a book *The Ideal of a Christian Church* for which he was censured by the Convocation of the University of Oxford in 1845.

In outline *The Ideal* resembled Palmer's *Church of Christ. The Church of Christ,* however, was an Anglican book and Palmer remained an Anglican throughout his life. *The Ideal* was only dubiously Anglican. It had been started as an answer to the attack which Palmer

---

[1] William George Ward (1812–82). Educ. Winchester and Christ Church, Oxford. Fellow of Balliol College 1834–45. Renounced Anglican orders, married and converted to Roman Catholicism 1845. Author of *A Few Words in Support of Tract 90* 1841, *A Few More Words in Support of Tract 90* 1841, *The Ideal of a Christian Church Considered in Comparison with Existing Practice* 1844.

had made on Ward's *British Critic* articles after Newman had refused to provide one, and had then grown into the quarter-of-a-million words of which the finished book consisted.

The Ideal displayed Ward's hatred of the Reformation, of the Lutheran doctrine of justification, and of the Protestant principle of private judgment, all of which by nature and tendency 'sank below atheism itself'. Its tone was Hildebrandinian, with Christianity being suspicious as well as appreciative of 'heathen' culture and having a duty both to control the education of the upper classes and to show a 'quasi-sacramental' concern for the 'troubles of the poor'.

In *The Ideal,* Ward referred to the break-up of 'old philosophical systems ... and religious prepossessions' and added that, 'if ever there was a period when just hope existed that sceptics or infidels might be caught ... on the rebound, that period was the present'. In holding up something for sceptics and infidels to rebound to, *The Ideal* and the *British Critic* articles criticized the Church of England for failing to do this.

In the long review of Mill's *A System of Logic* that he wrote in 1843, Ward praised Mill for his addiction to argument and system, and for his St Simonian belief that the age was an age of unfixed opinions which it was the business of the thinking classes to fix. A great deal of the review was given up to philosophical discussion of the superiority of Kant's to Mill's account of mathematics, and to an expression of the view that Mill's laws of human nature operated only under bondage to sin and not in conditions of Christian liberty. But Ward saw in the inverse-deductive method described in Book VI of *A System of Logic* the foundations of the 'real science of history' and Mill was right, despite Ward's unfavourable judgment of his religion, to interpret the review as the work of a fellow-travelling enemy of unthinking Conservatism.

Ward's eight articles in *The British Critic* translated into a contorted prose all the doubts that the Tracts had raised about Anglican attitudes towards dogmatic theology, ecclesiastical authority and private judgment. No Tractarian made so passionate a statement of antagonism to the 'sarcasm' and narrow-mindedness of the 'man of the world', to Erastianism's unChristian way of thinking about the poor and to the 'delusive sophisms' which 'the Protestant schools' had taught about almost all the articles of Christian belief.

In *The British Critic* Ward professed to be doing no more than restating what 'the Oxford writers' had established already. But he did this with a sharpness and venom which were heightened by the fact that he named names and specified persons – not only persons of the second rank but also, for example, the 'open disbelief' that he found in Milman, the 'irreligious' tone that he found in Macaulay and the Sabellian and quasi-Nestorian dryness that he found in so eminent an Anglican as Whately.

As in other Tractarians, so in Ward there was the certainty that 'the truths of natural religion addressed themselves to men's moral, not their intellectual, nature' and that Christianity's republication of natural religion merely increased the 'mystery' by which the intellect was confronted. The Christian method was to deepen and stabilize apprehension of doctrine by acknowledging the mystery and practising the truth, and by accepting the fact that it was only through moral action exercised on 'knowledge already acquired' that 'real synthetical judgments' could be made about moral and religious questions.

The idea of theory's dependence on practice was present throughout Ward's theology. It underpinned the conceptions of the will's power over belief, of mortification as the starting-point for holiness, and of 'holy men ... teaching with authority and rebuking with dignity' as the channel by which 'moral truth' flowed into the world.

Ward believed in Christian liberty but associated it with obedience to the Church rather than with the secular liberty characteristic of modern societies. He brought Carlyle into play and used Carlyle's authority to condemn 'that one principle which as differently developed was Eclecticism in religion, Protestantism in Christianity and Benthamism in morals and politics'.

Ward was an improbable Tractarian – sceptical as well as engaged, mathematical as well as musical, volatile, exuberant and fat, and through the vigour of his personality exercising a confusing influence on pupils like Jowett and Stanley who were attracted by Tractarianism almost as much as they were attracted by the latitudinarianism that they arrived at eventually. In reacting to Tractarianism, indeed, Ward himself might have jumped in any direction; it was in a sense an accident that the conclusion at which he arrived was that the Church of England was doing Rationalism's work and had to be abandoned, and that the loyalty which he was to give later to Manning was to be given to Newman.

In the 1830s the Tractarians had conducted two separate campaigns. On the one hand they had conducted a campaign to improve the tone of public religion, to tighten up religious practice and to give back to the Church of England the features which they supposed belonged to a properly constituted clerical Church. On the other hand they conducted a campaign to confute the intellectual enemies by which the Church was confronted and to show that Rationalistic Liberalism was self-contradictory and untrue. The two campaigns went hand in hand and almost all the important Tractarians contributed to both. Not all, however, were equally engaged with each. Keble and Pusey, for example, caused intellectual offence, Pusey by his Confessional and Eucharistic excesses, Keble by reason of Tract 89, his support for the doctrine of Reserve in Communicating Knowledge and his part in publishing Froude's *Remains*. But Ward and Froude addressed themselves more directly to problems of intellectual strategy than either of these had done by 1845 and it is for this reason that they have been considered out of their chronological sequence. Similarly, though Keble and Pusey had an intellectual coherence, they were far less advanced than Newman in expressing it. In the 1830s Newman was the most systematic of the Tractarians, and it is because he came closest to making an Anglican coherence out of the insights described in the last three sections that he will be considered next.

IV

When Newman [1] left for the Mediterranean in 1832, he had not established himself as an author. He had published articles and letters

---

[1] Rev. John Henry Newman (1801–90). Educ. Ealing and Trinity College, Oxford. Fellow of Oriel College, Oxford, 1822–45 and Vicar of St Mary's, Oxford, 1828–43. Converted to Roman Catholicism 1845. Author of *Cicero* and *The Life of Appolonius Tyanaeus* in *Encyclopaedia Metropolitana* 1824, *The Arians of the Fourth Century* 1833, ed. and contributor to *Tracts for the Times* 1833–41, *The Restoration of Suffragan Bishops Recommended* 1833, *Parochial Sermons* 1834–6 etc., *Elucidations of Dr Hampden's Theological Statements* 1836, contributions to *Lyra Apostolica* 1836, *Lectures on the Prophetical Office of the Church* 1837, *A Letter to the Rev. Godfrey Faussett* 1838, *Hymni Ecclesiae* 1838, *Lectures on Justification* 1838, joint ed. and contributor to *A Library of the Fathers of the Holy Catholic Church* 1838– , *The Church of the Fathers* 1839, ed. C. Sutton: *Disce Vivere*, 1839, ed. E. Wells: *The Rich Man's Duty*, 1840, ed. Bishop Wilson: *Sacra Privata* 1840, *The Tamworth Reading-Room* 1841, *A Letter Addressed to Rev. R. W. Jelf* 1841, *A Letter to the...Lord Bishop of Oxford* 1841, *Catena Aurea* 3 vols. 1841–3, *An Essay on the Miracles Recorded in the Ecclesiastical History of the Early Ages in Fleury's Ecclesiastical History* 1842, ed. *The Devotions of Bishop Andrewes* 1842, *Sermons Bearing on Subjects of the Day* 1843 etc., *Sermons...Preached Before the University of Oxford* 1843, reprinted as *Fifteen Sermons Preached Before the University of Oxford 1826–43* 1872, ed. *The Cistercian Saints of England* 1844, *An Essay on the Development of Christian Doctrine* 1845.

to newspapers, and had prepared and preached a large number of sermons. He had written a book, *The Arians of the Fourth Century* which, after being rejected by the series for which it had been commissioned, had been accepted for publication after his return to England. When he left England, he was run down after a number of years hard work as a tutor of Oriel and a parish priest, and a period of difficulty in which he had in effect been deprived of his tutorship because of his religious conception of its function. As he sailed towards Rome he displayed no sense of the prophetic work he was to do in the next twelve years or of the high written output that he was to achieve. Least of all did he understand that in thirteen years time he would become a Roman Catholic.

In Newman's life and in the development of his thought, the decade that followed his return from the Mediterranean in 1833 was crucial. It was then that he began to write prolifically, then that the publishing enterprises he was involved in, the tracts, reviews, introductions and pamphlets that he wrote, and the three major books that he published, established that he was destined to do some great work in English religion.

Newman's father was a Broad Churchman and a banker who went bankrupt in 1821 when Newman was twenty. Newman had been at school at Ealing, where he had had an Evangelical conversion. From there he had gone to Trinity College, Oxford, and, after failing to achieve the highest honours in the Oxford examinations, had become a Fellow of Oriel College in 1822. After ordination, he thought of becoming a missionary but on appointment to a tutorship gave up the idea definitively.

As an Oriel tutor, Newman contributed to that intensification of *teaching* which was one of the salient features of that College in the first quarter of the nineteenth century. From his appointment to the University Church of St Mary the Virgin in 1828 he acquired a wide following and exerted a deep influence on undergraduates with whom he would not have come into contact as a college tutor. By the time he went to the Mediterranean, he had become a significant Oxford figure. On returning to Oxford in the following year, he became the leader of that demand for the intensification of *religion* which is what we mean by Tractarianism or the Oxford movement.

Between 1833 and 1843 the intensification of religion became the centre of Newman's life, supplying the basis for a fashion and an opportunity to exercise leadership over a generation of undergraduates and dons. Intensification of religion, like intensification of teaching, however, was a practical matter, the demand to adopt a tone, manner or way of life which could have been made without systematic proclamation of the desirability of dogma. In these years Newman addressed himself to the question of the desirability and content of Christian dogma.

In the first decade of his adult life, Newman had given random and disjointed expression to a distinctive combination of positions which had not yet been cast in the massive form that they were to receive later. At this time there was Evangelical solemnity and Evangelical priggishness. There were also, however, strong convictions – of the importance of celibacy and the 'superiority of the celibate mentality', of the significance of poetry and scientific investigation and of the differences between 'holiness' and 'sensuality', the Church and the world and 'Christian' faith and virtue and 'human' faith and virtue.

Newman thought of himself as an Oxford man to whom it seemed that Oxford had a national duty to fulfil. He felt this with reference to Wellington. He felt it with special reference to Peel for imagining that 'religious, straightforward, unpolitical Oxford' could be used in support of Catholic Emancipation and he welcomed Peel's defeat in the university election of 1829 as a defeat for the 'rank and talent of London' by the 'inferior colleges' and 'humbler style of men' who had 'done a good work' and achieved a 'great victory' by demonstrating the independence and character of the Church of England.

At this time Newman was a Tory, but his Toryism had a pungent non-party character. He treated Catholic Emancipation as an irreversible work which 'the intelligence of the country' had demanded. It was also, however, the fruit of 'indifference' and 'hostility to the church', a prelude to the removal of Anglican influences from English life and a threat to the existence of the Conservative Party, while 1688 had been a republican revolution which had established the erroneously cheerful beliefs that 'sin was merely venial', that 'opinions do not influence character' and that there is 'no great evil in the world'.

Newman felt no confidence in the régime of rank and wealth which had been established in 1688. He expressed the hatred which Burke had felt in the 1790s, and Wordsworth later, for those who subordinated the duties of rank and wealth to comfort or convenience, and he judged that 'something was rotten' among the 'upper classes' who were 'liberal' rather than 'Christian' in their thinking. He despised the Whigs for being bogus revolutionaries and thought that a repetition of the riots of 1819 would be needed to knock sense into the minds of their supporters.

Consideration of the Whigs helped Newman to the view that they were 'vermin' who had no 'root in the heart', and that there was no long-term future for their 'cold and scoffing belief' that all religions were 'about the same'. At the same time, since they were in the saddle and in tune with the spirit of the age and were going to do a great deal of harm in the short run, he looked forward without pleasure to a future in which dissenters would be conciliated 'at the expense of truth' and Christianity replaced by universal education and the March of Mind.

In thus prophesying disaster, Newman identified enemies. In poetry there was Shelley. Among churchmen there were Milman for being virtually a Socinian and Arnold for wanting the Church of England to 'pig' it 'three in a bed' with the Socinians and the Baptists. The 'Utilitarians, Political Economists and useful knowledge men' were among intellectual enemies. The Unitarians had drifted into pantheism and, in abandoning Christ's divinity, had abandoned the chief advantage which revealed religion had over natural religion. Temperance institutions were an attempt to do without religion on the part of persons who were 'puffed up by their sense of superior decency'. 'High circles in London' were perceived as a threat from one end of the spectrum, the 'uneducated or partially-educated masses' sustained by radical pamphleteering were perceived as a threat from the other. So were the 'supercilious ignorance' of newspaper journalism, and the fact that the church party was 'poor in mental endowment' and faced by almost all the mental talent of the age.

These opinions were paramount in Newman's mind from Catholic Emancipation onwards. They issued in fears that a Whig government or 'infidel parliament' might attack church endowments or support unbelieving bishops, and that the Church might want to be severed from her endowments if they did. These fears created a sentiment of militancy of which *The Arians of the Fourth Century* was an outcome.

The Arians of the Fourth Century was published in 1833 after Newman's return from the Mediterranean. But it had been written between 1830 and 1832 in reaction to Catholic Emancipation, with

Arius and Athanasius as villain and hero and the Arian controversy as the central battle in which Athanasius rescued the early Church from its enemies.

The Arians of the Fourth Century was a polemical book, the taking of sides in a distant conflict which was rendered immediate by the arguments through which Catholic Emancipation had been justified. No doubt was left that Athanasius was right, and that Arius and the Arians were wrong and evil and afforded an open manifestation of the spirit of Antichrist.

Newman was at pains to emphasize that the Alexandrian Church had extirpated Arianism as soon as it had emerged, and that the soil in which it had flourished was in Antioch. Antiochene Arianism was explained by reference to Platonic and Aristotelian sophism, with their lack of seriousness and simplicity, their preference for dialectical and disputatious over dogmatic theology and their tendency to subject 'God's incomprehensibility' to the 'analogies of sense and the rules of physics'. It was further explained by reference to the luxuriousness and materialism of Syrian society and the sensual and carnal character of Syrian Judaism, Judaism itself being associated with an 'obsolete' ceremonial, the 'pestilence of unbelief' and a 'humanitarian ... error' about Christ's Person.

These were not only ancient heresies but also modern heresies, and Arianism was described in modern terms. It was described in part as being neological ('keeping the form while destroying the spirit of Christianity'); in part as being humanitarian; in part as embodying a 'systematic infidelity' which had 'hated' the sacred mystery. The Arians were said to have had a 'shrewd secular policy' which was pursued with cunning and craft and cruelty and atrocity, and with a duplicity and worldliness which Newman was later to find characteristic of the modern Papacy. Arians accommodated themselves to the 'humour of earthly sovereigns' and the judgment of the populace 'which was ever destructive of refinement and delicacy'. Their 'idle subtleties', 'irreverent enquiries' and 'ingenious disputations' had accommodated 'the superstitions of paganism' and the 'virtual atheism of philosophy' and would have succeeded in establishing a 'reckless profanation' of all things sacred had it not been the destiny of Athanasius's 'ubiquity', 'activity', 'tenderness', 'forbearance', 'maturity', 'prudence', 'meekness', 'liberality of mind', 'completeness of character' and uniform Christian charity, to resist them.

The Arians of the Fourth Century was a powerful book, with a

positively full synthesis of history and doctrine, and continual relevance as a contemporary tract. It distanced Newman from democratic
and rationalistic thought and from the 'spirit of men-of-the-world in
every age'. It stated a preference for Truth to Peace, and denied that
'they who received scarcely more of Christ's teaching than the instinct
of civilization recognised' were right to regard the 'religious dissensions
of the Church as ... simply evil'. Above all, it laid out the attitude
which Orthodoxy should take to the conflict of creeds in fourth-
century Alexandria and the conflict of creeds in nineteenth-century
England.

The Arians of the Fourth Century was an analysis of England's
problem. The 1832 Reform Act, the Whig victory at the 1832 election
and the beginning of the Whig asault on the Irish Church while
Newman was in the Mediterranean, then showed that its analysis was
correct. The connection Newman saw in Italy between the Napoleonic
invasions and clerical profligacy and Infidelity lent weight to the fears
that he had felt before he left England. These fears were expressed to
some extent in letters, to some extent in poetry, throughout in a
growing sense that 'agitation and tumult' were a duty. From his return
to England, just before Keble preached his Assize Sermon in July 1833,
Newman began an extraordinary output of prose which went on
continuously until he retired to Littlemore in 1843. In these years he
laid the foundations of a revivified Anglicanism and reached the
conclusion that a revivified Anglicanism could not reconvert England.
   In Newman's Anglican history there were no evasions. Newman did
not argue or ask; he asserted. He used literary art to promulgate a
doctrine, and to demand recognition of the primacy of doctrine. It was
the rhetorical promulgation of doctrine that was at the centre of his
undertaking, and if we are to understand its strength and weakness, it
is necessary to understand its purpose and content, the situation to
which it was addressed and the agency through which it was to be
promulgated.

Newman's doctrine was anti-aristocratic, not because Newman objected in principle to leadership by the 'eminent' but because of the
character of the only aristocracy of which he knew anything. This was
the Whig aristocracy along with the links of affiliation that bound the

Whigs of 1688 to the Whigs of 1832. These links were political –
between the decision to Protestantize the monarchy by law in 1688 and
the demand to emancipate Roman Catholics in 1829. They were also
intellectual, arising from the latitudinarianism of the Whig apologists
and the irreverence, hedonism and ignorance of religion that were to be
found in Hume, Locke, Bentham and Brougham.

. With Hume, Newman's engagement was random. With Locke, he
engaged more closely. Having interpreted Bentham as reducing all
motivation to the pursuit of interests, he decided that Brougham was
superior by reason of his 'lofty' enthusiasm.

Newman's most extensive discussion of Brougham appeared in the
celebrated letters that he wrote for *The Times* in 1841 under the
pseudonym Catholicus. These, however, were primarily an attack on
Peel. They were a smear by association, a continuation of the claim
that the Conservative Party had ceased to stand for anything in
particular, and that Peel as an Anglican should have known better than
adopt opinions which linked him with Benthamite realism, Ciceronian
paganism and Brougham.

In Newman's writing Brougham was a symbol. It was through
Brougham that Newman attacked the idea of 'physical and moral
science' as a 'neutral ground on which men of every shade of politics
and religion could ... disabuse each other of their prejudices'. It was
through Brougham that he dismissed the 'infidel principle' on which
University College, London had been founded, on which Brougham
had expatiated in a famous inaugural discourse at Glasgow and which
Peel had appeared to enunciate in opening a Reading-Room at
Tamworth in 1841 – the principle that 'dogmatism' and 'controversial
divinity' were undesirable, that there should be no monopoly of
education for 'the few who are of one denomination of the Christian
Church only' and that 'you have but to drench the popular mind with
physics, and moral and religious advancement follows'. These were, as
Newman understood them, not the principles on which education had
been conducted in England hitherto, and they were not principles on
which a Christian education could be conducted in the future.

For these judgments Newman offered two sorts of reason. On the
one hand, an education of this sort, so far from attempting to 'subdue'
human nature, 'offered merely ... gifts ... to bribe it with' and ignored
the fact that a 'mastery over the mind' would have to be sought in
'graver and holier places' than the 'libraries and Reading-Rooms' to
which Peel attached so much importance. On the other hand a non-

denominational education was not only not a 'direct means of moral improvement', it could not supply a 'principle of social unity' either.

No less than Mill, Comte or Marx, Newman was conscious of the social implications of belief and the political implications of error. He was acutely aware of the vast number of souls of whom the modern world consisted. And he believed that Liberals, Socinians, latitudinarians, Whigs and the advocates of Useful Knowledge were not only incapable of making religion intelligible to them but were also part of a 'conspiracy' which was 'marshalling its hosts, ... enclosing the Church ... as in a net, and preparing the way for a general apostasy from it'.

The difficulty Newman felt in conceiving of Anglicanism as the antidote to Infidelity was that its chief seminaries, Oxford and Cambridge, were threatened with Nonconformity and that 'our rulers' did not want a powerful Church. What English rulers wanted was what French rulers, even the Bourbons, had wanted – a 'tame Church', a Church that would keep the people quiet. This was what the English Church had been made in 1688 and had remained subsequently as she became socially reliable, suppressed 'enthusiasm and extravagance' and developed that patriotic politics which was 'so fully understood and so eloquently stated at Conservative dinners and meetings'. And this, moreover, was what had 'shut' her 'up within walls', given her 'golden chains' and prevented her absorbing Wesley and Whitfield as the Roman Church had absorbed St Francis and St Philip Neri in Italy.

There is no reason to think that Newman wanted the Church of England to be disestablished or had worked out the ways in which it could go on keeping its property and yet 'not be dependent on the state'. Believing that the writing was on the wall, he drew the conclusions that 'party strife' was essential, that the Church must regain the influence which the State had denied her, and that Protestantism must be extirpated from the English mind.

V

In attacking Protestantism Newman believed himself to be attacking a system which was spiritually dead. But he also knew that he was attacking prevailing respectability. 'Viewed politically' Protestantism was a 'rallying point of all that was loyal and high-minded in the nation' and in pointing out that it was not the authorized doctrine of the Church of England, he was conscious of affronting a large and influential segment of established opinion.

Newman's objection to Protestantism was that it was theologically erroneous and morally dangerous – that private judgment induced pride, that, in playing down works and the Sacraments and in playing up Faith as an instrument of justification, it permitted Christians to 'contemplate themselves instead of Christ', and by dwelling to a fault on the 'sin and misery' of 'man's unrenewed nature' had established as 'carnal and hollow a pharisaism' and as lifeless a 'formalism' as Protestants thought they saw among the superstitions of Roman Catholicism. English Protestantism, indeed, was described as 'lingering in the tomb' and sitting down with 'Job among the ashes', and the challenge it presented as being to show why theology could do better with grace than with depravity.

Newman's distaste for Evangelical depravity was expressed in his *Lectures on Justification,* his distaste for private judgment in *Lectures on the Prophetical Office of the Church.* In both respects he was differentiating Catholicism from Rome as much as from Wittenberg and Geneva.

In Newman's writing in the middle 1830s, it was a common subject of complaint that since the Bible had failed to mention 'nearly all the doctrines' that were to be found in historic Christianity, private judgment, once accepted as the practice of the Church, would establish 'sincerity' as the sole test of thought and conduct, and permit each man to 'decide for himself what was Gospel truth and what ... not'. 'This was what the age was coming to' and Newman 'wished it observed.' Unless something drastic was done, the Bible would be given up as well as the Church until all that remained would be a pantheistic religion of beauty, philosophy and imagination. That was what Protestantism was becoming. It was because Protestantism lacked a 'correct theory' of the 'duties and office' of the Church and of the nature of 'tradition, Catholicity, Learning, Antiquity and the National Faith' that it was failing to protect the 'mass of Christians' from the heresies to which they were succumbing and degenerating into a 'vague ... creed' which explained less what was believed than what Protestants 'doubted, denied, ridiculed or resisted' about Rome.

Until late in the 1830s Newman's view of the Roman Church was that, though possessed of a capability for truth which the Protestant Churches lacked, it was distanced from truth both by the pragmatic corruptions which had grown up in the mediaeval Church and by the deliberate corruptions which had been established at Trent – not only corruptions of rite and observance and the political corruptions which he associated with 'jesuitism' and 'intrigue' but also a doctrinal corruption which assumed a false view of the powers of the human mind and promulgated an 'unclouded certainty' involving a 'complete theology' resting on 'abstract arguments' to which 'obedience' was required necessarily. Like Rationalism, that is to say, Tridentine Catholicism subjected God's Word to 'the intellect', justified the Christian scheme on 'antecedent ground' and assumed that 'any degree of doubt' needed an 'external, infallible assurance' to resolve it; and just as respectability had bound the Church of England in chains, so it was their 'science of gaining Heaven' which had bound Roman Catholics in chains and made it necessary to throw Papalism onto the rubbish heap on which Rationalism was lying already.

In the 1830s Newman was obsessed, initially in an Evangelical but then in a wider and more intellectual way, with the inroads which Christianity had suffered in the previous three centuries from rationalistic varieties of science, literature and philosophy. Rationalism was the disposition to ask for reasons when to do so was 'out of place' and then, having asked for them once, to keep on asking until enquiry reached the point at which it had to refer to 'self'. 'Self' was the enemy. It was by reference to 'self' that Rationalism made 'system' depend on 'sense', reduced religion to a human invention and ignored syllogistic reasoning's dependence on 'antecedent grounds' which, being 'incapable of proof', depended on faith in the absence of proof. It was faith, therefore, that was fundamental to thought, and through faith in some non-Protestant sense that Christianity was to receive the rehabilitation which Newman gave it in *Tracts for the Times, Lectures on Justification, Fifteen Sermons Preached Before the University of Oxford* and *Lectures on the Prophetical Office of the Church.*

In these works faith was a 'venture' which was necessary to salvation and was given by God without the intervention of human reasoning. Faith was necessary because rational certainty was impossible, but the fact that Christ had given truth, however mysteriously, meant that his own words had to be the yardstick of any interpretation they received. 'The words of Scripture, as of every other book ... had their own meaning.' It was the duty of Christians to 'find the real meaning, not to impose what would serve for a meaning', even when they lacked infallible assurance that their interpretation was correct. And this, moreover, was the reason for the tone of Anglican theology – its insistence on 'unclouded certainty' not being 'necessary for a Christian's hope and faith', on 'doubt' being not 'incompatible with practical abidence in the Truth', and on an 'external infallible assurance' not being 'necessary to exclude doubt'.

Newman was in no doubt that the Church of England had authority to declare and enforce the 'Apostolic Tradition', even when it did so in a cautious and limited way. Creeds had to be taught as dogmas and accepted in obedience, but the obedience that God wanted was 'Gospel' obedience – a 'law of liberty' which treated men not as 'servants ... subject to a code of formal commands' but as 'sons' who were asked to 'love Him and wish to please Him'. This was *Christian* freedom. It was crucial to Newman's rebuttal of both Protestantism and Roman omniscience and systematization and in *Lectures on Justification* was related to God's action in giving it.

In *Lectures on Justification* the central claim was that the Protestant doctrine of justification by faith was meaningless and the Roman doctrine of justification by obedience imperfect, and that a Catholic doctrine existed which made sense of the truths which Christ had disclosed. This began from the Pauline affirmation that, though in their 'natural state' and through their 'own strength' men could not be 'justified' by observance of the moral law, they '*could* obey unto justification' once Christ's atonement became 'inherent' in them. Human depravity, in other words, was remediable and, even if men were still sinful after justification, justification released them from natural bondage, made them 'Temples of the Holy Ghost', and enabled them to obey 'not as instruments merely but as agents, freely accepting or rejecting what they were offered'.

Newman wrote about the soul's life in terms that were personal and dramatic. Righteousness had to 'force its way in' in order to 'overcome pride and sloth'. The 'shame' that sinners felt when they realized their sin was 'agonizing', and Christ's entry into the soul brought 'fear and trembling'. Justification itself, indeed, was a 'spiritual circumcision or ... crucifixion of the flesh', the Cross being 'brought home' to men 'not in word but in power', healing, purifying, glorifying, but also 'drawing blood'.

The Cross ... in which St Paul gloried was not (what the word will literally mean, and which the Romanists sometimes seem to make it mean) the *material* cross on which Christ suffered – as little is it (what persons among ourselves would take it to be, without even the plea of being literal) the actual *Sacrifice* on the cross, but it is that Sacrifice coming in power to him who has faith in it, and converting body and soul into a sacrifice. It is the Cross, realised, present, living in him, sealing him, separating him from the world, sanctifying him, afflicting him. Thus the great Apostle clasped it to his heart, though it pierced it through like a sword; held it fast in his hands, though it cut them; reared it aloft, preached it, exulted in it. And thus we in our turn are allowed to hold it, commemorating and renewing individually by the ministry of the Holy Ghost, the death and resurrection of our Lord.

Newman's main object in the *Lectures on Justification* was to reaffirm the truth of the doctrine of Baptismal Regeneration. It was of the essence of his position that faith did not precede justification but justification faith, that justification made faith its instrument, and that faith was to be played down not only by comparison with Baptism but also by comparison with the rest of the Sacraments. The Sacraments were preserved by the Church, and it was by emphasizing the inseparability of reason's dependence on faith from faith's dependence on the Sacraments that Newman took his most distinctive steps towards providing the nation with a doctrine.

When Newman asked what it was that the nation should be taught, his answer was the 'Catholicism' which had been the religion of Christendom 'at least down to the Reformation' and had been taught in the English Church from Augustine's arrival in 597 until some time between the martyrdom of Charles I and the revolution of 1688. It was Catholicism to which the Church of England had to be restored, not just because that was her birthright and the religion of her founders, but also because that was what she had been protecting, whether she had known it or not, throughout her period of imprisonment. It was the 'Holy, Catholic and Apostolic Church' that the English people had had 'amongst them' through the years in which their rulers had tried to 'hide her divine tokens' from them, and in restoring these tokens, including miraculous tokens, to them, Newman provided for Monasticism, Confession and Excommunication, and the sort of reading clergy to which Palmer's *Church of Christ* had been addressed.

In the 1830s Newman held out the prospect of the Church of England becoming a universal Church. It was no merely insular Anglicanism that he claimed to be propagating, but the patristic Catholicism which ought to have been allowed to convert the British Empire in the eighteenth century. In regretting the opportunity which had been lost then, as in anticipating the opportunities which might be taken in England, in the Empire and eventually in Rome in the future, he alleged the crucial significance of the continuity of belief that linked Christ and the Apostles to the Bishops and Fathers of the undivided Church and to the Bishops of Churches which had preserved the faith of the undivided Church thereafter. It was episcopal Catholicism that he thought of as transcending the poetic Romanticism of his generation, episcopal Catholicism that would provide leadership against Democracy and the Rights of Man, episcopal Catholicism that alone had any chance of instilling 'humility' into the poor.

In 1837 Newman wrote of the Papacy as being 'aristocratic in carriage', while depending 'for its true power' on 'the multitude'. In attributing these characteristics to the Papacy which, though corrupted, was the corruption of an essentially spiritual power, he argued that 'the multitude' needed neither the revolutionary leadership which they were being offered on the Continent nor the political leadership which the Conservative Party was failing to offer in England. What 'the multitude' needed was the religious leadership which 'Catholicism' was capable of providing, since Catholicism alone, in supplying a dogmatic religion in place of a rationalistic religion which they did not understand, would hold up to 'thousands of hungry souls in all classes of life' the 'image of a true Christian people' living in 'apostolic ... strictness and awe'.

This was a demand for a public persona, not the crafty persona of the Popes nor the ranting persona of dissent, and certainly not the emotional abasement favoured by the evangelical personality. The demand was for plainness, simplicity, dignity and reserve, and for a personality which, when it 'hazarded', as in 'right Faith' it had to, did so 'deliberately, seriously, soberly, piously and humbly', substituting for the hitherto existing respect for 'birth, education, wealth and connections' the demands that were made by 'holiness of life'.

These conceptions were designed to rescue Christianity from extinction. In this phase of Newman's life, though 'Catholic' they were also Anglican. After 1845 they ceased to be.

2

Ruskin and Protestantism

'The civilised world is at this moment collectively just as Pagan as it was in the second century; a small body of believers being now as they were then representative of the Church of Christ in the midst of the faithless but there is just this difference, and this very fatal one, between the second and nineteenth centuries, that the Pagans are nominally and fashionably Christians.' John Ruskin *The Stones of Venice* 1853 vol. iii p. 109.

'I did not in my Good Friday's letter explain enough what I meant by saying I had come to the place where the "two ways met". I did not mean the division between religion and no religion; but between Christianity and philosophy: I should never, I trust, have become utterly reckless or immoral, but I might very possibly have become what most of the scientific men of the present day are: they all of them who are sensible believe in God, in *a* God, that is: and have I believe most of them very honourable notions of their duty to God and to man: but not finding the Bible arranged in a scientific manner, or capable of being tried by scientific tests, they give that up and are fortified in their infidelity by the weaknesses and hypocrisies of so-called religious men (who either hold to what they have been taught because they have never thought about it or pretend to believe it when they do not). The higher class of thinkers, therefore, for the most part, have given up the peculiarly Christian doctrines, and indeed nearly all thought of a future life. They philosophize upon this life, reason about death till they look upon it as no evil: and set themselves actively to improve this world and do as much good in it as they can. This is the kind of person that I must have become, if God had not appointed me to take the *other* turning: which having taken, I do not intend, with His help, ever to look back: for I have chosen to believe under as strong and overwhelming a sense of the difficulties of believing as it is, I think, possible ever to occur to me again ... To believe in a future life is for me, the only way in which I can enjoy this one, and that not with a semi-belief which would still allow me to be vexed at what occurred to me here but with such a thorough belief as will no more allow me to be annoyed by earthly misfortune than I am by grazing my knee when I am climbing an Alp.' John Ruskin to his father, Easter Day [11 April 1852] in J. L. Bradley *Ruskin's Letters from Venice 1851–2* 1955 pp. 246–7.

'We cannot reason of these things. But this I know – and this may by all men be known – that no good or lovely thing exists in this world without its correspondent darkness; and that the universe presents itself continually to mankind under the stern aspect of warning, or of choice, the good and the evil set on the right hand and the left. And in this mountain gloom, which weighs so strongly upon the human heart that in all time hitherto, as we have seen, the hill defiles have been either avoided in terror or inhabited in penance, there is but the fulfilment of the universal law, that where the beauty and wisdom of the Divine working are most manifested, there also are manifested most clearly the terror of God's wrath, and inevitableness of His power.' John Ruskin *Modern Painters* 1856 vol. iv p. 351.

The wave of conversions to Roman Catholicism in the early 1840s marked the first rift in High Anglicanism and the first sign since Wesley that loyalty to the Church of England would be called in question. It was paralleled at the same time and as a result of some of the same influences by a series of symbolic transformations through which Evangelicalism was to lose its authority.

In early nineteenth-century England Evangelicalism was the strongest form of practical religion and an integral part of established Anglicanism. It produced a large devotional literature and a perpetual call for amendment of life. In Simeon it had a major preacher, from Wilberforce a seminal work, and through Shaftesbury a major influence on public action; as the Evangelical party, it exerted a decisive effect on the government of the Church of England.

The Evangelical party, though practical and political, was not gifted intellectually, became less gifted as the century proceeded, and showed increasingly little grasp of the intellectual dangers by which Christianity was confronted. Though it will appear in Volume III, therefore, as an aspect of Anglicanism and dissent, it will appear in this volume through thinkers who were easing themselves out of its framework. Newman has appeared already; Manning, Stephen, Huxley, George Eliot, Ellis and Patmore will appear later. In this chapter and the next, two brilliant Evangelicals will be shown prising open narrownesses and inserting elements which were to transform their view of Christianity.

Gladstone was born in 1809, Ruskin in 1819. Both were brought up in Evangelical homes. Both wished to distance themselves from the eighteenth century; both absorbed the Romantic and Tractarian conceptions through which in their generations distancing was conducted. Both began by defending Evangelicalism against subversion but both failed to make it the controlling principle of a wider culture. In the course of failing to do this, both helped to transform Evangelicalism's substance.

The insertion of a wider culture was crucial and ambiguous; it created a relevant, modern idiom but it also submerged the substance of the message – in party Liberalism in Gladstone's case, in romantic pantheism in Ruskin's.

I

Ruskin[1] had a comprehensive mind which he turned to most aspects of life. It is not, however, because Gothic was good or Turner the only real painter, or because the architecture of the High Middle Ages was the greatest achievement of European Art, that Ruskin is significant here. Neither is it because of his rejection of Political Economy, his concern for the craftsman or his belief that a universally available education was a remedy for the oppressions of industrialism. What deserves attention is his sense of the relationship between history, religion, aesthetics, literature, politics and morality which he helped to insert at the heart of Victorian high thinking as holes were plugged in the walls of authority which had been left by what he took to be the well-deserved death of aristocratic England.

Ruskin wanted the 'multitude' to believe in the things that he believed in. In the first phase of his career these were more Protestant then Turnerian, in the second phase more Socialist than Protestant. In both phases and at all times, Ruskin addressed himself not just to the technical problems raised by the subjects about which he was writing but also to the rôle they should play in the creation of a social doctrine.

The greatest phase in Ruskin's thought was between 1843 and 1860. In the 1860s and 1870s he made a far-reaching statement which bit deeply into the mind of the Victorian intelligentsia and the English Labour movement. The Ruskin of the 1860s and 70s, however, had been stranded; whatever effect his writing may have had on other thinkers, it had arisen in such intimate connection with religion and

---

[1] John Ruskin (1819–1900). Educ. Camberwell, King's College, London, and Christ Church, Oxford. Author of *Modern Painters* 5 vols, 1843–60, *The Seven Lamps of Architecture* 1849, *The King of the Golden River* 1851, *The Stones of Venice* 3 vols. 1851–3, *Notes on the Construction of Sheepfolds* 1851, *Pre-Raphaelitism* 1851, *Giotto and His Work in Padua* 1854, *Lectures on Architecture and Painting* 1854, *The Opening of the Crystal Palace* 1854, *Notes on Some of the Principal Pictures Exhibited in the Rooms of the Royal Academy* 1855, *The Harbours of England* 1856, *Notes on the Turner Gallery* 1856, *The Elements of Drawing* 1857, *The Political Economy of Art* 1857, *The Unity of Art* 1859, *Unto This Last* 1862.

embodied so magnificent a failure to make religion central to life that the genesis must be judged to have been more interesting than the outcome, and *Modern Painters, The Stones of Venice* and *The Seven Lamps of Architecture*, strange and curious as they are, more worthy of attention and profounder in their implications than all his other works put together.

In Ruskin's life there were two transitions – the first involving an attempt to reconcile Protestantism with Art, the second involving Art and Socialism taking over from Art and Protestantism. Just as 1842–5 was the important turning-point in Newman's life, so 1858–61 was the important turning-point in Ruskin's. By 1861, in his early forties, Ruskin had flown off into the stratosphere as certainly as Newman had flown off in his early forties in 1843. By then Ruskin had had his marriage annulled, had fallen in love with a nine-year-old girl and lost faith in the Protestantism of his parents, and had begun to teach and preach the doctrine that he was to teach and preach in the last thirty years of his life. It is true that *Modern Painters* was a Christian document right up to the end of the final volume in 1860, that Ruskin was re-Christianized in the 1870s and that in the 1880s, when mad, he thought of becoming a Roman Catholic. But what had been abandoned between 1858 and 1861 was not really restored, and Ruskin was right to believe, as he did, that a faith which had once been lost was unlikely ever fully to be regained.

Ruskin's later doctrine exercised an uplifting influence on many writers and in all classes. But it was a sociological rather than a religious doctrine or, if religious, was so much dominated by its sociological, as to have lost its Christian, content. In this chapter we shall confine ourselves to the attempt which Ruskin made between 1843 and 1860 to provide a Protestant content for Art.

When Ruskin began his literary career, precociously at the age of seventeen, he was a defender of Turner, a competent poet and the exponent of the view that poetry, painting, architecture, politics, religion and morality had to be understood in connection with one another. In an article and in an unpublished essay about literature in 1836, and in a more or less contemporaneous essay on painting and music, he gave expression to the connected views that Turner's imagination was 'Shakespearean' and that, 'with the sole exception of Shakespeare, Byron was the greatest poet' because he was the 'most

miserable man' that had ever lived. In another essay he ascribed
the shortcomings of contemporary architecture to the insensitivity
which architects were displaying towards architecture's 'poetry' and
their failure to understand that a man could not really be an architect
unless he was also a metaphysician. It was through the 'intricacy of
feeling' involved in the 'raising of an edifice' and through the connection between a nation's architecture on the one hand and skies and
scenery and 'prevailing turns of mind' on the other that Ruskin discerned that 'unity of feeling' on which the poetry of architecture
depended.

These were occasional, juvenile and not very systematic intuitions.
They were sustained by assumptions about the priesthood of all believers, the relevance of poetry and geology to the 'great end of salvation'
and the belief that 'Galileo, Newton, Davy, Michel Angelo, Raphael
and Handel' had been 'employed more effectively to the glory of God
... than if they had been occupied ... in direct priestly exertion'. There
was Carlylean heroism and a doubt whether the 'plain duties' that
Ruskin might perform as a clergyman if he were to be ordained could
properly be renounced on the off chance that he might become a
Galileo, Raphael, Wordsworth or Bacon. When Ruskin was twenty-
four these undergraduate fantasies were subsumed and achieved in
volume i of *Modern Painters*.

When volume i of *Modern Painters* appeared in 1843, it established
that conflict was likely between 'the multitude' on the one hand and
those who established taste on the other, between Ruskin, Turner and
Turner's associates on the one hand and the taste of the age on the
other, and between Turnerian painters and the historical painters of
the fifteenth century on the one hand and the landscape painters of the
seventeenth and eighteenth centuries on the other. Above all, it established that there was a fundamental difference between painting as a
language or technique which had to be mastered by anyone who
wanted to be a painter, and painting as thought which related the
excellences characteristic of the painter 'as such' to the excellences
which belonged to the painter 'in common with all men of intellect'.

In volume i Ruskin wrote as a 'man of intellect' and in full consciousness of the responsibility which the 'man of intellect' had to
determine taste. He wrote for his equals, not for the multitude. He
wrote for minds which were 'educated ... and capable of appreciating

merit'. He was willing to encounter 'whatever opprobrium' he might encounter in demonstrating whatever 'points of superiority' he might discern in the modern painters whose works he was celebrating, and he made it characteristic of the 'great picture' that it conveyed the 'greatest number of the greatest ideas', invited 'communion with a new mind' and brought the 'impetuous motions of a noble ... intelligence' to bear upon the 'repetitive, rule-regulated standard painting' with which 'half the walls of Europe' were said to be covered.

In volume i Ruskin did not push these ideas to their conclusion; the central sections discussed merely the need for painters to begin by recording the truths of nature, and described at length the truths that were to be found in Tone, Colour, Space, Water, Mountains, Vegetation, Clouds and Skies, along with the demonstrations which had been given by Prout, Harding, Stanfield, Fielding and Turner of the truths he was proclaiming.

Ruskin, though he may not quite have known it, was contributing to a revolution in taste and, in doing so, was equipped with both an existing body of painting and a set of theoretical justifications derived from Hooker and Dante, Plato and Bishop Butler, Wordsworth and Coleridge and as a facet of Romanticism generally. He distinguished sense-impressions from comprehension and argued that the historic task was to convert sense-impressions *into* comprehension. For the highest kinds of comprehension love was said to be needed in its 'intimate and holy functions', and it was only when love was present that a painter could understand Nature's detail and variety, and convey the truths which it was his business to convey.

The chief reason that Ruskin gave for writing volume i was to defend Turner against the accusation of painting 'more falsehood and less fact' than any other contemporary painter. From that point of view, the analytical sections of part i were designed to show that Nature was as Turner had painted it. It was not only in this sense, however, that Turner's supremacy was affirmed; it was also made clear that Turner was playing in Ruskin's mind an even more fundamental role than Athanasius had played in Newman's mind in *The Arians of the Fourth Century* ten years earlier – 'as a prophet of God' who had been sent to reveal 'the mysteries of His Universe'.

There is no reason to suppose that Turner had strong religious feelings, was pleased to have been taken for a Messiah or could really have understood what Ruskin was talking about. Nor need we explain this defect in Turner's mentality, as Ruskin did, by referring to Turner's lack of education. Least of all is there reason to suppose that Turner felt himself to be a 'prophet of God'.

In volume i of *Modern Painters*, nevertheless, God appeared often. The Truths of Nature were His Truths which were traced out by those whose lamps had been lit by Him, and a man of taste was a man who gained pleasure from objects which God intended should give pleasure. God alone knew the body and soul of Nature in its inwardness and individuality, and it was painting's highest achievement to represent the 'depth and mystery' of Nature's spirit in its 'secret and high operations'. The soul of Nature, indeed, was said to be 'the deity', and the poet (and presumably the painter) in providing a representation of Nature to be supplying not only 'prophecy and revelation' for Man but also 'adoration' and a history of His Universe for God.

Volume i attracted criticism; in face of criticism Ruskin insisted that it had been only a preliminary. Moreover, between volume i and volume ii, he became aware of Lord Lindsay and a feeling for Christian art of which he expected Lindsay to become the spokesman. He also revisited Italy and discovered in Fra Angelico and Giotto a fertility of Christian painting which he had not appreciated before. At the same time he was moving against ordination and felt obliged to establish that he was not neglecting his duty in choosing to be a painter and critic rather than a clergyman. Volume ii of *Modern Painters* made a systematic statement both about the high functions that the painter could perform and about the extent to which Art could be justified even when a man's primary duty – perhaps the primary duty of every 'man of intellect' – was to save souls.

What distinguished volume ii was its dogmatic and theological content, the Christian function that was claimed for the painter and the implication that painting involved a discerning of God's will. Volume ii was 'God-intoxicated'. It saw God everywhere and presented God's will as the object of all the actions of the painter. There was also, however, an argument about painting, and it is likely that even the argument about God, and certainly its connection with the argument about painting, will be understood best if the argument about painting is discussed first.

II

In *Modern Painters* ii, Ruskin made his statutory declaration against Utilitarianism. He dismissed the 'calculating metropolis of manufactures' into which Europe had been 'contracted' and argued that Art had 'functions of usefulness' which were addressed to the 'weightiest human interests'. In establishing the 'weight' of these 'interests', he explained why it was that he wished to turn 'Aesthetics' into *'Theoria'*.

What *Theoria* meant in volume ii was distinguished from aesthetic appreciation by the fact that aesthetic appreciation was, where *Theoria* was not, a 'mere operation of the sense'. *Theoria* gave to the appreciation of beauty an elevating, indeed a moral, character, being no 'mere amusement' designed to 'tickle' the 'soul's sleep' but an 'eternal and inexhaustible fact', issuing in an 'exulting' perception which rendered even the 'lower and more sensual pleasures' theoretic. Only by engaging their moral capability and dedicating their lives to Art could painters disclose the beauty of the physical universe; only when their moral capability was in common operation could there be widespread public appreciation of the beauty which painters displayed. Volume ii left no doubt that without a 'pure, right and open state of the heart' the appreciation of beauty would be impossible.

The range of beauty that was open to the theoretic faculty within its limits thus conceived, was universal. The chapters on Physical Beauty identified the types of loveliness in Inorganic Nature; subsequent chapters described the 'vital healthy beauty' that was created by the sight of living beings, including men, 'solicitously fulfilling' their 'functions'. Both types of beauty were said to be discernible by the theoretic faculty. What the theoretic faculty could not discern, since it did not exist on earth, was 'consummate beauty', a 'beauty ... greater than we see', whether in relation to Nature or Man, and it was in dealing with this that the Coleridgean and the Platonic Imaginations were brought into play.

In describing the 'penetrative' function of the Imagination, Ruskin claimed to be describing the 'highest intellectual power of man', and it was said to be as true of great painting as of great poetry that, though often 'obscure, mysterious and interrupted in the giving of outer detail', it did not stop short at 'crusts, ashes, or outward images' but, 'cutting down to the very root', drew the 'vital sap of that it dealt with'. It was of a moral as well as of an artistic function that Ruskin was thinking when he wrote of the Imagination 'revealing by intuition and intensity of gaze ... a more essential truth than was seen on the surface of things' and of it doing this in ways which were 'mysterious and inexplicable', owning no laws and denying all restraint, carrying the painter over 'untrodden plains' towards the end that he sought and integrating the ideas that he used until the 'whole' of a picture could be seen before him.

This was the argument of *Modern Painters* volume ii – put secularly, as it were – that it was the painter's mind which transcribed Nature or Man, and disclosed truths about their inner relations. In terms of religion its argument was that Man's end was to 'witness to the glory of God' by producing a Christian painting which 'evidenced ... the universal dominion of ... God's chastising, animating and disposing Mind'.

Ruskin's conception of a Christian painting was connected with his conception of a non-Christian painting. By non-Christian painting he meant a painting that was acceptable to a Whig or Utilitarian paganism based on sense-impressions and the philosophy of sensation and allowing the lust and luxuries of a 'sensual art' to overlay the joy, love, thankfulness and veneration characteristic of man's moral nature.

In *Modern Painters* ii, Ruskin did not develop the historical structure that he was to develop later about the delinquencies of the Renaissance; he did not get far beyond explaining that secular painting lacked joy, love, thankfulness and veneration, and that it was the business of a Christian painting to break in on its defects of sympathy and sensibility. It was because harshness and fearfulness had eluded paganism as they were eluding Whiggish sarcasm and Utilitarianism that Christian thinking alone could rise to the level of the painter's opportunity.

Christian Theoria [went a typical passage] ... finds its food and the objects of its love everywhere, in what is harsh and fearful as well as what is kind: may, even in all that seems coarse and commonplace, seizing that which is good, and sometimes delighting more at finding its table spread in strange places, and in the presence of its enemies, and its honey coming out of the rock, than if we all were harmonised into a less wondrous pleasure; hating only what is self-sighted and insolent of men's work, despising all that is not of God, unless reminding it of God, yet able to find evidence of Him still where all seems forgetful of Him, and to turn that into a witness of His working which was meant to obscure it; and so with clear and unoffended sight beholding Him for ever, according to the written promise 'blessed are the pure in heart, for they shall see God'.

In considering the types of beauty to be found in Inorganic Nature, Ruskin elaborated a scholastic synthesis in which the painting that

displayed them was conceived of as being beautiful because it represented attributes of the Divine Nature. This synthesis was worked out
in considerable detail. Thus Infinity was treated as representing God's
incomprehensibility, with the sky being seen as the 'glory of His dwelling place'. Repose represented God's permanence along with 'trustful-
ness in His presence ... under the Christian dispensation', while divine
justice was embodied in symmetry, divine energy and spirituality in
purity, and the divine capacity for governing by law in the effortless
restraint through which 'the very being of God was a law to His own
Being'. The same line of argument was applied to the types of beauty
that were to be found in Organic Nature and to the divine function
which the painter performed in disclosing beauty in Human Nature.

In accounting for human beauty, Ruskin both alleged an idio-
syncrasy and gave a Christian reason for it. Whereas in all non-human
creatures, there was said to be a high degree of completion, in man
alone there was no 'fixed type'. In fallen man, moreover, as Christians
understood him, there was an 'evil diversity': there were bodies
wracked by 'sickness, sensuality, passion, poverty, sorrow, remorse,
sloth, labour, and disease', and in relation to these, the painter had a
task to perform – a task which had not been performed by Greek
sculpture – to restore to the human body the 'grace and power' which
'inherited disease' had destroyed and to the human spirit and intellect
the purity and grasp that they had had in paradise. This was described
as undoing the work which the devil had done, and the reason why the
Christian painter could do it, where others could not, was because of
the mentality into which he had been inducted by Christ.

This was a mentality which felt love and charity towards everything
and assumed that everything that existed, however harsh and imperfect, had a part to play in God's providence. It was a mentality which
was 'patient' and 'retentive', and was for ever 'growing, learning, reading and worshipping'. It was a mentality above all which knew that
true taste was not proud, fastidious or self-regarding, that 'he drew
nothing well who thirsted not to draw everything' and that there was
'that to be seen in every street and lane of every city, that to be found
and felt in every ... heart and countenance, that to be loved in every
roadside weed and moss-grown wall which, in the hands of faithful
men, might convey emotions of glory and sublimity continual and
exalted'.

In justifying the conception of a Christian painting, *Modern
Painters* ii attempted to establish a social and theological function,

indeed a social and theological utility – 'witnessing to the glory of God' – to replace the practical, mechanical utility which the first twenty pages had shown 'drawing and twitching the ancient frame and strength of England'. It was in protest against the 'iron roads' that were 'tearing up the surface of Europe' and the 'cafés and gaming houses' that were superseding the monuments of the past, that Ruskin offered his Evangelical 'summons' to resist relaxation, reject sarcasm and remind the 'holy mind' and 'moral energies' of the nation that painting had as high a function to perform as the function that Ruskin had abandoned in abandoning ordination. In *The Seven Lamps of Architecture* a similar function was established for architecture through consideration of the 'magnificently intellectual schools of Christian architecture' that Ruskin had found in mediaeval Venice and Verona, in the Val d'Arno, and in Rouen, Caen, Bayeux and Coutance.

III

At the beginning of *The Seven Lamps of Architecture* Ruskin drew a distinction between building – 'putting together and adjusting the several pieces of any edifice' – and architecture, the art which 'so disposes and adorns ... edifices ... that the sight of them may contribute to man's mental health, power and pleasure'. All architecture 'impressed' on the 'form' of a building 'certain characters' which were 'venerable or beautiful' but otherwise unnecessary. In Chapters i to vi, Ruskin listed the lamps that architecture ought to light. These were the lamps of Sacrifice, Truth, Power, Beauty, Life and Memory and they were represented as showing how 'every form of noble architecture was in some sort the embodiment of the polity, life, history and religious fate of nations'. In discussing these lamps, Ruskin began significantly with Sacrifice.

In criticizing the contemporary desire to produce 'the largest results at the least cost', Ruskin made the point that God wanted Sacrifice, and that it was the 'failing faith' of the modern world which had been responsible for providing a luxurious domestic architecture where 'the tenth part of the expense' that was used on it, if 'collectively offered and wisely employed', would have been sufficient to build a marble church in every town in England.

Ruskin claimed not to want marble churches 'for their own sakes' since, for example, in a village the 'simplicity' of a 'pastoral sanctuary' would be lovelier than the 'majesty of an urban temple'. The reason for wanting an improved church architecture was the aid that this would give to the piety of the builder. It was not 'the church' that Ruskin wanted 'but the sacrifice'; not the 'emotion of admiration, but the act of adoration; not the gift but the giving'; and this because, like all other arts, architecture would 'never flourish' until it was 'primarily devoted' by 'both architect and employer' to the service of religion. There had to be restraint and thankfulness, an avoidance of idolatry and superstition and a Protestant simplicity, integrity and unpresumingness. But it was assumed that work done in adoration of God would be done better than work that was not so done and that, since God 'never forgot any work of labour or love', it would follow that 'whatever it might be of which the first portion or power had been presented to Him, He would multiply and increase sevenfold'.

These conceptions were most apparent in Chapter i. But it was apparent throughout Chapters ii to vi that the Truth, Beauty, Life, Power and Memory, which a 'living architecture' ought to embody, ought to be offered to God, that all six Lamps were aids that architecture gave men to become what God intended them to be, and that, when properly lit, they signified the victory of true life over the false life of custom and accident in which external objects moulded and assimilated men instead of men moulding and assimilating *them*.

In these chapters Ruskin was trying, rather cunningly, to absorb architecture – all architecture – into a Protestant system which combined an adoring Gothic demonstrativeness with warnings against popish exhibition and vulgarity and the advance of papal power in England. He left no doubt that, despite a 'natural disposition' towards Roman Catholicism and ties with friends who had become Roman Catholics, he regarded the Roman Church as 'in the fullest sense anti-Christian' and that Catholic Emancipation had been so 'capital an error' in treating a 'purely religious' as though it was a 'purely political' question, that it was doubtful whether England would ever again be what she should be 'until the Romanist was expelled from the place which had been impiously conceded to him among her legislators'.

All this implied the need for a doctrine, but the difficulty as *The Seven Lamps of Architecture* presented it, was that England was not in a frame of mind to have a doctrine. In the concluding chapter, Ruskin argued the need for a doctrine, presenting the lamp of Obedience as 'the saving grace of all the rest' and the principle to which 'polity owed its stability, Life its happiness, Faith its acceptance and Creation its continuance'. The lamp of Obedience alone showed the way to the need for authoritative teaching both as an aid to the establishment of taste and as an antidote to liberty and license, and it was the need to associate liberty with obedience which justified the conclusion that the essential preliminary to social and political, as well as to artistic, achievement, was the entrenchment of a style, the establishment of a school of thought and the promulgation of a doctrine to which obedience could be given.

It does not matter one marble splinter [Ruskin wrote in the concluding chapter of *The Seven Lamps of Architecture*] whether we have an old or new architecture, but it matters everything whether we have an architecture truly so-called or not ... whether an architecture whose laws might be taught at our schools from Cornwall to Northumberland as we teach English spelling and English grammar, or an architecture which is to be invented fresh every time we build a workhouse or a parish school.

As between architectural styles Ruskin had preferences and also reasons for his preferences – Romanesque, Early Western Gothic, Venetian Gothic and Early English Decorated being expected to break down social emulation and ritualistic conflict and, in helping the poor to view their 'tenements' as 'sacred temples', to enhance 'fellowship' and 'natural virtue' and spare England the horror and discontent which had been God's judgment on the idleness of the revolutionary and governing classes on the Continent.

In identifying 'idleness' as the cause of revolution, Ruskin specified two forms of under-employment – the under-employment which was created when 'semi-gentlemen' who ought to have been shoemakers or carpenters spent their time 'disturbing governments', and the under-employment which was created when 'railway navvies and iron founders' performed feats of 'mechanical' ingenuity when they ought to have been building 'houses and churches'. An Evangelical distaste for idle luxury and the need to revive mental occupation amongst the educated young provided reasons for encouraging handicrafts as the antidote to revolution in the future.

In providing for resistance to revolution, Ruskin, though reactionary, was in no way aristocratic. On the contrary, his virtue was gnarled and republican. He condemned the principles of 1789 and 1848, but he also condemned the society in which he lived. It was not in order to protect the interests of any existing class or group, far less to defend an effete aristocracy, that he conceptualized a coincidence between the 'constant, general and irrefragable laws of right' through which God governed 'the moral world' and the spiritual rôle which landscape painting and architecture had taken over from the 'fields and woods' as Nature had withdrawn and modern men had been 'thrown back upon the city gates'.

The Seven Lamps of Architecture, like *Modern Painters* i and ii, though thóroughly naturalistic, was the work of a romantic historical sensibility. In these volumes, however, history was in the background. It was not until the three volumes of *The Stones of Venice* that it came to the forefront.

IV

The Stones of Venice did three things. It was an essay, first of all, about the decline in Venetian power down to the Napoleonic occupation of 1797. Secondly, it recovered from their present, and established a chronology for, the past forms which Venice's buildings had taken before restoration and rebuilding had obscured them, and used the chronology it discovered to show how the buildings that still stood in the nineteenth century were related to the mentalities that had conceived them. Finally, it gave an historical evaluation of Venetian architecture which was alleged to contain in the Doge's Palace 'the central building in the history of the world'. The book was bound together by its conclusion, that the deterioration in Venetian architecture and painting, and the decline in Venetian power, were facets of the Venetian neglect of private religion from the fifteenth century onwards.

This was historical writing grandly conceived and magniloquently executed. It was not, however, a history of material difficulty. It recognized the existence of, but did not discuss, markets and trade rivalry and the strategy of war, the decline it discussed beginning somewhat arbitrarily with two deaths in 1418 and 1423. Its subject was national heroism and solidarity, not national commerce; it explained decline by reference to politics and religion, and drew the conclusion that England must suffer the fate of Venice if she did not read in the history of Venice a warning variant of the 'exaltation, sin and punishment of Tyre'.

In discussing what after all was a Catholic city, Ruskin praised not Venetian Catholicism but the 'deep ... tone of individual religion' which had defied the Church of Rome and effected the 'total exclusion of ecclesiastics' from all share in government. Venetians were praised for being in their period of glory so thoroughly unified by earlier experience of adversity and death that Venetian greatness was no mere aristocratic achievement but the outcome of a 'training' which had enabled all Venetians to be 'masters of themselves' and 'servants of their country'.

The central statements in *The Stones of Venice* were made in the two hundred or so pages entitled 'The Nature of Gothic' in volume ii and the two hundred or so pages entitled 'The Renaissance Period' in volume iii. Between them these sections said almost everything that Ruskin wished to say about the religious function of architecture and about the rôle which Venetian architecture had played in the development of architectural style.

In describing the Doge's Palace as 'the central building in the history of the world', Ruskin meant that Venice had been the meeting point of three pre-eminent architectures, each of which had expressed 'a condition of religion'. It was by synthesizing the principles embodied in Roman, Lombard and Arab architecture that Venice had created 'all that was greatest in Christian art in the thirteenth century' and it was the disintegration of this synthesis which had been responsible for failure thereafter.

At the beginning of volume i the principles were described with a degree of personification. To the 'shaft' and 'arch' which had been created by the Greeks and Romans were attributed architecture's 'framework' and 'strength' and to the 'pointing' and 'foliation' of the arch which had been introduced by the Arabs architecture's 'sanctity' and 'spirituality'. Christianity's seizure of the arch 'as her own' was explained, along with the childlike radiance which had 'flamed up under Constantine' and 'illumined the shores' of the Bosphorous, the Aegean and the Adriatic. Romanesque was shown declining with the decline of the type of Christianity which had 'animated' it, and then being swept away by Lombard energy and system from one direction and by Arab iconoclasm from another.

The Stones of Venice dealt with the successive phases of this history – initially in the Byzantine, Romanesque and Arab phases, then in the Gothic phase which prevailed during the 'central epochs of Venetian life'; finally during the degradation of the Renaissance. In each of these periods Venice was shown to have been central. And just as in her 'strength' she had been at the 'centre of the past currents of Christian civilisation', so in her decline she had given Renaissance architecture the pre-eminence it had acquired in the eyes of Europe. In Venice

Ruskin claimed, in a famous and significant conception, the hand of God could be shown disappearing visibly from the Doge's Palace in the course of the fourteenth century. It was in Venice therefore, and in Venice alone, that 'effectual blows' could be 'struck' at the 'pestilent' character of Renaissance art and architecture, and it was the most important aim of volume iii to destroy the 'admiration' these had attracted by connecting them with the decline of national heroism and solidarity.

This decline, or 'fall', was described at length. What matters for understanding Ruskin's doctrine, however, is not so much *The Fall* by itself or *The Nature of Gothic* by itself as the melodramatic conflict that was symbolized by the contrast Ruskin drew between the Gothic cathedrals which were good and Bellini's St Peter's and Wren's St Paul's which were bad, and between the empty classicism of 'Harley Street, Baker Street and Gower Street' and the 'rich sculpture' and 'glowing colour' that would have been found in the streets of thirteenth-century Venice.

Volume iii of *The Stones of Venice* made the most sustained statement of the hatred that Ruskin felt for the modern world. It was by exposing the religious foundations of evil as they appeared in all Renaissance activities that he showed most clearly why he wanted to 'cast out' of the modern world anything that was in any way connected with the 'proud', 'cold', luxurious', 'rule-regulated' characteristics that he associated with 'Greek, Roman and Renaissance architecture'.

In explaining Venice's decline in terms of religion, Ruskin did not mean by religion only worship, prayer or the reading of the Bible; he also meant the fundamental assumptions within which life was lived, society governed and buildings built. He meant 'the formalism' of the Renaissance, its subordination of religious subjects to 'purposes of portraiture and decoration' and its mistrust of the 'tenderness and feeling' that had been manifested in the spontaneity of Gothic ornament. He meant Renaissance humanism's pride and insolence, an 'infidelity' that was 'the more fatal' for retaining 'the form and language of faith', and the aristocratic isolation which the Renaissance had created between workmen working slavishly in pursuit of an unattainable perfection, and an architecture which 'insulted the poor in its every line'.

The defects of the Renaissance thus had socio-political as well as religious aspects. But it was its religious defects which were represented as having provoked both the Protestant attempt at reanimation and the Tridentine attempt at control, and as producing in reaction to both the aristocratic Rationalism which had received its just reward when 'liberty' and 'license' had destroyed it in 1789. Most significantly of all, Ruskin asserted that the disintegration which had begun in the fifteenth century had not yet been halted, that the 'civilised world' of 1853 was 'collectively, just as pagan' as 'the civilised world' had been in the second century, and that it was to this situation that Gothic had to address itself.

In *The Stones of Venice*, no less than Turner in *Modern Painters* i and ii, Gothic was the hero, and the essence of Gothic was that, though visibly distinguished by pointed arches, vaulted roofs, flying buttresses and grotesque sculptures, it was in fact a 'faithful' expression of the savageness, love of change, love of nature, obstinacy, generosity and disturbed imagination which had constituted the 'mental character' or 'soul' of the Gothic builder.

In elaborating this description, Ruskin reproduced in relation to Gothic the compliments that *Modern Painters* i and ii had paid to Turner. He emphasized Gothic's interest in man's 'mortal as well as his spiritual aspects' and its ability to bring a 'majestic harmony' out of man's 'haste, anger, pride, sensuality, fortitude and faith'. He associated Gothic with 'truth' and a religious confidence that even imperfection would 'work ... for good'. He described Gothic ornament as displaying a Christian recognition of the 'value of every soul' and presented the Gothic workman as being free to do what he did to God's glory, however imperfect the resulting ornamentation might be. It was by 'confessing ... imperfection' and by recognizing that the workman was not 'meant' to work 'with the accuracy of tools' or his soul's eye 'bent upon the finger point' as Renaissance workmen had done that the primary justification was given for admiring Gothic's adaptation of Christian principle.

Ruskin's account of the Gothic soul had important implications for the English soul. It deplored the 'slavery' which England had suffered as craftsmen had been yoked to 'machinery', the grand mockery of the High-Gothic craftsman reduced to the 'word-wit' of the modern workman and the 'animation' of the 'multitudes sent like fuel to feed the factory smoke'. Long before *The Political Economy of Art* Ruskin made it obvious that he had Gothic as well as Turnerian reasons for disliking Adam Smith and Political Economy, for remembering that the Protestant virtues had been expressed in Gothic's 'every line' and for understanding that it was only in the 'veined foliage ... thorny fretwork, shadowy niches, buttressed pier and fearless height of ... pinnacle and ... tower' which had been 'the distinctive creation of the Gothic school' that could be traced any sign of the 'moral habits' to which in the 'present age' England owed the 'kind of greatness that she had' – 'the habits of philosophical investigation ... accurate thought ... domestic seclusion and independence ... stern self-reliance ... and sincere upright researching into religious truth'.

In *Modern Painters* i and ii Ruskin had considered painting as a contribution to public doctrine. In *The Seven Lamps of Architecture* and *The Stones of Venice* he had considered architecture. In *Modern Painters* iii he considered literature.

V

When young, Ruskin had intended to be a poet as much as he had intended to be a painter or a critic: renunciation of the attempt to be a poet coincided with rejection of the idea that he should be ordained. Almost all of his poetry was written before 1845, and he seems to have taken little interest when his father published *Poems by John Ruskin* in 1850. Poetry and literature, however, he thought of as contributing no less to public doctrine than painting and architecture, and volume iii of *Modern Painters* was about poetry and literature at least as much as it was about painting.

Modern Painters iii–v was a series of essays rather than books and to a large extent merely repeated what Ruskin had written in the previous ten years about the 'poison of Raphael and Palladio', the pride and irreligion of the Renaissance and the effect which Art, including pre-Raphaelite Art, could have on men's minds and spirits. What was new in these volumes was the treatment of literature.

In a course of lectures that he gave on architecture and landscape painting in Edinburgh in 1853, Ruskin proclaimed it his aim to insert into the minds of the 'practical men' who ruled the city what he thought of as a romantic component – a 'secret enthusiasm' which practical men tried to 'resist' but which was not only 'one of the holiest parts of their being' but was also a truer part of their being than their consciences. Though Ruskin called on his audience to make up their own minds, what he really meant was that they should defer to the 'geniuses' or 'great men' who were better guides to taste than they were. It was to the 'high mental supremacy' of 'genius' that he wished 'practical men' to defer, and the claims that he made on behalf of the 'god-made great man' in art were vast, far vaster than those he made for 'genius' in any comparable activity, and at least as significant as anything that he had claimed for priestly inspiration in the past. Given the assumption that 'great art' was the work of the 'whole living creature' addressing the 'whole living creature' and that it was the architect's 'duty' to 'evoke' an 'answering call' from the souls he addressed, one can see why relations between *genius* and *practical men* were so central to any plan that Ruskin might have had for a Gothic restoration.

In the central chapters of *Modern Painters* iii, Ruskin discussed landscape as it appeared in the poetry of three of the 'greatest geniuses' the world had known. These geniuses were Homer, Dante and Sir Walter Scott, and they were dealt with not only in connection with Turner, but also because their attitudes towards landscape reflected or represented the religious attitudes of the Greek, the mediaeval and the modern worlds.

In comparing attitudes Ruskin aimed to show how distinctive modern attitudes were, how peculiar when compared with the attitudes that had prevailed in the previous three thousand years, and how important it was that modern attitudes should not be sustained by modern complacency about them.

In this connection Homer was a shadowy figure, little more than a stick with which to beat modern hypocrisy. Dante also was used polemically and by way of contrast as Gothic had been used in *The Stones of Venice*. But the central features of the mediaeval chapters of *Modern Painters* iii were the descriptions of 'humility' and 'joy under trial' as distinguishing the Christian from the pagan spirit, of the contemplation of Christ's beauty and the working of Christ's mind as the antitheses to the Greek's contemplation of 'his own beauty and the working of his own mind', and of Dante – the 'great exponent of the heart of the Middle Ages' – as embodying the discovery that men's happiness lay 'not in themselves' but in 'delight in God's work'.

In Chapter xvi, not for the first time in Ruskin's writing, the modern world was evaluated. But on this occasion it was double-faced, not only a child of the Renaissance but also beginning to rebel against it. Modern life was described as being sadder than mediaeval, but sadder

in a 'dim' and 'weary' way, to deserve the judgment which 'the laws of
the universe' imposed on those who shared the Renaissance preference
of beauty to truth, and to have created the 'deserts of Ugliness' that
were to be found in modern dress, painting and architecture. All the
modern world's 'powerful men' were said to be 'unbelievers' who could
offer only substitutes for belief, like Scott's Nature, Dickens's and
Thackeray's 'truth and benevolence', the 'careless blasphemy' of Byron
and Béranger, and the 'bitter and fruitless statements of fact' that were
specified as Balzac's contribution to public thinking.

In the central chapter, 'The Moral of Landscape', which came towards
the end of *Modern Painters* iii, and throughout volumes iv and v,
Ruskin explained the benefits that he expected from bringing
Turnerian landscape into connection with the public mind. He differentiated his own self-justifications from the half-hearted self-justifications which Wordsworth and Scott had provided for their love of
nature, connecting his own adolescent feelings with the painter's
'power of imagination', and presenting Turner as supplying, in a
maturer form, as valid a science – the 'science of Aspects' – as Bacon
had supplied in the *Science of Essences*. 'The whole force of education'
having hitherto been directed to the 'destruction of the love of nature',
however, the love of nature was said to have become associated with
rebellion against education and faithlessness towards God, and it was
of the essence of the argument not only that Job and Jesus had called
on men to 'watch' God's 'wonders and works in the earth' but also
that, in the present 'crisis of civilization', to do so alone could rescue
them from the 'mechanical impulses' which the age was forcing upon
them. It was landscape painting alone which would help men to
remember what the speed and inventions of modern science were making them forget – that the 'precious things' in life consisted not in
'doing' but in 'being', and that 'nobleness' was to be found in 'watching
the corn grow and the blossoms set, enjoying hard breath over the
ploughshare and the spade, in reading, thinking, loving, hoping, pray-
ing', and not in 'iron, glass, electricity, or steam'.

How far Art could help men to achieve happiness and nobility they
'hardly yet know'. What Ruskin knew in *Modern Painters* iii and in his
discussions of Millais and the pre-Raphaelites was that it was by entering into a communion of humility with Nature that the chief hope for
the future was to be found.

Ruskin's social doctrine was a facet of his doctrine about life, and the reason for being interested in it in the order in which it has been considered is that Ruskin was at the same time assaulting the enemies of Christianity and contributing to Christianity's erosion. By the time he wrote the essays that made up *Unto This Last, Sesame and Lilies, Munera Pulveris* and *The Political Economy of Art* he had been expounding his doctrine for about fifteen years, and the question we have to ask is, how did it come about that he replaced Evangelicalism by Socialism?

By origin Ruskin was a Tory; in early middle age, he meant by Toryism not the romantic Jacobitism that he had believed in when he was an undergraduate, but the Protestant Gothic that he imputed to Venice in the period of its greatness – a Protestant Gothic which accepted inequalities of authority, wealth, power and education but made them tolerable by involving all Venetians in the national sentiment on which the city's greatness had depended.

In the English context, Ruskin accepted the social mobility which had succeeded the stratified society of the past but attacked the 'unreasonable luxury of the rich' as a main cause of the 'downfall of nations'. He despised parliamentary government and was willing to support safeguards to prevent 'the mob' acquiring the whiphand through universal suffrage. His conception of government was monarchical in Carlyle's sense; he thought it the duty of those who had power both to govern and to avoid consulting their subjects in governing; in describing the duties which rulers owed, he made it clear that they were owed neither to the people nor to themselves but to God, and, moreover, that a nation which had been properly constituted was in some sense a church. That was why Gothic Venice was so attractive, because its ecclesiastical politics were Gallican, not Ultramontane. It was also the point of England – that England's cohesion had been achieved when Ultramontane complications had been removed at the Reformation and the national Church, however inadequate in fact, in theory had begun to supply the religion that the nation needed.

After an Evangelical upbringing, Ruskin's irregular undergraduate career had been spent in Oxford where he admired the culture and intelligence of his Tractarian friends but where from an early stage he had been hostile to Tractarianism. On the other hand, while retaining Evangelical assumptions, he professed, when young, to prefer popery to dissent and also to the Church of Scotland. He was exercised by the problems connected with the nature of the Church and its relation to private judgment and he rejected the Tractarian claim that the Anglican clergy was a priesthood. Nor was his religious position very much altered by the experience that he had of religion on the Continent. He made heroes of some of the Protestant communities that he visited, and was overwhelmed by the religious painting that he saw in Italy in 1845. In general, however, he developed a Protestant reserve about religious art and doubted whether Roman Catholic art had had a good effect on the 'minds of the common people'.

These experiences may ultimately have undermined Ruskin's regard for his parents' Protestantism, but the outcome of doubt was usually a reaffirmation of belief. It is unlikely that either travel or marriage effected any of the permanent inroads in Ruskin's Protestantism that were to be effected in the La Touche period at the end of the 1850s.

During this phase of his life, Ruskin was conscious of difficulty in keeping up spiritual tension, in relating the motions of the soul to the actions of the body and in establishing connections between the practice of religion and the criticism of painting: in preparing *Modern Painters* ii he was 'pretty sure' that he would not 'use the language of any particular church' because he did not know which one he belonged to. In the 1840s and 1850s, nevertheless, he continued to 'hold by' Protestant Evangelicalism at the same time that his faith in it was 'fluttering in weak rags from the letter of its old forms', disliking its philistinism as much as he disliked the pharisaism of the Tractarian Aesthete but convincing himself that he was doing God's work by showing that landscape painting and appreciation of it, when properly conducted, provided both as 'earnest and elevated' a 'moral influence' and as 'gigantic' an 'instrument of moral power' as even the Church of England could bring to bear on the English people.

If one asks what was the content of Ruskin's Christianity, the answer is that at one level it was simply *conduct*, that in the 'early ages of Christianity' the 'love of Christ' had been the only thing which mattered, and that it had been a mark of the decrepitude of the late mediaeval Church that the 'law of love' had been obscured by the 'logical quibbles' and 'detestable formalisms' characteristic of Aristotle's legacy to Christendom. It was in reaction against Scholasticism on the one hand and against Classical Paganism on the other that Ruskin rejected doctrinal Christianity in favour of the view that the Christian life involved only 'plain application of and obedience to the

Sermon on the Mount', along with the revival of excommunication for criminal or immoral conduct for which he argued in his famous pamphlet *Notes on the Construction of Sheepfolds*.

All this at first sight looks obvious; it looks as though Ruskin was simply making a Protestant affirmation. Yet there is a sense in which Ruskin's doubts before 1858, his abandonment of Protestantism after 1861 and the diversion of his attention to sociology in the 1860s externalized a weakness which had always been present. The disregard that he had shown for doctrine and metaphysics in religion, when considered in the light of his obsession with doctrine and metaphysics in painting, literature and architecture, suggests that the crisis of the late 1850s was the outcome of a prolonged shift in which the conceptions he had associated with literature, painting and architecture took over from the conceptions he had associated with religion. Moreover, whatever he may have believed, or affected to believe, it was not conduct with which he was engaging intellectually, except in the Carlylean sense that conduct was what his doctrine suggested that he ought to be engaging with. What he was engaging with intellectually, however much he may have felt obliged to deny this, was precisely the doctrinal element which he insisted should be expelled from religion, and it was as true of his doctrine as it was of Carlyle's doctrine of silence that its anti-doctrinal content was merely a trick designed to conceal the fact that it attached the highest importance to the modification of sensibility.

What Ruskin was demanding, indeed, was mainly a modification of sensibility as the recipe for national regeneration and this in its turn depended on the view that God, so far from being merely a God of wrath who wanted responses born in fear and trembling, was also a God who gave love and encouragement to his children.

This was God's first characteristic in Ruskin; it was connected with the second – that God had given His love not only to His Church but through all His words and works. Ruskin treated God's Revelation as having been manifested not in the Bible only but in the whole of the universe as God had made it, and he regarded as vital not the ecclesiastical or strictly religious sensibility but the sensibility that was manifested in literature, art and science as well.

About science Ruskin was reluctant because he wanted, more than he wanted to protect science, to protect art, literature and religion against it. He had, nevertheless, a Spencerian attitude to science as a discloser of Nature, and was as clear as Darwin that, in its place and within the limits of its competence, the scientific sensibility, no less than the literary, religious or theoretic sensibilities, had a part to play in the full response that God demanded from mankind.

The response that God demanded, though it absorbed intellectual responses, was not, however, an intellectual response. The most important response that men could give God was not rational argu-ment, enquiry and understanding, but action; the decision to trust Him in the expectation that rational understanding would follow. In this Tractarian sense, Ruskin was a follower of Pascal, emphasizing that God had given 'a mysterious and questionable Revelation' which could be believed securely only when action and commitment had been undertaken and that the action to which God was calling was not *any* action or commitment but the action and commitment which Ruskin had extracted from Turner since he began writing about him in the 1830s.

Modern Painters iii was concerned with man's past on the one hand and with theoretical justification of Ruskin's methods and opinions on the other. Volume iv contained an account of Turner's attitude to mountains and a discussion of the effects which mountains could have on men. In volume v, published four years later, a similar discussion of leaves and clouds was followed by a restatement of Ruskin's view of the inventive character of the painter's imagination.

The ultimate aim in these volumes was a social one – to examine the influence which 'country life' had had on mankind in the past and to suggest the kind of influence which landscape painting could have on urban society in the future. Even the final volume, written at the point at which Ruskin had had his main crisis of doubt, assumed the signifi-cance of a secularized Protestantism in which the instrument of social teaching was to be the principles of Turnerian painting.

Like much of the rest of *Modern Painters*, the last half of volume v was an historical survey of past painters, in this case of landscape painters from the Venetian painters onwards. At the same time it reached the conclusion that 'landscape' achieved its true significance only when it connected appreciation of God with appreciation of 'humanity'.

This was a new conclusion, and it registered the most important transition in Ruskin's thought. For the 'directest manifestation' which God had given of Himself was not now Nature, as it had been in *Modern Painters* i and ii but Man, and not Man's body but his soul which, though subject to the death that had been brought by Adam's sin, was capable of reflecting as in a 'mirror wherein might still be seen, darkly, the image of the mind of God'. It was only by such a soul that revelation could be received and understood, only through the 'flesh-bound volume' it contained that God's image could be painted and only by concentrating attention on it that Ruskin felt able to establish the necessary nature of the connections between landscape and the 'digressions respecting social questions' which he came to believe had always for him had 'an interest tenfold greater' than the work he had been 'forced into undertaking' about painting and architecture.

Like its predecessors, this landscape or architectural sociology was expected to produce all the consequences that Ruskin had anticipated in the 1840s and 1850s – an enhancing of mutual aid, a propagation of religion where modern art had been profane and the creation of conditions in which, by developing the qualities of the 'gentleman', artists and workmen would become as happy as the Gothic artists and workmen whom the Renaissance had destroyed. In discussing it, Ruskin gave his culminating account of Turner as the high priest of a divine sensibility, creating for himself an identification of self-pity in which he suffered an isolation such as not even Columbus or Galileo had had to suffer – the isolation which genius suffered when it followed its lights and did its own work as Turner had done his, even when it knew that 'no man living in Europe' could understand it.

This would have been nonsense even after Thackeray's *Cornhill* had rejected parts of *Unto This Last* in 1860 since it was among other things by *claiming* to be morally isolated that Ruskin made himself attractive to the young. If, however, one asks what it was that Ruskin wanted support for, the answer is that he wanted it for 'all the great men whose hearts had been kindest and most perceptive' of God in nineteenth-century England – not clergymen or priests but novelists or poets like Scott, Keats, Byron and Shelley who had called on England to 'end its sleep', stop 'passing by on the other side' and recognize both the primacy of love and the need to act on the recognition. This was the central feature of Ruskin's doctrine after 1860 – the sociological doctrine for which he is famous – and the point of this chapter has been to show not only that in origin it was inseparable from his Evangelicalism but also that it was disengagement from Evangelicalism which enabled him to make as central, earnest and morally elevating a contribution as Gladstone was making at the same time to the creation of a resurgent, self-conscious Christianity.

3

Gladstone, Oxford and Christianity

'As, therefore, it is rationalistic to say, Christian doctrine must be true or false, according as it is agreeable or repugnant to our natural perceptions, so also is it rationalistic to ... maintain that intellectual apprehension is a necessary or invariable precondition of spiritual agency upon the soul. As the need and the applicability of Divine influences are so large in extent and embrace so many more persons than possess an active understanding, the rationalism which makes these influences dependent on doctrine only as the medium of their conveyance to men, is exceedingly dangerous to Christianity. By all these considerations we are prepared to anticipate, in a religion having the wide scope of the Gospel, some distinct provision for the conveyance of grace otherwise than through the understanding or in connexion with its agency; and some rites or institutions which should both convey grace in this separate and transcendent manner, and likewise mark, to the view of men, in the most forcible manner, the distinctness of these channels; and the complex and mystical constitution of all religious ordinances whatever, as consisting of an outward representation or instrumentality, and an inward living power.'
W. E. Gladstone *Church Principles* 1840 p. 84.

'It has indeed been said that the old phrase of "saving one's soul" has ceased to have much meaning for the religion of educated people in the present day. If this be indeed true, we can only rejoin in all truth and sorrow, so much the worse for the "educated people". Whatever be a man's place in society or in letters, whatever his circumstances in this earthly scene, it remains true that, to close with the offers which Christ makes to sinners, to "work out his salvation with fear and trembling", is his one most important business here. The eternal realities do not change with our intellectual fashions; and like the laws which govern our physical frames, the spiritual rules under which men live or die are the same for all of us. The day will come when the God-fearing peasants of Devonshire or of Yorkshire will rise in judgment against the cultured irreligion of the centres of our modern civilization: not because it is cultured, but because it is irreligious.'
Rev. H. P. Liddon *Some Elements of Religion* 1872 (1881 edn) pp. 123–4.

'There is a religious scepticism as well as a philosophical scepticism; and the two have not merely no natural connection with each other, but each may frequently be called into existence as the antagonist and antidote to the other.' Rev. H. L. Mansel *Philosophy and Theology* (1866) in H. W. Chandler (ed.) *Letters Lectures and Reviews* 1873 p. 342.

Like many Oxford undergraduates of his generation Ruskin was influenced by Tractarianism, which played a part in transforming his Evangelicalism into Sociology. The transformation, however, was painful and the outcome for many years in doubt. In Gladstone's case, though the Evangelicalism was initially as strong as in Ruskin, the Tractarian impact was stronger, the sense of European literature acuter and the impact of political engagement decisive.

In Chapter 1 Tractarianism was examined as a negative assault. But Tractarianism also had constructive characteristics which entered into Anglican thought through *The Christian Year* and the polemical and scholarly writing that was done in Oxford in the forty years after *The Arians of the Fourth Century*. In considering Gladstone as a transformed Evangelical, this chapter will examine first the constructive polemic of Keble, Pusey, Liddon and Mansel.

I

Keble[1] was the first of the Tractarians to become famous, not only through the publication of *The Christian Year* in 1827 but also when the author of *The Christian Year* delivered a sermon on *National Apostacy* in 1833. It was the sermon on *National Apostacy* which announced the Tractarian crisis and the Tractarian attitude to it, and argued that something drastic would have to be done if the crisis was to be resolved.

---

[1] Rev. John Keble (1792–1866). Educ. at home and at Corpus Christi College, Oxford. Fellow of Oriel College 1811–23. Curate of Hursley 1825–6 and of Fairford 1826–36. Vicar of Hursley 1836–66. Author of *The Christian Year* 1827, *National Apostacy Considered in a Sermon* 1833, contributor to *Tracts for the Times* 1833–41, contributor to *Lyra Apostolica* 1836, *The Case of Catholic Subscription to the XXXIX Articles* 1841, *Praelectiones Poeticae* 1844, *Lyra Innocentium* 1846, *Sermons Academical and Occasional* 1847 etc., *The Life of Thomas Wilson* 1863, *Occasional Papers and Reviews* 1877.

In the 1830s Keble was part of the Tractarian triumvirate, wrote a number of the Tracts, and made a succession of statements about the condition of English religion. Throughout his life he wrote devotionally, produced works of spiritual counsel and published a very large number of sermons. In the years that followed Newman's conversion, Pusey was Tractarianism's strong arm in Oxford, but Keble was his closest adviser, indeed his confessor, made many important interventions and wrote important pamphlets including *A Very Few Plain Thoughts on the Proposed Admission of Dissenters to the University of Oxford, An Argument for not Proceeding immediately to Repeal the Laws which treat the Nuptial Bonds as Indissoluble, Eucharistical Adoration* and *Considerations Respectfully Addressed to the Scottish Presbyters on the late Pastoral Letter of the Six Bishops.*

Keble had been elected to a Fellowship at Oriel College before he was twenty. Except for a brief curacy, he had stayed in Oriel until 1823 when he left Oxford for good. His life thereafter was exemplary. Having been a don, for most of his life he was not one and acquired additional authority from that fact. He mattered not only because he was learned but also because he embodied the pastoral and practical character of Anglican learning while incorporating, even when most resistant to their consequences, the romantic, and to some extent the Coleridgean-German, mentalities which were to be such central features of all mid-Victorian intellectuality.

Keble emphasized human ignorance, and was both mistrustful of the 'intellectual' faculties and cautious about their 'depth and originality'. While denying that the Bible enjoined a 'blind' or 'unreasoned' obedience or was hostile to 'free ... enquiry', he emphasized that 'uprightness' was as important as 'ability' in interpreting it. In *Sacred Poetry, The Christian Year* and the *Praelectiones Poeticae* that he gave as Professor of Poetry at Oxford in the 1830s, it was poetry's 'higher associations' that played the central rôle in the fostering of piety and the elevating of the mind.

In *Sacred Poetry* Keble's interest had been less in poetry's public relevance than in the subjective devotion that it could induce. *Sacred Poetry* did not get far beyond devotional poetry, and, when it did, in discussing oblique sacredness from *The Faerie Queen* onwards, did not do so convincingly. In the Oxford Lectures Keble made an important statement about poetry's relevance to the nation's problems.

The Oxford Lectures surveyed classical poetry in the shadow of Homer, and discussed Virgil's influence down to Tasso and Spenser. Their argument was about the 'decadence and deterioration' of contemporary poetry, the 'smartness and pretentiousness' of contemporary criticism and the duty of 'order and submission' as remedies for them. Their tone was the opposite of Byronic flippancy, was neither 'meretricious' nor journalistic, and presented poetry as 'high-born ... handmaid to religion' and an antidote to revolution 'among the many'.

The connections between poetry and citizenship were prominent in the Oxford Lectures. While touching on relations between rich and poor, however, the lectures said nothing about the Industrial Revolution and drew a merely Wordsworthian contrast between the noise and energy of modern life and the quiet emotion on which poetry depended. Emotion was said to be good and 'glowing emotion' to be better, and good men to feel it even when a 'modest reserve' was needed in expressing it. Poetry was described as God's way of relieving 'over-burdened minds' without the shame and insanity for which over-burdened minds could easily be responsible, and the prospect was held out of a 'new order' in poetry preparing for a 'new order' in religion in the way in which Shakespeare and Spenser had prepared for the new order for which Charles I had been martyred.

Keble did not give wide circulation to his lectures which, on publication in 1844, were still in Latin as they had been when delivered. But they made an important announcement of the view of Tract 89 that poetry mattered theologically, that poetry and mysticism were interrelated and that poetry, mysticism and theology had to impregnate patristic scholarship.

On the Mysticism Attributed to the Fathers of the Early Church was a Tractarian rescue-operation – an attempt to transcend the evidential theology of the eighteenth century and to refute the 'coarse smears' with which its subject had been treated by Gibbon and Conyers Middleton. It argued that mysticism had from the beginning been 'inwrought into the thought and language of the Catholic Church', supplied antidotes to rationalistic science and the 'complacency' felt by modern men at their 'command of the power of nature' and, when properly conducted, would dispose of the 'cheerful indulgence' characteristic of 'liberal' ethics and the 'idolisation of the material world' which all the Tractarians regarded as Christianity's enemy.

Keble emphasized that theology should be characterized by 'doubtfulness' and a deep sense of man's ignorance of the nature of the universe, and that God's 'words and doings' being 'too deep' for men must have been charged with 'heavenly and mysterious meanings'. It was the business of mystical theology to discover these meanings, to treat the 'world of sense' as a 'token from the Almighty' and to examine the exemplifications it supplied of the ways in which God had turned His 'outward and visible work' to 'moral or spiritual uses'. In the 'final causes' disclosed by 'natural philosophy and history', Keble found testimonies to the limited character of human knowledge, and in the 'poetical forms of thought and language' which had been used in the Bible before God had manifested himself in the flesh a 'deep mystical import' which was relevant to the 'whole material world' and to all parts of it.

The exposure of the finiteness of physical science was a romantic undertaking. It denied that science had anything to do with duty or happiness and, while claiming that the moral and mystical transcended the poetic, saw in the connection between the three both a necessary antidote to human pride and a groundwork for the 'knowledge of man' which the Tractarians believed had been destroyed between the Reformation and the nineteenth century.

If we suppose poetry in general to mean the expression of an overflowing mind relieving itself ... of the thoughts and passions which most oppress it, [went the continuation of the argument of *Praelectiones Poeticae*] it will not perhaps be thought altogether an unwarrantable conjecture ... that our blessed Lord in union and communion with all His members, is ... in a certain sense one great and manifold Person into which, by degrees, all souls of men who do not cast themselves away, are to be absorbed. And, as it is a scriptural and ecclesiastical way of speaking, to say, Christ suffers in our flesh ... and ... is put to shame in our sins ... so may it not be affirmed that He condescends in like manner to have a Poetry of His own, a set of holy and divine associations and meanings wherewith it is His will to invest all material things. And the authentic records of His will, in this, as in all other truths supernatural, are of course Holy Scripture, and the consent of ecclesiastical writers.

For all his influence in the 1830s, Keble's decision to be a country vicar detached him from the rancour and resistance that Pusey was to encounter in Oxford after Newman's conversion. Keble was Pusey's most intimate colleague and made an important contribution as a scholar. But it was Pusey who bore the heat of the day in face of assault of the 1850s and 1860s.

II

Pusey[1] was the son of an elderly High-Church father. He was at school at Eton where he swam and rode, and was at Christ Church, Oxford, where he hunted and suffered a Byronic depression occasioned by his father's refusal to allow him to marry. Having taken a First in the Oxford Schools, he was elected to a Fellowship at Oriel at about the point at which Keble left. In 1825/6 he went to Göttingen and Berlin where he studied Theology and Oriental Languages, heard Schleiermacher and Strauss, and began working on both German theology and the Old Testament. In 1827/8 he was allowed to marry, was appointed to the Chair of Hebrew at Oxford and was ordained in order to become a Canon of Christ Church.

Pusey supported Catholic Emancipation where Keble opposed it, and voted against Keble for the Provostship of Oriel. Between 1829 and 1833 his main work was the cataloguing of the Arabic manuscripts in the Bodleian. In 1832 he made his first public attack on Infidelity and began a longstanding collaboration with Keble and Newman in the course of an unsuccessful campaign to appoint W. H. Mill to the Chair of Sanscrit.

Pusey was socially secure, academically entrenched and for the last thirty years of his life a deranged widower. He remained Professor of Hebrew and a Canon of Christ Church for over fifty years and despite indifferent health provided leadership for a growing party inside the Church of England. However unsuccessful intellectually, in this he was successful, building on the work which had been done before the seces-

---

[1] Rev. Edward Bouverie Pusey (1800–82). Educ. Eton and Christ Church, Oxford. Fellow of Oriel College 1822–8, Regius Professor of Hebrew at Oxford and Canon of Christ Church 1828–82. Author of *An Historical Enquiry into the Probable Causes of the Rationalist Character Lately Predominant in the Theology of Germany* 2 vols. 1828–30, *Remarks on the Prospective and Past Benefits of Cathedral Institutions* 1833, contributions to *Tracts for the Times* 1833–41, *Dr Hampden's Theological Statements and the Thirty-Nine Articles Compared* 1836, *Dr Hampden's Past and Present Statements Compared* 1836, *Churches in London* 1837, ed. *The Confessions of St Augustine* 1838, *A Letter to Richard, Lord Bishop of Oxford* 1839, *A Letter to the Archbishop of Canterbury* 1842, *A Letter to the Bishop of London* 1851, *Parochial Sermons* 3 vols. 1852–73, *Collegiate and Professorial Lectures and Discipline* 1854, *The Doctrine of the Real Presence* 1855, *The Councils of the Church* 1857, *The Minor Prophets* 1860, *Daniel the Prophet* 1864, *An Eirenicon* 3 vols. 1865–70, *Historical Preface to Tract No. 90* 1865, *Eleven Addresses during a Retreat of the Companions of the Love of Jesus* 1868, *Sermons Preached Before the University of Oxford 1859–72*, 1872, *Lenten Sermons 1858–74* 1874, *Unscience not Science Adverse to Faith* 1878, *What is of Faith as to Everlasting Punishment* 1880.

sions to Rome had started in the 1840s and succeeding in the company
of Keble and Marriott until their deaths and of Liddon, Forbes,
Bishop Hamilton and William Bright thereafter in constructing an
oeuvre which was to affect all strands of Anglicanism to some degree
subsequently.

Pusey's first major work was *An Historical Enquiry into the Probable
Causes of the Rationalist Character Lately Predominant in the Theology
of Germany* which among other things attacked Rose for providing a
superficial account of the connection between Rationalism and Protestantism. This part of the work created the impression, which his critics
were to recall in his period of manifest orthodoxy, that Pusey himself
held Rationalistic opinions. The main part of the work provided an
anti-Rationalist account of the crisis which had resulted in the 'temporary unbelief of ... a large part of the speculating minds of Germany.'

Pusey's explanation went back to the Reformation and contrasted
Luther's 'intuitive insight into the nature of Christianity' at the beginning of his public career, the 'practical' distractions he suffered *during*
his public career and the 'polemical' developments which inferior successors had made of 'subordinate ... points in his system' after his
death. Luther was appealed to against Lutheranism and the 'minute
and detailed confessions' which had been established by secular
authorities criticized for converting the Gospel from a 'motive for
practice' into a 'matter of speculation'.

An Historical Enquiry rooted Christianity in the Bible. But it also
distinguished theology's 'religious basis' from its 'scientific form' and
argued that the defect of German theology had been its interest in the
'scientific form' at the expense of the 'religious basis'. It emphasized
that practice was superior to theory and the 'heart' to the
'understanding', and that the Bible should not be forced into a 'monot-
onous conception of system'. Biblical interpretation which ought to
have been the 'mistress and guide' of doctrinal theology, however, had
become its slave, and the religious crisis which Germany was
undergoing was a crisis of reaction leading to unbelief.

An Historical Enquiry described Protestant narrowness and the
unsuccessful efforts which had been made to remedy it from the seventeenth century onwards. In the deterioration which Pietism had suffered from being a genuine religion into being a test for office or
advancement and in the undiscriminating nature of the Orthodox resis-

tance to Leibniz and Wolff, it found explanations of the 'dry', 'abstract', 'dialectical' character which had made German Protestantism incapable of dealing with the damage that was done by Frederick the Great's introduction of French unbelievers to the Prussian court.

The first two-thirds of *An Historical Enquiry* was about the 'dark side' of Rationalism's penetration of German theology in the past. The last third was about the prospect of turning German philosophy to Christianity's advantage in the course of which Pusey presented the 'Christian meaning' that was to be found in Herder and Schelling, the 'services' which Lessing had rendered to Christianity and the aid which Kant had given in establishing a consonance between Christianity and man's 'moral nature'. Pusey did not capitulate to Rationalism, or, quite, to Romanticism. In relation to Kant's anthropomorphism in particular he kept a firm grasp on fundamentals which he restated when Part II of the *Enquiry* was published two years later, and at the same time as *The Christian Year* was bringing poetry into play against the 'lifeless formalism' of Protestantism in England, brought the 'feelings' into play against the 'mere intellectual recognition of Christianity in Germany'.

In approaching Pusey, it is necessary to understand not only his manner – the silky combination of gentleness, meekness, submissiveness, humility and resignation with which, like Keble, he surrounded the self-assertive apologetic of the 1830s and 1840s – but also the problem to which he pointed, of infusing Catholic practices and dispositions into a nation too 'gorged with wealth' to cope with the Malthusian 'torrent of human souls'.

Like most of the Tractarians, Pusey discovered in English history both evidences and explanations of Christianity's decline. On the one hand, in England's 'towns and spires', he found reproaches to the paralysing Protestantism which represented piety as a branch of 'popery'. On the other hand, he criticized Hume's and Hallam's understanding of the seventeenth century, the damage which the first two Hanoverians had done to the Church of England and the 'sin' of 1688 as 'scheming ... precursor' of the 'lax ... low and ... unChristian' standards of the world around him. In connecting the Sabellianism of Hampden and the Noetics with the 'moral contagion' which was 'polluting the atmosphere' among the 'heathen population of our ... mines and ... places of manufacture', his answer to Chartism was that only a 'moral and religious revolution' could prevent a 'political revolution'.

In the 1830s and 1840s Pusey was an acknowledged leader; he led the fight in favour of subscription to the Thirty-Nine Articles and was suspended from preaching for his Sermon on the Eucharist. It was not, however, until after Newman's secession that he exercised the leadership he was to exercise in the 1850s, 1860s and 1870s.

Between 1846 and 1882 Pusey aimed to create conditions in which re-Christianization could begin. He preached extensively, wrote large works of scholarship and engaged in spiritual counselling and the production of handbooks relevant to it. Most of all he defended and defined the Church of England both constitutionally and in the theological and intellectual sense which reached its climax in *An Eirenicon* that he began publishing in the year in which Gladstone left Oxford and Manning became Archbishop of Westminster.

Pusey feared the 'Naturalism, Rationalism, Socinianism and Indifference' which were being propagated by the newspapers and the effect they would have on the unconverted cities. At the same time he believed that 'unbelief, scepticism, rationalism and doubt floated harmless around the heart which believed in Jesus and meditated on him'. He praised the 'training of the mind' and 'schooling of the heart' which universities provided, and argued that the professional education conducted by the teaching hospitals and Inns of Court should be matched by a similar professional education for the clergy. In facing the challenges presented by poverty on the one hand and Infidelity on the other, his *Letter to the Archbishop of Canterbury* in 1842 contained a classic statement of the Tractarian illusion that Tractarian Anglicanism was so attractive that even the Roman Church would move towards it.

Letter to the Archbishop of Canterbury was a subtle piece of spiritual blackmail in which Pusey wrote on behalf of the 'younger men' who had heard more and better of the Church of Rome than his own generation had heard when young. It emphasized that the Church of England's 'island situation' made Rome attractive but that Tractarianism, so far from being a concealed form of Popery, was the best antidote to it. It also hinted that one bishop was in a state of 'unconscious heresy', that other bishops were 'baldly ... Genevan' and that the negotiations about the Jerusalem bishopric raised the prospect of an 'experimental church ... of Lutheran and Jewish converts' which the presence of an Anglican bishop would do nothing to stabilize.

In the 1850s and 1860s, Pusey's problems were that latitudinarianism not only would not go away but was making its mark on university reform, that it had powerful allies in parliament as well as a party in Oxford and that there was, as he supposed, the prospect of the colleges being submerged by the expanded professoriate proposed by Jowett, Stanley, Lake, Goldwin Smith, and the University Commissioners appointed by Russell in 1850.

Pusey was neither inflexible about university reform, nor incapable of responding intellectually once the battle had been lost. But he felt it necessary to fight the battle and conceptualize a crisis, and in reacting to the Commission made a fundamental statement aobut the relationship between learning and life. It was not the endowment of colleges that he argued for but the method of teaching that they pursued and the critical character of the change which was envisaged – the emphasis on lecturing as opposed to the catechetical instruction, the willing acceptance of the balkanization of knowledge and the conception of professorships dedicated to the 'promotion of science' as being beneficial in itself and useful to the education of undergraduates.

What Pusey predicted was an enslavement of the intellect such as had occurred in Germany, the establishment of an irreligion such as had followed the destruction of colleges and universities in the French Revolution and the licensed propagation of Infidelity through the 'rigid conformity' and preference for 'novelty and truth' which he identified as concomitants of professorial authority. What he advocated was an English mistrust of philosophical systems and a refusal to turn the university into a 'forcing-house for intellect'.

Pusey believed in the unity of knowledge, the inseparability of theory from practice and the ultimate reconcilability of 'real science' with 'real theology'. Scholarship and learning were to be admired for the discipline they supplied to the mind, the proof they suggested of God's providence and the help they gave in providing a religion for the poor. Since 'acute and subtle intellects' were 'not needed' for 'most offices in the body politic', moreover,

the problem and special work of a university was not ... to advance science ... make discoveries ... form new schools of mental philosophy or ... invent new modes of analysis; nor to produce works in medicine, jurisprudence or even theology; but to form minds religiously, morally, intellectually, which should discharge aright whatever duties God in his Providence shall appoint them to.

These conceptions were apparent in most of Pusey's works, not only, for example, in the account that *The Doctrine of the Real Presence* and *The Councils of the Church* gave of the connection between the real presence, synodical government and the conversion of the poor, but also, and especially, in the six hundred or so pages of *Daniel the Prophet*.

In *Daniel the Prophet* Pusey made his contribution to the demolition of *Essays and Reviews*, picking on *Daniel* as the field of battle because of its testimony to miracle and supernatural prophecy, and criticizing the cowardice and ambiguity with which the authors of *Essays and Reviews* had kept their 'positions ... as ministers of the Church of England' while claiming that 'the old faith was no longer tenable'. Disbelief of *Daniel* had been one of the 'greatest triumphs' of the 'unbelieving critical school', so success in re-establishing its chronology would provide an evidence of 'supernatural prophecy' such as could only be explained away by those whose unbelief prevented them considering the possibility in the first place.

Unlike Westcott, Pusey met issues head on and drew lines between those who did and those who did not deny that God had 'revealed Himself to men in any other way than by the operation of man's natural reason'. This, as he criticized Tait for implying, was no mere matter of 'reconciling physical science and theology'. What was at issue was whether Renan's 'supercilious ... superiority' was insolent towards God, whether 'exclusive adherence to definite truth' was as 'antagonistic' to Christ's mind as Dean Stanley had suggested and whether thirty years of Anglican open-mindedness had not made theology into a 'corpse'. Those who 'had that one truth which God had revealed' were bound not to 'soften it' and the purpose of *Daniel the Prophet* was to compel an 'already alienated world' to choose between a 'patronizing blasphemy' which emptied God's word of its meaning and the 'glimpses' of truth which God had given 'even in this world' to the 'soul which resigned itself wholly to Him'.

Daniel the Prophet included an attempt, like the attempt which Gladstone was to make later, to reconcile Genesis with Geology and Old Testament cosmogony with the conclusions of modern science. These were unconvincing and at variance with the separation which Pusey also affirmed between science and theology. They did nothing to diminish the claim that Rationalism had to be destroyed, and that 'rebellion' had to be replaced by a submission to revelation which would make those who gave it as 'certain of what rationalism impugned as of their own existence.'

The preface to *Daniel the Prophet* was the most formidable statement that Pusey was to make of his contempt for the latitudinarian Rationalism against which he had been arguing since 1828. It was followed in *An Eirenicon* a year later by the most formidable statement that he was to make of the Catholic credentials of the Church of England.

After the Gorham Judgment and the anti-Erastian secessions which followed, Pusey's first concern had been to establish that the Church of England was not an Erastian Church. This was implicit in *The Councils of the Church* and in a number of the pamphlets that he wrote between 1857 and 1881. It received its first and most emphatic statement in *The Royal Supremacy* in 1850.

The Royal Supremacy was written during the proceedings that led up to the Gorham Judgment and reflected the shock induced by the prospect of a Court which derived its sanction from the Church deciding that 'what was contrary to Truth' was 'consistent with the discipline of the Church of England.' The Gorham Proceedings were about baptismal regeneration but they might have been about any of the main articles of Christian doctrine. The question they raised was whether the Gorham situation was one to which Anglicans were 'bound by their acknowledgment of the Royal Supremacy'. Pusey's answer was that except under Henry VIII, the Church of England had never given up its right to determine doctrine and discipline and that the history of France, Spain, Germany, Rome and Byzantium justified the conclusion that, in matters of legislation affecting the Church, the Church not the State ought to have the 'initiative'.

In *The Royal Supremacy* Pusey made a primarily constitutional point. In *An Eirenicon* he justified the Church of England as England's 'real and chief bulwark against Infidelity'.

In explaining this conception, Pusey referred not only to the size of the Anglican clergy and the affection in which the English held the Church of England but also to the influence which its maintenance of 'Catholic truth' had had in preserving the faith among dissenters. He drew attention to the enormous scale of the unbelief which had occurred in Roman Catholic countries and to the importance of the Renaissance and the French Revolution in establishing it. In coming close to absolving the Reformation from responsibility for it, he did not abandon either his Tractarian mistrust of the Reformers or his rejection of Lutheran and Calvinistic theology.

In *An Eirenicon* Pusey repeated much of what the Tractarians had established before 1845, large parts of it simply listing the respects in which Anglican Christianity was more consonant with the primitive and patristic versions than the Roman version had become. While rejecting the Roman doctrine of Infallibility, the Roman preference for 'monarchical' over 'aristocratic' rule and the Roman practice of elevating the Virgin to a position of equality with Christ, it affirmed, nevertheless, that Rome and Canterbury shared a unity in Christ which transcended the 'interruptions' of 'intercommunion' of the past.

Pusey recognized in the Orthodox Church an antidote to Rome which, in any case, he claimed, was in retreat in Ireland, Italy and the United States. But his main interest was in Rome and in the prospect, however impossible in his lifetime, of restoring communion with her.

Pusey was surprised by the vigour of the Roman attack on *An Eirenicon*. He counter-attacked on Conciliar lines, called Bossuet into play and, while reaffirming his objections to Papal Infallibility, affirmed that upon any point which a General Council received by the whole Church should pronounce to be 'de fide', private judgment should be abandoned.

In volume iii of *An Eirenicon*, not for the first time, Pusey disclaimed leadership and denied that Puseyism was the name of a 'party'. He wrote as an Englishman with a 'Saxon' dread of 'irresponsible power' and the historic memory of resistance to the Papacy. In face of Gladstone's removal from Oxford, he wrote of 'severing his last link with earthly politics' and of believing, disingenuously considering that he had never been a Tory, that the Toryism of the 1830s had now been replaced by a grasping Conservatism. On Keble's death in the following year he found consolation in the 'thousands upon thousands of English hearts both ... in England ... and the United States who believed that if ... accredited Roman authority could present Reunion' as involving merely a 'profession of belief', the 'wall of partition which had existed so long ... would be ... shattered'.

Pusey was unreasonable and intense, and, even when most insistent on curbing the extravagances of his followers, suffered the delusion, with which Halifax was to become infected, of believing that his type of Anglicanism would act as a magnet in Rome. He had an unhelpfully unmodern mind, was insulated to a fault against modern modes of feeling and apart from Liddon was the most uncompromising thinker by whom Anglican Tractarianism was to be defended.

III

Liddon[1] left school in 1845, entered Christ Church in 1846 and spent the next ten years becoming Pusey's right-hand man in the politics of the university. His formative years were spent in the shadow of the Gorham Judgment. Many of his undergraduate friends became Roman Catholics, and he thought about becoming a Roman Catholic himself. Having decided not to, he became Vice-Principal of Cuddesdon Theological College and of St Edmund Hall, Oxford, and a Student of Christ Church and a Canon of St Paul's. He was Pusey's candidate to be first Warden of Keble College, which he declined to become, and for the Ireland Chair of Exegesis, which after difficulty he was offered and accepted in 1870. Though he resigned the Chair on Pusey's death in order to begin work on Pusey's biography, he had not completed the biography by the time he died eight years later.

Liddon was an arresting preacher who commanded large audiences in Oxford and London, and wrote a good deal of controversial theology; but there is a serious sense in which his memorial was his share of the four-volume *Life of Pusey*. It was there that Puseyism was described in its spiritual and religious setting, there that the Puseyite position was encapsulated in the life of its inventor. If the political parts of the biography were less sophisticated than the subject required, they made it clear that Puseyism had rancorous ramifications arising from its rôle in the politics of a university.

For the purposes of Westminster politics Liddon was a Gladstonian Liberal. For the purposes of religious politics, his opinions during forty years of preaching and writing may be found most readily in the Bampton Lectures that he gave at short notice in Oxford in 1866 after illness had compelled Haddan to withdraw, and in the eight sermons that he preached in St James's Church, Piccadilly, in Lent 1870 and published subsequently under the title *Some Elements of Religion*.

---

[1] Rev. Henry Parry Liddon (1829–90). Educ. King's College School, London, and Christ Church, Oxford. Student of Christ Church 1846–90, Curate of Wantage 1852–4, Vice-Principal of Cuddesdon College 1854–9, Vice-Principal of St Edmund Hall 1859–70, Ireland Professor of Exegesis 1870–82, Canon of St Paul's 1870–89. Author of *Some Words for God* 1865 etc., *The Divinity of Our Lord and Saviour Jesus Christ* (Bampton Lectures for 1866) 1867, *The Priest in His Inner Life* 1869, *Some Elements of Religion* 1872, *Thoughts on Present Church Troubles* 1881, *Easter in St Paul's* 2 vols. 1885 etc., *Advent in St Paul's* 2 vols, 1889 etc., *Christmastide in St Paul's* 1889, *Sermons on Old Testament Subjects* 1891, *Essays and Addresses* 1892.

Liddon's Bampton Lectures dealt with the question whether Jesus was divine and concluded that Christianity differed from other religions in believing that its founder was the 'True Saviour of the World because He was ... the Being who made it'. This was asserted powerfully and with a belligerent expressiveness which stood out even in a belligerent literature like the Tractarian.

The Bampton Lectures were eloquently uncompromising. They made no concessions to modern criticism which, though 'destructive' in intention, had left the main features of Orthodoxy unchanged and vindicated the 'great theologians' of the past, whether in the shape of Waterland's 'genius and energy' or in the 'wider field of Catholic Christendom'.

Liddon's central contention was that all religions had to have an Object, that they must 'rest consciously' on it and that the Objects that were to be found in modern religion were inadequate. Consideration of modern religion led to the conclusion that, since religion's proper Object was 'God', it 'could not exist without a theology' and that not only historic Christianity's but also Christ's theology had been 'dogmatic'. Christ's claim to be the sharer of 'God's Throne' was pointed menacingly at religions which denied it.

The Bampton Lectures were both negative and positive. They blew on the human Jesus as he had appeared in modern thought since Kant and dismissed the heresies that were to be found in Strauss, Colenso, Seeley and Renan. At the same time they argued that Naturalism was self-contradictory, that the 'Catholic Creed' resolved its contradictions and that the relationship between Christ and Christianity was so far superior to the relationship between a philosopher and his philosophy that it had enabled 'millions of souls' which would otherwise have been 'sensual and selfish' to 'shed ... blood' for Christ, 'die for Christ' and become 'pure, humble and loving' in imitation of Christ.

In the Bampton Lectures Liddon investigated the contrasts which Naturalism had drawn between the 'historical spirit' and 'the spirit of dogmatism', and between the 'prophet of Nazareth' or 'real person of Jesus' and the 'bandages' or 'metaphysical envelopes' which supernatural theology had 'wrapped around him'. Theology, he argued, was necessarily 'inferential'. All that the 'illuminated reason of the collective Church' had done was to 'systematise inferences' from the 'original materials of the Christian revelation', so there was no disparity between the Christ of Catholicism and the historical record of the Bible. Not only did the 'only records we possess' show that Jesus 'claimed to work ... miracles' and to be God's son, they also made it impossible to take a 'neutral attitude' towards him. Renan's Jesus, as the 'conscious performer of thaumaturgic tricks', could not have had the 'humility and unselfishness' with which the 'ethical Jesus' had been credited and Strauss's Jesus must have been so insignificant as to have been 'compressible within the limits of a newspaper paragraph'. Jesus either performed miracles, or he did not perform miracles. He was either God's son and infallible or he was not, and there was no stopping-point between Catholic preconceptions and the crudely negative preconceptions which ignored 'Bethlehem and Calvary' and treated Christ's birth, crucifixion and resurrection as of no more importance than his ministry and moral teaching.

Liddon can no more be said to have proved the possibility of a supernatural Christianity than Westcott did. But whereas Westcott was content to establish that supernatural Christianity was the religion of the Bible, Liddon went far beyond him in asserting the unreasonableness of the preconception that a supernatural religion was an impossibility.

The Jesus who emerged from the Bampton Lectures was neither a happy memory, a 'theme for ... poetry' nor a 'human ideal'. He was a personal saviour – the second person of a Triune God whose divinity 'transfigured men's inward being' and provided a 'deeper motive' for their 'every action'. The dogmatic and devotional asseverations of these facts were said not only to provide no obstruction to 'piety' and the 'practical obligations of life' as the enemies of dogmatic theology had suggested, but also to be crucial to them and to command action in conformity with them.

Liddon equated 'the progress of the human race' with the spread of Christianity and pessimism about progress with rejection of Christianity. Christianity was said to have given 'new ideals to art', a 'new world' to literature and 'new graces and refinement of mutual intercourse' to civilization, and to have made society 'more kindly and humane' by proclaiming the 'dignity of poverty'. Christianity had transcended the nation in a way that Confucianism had failed to do, had expanded more widely than Buddhism or Mohammedanism had done, and had elevated women, abolished slavery and invented both the modern hospital and international law. At times Liddon's tribute sounded like a Gladstonian tribute to the Liberal Party, a celebration of mid-Victorian virtue, or a commination against what were darkly described as 'habits which were treated as matters of course by the friends of Plato'.

These claims, though evidences of Christianity's worth, were even more important as evidence of its inexplicability, and of the inadequacy of Gibbon's explanation of its success. 'Natural' explanations were said to be 'out of date' and Gibbon's explanations to be flawed by the assumption that merely historical conceptions could account for the success of a religion that was divine.

In dismissing Gibbon Liddon was doing what Newman was doing in dismissing him in *A Grammar of Assent* – insisting that historians' preconceptions must yield to theological preconceptions. This was a problematical position, even when Napoleon was called into service against Renan to support it. Yet the Bampton Lectures expressed it with energy and power and, in doing so, were reacting against claims which Liddon was by no means alone in mistrusting.

Liddon's Bampton Lectures were designed for dons and undergraduates. *Some Elements of Religion* was designed for ordinary congregations and was later printed for the benefit of 'working men in London'. It touched on many of the errors of the present and preceding ages, including Pantheism, Deism, Materialism and Agnosticism. Feuerbach, Schleiermacher, Goethe, Buckle, Shelley, Hegel, Kant, Büchner, Spencer, Comte, Diderot, Robespierre, Schopenhauer, Strauss, Seeley and Goldwin Smith were despatched summarily while the success which Christianity had had in 'making Christians feel the value of each separate life' was rooted in the cycle of sin, prayer, redemption and immortality.

In Lectures I to III Liddon played with the problem, showed that a secular religion could not meet the requirements of a romantic psychology and led towards the conclusion that these requirements could only be met by a Christian psychology. He drew attention to the fact that whatever else science could do it could not prevent death and that it was the 'solemnity' of death which gave religion its natural place in the human mind.

In Lecture I Liddon analysed 'feeling' as the test of acceptability and criticized Wesleyanism for making it the sole test. He argued that Kant had been wrong to identify religion with morality, that Gnosticism and Hegelianism had been wrong to identify it with knowledge and that knowledge of 'intellectual truth' had to be supplemented by action if it was to contribute to religion. Though religion included poetry, feeling, mental illumination and moral effort and spoke in terms that were appropriate to these activities, its essence was that 'unquenchable passion' for the 'Highest and Invisible Object' through which the 'large masses of mankind' were moved.

The object of religion, in other words, was God, and the purpose of the earlier Lectures was to show that merely moral and merely intellectual approaches to Him would be unsuccessful. In showing why Christianity alone could be successful, Liddon rejected both the 'sterile deism which had banished God from the world' and the 'reactionary pantheism which had buried Him in it', and proposed instead a Christian conception of man as a person, of God as a moral person and of a 'personal and moral God' as maintaining a 'real bond' between Man and Himself.

This was the central argument of the Lectures which aimed to show how all other views of religion were superseded by it. It was this that had been taught by Christ and attested by the resurrection, this that issued in the cycle of sin, prayer, redemption and immortality, this alone that could transcend paganism's contempt for life by displaying religion as man's 'most reasonable field of thought and work'. In discussing sin, Liddon recognized the importance of man's 'sensuous nature'. But he did not identify sin with sensuality, on the one hand because the 'seat of sin' was 'the will', on the other because body and soul were united to eternity. In affirming the reality of sin in face of modern attempts to disregard it, he emphasized its character as an 'internal offence against God's Law'.

God's Law was 'Eternal', and Liddon differentiated between the Eternal Law and the 'laws and facts of the physical universe', the latter being laws which God need not have made, the former being 'necessary truths' of Man's Nature which God could not have given men authority to break. A 'moral truth', like a 'mathematical axiom', was said therefore to be seen 'intuitively', to be binding for ever, and to be 'formulated into rules' to suit the 'conditions of creaturely existence'. It was the freedom which creatures had to obey or not to obey that rescued God from responsibility and Christianity's recognition of man's freedom that gave Christianity its distinctiveness as a 'life-controlling' principle; it was because suffering and crime were aspects of sin that modern attempts to deal with them through philosophy and education were encouraging pride and ambition where they ought to have been encouraging faith and prayer.

In *Some Elements of Religion* prayer was central. It 'opened the heart' and 'put the affections in motion', impelling a 'joint act of the will and the understanding', and revealed men to themselves as 'immortal spirits, outwardly draped in social forms ... and linked to a body of flesh and blood ... but in ... conscious spiritual solitude looking steadily upwards at the Face of God'. Prayer was 'religion in action'; it was men in 'real and effective communication with God', and it was much more religion's 'peculiar work' than any of the other works that religion actually did.

Liddon said little about Christianity as a social doctrine, far less than Westcott or Scott Holland, despite Gladstonian affirmations and a long period as a Canon of St Paul's. What he offered was a serious version of Disraeli's claim that without dogmas, there would be no Deans, that Christ was less the perfect man than he was God, and that the social offering which Christianity had to make was of Grace and the possibility of Everlasting Life.

'My soul is athirst', not for pleasures which may degrade, nor yet for philosophies which may disappoint, but for the Pure, the Absolute, the Everlasting Being. 'My soul is athirst for God: when shall I come to appear before the presence of God?'
Was this cry ever heard more distinctly by those who have ears to hear the voices of the spiritual world than in our own generation? The passion, or, as the Psalmist phrases it, the thirst for God – the strong desire of the soul mounting towards Him with all the agonized earnestness of a disappointed and tortured sense – speaks, not merely or chiefly in churches and pulpits, but in magazines, in newspapers, in social gatherings, in political assemblies, with a fervour and decision which would have startled the age of George III. The pulse of this desire is felt outside the Christian camp: it quickens the very enthusiasms of error and paradox; often enough, it mistakes friends for foes and foes for friends, but it is generally sincere, vehement, intolerant of trifling and delay. 'My soul is athirst for God, yea even for the living God' is the desire of desires; it really underlies and explains all others that are not purely brutal in this Europe, this England of the nineteenth century.

Pusey's, Keble's and Liddon's achievement in Oxford was to have entrenched a tone, a body of scholarship and an academic party. What they fought for and failed to win was command, and the re-entrenchment of Christianity as institutionalized Truth. Their defeat was the symbol of an intellectual future in which Keble College was to provide a meagre antidote to the emasculated Christianity of a secularized university. In Mansel and Gladstone, along with a counter-revolutionary polemic, there were other symptoms of retreat.

By the middle of the 1860s Gladstone had abandoned Oxford as much as it had abandoned him. His defeat at the General Election of 1865 was the conclusion to a twenty-year transition in which he had come to understand that the future could not be controlled by the Conservative Anglicanism that he had believed in from the Reform agitation of 1832 onwards. For Conservative Anglicanism as intellectual counter-attack, it is necessary to look at Salisbury and Mansel.

V

Like Salisbury, Mansel[1] was a Church–State Anglican who wrote gratefully of the 'Catholic' movement inside the Church of England. Mansel, however, though politically active in Oxford, was neither a politician nor a political writer. Apart from a slim volume of undergraduate poems, a handful of articles in a Disraelian newspaper, and a satire – *Phronisterion* – on Lord John Russell's view of the future of Oxford, his writing was theological, philosophical and historical. Salisbury had the wider experience and the more conspectual mind, combining a Christian cynicism with disparagements of the academic and clerical mentalities, and giving a better account than Mansel could have given of the national character of the Church of England. Since, however, Salisbury was discussed at length in Volume I, the Conservative–Anglican assault will be considered here by reference to Mansel alone.

Mansel shared neither Pusey's obsessions nor Pusey's Gladstonianism. As a Fellow and Tutor of St John's College, Oxford, as Reader and then Waynflete Professor of Moral Philosophy and as Regius Professor of Ecclesiastical History, which he became during the short-lived Conservative ministry of 1866, he was an influential teacher and one of the most important party Conservatives in the University. Election to the Hebdomedal Council at the age of thirty-four, a breakdown in 1865 and death in 1871 at the age of fifty-one, three years after Disraeli had

---

[1] Rev. Henry Longueville Mansel (1820–71). Educ. Merchant Taylors' and St John's College, Oxford. Fellow of St John's College 1844–55. Reader and then Waynflete Professor of Moral Philosphy 1855–66, Regius Professor of Ecclesiastical History 1866–8, Dean of St Paul's 1868–71. Author of *Prolegomena Logica* 1851, *The Limits of Religious Thought Examined* 1858, *An Examination of Rev. F. D. Maurice's Strictures on the Bampton Lectures of 1858* 1859, *Metaphysics* 1860, *A Letter to Professor Goldwin Smith* 1861, *A Second Letter to Professor Goldwin Smith* 1862, H. W. Chandler (ed.) *Letters, Lectures and Reviews* 1873, J. B. Lightfoot (ed.) *The Gnostic Heresies of the First and Second Centuries* 1875.

made him Dean of St Paul's, all helped to deprive Conservative Anglicanism of a more extended justification of 'the principles of religious faith' than Mansel was able to give it in his lifetime.

Mansel was born in a Northamptonshire rectory of a well-established naval and military family. He was at school at Merchant Taylors' and was an undergraduate at St John's College, Oxford. Apart from his poems, his first book was *Prolegomena Logica* of 1851; his last were the contributions he made to *The Speaker's Bible* in the late 1860s and *Gnostic Heresies of the First and Second Centuries* which Lightfoot, who had known him at St Paul's, edited and published after his death.

Mansel's interest in ecclesiastical history was occasioned rather by the requirements of the Regius Chair than by personal preference. His preference was for logic, especially formal logic, and it was through philosophy and philosophical theology that he became famous as an apologist.

When Mansel's Bampton Lectures were delivered in Oxford in 1858 they were an astonishing success; when published in the same year they received extensive criticism. In the course of the 1860s Mansel replied to his critics and made himself a spearhead of attack on Mill and *Essays and Reviews*. Throughout the 1860s he was one of the most powerful Anglican critic of Infidelity, causing alarm among Anglicans but attracting reasoned and respectful attention from the anti-Christian thinkers he was attacking.

Mansel's defence took the form of a negative assault on Christianity's enemies. It was in criticism of German philosophy between Leibniz and Hegel, and of its successors and imitators in Germany and England down to Strauss and Baur, that he deployed classical and patristic learning, the opinions and assumptions of Sir William Hamilton and Bishop Butler, and the testimony that was available from all ages of Christian theology to the 'incomprehensibility of the Divine Nature'.

Mansel had a tough mind; he knew what he was defending, and his attitude to German philosophy, though sceptical, was in no way latitudinarian. It was apparent throughout that he was making no concessions, was making a cunning attempt to turn German philosophy against itself and was in relentless pursuit of the 'a priori prejudice against revelation'.

Mansel stated his position twice, first negatively in *Prolegomena Logica*, *Metaphysics*, and the Bampton Lectures; then, more positively, in the Bampton Lectures and the notes, prefaces and defences of the Lectures that he published subsequently. In both phases his argument was that his criticisms of German philosophy were as firmly rooted in Orthodoxy and as much devoted to extirpating Rationalism as Newman had been in his university addresses in Oxford and Dublin.

What Mansel meant by Rationalism in the 1850s was not exactly what the Tractarians had meant twenty years earlier since in his view Deism was dead and eighteenth-century free-thinking a 'coarse relic from the past'. The real target now was not the 'cast-off goods' of the eighteenth century, which *Essays and Reviews* was said, unfairly, to have picked up, but the 'metaphysical profundities' of Kant.

In dealing with Kant, Mansel's tactic was to pinpoint a contradiction. He approved of Kant's epistemology and echoed Hamilton's belief that Kant had annihilated metaphysics as a 'science of the ... absolute' by establishing that the 'absolute' was 'inconceivable by the human consciousness'. On the other hand, also like Hamilton, he rejected Kant's exaltation of the 'speculative reason' above the Understanding, and of the 'practical reason' above the 'speculative', and criticized not only Kant's attempt to reconstruct 'that fabric of metaphysical philosophy which his previous criticism had pronounced a delusion' but also his attempt to establish a 'profane' philosophy in which the 'contemplation of the world was identical with the creative thought that brought it into being'.

What Mansel did in the 1850s and 1860s was to subvert Kant's religion and to turn Kantian dualism against Fichte, Schelling, Strauss, Feuerbach, Comte, Emerson and Hegel.

Though Hutchison Stirling's *The Secret of Hegel* was published in 1865, Mansel died before Hegel's full force was felt in England. Consequently it is impossible to know what he would have made of subsequent attempts to marry Hegelianism and Christianity. What can be known is that he attributed an 'atheistical' or 'pantheistical' quality to Hegel's identification of 'thought' with 'being', discerned difficulties in the Hegelian doctrine of the 'identity of contradictories' and called Kant into play against the Faustian arrogance involved in Hegel's destruction of the divine dualism. To the question, how could dualism be justified philosophically, he answered with a set of evidential and historical considerations which depended on a set of psychological and ontological considerations.

Like many of his contemporaries Mansel disparaged Paley while declining to disparage the evidences for Christianity or the improbability of the 'civilized world' having been 'deluded by a ... fable for eighteen hundred years'. Moreover, he attached importance to the similarity between the 'principle of causality' as the presupposition of philosophy and the existence of God as the presupposition of theology. Even these positions, however, though important, were of little importance beside the resolution which Christianity was alleged to offer of the question which psychology asked about the possibility of ontological knowledge.

By Psychology Mansel did not mean remedial therapy: he meant Kantian doubt about the powers of the human mind and the question whether ontology was a possibility. His answer was that it was not, that the 'Absolute' and 'Infinite' were beyond Philosophy's grasp, and that 'deductive ontology' involved the abandonment of thought in order to 'struggle wiith words'. In the twilight which men enjoyed on earth it was philosophy's task to show this, and psychology was central because its investigation of the human mind showed that the psychological dualism implied in 'the very notion of consciousness' necessitated the 'ontological dualism' which German philosophy had abandoned.

Prolegomena Logica and *Metaphysics* laid down the guidelines on which the Bampton Lectures were to run. Both questioned the connection between Logic and Metaphysics which had been asserted from Aristotle onwards, and supported Kant's attempt to define the proper relationship between psychology and the 'science of the laws of the thinking subject'. Both denied that the thinking subject could know reality; both limited human thought to the phenomenological. Both attacked German philosophy for claiming to do more, and both claimed that the attempt to do more led to pantheism or atheism.

These were the central arguments, and their polemical relevance arose from the belief that German Rationalism was claiming a knowledge of existence which was outside the range of human thought. Psychology had established this and it was through psychology that philosophy would show that the philosophical difficulties which free thinkers professed to find in Christian thought were present in free thought, that the 'insolubility' of ontological questions had made ontology into a 'higher kind of phenomenology' and that the time mankind had spent 'among the mazes of metaphysical speculation' would turn out to have been justified once it came to be understood that philosophy was useful chiefly as a means of 'proving its own uselessness'. It followed that natural religion and rational theology were 'self-destructive impossibilities' and that the proper concern of the philosophy of religion was 'the human mind in its relation to religion' – and especially the sin, suffering, prayer and redemption which were experienced when men related themselves to God as 'persons' to a 'person' and as consciences dependent on Him.

As it was presented in the Bampton Lectures, the special function of 'revealed religion' was to indicate the existence of truths that were 'beyond human intelligence' and to show God using 'human images' which enabled men to practise where they were unable to speculate. This led to the conclusion that, though men were bound to believe in God as their 'moral ... governor', they should not claim to understand His nature, that the doctrines of Christianity were 'eternal riddles' which could not be demonstrated from 'philosophical premises' and that in relating God to man Christianity was a relationship of mystery as deep and unfathomable as the metaphysical relationship of which philosophy had failed to achieve a resolution in the past. The high negative defence was completed when Law as a 'periodical recurrence of phenomena' derived from 'observation of facts' was differentiated from Law as a 'supposed characteristic of the divine nature' and human thought was declared to have no ground for denying that God could suspend the laws of nature through the operation of His will.

The flaming sword turns every way against those who strive in the strength of their own reason to force their passage to the tree of life [went an Islamic denunciation of those who denied that miracles could have occurred]. Within her own province and among her own objects, let Reason go forth, conquering and to conquer ... But when she strives to approach too near to the hidden mysteries of the Infinite, when, not content with beholding afar off the partial and relative manifestations of God's presence, she would ... know why God hath revealed himself thus, the voice of the Lord himself is heard ... speaking in warning from the midst 'Draw not nigh hither; put off thy shoes from off thy feet; for the place whereon thou standest is holy ground.'

In turning a negative criticism to Christianity's advantage, Mansel declined to diminish Christ's divinity since, if Christ was merely a man, then every man was his own redeemer and 'we of the nineteenth century could no more be Christians than we could be Platonists or Aristotelians' while, if Christ *was* the 'Son of God' and different, therefore, from all other human teachers, then he *could* 'save us from our sins', *could* be something more commanding than a 'republication of natural religion' and *could* require the attention that was required by a 'regulative truth'.

What Mansel meant by 'regulative' truth was a truth which was 'necessary and valid within the legitimate bounds of human intelligence' but was not necessary or valid beyond it. He agreed that there was an 'Absolute Morality' which was part of God's 'nature' but was equally emphatic that it could no more be defined than God's other characteristics could be. The concept of a human morality was as self-contradictory as the concepts of 'Infinite Number and Magnitude', and the 'very conception of moral obligation' implied not only 'a superior authority' to which obedience was due and an 'ability to transgress what that authority commanded' but also a 'complex and ... limited nature in the moral agent' which operated in conditions very different from the conditions in which God operated.

In his seventh Lecture, Mansel differentiated the 'Absolute Morality' inherent in God from the morality which God had delivered in Christ and left men to interpret and observe. It was by reason of men's 'sinfulness and ignorance' that men had neither the right to judge God's revelation nor the capacity to receive it in any but an analogical and anthropomorphic way, and because mysteries existed and would not go away that human life had necessarily to be lived in their shadow. The beginning of wisdom in these circumstances was to realize that mysteries would not be dispelled either by a philosophical science or by a science of theology, and that

the instant men undertook to say that this or that speculative or practical interpretation was the *only real meaning* of that which Scripture represented to them under a different image ... they abandoned at once the supposition of an accommodation to the necessary limits of human thought, and virtually admitted that the ulterior significance of the representation fell as much within those limits as the representation itself.

Thus interpreted [went a passage towards the end of the Lectures] the principle no longer offers the slightest safeguard against Rationalism; – nay, it becomes identified with the fundamental vice of Rationalism itself; that of explaining away what we are unable to comprehend.

The adaptation for which I contend is one which admits of no such explanation. It is not an adaptation to the ignorance of one man, to be seen through by the superior knowledge of another; but one which exists in relation to the whole human race, as men, bound by the laws of man's thought: as creatures of time, instructed in the things of eternity; as finite beings, placed in relation to and communication with the Infinite. I believe that Scripture teaches, to each and all of us, the lesson which it was designed to teach, so long as we are men upon earth, and not as the angels in heaven. I believe that 'now we see through a glass darkly' in an enigma; but that *now* is one which encompasses the whole race of mankind, from the cradle to the grave, from the creation to the day of judgment: that dark enigma is one which no human wisdom can solve; which

Reason is unable to penetrate; and which Faith can only rest content with here, in hope of a clearer vision to be granted hereafter. If there be any who think that the Laws of Thought themselves may change with the changing knowledge of man; that the limitations of Subject and Object, of Duration and Succession, of Space and Time, belong to the vulgar only, and not to the philosopher: if there be any who believe that they can think without the consciousness of themselves as thinking, or of anything about which they think; that they can be in such or such a mental state, and yet for no period of duration; that they can remember this state and make subsequent use of it, without conceiving it as antecedent, or as standing in any order of time to their present consciousness; that they can reflect upon God without their reflections following each other, without their succeeding to any earlier or being succeeded by any later state of mind: if there be any who maintain that they can conceive Justice and Mercy and Wisdom, as neither existing in a just and merciful and wise Being, nor in any way distinguishable from each other: if there be any who imagine that they can be conscious without variety, or discern without differences – these and these alone may aspire to correct Revelation by the aid of Philosophy; for such alone are the conditions under which Philosophy can attain to a rational knowledge of the Infinite God.

Mansel was a powerful writer, sawing off the branch on which he was sitting as his critics alleged, and needing at times to protest his appreciation of mysticism, but sawing off even more of that 'philosophical improvement' of the Bible which linked the Sadducees to Modern Rationalism. It may be that Mansel's Hamiltonianism was too strong, his Butlerianism too bare and his Kantianism unnecessary and confusing. But there can be no doubt that they gave him a coherent idiom with which to capture ignorance for faith, pyrrhonism for religion and modern doubt and indifference for Christianity.

Mansel's strength, and also his weakness, was that Christian agnosticism reflected the loss of authority which Christianity had suffered at the hands of philosophy and science. Because he knew what he was doing, Mansel was able to be intellectually aggressive but he also reflected the loss. Retreat, doubtless, was essential, if the ramparts were to be manned or an equality of esteem to be established for religion and theology in relation to science and philosophy, and so long as the Church of England had objective authority as a social and educational force, Mansel's tactic may well have been right. In leading a retreat, however, he was assisting at the slide which led through 'incognoscibility' to the subjective religion of the Aesthetes and the intellectual anarchy of modern Anglicanism. In Gladstone, though in a different form, retreat was a central and significant feature.

V

From an early point in his life Gladstone[1] was conscious of belonging to the nation. But he was also conscious of belonging to Oxford. For him, as for Jude, Oxford meant scholarship and Christianity, to which, as for the Tractarians, the central challenge had emerged between the emancipation of Roman Catholics in 1829 and the Gorham Judgment in 1850.

Gladstone was not in any sense a liberal latitudinarian. By his middle thirties he had come to believe, and continued thereafter to believe, in miracle, the Incarnation, the Church, the Apostolic Succession, the Sacraments, including the irreversibility of marriage, and supernatural Christianity's superior suitability as the remedy for sin and a religion for the multitude. But whereas, at first, he had been certain that those things could be preserved by a confessional state, he came slowly to the conclusion that in modern conditions they would be preserved best by abolishing the confessional state and modifying the exclusiveness of the confessional university.

At home and at Eton Gladstone did not really understand that Christianity was being assaulted. He was an undergraduate before he understood this; as soon as he did understand it, he reached the same conclusions as Newman had reached and expressed the same distaste as Newman had expressed.

At this time Gladstone's awareness of depravity was Evangelical. By the early 1830s it had become political and was reflected in his decision to enter parliament rather than the Church. In face of the agitation which preceded the 1832 Reform Act, he became an anti-Jacobin and for the rest of the decade was less the Canningite Tory he had been beforehand than a replica of Newman's hatred of Whiggery.

Gladstone's mind, though eventually complicated, was not so originally; until fertilized by transitions, his complication was a complica-

---

[1] William Ewart Gladstone (1809–98). Educ. Eton and Christ Church, Oxford. Author of *The State in Its Relations with the Church* 1838, *Church Principles* 1840, *A Manual of Prayers for the Liturgy* 1845, trans of L. C. Farini *The Roman State 1815–1850* 4 vols. 1852–4, *Studies in Homer and the Homeric Age* 3 vols. 1858, *Speeches on Parliamentary Reform in 1866* 1866, *A Chapter of Autobiography* 1868, *Juventus Mundi* 1869, *Rome and the Newest Fashions in Religion* 1875, *The Church of England and Ritualism* 1875, *Homeric Synchronism* 1876, *The Bulgarian Horrors and the Question of the East* 1876, *Gleanings of Past Years 1843–78* 7 vols. 1879, *Landmarks of Homeric Study* 1890, *The Impregnable Rock of Holy Scripture* 1890, *The Odes of Horace* 1894, *On the Condition of Man in a Future Life* 1896, *Studies Subsidiary to the Works of Bishop Butler* 1896, *Later Gleanings* 1897.

tion of style rather than substance. Having come to manhood as an Evangelical, he continued to be one until friendship with James Hope and the events of the mid-1830s made him waver. *The State in Its Relations with the Church* and *Church Principles* were para-Tractarian tributes to High Anglicanism.

In relation to Tractarianism, Gladstone was a fellow-traveller; he both responded to it, and resisted it. Manning, also in the 1830s a fellow-traveller, was a close friend and Palmer's *Church of Christ* a profound influence. Gladstone approved of Pusey, though not of Pusey's view of the Papacy, was at once sympathetic to and appalled by Froude's *Remains* and *Tract 90* and, while voting against the proposal to censure them in 1845, disapproved of both Ward's and Newman's sympathy for Roman Catholicism. In this phase he assumed that a confessional state could survive, that the Romanizing movement could be checked and that the Catholic Anglicanism of 1833 should take the lead in checking it.

In defending the Church of England, Gladstone argued that it was not only the only Church that could face up to the political problem, but was also the only Church that could face up to the philosophical problem. *Church Principles* was written in the idiom which the Tractarians had borrowed from Coleridge and Bishop Butler, the central chapter being entitled 'Rationalism' and setting out from the negative propositions that 'rational understanding' was not the 'final judgment ... of matters purporting to be revealed' and that its 'concurrence' was not a 'necessary ... condition of the entrance of ... religion into the human being'.

The positive argument of *Church Principles* was that 'the affections preceded the understanding', that man's 'need' was larger than the 'measure of his intellect' and that a 'spiritual process' was necessary if the understanding was to set out from 'right premisses'. 'Right premisses' required a 'right disposition of the affections'. It was through the right disposition of the affections that belief was achieved, the Sacraments received and men made 'partakers' in God's grace, and because the Church was the transmitter of the Sacraments that it alone could convey the 'primaeval image of holy love' which was its principal justification in face of the attacks it was to suffer in the forty years that followed.

After his resignation from Peel's government in 1845, Gladstone replaced the idea of a confessional state based on a Church in which less than half the population believed by Froude's idea of the limb which had been set at the Reformation being broken, of the Church 'descending' to 'the people', and of 'asceticism and faith' bringing back to at least the 'habits of Christianity ... the millions ... who had lost all but its name'. In the process Gladstone abandoned his Toryism, anticipating and, by his votes in parliament, assisting in the creation of a non-confessional state and university system, and expressing the gloomiest prognostications about both the continued establishment of the Church of England and the damage which Pius IX was doing to Christianity. Gladstone's most striking attacks on the Papacy were made in the wake of the Vatican Council of 1870. But he had made similar attacks earlier, not least in the course of the scathing account that he gave of Montalembert on the rebound from Manning's conversion and the 'papal aggression' of 1851.

What the attack on Montalembert defended was the conception of 'authority' as 'helpful ... for the attainment of truth' and of freedom as the means by which truth 'entered into and moulded ... man's composition'. What it attacked was the fraudulent nature of Montalembert's claim to have reconciled freedom and Roman Catholicism and the 'change of spirit' which had come over the Papacy during Pius IX's pontificate. The rehabilitation of the Jesuits and the proclamation of the Immaculate Conception as an article of faith were precisely what Gladstone's analysis suggested that Christianity did not need, and he expected the damage which had been done to go on being done so long as the 'withering hand' of De Maistre and Ultramontanism neglected biblical and patristic in favour of 'hierarchical and mystical' Christianity, and replaced the 'individual responsibility' of 'inward freedom' by the illiberal tyranny of a 'sacerdotal caste'.

The more perfect the organisation of the Roman Catholic clergy shall become ... the more glaring ... will it be ... to all except itself ... that it is an army and nothing else, a fortified camp in the midst of Christian society ... and that ... for others less equipped in high pretension but better grounded upon homely truth was reserved the ... best approach to solution of the great and world-wide problem, how, under the multiplying demands and thickening difficulties of the time coming upon us, to maintain a true harmony between the Church of Christ and the nations it had swayed so long, to reconcile the changeful world and that unchanging faith on which all its undeceptive hopes were hung.

Gladstone thought of the Church of England as a national branch of the Catholic Church. He believed that it was better equipped than Rome to establish by persuasion the truths which could no longer be established by law, and he claimed for it a leading rôle in a Mill-like competition in which Christianity and secular thought would compete for the allegiance of educated opinion.

Gladstone's aim was to contribute to this competition, and much of his religious writing had it in mind. In some respects he was successful. In other respects he was confused; it cannot be said, for example, that he differentiated consistently between Christian and secular thought, explained the sympathy which he alleged between Christianity on the one hand and Homer's and Tennyson's poetry on the other, or in his own '*Ecce Homo*' showed any sense of the Goethean agnosticism which Seeley displayed in his and was to display subsequently.

About art and literature as contributions to the restoration of Christianity, Gladstone expressed himself in two separate ways. On the one hand he was a laureate of the 'cheap press' and 'cheap literature' which had emerged with the removal of the penny stamp on newspapers in the 1850s. On the other hand he left no doubt about the 'liberalizing and civilizing power' of art, about the Christianizing influence which literature had had when conducted as Dante had conducted it and about the anti-Christian influence it had had when improperly conducted by Leopardi, and by Boccaccio and Shakespeare who had carried 'religious desolation' and 'Renaissance paganism' into the 'heart of the ... Christian world'.

Gladstone's mind and education were literary; unlike Salisbury he had no first-hand acquaintance with scientific thought and experiment. Science impinged only in so far as it threatened Christianity, and he reacted to the threat in two distinct ways – by trying to limit science's authority, and by reconciling its conclusions with the conclusions of the Bible. The former reaction was displayed unsystematically and by implication in *Studies Subsidiary to the Works of Bishop Butler*, the latter in defending his Homeric writings, controverting Huxley and constructing an absurd but ingenious reconciliation between Orthodox opinions about prayer, miracle and the biblical account of Creation and modern developments in astronomy, geology, history, archaeology and Darwinian evolution.

Gladstone believed himself to be living in the shadow of a threat by which every aspect of life was being affected. The threat was not just a threat to personal Christianity but to Christianity's central position in public intellectual life. He expressed his fears most strongly in relation to universities.

Gladstone believed that in the modern world university education was sought for the sake of its 'bearing on the professions and the pursuits of life' and he offered as an antidote the 'mediaeval' conception which had been invented by Christianity. This was the conception of a university as a 'telegraph for the mind' which fused together 'all the elements of intellectual culture' and achieved a 'completeness' that united 'old and new', 'high and low', 'authority and freedom', and 'speculation and action'. This was the point from which the Tractarians had begun, and Gladstone agreed that a Christian university should assert on behalf of the 'Christian ministry' and against the modern obsession with wealth an 'intellectual dignity' which the ministry was in danger of losing.

Gladstone was M. P. for the University of Oxford for eighteen years, was intimately associated with everything that happened in the university in that period, and alienated many of his followers by insisting, after much uncertainty, on dragging it, however cautiously, into the nineteenth century.

Gladstone did not create the climate in which the Russell government took up the Oxford problem in 1850; in reacting to it, he aimed, doubtless, to preserve Anglican influences by retaining for them as much as could reasonably be retained once parliament had been persuaded of the need for 'progress'. In piloting the 1854 Act through the Aberdeen Cabinet and parliament, nevertheless, he accepted many of the assumptions of Stanley and Jowett and made striking statements of the view that if Anglicanism was to retain its academic and intellectual pre-eminence, it must do so with rather than against the grain of modern knowledge and through an Oxford where Nonconformists had a place, however irregular and obscure, and academic strenuousness and professorial authority would shame collegiate idleness and parochiality into justifying the endowments on which the collegiate university depended.

Gladstone expressed doubts about the effect of endowment on effort, concluding, however, in the 1870s, that endowment created 'traditions', that a spirit of improvement was at work and that universities ought not therefore to be 'stripped ... of their trappings'. In considering the content of their teaching, he attached particular importance to theology and history, the former because of the encouragement it gave to ordination, the latter because, as Stubbs's *Constitutional History* was instanced as showing, the 'historical treatment' of religion would discourage the 'unbelief' which physics and metaphysics were encouraging.

Gladstone's optimism was misplaced, as the development of histori-cal thought since 1875 has shown. But it was based on an existing fact – the connection since Sir Walter Scott between the historical imagination and the reinvigoration of Christianity – and the hope that the Christian civilization which had begun in the time of Charlemagne and 'now presented the mingled signs of decrepitude and vigour', would be able to see off the 'pretenders' by which it was threatened. In addressing the students of Glasgow University during the Midlothian campaign in 1879, Gladstone specified the errors of the 1870s with regard to Christi-anity. These were the errors which had arisen when dogmatic religion was dismissed, 'specialisms' masqueraded as 'universal knowledge' and an 'advanced morality' was based on 'natural science'. It was the pro-vince of a university to disturb the 'levity' and 'scepticism' from which these errors had emerged, and to challenge sceptics to provide 'proof' of what they had become accustomed to asserting without proof. 'Scepti-cism' had to be met with scepticism: the 'wanton scepticism' which 'levity' had induced with the 'legitimate scepticism' – though Gladstone did not say so at Glasgow – of Bishop Butler.

For Gladstone, Butler was the most important Christian thinker after Dante and Augustine, and *Studies Subsidiary to the Works of Bishop Butler*, though not published until he was eighty-seven, had been started in his twenties. Moreover, it was important not only that Butler was an Anglican bishop but also that he had been brought up a dissen-ter and latitudinarian, was not to be identified with either the Nonju-rors or the seventeenth-century Anglican divines and was a symbol of the hard-working, Nonconformist mentality into which, as Liberal leader, Gladstone had made it his business to incorporate himself. Butler was supremely important, however, because of his 'method'.

What Gladstone meant by Butler's 'method' was expressed in the dictum that 'probability is the guide of life', by which he meant that in no case could 'the reasons upon which human judgment rested' be supported by more than 'probable evidence'. Man was a 'being of limited powers', and since the 'law' by which God had 'furnished him with evidence to govern conduct' was a law of 'sufficiency' not 'perfec-tion', it followed that the search for truth, of which God had not guaranteed the outcome, put a stigma on humanistic pride and necessi-tated the 'effort' or 'wrestling' that was characteristic of 'great and noble ... manhood'.

These were the conceptions which Mansel had used in the 1850s and 1860s and, though Gladstone's Butler was more straightforward than Mansel's, Gladstone assumed, like Mansel, that Orthodoxy should be defended through the connected conceptions of 'life' being 'charged with duty', of 'duty' being 'religious' and of the truth of religion being 'so well worthy of enquiry' as to impose a duty to enquire.

The Christianity that Butler was used to defend included miracle, immortality and the authority of the Church. In these respects, however, the arguments that Gladstone extracted from Butler were low-keyed. What was not low-keyed was Gladstone's use of the argument from history – the claim that the Christian mind was so much more complicated than the pagan mind, and Christian vices and virtues so much 'larger and deeper' than their pagan equivalents, that Christianity imposed 'graver' duties and 'heavier' burdens, and had created a human nature so much subtler than the human nature with which Aristotle had had to deal that Butler's moral philosophy had been better than Aristotle's moral philosophy.

In later life Gladstone assumed that the positions he had adopted in his thirties would not achieve the objectives at which they were aimed. Situational compulsions and personal tensions determined his movement from the Conservative into the Liberal Party and did nothing to make him a disestablishmentarian in England. But the movement was also a conversion, or produced a conversion which left intact the articles of faith and belief while issuing in the realization that Nonconformity was free in a properly Tractarian sense, that it was the Liberal Party's function to preserve a free Christianity by giving up whatever had to be given up in the schools, the universities and parliament in order to keep parliament and the Privy Council away from the Creeds, and that this was a crucial contribution to the assault on Infidelity since a free credal Christianity alone could win the battle for the mind which was to be the preliminary to re-Christianization.

In envisaging re-Christianization Gladstone specified his allies – Manning across the years; Acton since Acton kept suggesting this; Döllinger whose mental development resembled his own far more than Acton's did; Wilberforce; Church, the only really central Tractarian; Liddon and Pusey with reservations; MacColl, Hook, even Frederick Temple in spite of *Essays and Reviews*; Hutton and Spurgeon across the divide; Dale. Gladstone also specified the enemy; not, since sincerity made any argument fruitful, the 'attenuated' Unitarianism of Martineau, Greg, Carpenter and Jevons nor even, since he had rescued Rationalism from profligacy, the mistaken Rationalism of John Stuart Mill; but certainly Annie Besant's vacuousness about sin, Mrs Humphrey Ward's neglect of features which 'fifty generations' of Christians had regarded as the soul's 'wings' and the 'moral enormity' involved in an 'undenominational spirit of religion ... framed under the authority of the state'.

Gladstone was a generation older than Westcott – the most authoritative of Anglican scholars – and shared with him a certain complicated Byzantinism of mind. With Westcott, nevertheless, it is contrast that is particularly appropriate. With Newman, comparison is more appropriate since, except about Church government, Gladstone's critical Anglicanism was not very different from Newman's critical Catholicism. In the final chapter of this Part critical Catholicism will be contrasted with the authoritarian Ultramontanism which Gladstone deplored as a stimulus to 'secularism' but which Ward and Manning made their principal contribution to the counter-attack to which all four contributed equally.

4

Tractarianism as Constructive Assault

'No Catholic desires to see the Church of England swept away by an infidel revolution, such as that of 1789 in France. But every Catholic must wish to see it give way year by year, and day by day, under the intellectual and spiritual action of the Catholic Church; and must watch with satisfaction every change, social and political, which weakens its hold on the country.' Rev. H. E. Manning *The Workings of the Holy Spirit in the Church of England: A Letter to the Reverend E. B. Pusey* (1864) in *England and Christendom* 1867 p. 113.

'It is not the mission of the Church in England to conform itself to the varying currents of intellectual activity, philosophical and religious, which have passed and are still passing over the intelligence of the English people. For three hundred years what was thought to be the liberation of the English intelligence from the bondage of Catholic tradition has issued in what is called the progress of Modern Thought. I have no desire to wound or to offend, but truth must be spoken. There never was a time in the last three centuries when the religious diversities of the English people were so manifold, and the intellectual deviations in the higher education of England from the traditional philosophy of the Christian world so wide or so extreme.' Rev. H. E. Manning *The Office of the Church in Higher Catholic Education: A Pastoral Letter* 1885 p. 21.

'An internecine conflict is at hand, between the army of Dogma, and the united hosts of indifferentism, heresy, atheism: a conflict which will ultimately also (I am persuaded) turn out to be a conflict, between Catholic Theism on one side and atheism of this or that kind on the other. Looking at things practically – the one solid and inexpugnable fortress of truth is the Catholic Church, built on the Rock of Peter. But we cannot submit to the Church's authority by halves. We cannot accept what we please, and reject what we please. By rebelling against one part of her doctrine, we rebel against her doctrinal authority itself. But by rebelling against her doctrinal authority, we lay open our one position of security, and become an easy prey to our enemies. The Church's power as witness of the Truth cannot be duly brought into practical action, except so far as the Truth which she teaches is set forth in its full and genuine proportions. Its power, I say, cannot be brought into due action, if we choose merely to exhibit what after all are but fragments of her teaching; and very far less, if those fragments be united with other tenets which she actually condemns, whether that condemnation be definitional or merely magisterial. Such is the lesson which I had learned from my old friend Father Faber; and with which I have always sympathized most entirely. If I were not to edit the 'Dublin Review' on this principle, – such was my habitual conviction – I could not in conscience edit it at all.' W. G. Ward *Essays on the Church's Doctrinal Authority, mostly reprinted from the Dublin Review* 1880 pp. 24–5.

I

Between 1833 and 1843 Newman[1] had tried to make something of the Church of England. He had failed and had become a Roman Catholic. He had also shifted from aiming to understand Anglicanism as the religion of the English people to justifying religion as the truth of civilization.

In capitulating to Rome, Newman had lost a place in an influential establishment and had gained a future as a man of letters. From that point of view conversion was a gesture, the pulling of the only lever that could be pulled once normal methods had failed. Nowhere was this made more apparent than in the venomous account which he gave in *The Present Position of Catholics in England* of the complacency, materialism and Liberalism of the Protestant Establishment in face of the Great Exhibition and the Ecclesiastical Titles Act.

During the forty-five years that he spent as a Roman Catholic, Newman held official positions in Dublin and Rome, and an official position at Oscott. But he held no official position in the mainstream of English religion or education. He did not move in the world as Manning did, and he exerted an influence on English thought and religion almost entirely through his books.

[1] Rev. John Henry Newman (1801–90). Converted to Roman Catholicism 1845 and ordained 1847. Founder of Oratory in England 1847–54 and 1858–1890. Rector of Catholic University of Dublin 1854–8. Cardinal 1878. Author of *An Essay on the Development of Christian Doctrine* 1845, *Loss and Gain* 1848, *Discourses Addressed to Mixed Congregations* 1849, *Lectures on Certain Difficulties Felt by Anglicans* 1850, *Lectures on the Present Position of Catholics in England* 1851, *Discourses on the Scope and Nature of University Education* 1852, *Verses on Religious Subjects* 1853, *Lectures on the History of the Turks in its Relation to Christianity* 1854, *Callista* 1856, *The Office and Work of Universities* 1856, *Lectures and Essays on University Subjects* 1859, *Apologia pro Vita Sua* 1864, *The Dream of Gerontius* 1865, *A Letter to Rev. E. B. Pusey* 1866, *The Pope and the Revolution* 1866, *Verses on Various Occasions* 1868, *An Essay in Aid of A Grammar of Assent* 1870, *Essays Critical and Historical* 2 vols. 1872, *Historical Sketches* 3 vols. 1872–3, *The Idea of a University* 1873, *A Letter to the Duke of Norfolk* 1875, *The Via Media of the Anglican Church* 2 vols. 1877.

Newman's mind was heavily historical. In his Roman phase far more than in his Anglican, obedience to the historic Church was the resolution of the Tractarian dilemma, the embodiment of the faith by which reason had to be governed and the pre-eminent challenge to a world that was 'irreligious'. Though always assumed, however, this was not the central feature of his apologetic which after *Lectures on Certain Difficulties Felt by Anglicans* aimed less at elaborating a Roman doctrine or sensibility, as Faber's, Ward's and Manning's did, than at restoring to religion in general and to Christian theology in particular the credibility of which modern thought was depriving it. After 1845 Newman was as Roman a Catholic as Manning was to be after 1851. But Newman retained far more than Manning did the habits of thought he had acquired in Oxford, and throughout his long life as a Roman Catholic was governed not only by the ecclesiastical truths he had come to understand after 1839 but also by a literary desire to establish that ecclesiastical truths were a possibility.

In Oxford in the 1830s Newman had tried to insert historic Catholicism into Protestant Anglicanism. Once acclimatized as Rector of the Catholic University of Dublin, he tried to insert modern knowledge into Irish Catholicism. The aim in Dublin was the same, ultimately, as the aim in Oxford – the establishment of a university in which modern knowledge would be under Christian control. But the problem in Dublin was the opposite of the problem in Oxford since in Dublin Newman was defending modern knowledge against ecclesiastical mistrust.

During the Crimean War Newman published *Lectures on the History of the Turks in its Relation to Christianity* which was his attempt to interest his Irish audience in philosophic history. In predicting that the Turkish Empire would collapse because it lacked the culture and discipline of civilization, he used the same broad brush as in the three sets of lectures that he delivered in Dublin about university questions to assess the part which modern knowledge should play in a Christian civilization.

At all times in his life Newman was conscious of the power that had been generated by secular culture both in the Ancient World and since the Scientific Revolution. This had been the central problem in Oxford. In Dublin he faced the same problem in assessing theology's status as science, the difference between science and literature, and literature's significance as 'spokesman and prophet of the human family'.

In contrasting literature with science, *Lectures and Essays* argued that science had to do with 'things' rather than 'thought', and literature with 'thought' rather than 'things'. Positive testimony was given to science's autonomy and objectivity but the practical point was that literature had to be understood in its own terms, and that it was the coherence it established between 'thought' and 'word' which enabled it to remove grief, relieve the soul and open up the 'secrets of the heart'. This was the justification of literature and Newman explained why it was that, though a Catholic university could help to create a 'Catholic' literature to replace the Protestant literature of the past, theology was to be understood as science.

Newman's idea was that the function of a university was to preserve civilization as the Church had preserved it after the fall of Rome, and that the differentiating function of a Catholic university was to subject all study to the authority of a 'science of sciences'. The 'science of sciences' was not theology, but neither was it any of the sciences by themselves, and what he was at pains to explain was that it was less important to assert the emancipation of the separate sciences from theology than to assert the emancipation of theology from the separate sciences. Physical science was the 'philosophy of the natural', but theology was the 'philosophy of the supernatural' and since God had not 'superseded physical enquiry by revealing the truths which were its subjects', the physical sciences acquired inductive knowledge by reasoning from observation in terms of cause and effect where theology acquired knowledge of final causes by deductive reasoning from God's revelation of the infinite. In these circumstances, 'religious doctrine' was knowledge in as full a sense as Newton's doctrine was knowledge, and the task of the nineteenth century was to ensure that the knowledge it taught was the 'Catholic creed' which, as a 'living and breathing fact', was in irreconcilable antagonism to the 'specious nobleness ... of moral deportment' with which Gibbon, Shaftesbury and 'men-of-the-world' had emasculated sin, converted 'duty' into 'taste' and in rejecting confession made men shy, sensitive and self-obsessed.

In his Dublin period, Newman's defence of Christianity arose from the academic situation to which it was addressed, defined the respective powers of the university Faculties with which it dealt and discussed secular knowledge in the context of theological knowledge. In *A Grammar of Assent* these problems were raised to a higher level as questions were asked about the authority and impregnability of theological knowledge itself.

In *A Grammar of Assent* the principal assumption was that faith was natural and ubiquitous, and that the methods characteristic of the physical sciences were of limited applicability. Newman built on this assumption as the assailants of Christianity had built on the contrary assumption, advancing out from the ramparts, asserting on theology's behalf a standing as science which was not less real because it was based on revelation and pushing the *elenchus* of the Dublin Lectures to the conclusion that 'religious and ethical enquiries' took their starting-point in 'divine illumination'.

Chapter V of *A Grammar of Assent* found in the feelings of reverence, awe, hope, fear, responsibility and guilt realities as impregnable as memory, reason, imagination and the sense of the beautiful. Reverence, awe, hope, fear, responsibility and guilt enabled the conscience to 'reach forward ... beyond self', and it was said to be one of the most important of the nineteenth century's achievements to have understood that the conscience could only be excited by an intelligent Object which must be a 'divine ... holy, just, powerful, all-seeing and retributive ... Judge and ... Supreme Governor' of the world.

This was the basis of 'personal religion' which, though 'traced out' in natural religion, had needed the intellectual apprehension which Newman had described in *An Essay on the Development of Christian Doctrine* to achieve the 'fullness and exactness' of historic Christianity. In the 'brief, elementary declarations' of the Creeds, and in the assent which 'ordinary Catholics' had to give to the Church's theology, even when they did not understand it, he identified crucial lynch-pins of 'popular faith and devotion'.

In Chapter V the main line of argument had been about Christianity as the fulfilment of natural religion. What Newman meant by natural religion, however, was not the 'religion of ... civilization' with its soulless emphasis on the 'progress of the mind', but the cycle of sin, guilt, prayer, atonement and eternal punishment of which primitive religion agreed with the great religions in affirming the reality. This was the 'primary teaching of nature'. It denied that 'moral evil' was the offspring of physical evil or would be annihilated by mental progress, and it did not believe that 'knowledge was virtue, and vice ... ignorance; ... that miracles were impossible; that prayer ... was a superstition ... or that if men did their duties in this life, they might take their chance for the next'.

Newman attached importance to the fact that Christianity, alone among the religions of the world, had had a new message and revelation, and had conducted religious warfare through an 'aggressive' Church. He attached equal importance to the fact that it had been embraced 'in all climates ... and ... races, in all ranks of society, under every degree of civilization ... and in all parts of the world', and as against Gibbon drew the conclusion that a 'merely literary philosophy', so far from being able to explain this, needed the concept of supernatural intervention to account for the 'sanctity and suffering' which had enabled the early Christians 'without force of arms' to conquer the pagan world by which they had been confronted.

Throughout *A Grammar of Assent* Newman was aiming to remove the doubts about the reality of religious experience which had been infiltrated into the English mind. In affirming its reality and in conceptualizing the reality of Christian liberty, his most impressive weapon was the Illative Sense.

By origin the Illative Sense was Aristotelian phronesis – the agency through which the individual made something of the faculties he was born with and became 'his own ... teacher and judge in those special cases of duty which were personal to him'. There were as many kinds of phronesis as there were subject-matters, and though the process of reasoning was the same in all, the validity of reasoning depended on the subject-matter to which it was applied. An individual who had judgment in 'one department of thought' would not necessarily have it in another, but it was also the case that the Illative Sense of each individual person provided the 'only ultimate test of error' in choosing the 'assumptions ... often of a personal kind' on which all inference depended.

In this there was Aristotelian truth, but there was also a Tractarian, or Coleridgean, tactic. Newman was not just describing what the Illative Sense was and why the *elenchus* was significant in understanding its operation, he was also explaining why its 'elasticity' freed thought to be Christian by making it easier for free men to be Christians. In this argument fifteen pages about the choice of assumptions were central.

The ostensible object of these pages was to show that the assumptions which Newman found in the works of half a dozen historians reflected differences of 'intellectual complexion' which, though too 'spiritual' to be 'scientific', were a concomitant of all reasoning whatsoever. The tactical object was to show that 'universal doubt' was an impossibility, that reasoning should begin rather by 'believing' than by 'doubting' and that there was no 'ultimate test of truth' in religion apart from the 'testimony borne to truth by the mind itself'. This was what freed the mind to choose its starting-point, and it was the difficulty the mind encountered in doing this that made discovery of God dependent on God supplying the 'clue' which would enable men to discover Him.

A Grammar of Assent was Newman's unfriendly response to the unfriendly climate by which Christianity was being confronted and the institutionalized learning by which it was threatened. In both respects Newman presented the Church as the agent of counter-revolution. It was the Church's 'Infallibility' and the 'absolute submission' required of Christians which supplied the keynote even when they were grounded only in probabilities, but it was an infallibility and submission which embraced 'private judgment' as well as 'authority', was limited by the 'moral law, natural religion and scriptural and apostolic truth' and was designed not to 'enfeeble ... thought ... but to ... control its extravagance' and permit it to believe dogmas, like Transubstantiation, for example, which could not have been believed if obedience and submission had been absent.

Like Gladstone's, Newman's problem was to establish theology's authority and credibility within a pluralistic society. Unlike Ward and Manning, he did not assume that the pluralism of opinion could be superseded. On the contrary, he welcomed it, addressed himself to it and hoped to win the battle it involved. Most significant of all, he saw in the Roman Church a microcosm of a pluralistic society where 'every exercise of Infallibility', though 'brought out into act by an ... operation of the reason', provoked a 'reaction of reason against it', and

just as in a civil polity the state existed and endured by means of its rivalry and collision, the encroachments and defeats of its constituent parts, so in like manner Catholic Christendom was no simple exhibition of religious absolutism but ... presented a continuous picture of authority and private judgment alternately advancing and retreating as the ebb and flow of the tide ... a vast assemblage of human beings with wilful intellects and wild passions, brought together ... by the beauty and ... majesty of a superhuman power ... into ... a large reformatory or training-school; not to be sent to bed, not to be buried alive, but for the melting, refining, and moulding, as in some moral factory, by an incessant noisy process (if I may proceed to another metaphor) of the raw material of human nature, so excellent, so dangerous, so capable of divine purposes.

In the 1830s Newman had believed that Catholicism could become what Protestantism had failed to become – a religion for the masses. From that point of view his conversion implied the belief that the Papacy alone could cope with Democracy, and it was the tension he hinted at between the inferential theology of the Church and the simple religion of the masses that made *A Grammar of Assent* as political a book as *The Arians of the Fourth Century*. In his Roman phase Newman did not openly question the doctrine of papal infallibility. But he expressed reservations about the way in which it should be defined and in these respects differed sharply from Ward and Manning.

II

On conversion to Roman Catholicism Ward[1] reduced his credibility among some of his Anglican admirers by getting married. Thereafter he spent a number of years teaching at St Edmund's College, Ware, and lived on his estate in the Isle of Wight until Wiseman chose him to edit the *Dublin Review* in 1863. On Wiseman's death in 1865 he became an enthusiastic proponent of Manning's appointment to the archbishopric of Westminster and under Manning's supervision in the following thirteen years made the *Dublin Review* the leading organ of intellectual Ultramontanism.

Like Newman's, Ward's conversion had been governed by the perception that Anglican anarchy and Erastianism could only be ended by submission to Rome. Unlike Newman, Ward fitted easily into the Roman context and was not embarrassed, as Newman was, by real obedience. By the middle 1860s he had outshone Newman in loyalty and as a layman had responded in the manner of De Maistre to the need for a modern papal authority to fill the vacuum which had been left by the destruction of mediaeval papal authority.

Ward's Catholic writings dealt with the philosophical attack on Theism, gave an extended critique of Mill's religion and in *Nature and Grace* provided the beginnings of a systematic theology. His attitude to

---

[1] William George Ward (1812–82). Converted to Roman Catholicism 1845. Lecturer at St Edmund's College, Ware, 1845–58. Editor of *Dublin Review* 1863–78. Founder of Metaphysical Society 1870. Author of *On Nature and Grace* 1860, *The Relation of Intellectual Power to Man's True Perfection* 1862, *Authority of Doctrinal Decisions* 1866 *Essays on Devotional and Spiritual Subjects* 1879, *Essays on the Church's Doctrinal Authority* 1880, *Essays on the Philosophy of Theism* 1884.

Pusey's *Eirenicon*, to the Puseyite hankering after Reunion and to Pusey's attacks on mariolatry was unencouraging, not least because of the difficulties they raised about papal infallibility.

When Ward emerged from the seclusion in which he had lived after his conversion in 1845, he was moved principally by a desire to destroy Acton's Liberal Catholicism. This was a powerful motive even before he was given the *Dublin Review* in which to do it; the *Dublin Review* supplied a regular pulpit and episcopal authorization for opinions which he had expressed already. From the counter-attack which he had launched when Acton's *Rambler* attacked his book *The Relation of Intellectual Power to Man's True Perfection* in 1862, his message was that English Catholicism had to be protected from the pantheism, materialism and idolatry which were the inevitable concomitants of intellectual Liberalism.

In the 1860s Ward retrod Tractarian water about the Whigs, about the slide which led from Protestantism to Liberalism and about the contempt for Christianity which was expressed by thinkers who attached primary importance to the 'intellect'. He denied that 'intellectual power' had anything to do with 'spiritual perfection', imposed on intellectuals a special duty to recognize this and, in identifying spiritual perfection with the desire to serve God through 'free supernatural acts of the will' argued that, since spiritual was superior to intellectual perfection, Acton and the Liberal Catholics would have been better employed modelling themselves on popes and saints than on the 'disloyalty' of the secular intelligentsia.

As a proponent of papal infallibility, Ward's mentality was the Tractarian mentality of the 1830s, confirmed and strengthened by the counter-revolutionary leadership of Pius IX. While aiming to carry Gallican as well as Ultramontane opinion with him, he provided contentious accounts of the poison which Acton was spreading and the protestantizing tendency which he represented, of the intellectual 'captivity' which the Church of necessity 'imposed upon loyal Catholics' and of the importance of extending papal infallibility beyond 'actual definitions of truth' to the 'vast mass of ... heterogeneous error' about which Pius IX had declared himself in the Syllabus of 1864. From Ward's standpoint the Syllabus marked a 'momentous epoch in the Church's ... annals' because it subjected the intelligentsia to the discipline to which all other Catholics were subject and made it a condition of faith that the intellectual errors it was anathemizing were threatening Christian life and civilization.

For Ward in the 1860s this was the crucial problem – that modern knowledge was 'eating like a canker' into belief and that until Pius IX had taken control the Church had had no proper means of declaring herself about it. The Church had to declare herself, and the machinery of infallibility would enable her to do this by converting the 'dogmatic history and anti-Protestant controversy' at which she had been arrested for a very long time past into the authorized philosophy and dogmatic theology which the situation required.

In all these respects Ward was unyielding. Not only could the Church pronounce propositions to be erroneous 'if they tended by legitimate consequence to a denial of any religious doctrine which she taught', she should also recognize that Cartesian divisiveness had been the 'severest intellectual calamity' which she had ever encountered. The restoration of philosophical unity was as important as the restoration of theological unity, therefore, and it was only by giving infallible authorization to Scholasticism that a dogmatic theology would be restored, intellectual unity re-established and the 'Mills and Bains' confuted by a Catholic Crusade on behalf of 'Natural Religion'.

Ward was clever, vigorous and aggressive; his arguments, though circular, were no more circular than the circularities of the Liberalism he was attacking. As in many other respects, he saw eye to eye with Manning.

III

Manning[1] spent forty-one years as a Roman Catholic, twenty-seven of them as Archbishop of Westminster. He came of a once rich but insolvent family, was a sportsman, orator and scholar when young, and had had experience of secular employment as well as marriage. He could

---

[1] Rev. Henry Edward Manning (1808–92). Educ. Harrow and Balliol College, Oxford. Colonial Office 1830–2. Fellow of Merton College, Oxford, 1832, Rector of Woolavington and Graffham 1833–7, Rural Dean of Midhurst 1837–40, Archdeacon of Chichester 1840–51. Converted to Roman Catholicism and ordained 1851. Superior of the Congregation of the Oblates of Saint Charles 1857–65. Archbishop of Westminster 1865–92. Author of *The Unity of the Church* 1842, *Sermons* 4 vols. 1842–50, *Sermons Preached Before the University of Oxford* 1844, *Sermons on Ecclesiastical Subjects* 3 vols. 1863–73, *The Temporal Mission of the Holy Ghost* 1865, *England and Christendom* 1867, *The Fourfold Sovereignty of God* 1871, *The Four Great Evils of the Day* 1871, *The Vatican Decrees in Their Bearing on Civil Allegiance* 1875, *The True Story of the Vatican Council* 1877, *Miscellanies*, 3 vols. 1877–88, *The Eternal Priesthood* 1883, *Religio Viatoris* 1887, K. Paul (ed.) *The Temperance Speeches of Cardinal Manning* 1894.

have succeeded in almost any profession he had chosen, would have risen high in the Church of England if he had not left it and is the best disproof of the belief that Tractarian conversion was a sexual or psychological deformity. If he lacked Keble's poetry, Pusey's scholarship and Newman's intellectual breadth, if he had instead the tact and address which are necessary in a Prince of the Church, he must still be regarded as essentially a Tractarian – not in his Oxford period and not for many years, so to speak, as a comrade, but an unexpected consequence of the movement at its most versatile and the author of a popular and pastoral, but carefully considered, attempt to destroy modern thought.

Manning wrote devotional works and preached devotional sermons, made extended efforts to ally Catholic and Nonconformist hostility to the Education Act of 1870 and converted his Tractarian concern for the poor into a social doctrine addressed to the poor Irish congregations over which he presided. His main problem, however, was the prior problem, where authority lay, how Christianity was to be justified and protected in a democratic and rationalistic age and in what sense it could once more become the religion of European civilization in face of the anti-Christian forces by which it was being threatened.

Like Ward's, Manning's answer was Ultramontanism; between them Ward and Manning provided the only full English statement of the doctrine. It was under Manning's guidance that Ward made the *Dublin Review* an Ultramontane organ, and if one asks of what problem Manning presented Ultramontanism as the solution, the answer will be found in the running commentary on English religion that he gave from his reordination by Wiseman after he had resigned his Anglican Orders in 1851.

In justifying his conversion, Manning disengaged feelingly from his past, accusing 'rationalistic Protestantism' of taking 'half its people' from the Church of England. The task of the future was to redraw the lines between the Church and the 'solitariness and darkness of the human soul', and to allow a 'holy priesthood' to reinsert the 'science of the saints' into the 'heart and intelligence' of the people. There had to be 'conflict' between Rationalism and Rome, and it had to be fought in the knowledge that, though the 'mass of the people' were almost completely Godless, England could become the 'Evangelist of the world' if Protestantism could only be conquered.

In accounting for the English dilemma, Manning looked back to Anglo-Saxon England as the high point of English Christianity and dismissed the Reformation as the culmination of Norman secularity. English individuality was said to be 'exaggerated', denial of earthly infallibility to be the 'master-heresy' of the English race and Anglicanism to have degenerated into the 'naturalistic ... vagueness' which had enabled it to embrace not only 'Rationalism and Anglo-Catholicism' but also the 'Lutheranism of Edward VI, the hierarchical Calvinism of Elizabeth, the ceremonial Arminianism of James, the Episcopal Antiquarianism of the two Charles's, and the formalism and fanaticism of the Georges'.

Manning emphasized that Christianity and Ultramontanism were inseparable, that it was Rome's 'immortality' which had enabled the Papacy to integrate Europe into a 'Christian society' and that it was with the 'intelligence of the universal Church' in this sense that he wished England to resume its connection. He made no bones about the defeats which English Catholicism had suffered since the 1530s or about the materialism that had accompanied the 'rise of Empire' and the 'application of steam' to the world of the 'civil engineers'. Protestantism, he argued, had 'lost the respect of educated men', but since the Anglican Reformation had been the sin of the 'rulers' and an instrument of 'class interests' against the poor, it was to the poor that he looked to provide avenues for Catholicism's re-entry into English life.

In the 'wonderful expansion' which the Catholic Church had effected in England since 1830, Manning saw the tip of an iceberg so vast as to make these years the 'most prolific of change' since the Reformation. He thought of this as a European, indeed a world-wide, phenomenon, involving the revivification of Catholicism in the Far East as well as in Europe, and in explaining its significance for England attacked the 'anti-Christian' doctrine of 'national supremacy' with which English governments had made themselves the leaders of 'unbelief' and 'sedition' among 'every people' in Europe.

In aiming to subvert nationalism, except in Ireland, Manning required recognition of the 'unity' and 'liberties' of the Catholic world. It was in the name of the 'Red Revolution' that the 'anti-Christian hordes' were said to have invaded the papal states, and it was in order to prevent the dethronement not of the Pope only but of Christ also that 'brave men' had fallen in their defence. The 'tyranny of modern nationalism' was declared to be such that capitulation to it would involve the 'deification of the civil power' and the entrenchment of an 'anti-Christian hatred against the Church of God'.

Manning had adopted some of these opinions by the end of the Italian crisis of 1859. He adopted the rest in relation to *Essays and Reviews*, the Lushington Judgment and the Colenso controversy, and in the course of explaining the theological implications of Garibaldianism during Garibaldi's visit to London in 1864. He continued to maintain them in face of the threats presented by the Third Republic in France and by Bismarck and the 'anti-Christian ... hatred characteristic of German Liberalism' in Prussia.

Manning's account of the division between spiritual and civil authority had been given before the Vatican Council of 1870. In the 1870s he defended the Vatican Decrees against criticism, in particular against Gladstone's criticism, and endeavoured to establish that, so far from enlarging papal power, they merely reaffirmed it against aggression from the civil power. He differed from Newman in believing that the Pope's Temporal Power was the 'last witness' of a Christian polity which, if it were to be 'struck out', would be 'loosened to its base'.

Manning had an accurate sense of the English situation. He knew that Christians ought to be armoured against Locke, Comte, Renan, Mill, Lewes, Buckle, Thomas Arnold and Leslie Stephen, and believed that in existing English universities they would find it difficult to be so. He was not himself, however, locked up like Newman with his prayers and his books; at the Metaphysical Society, alongside Ward, he met and argued with some of Christianity's most important enemies.

Manning's public statements lacked Newman's subtlety and intellectuality. But they do not suffer by the comparison, not even in *Religio Viatoris*, certainly not in *The Four Great Evils of the Day* and *The Fourfold Sovereignty of God*.

The Four Great Evils of the Day made a virtue of facing the issue. The issue was plain and simple – that the modern world had questioned God's revelation, rejected God's authority and denied His existence, and in the process had turned not only the intellect but also the will against Him. 'Every act of the will' was said to require an 'act of the intellect or reason' and once the 'intellect' and 'reason' had been perverted, as they had been, it had followed that Christ's healing power had been destroyed, God's friendship rejected and men's 'passions and affections' freed to turn against their 'souls'.

In *The Four Great Evils of the Day* Manning proclaimed the twofold mission of the Church – 'the salvation of individual souls' and 'the sanctification of the civil society of the world' – and emphasized both the intimacy of the connections between 'private conscience' and 'col-

lective ... opinion' and the incompatibility between 'Christian civilization' and the 'varieties of lawlessness' that he described in Chapter I. In
the threats to 'manliness' and 'good sense' that were presented by
'luxury', 'worldliness' and 'superabundance of wealth', in the blows
which had been struck at the 'first principle of Christian love' by the
legalized dissolution of marriage and in the 'fearless and indiscriminate
reading' which sustained the dogmalessness licence of a secular education, he found explanations of that tendency to compromise to which
the spirit of the age was reducing even decent Christians.

What Manning demanded of Christians was a rejection of compromise and recognition of the need to mortify both the intellect and the
will. The religion of Christ was neither 'soft' nor 'easy'; neither did it
consecrate the godless world of the Commune. Christianity was related
to modern thought in the terms of the Syllabus of 1864 and the Vatican
Decrees of 1870 which were presented as the basis for believing that
papal authority over conscience, religion, and the State provided the
only means of controlling the 'masses'"who, as statesmen were called
upon to notice, having been 'robbed of their Christian education', had
grown up the 'scourge and ... overthrow of civil society'.

Manning's religion was a standing reproach to 'progress', 'civilization' and the modern world. It challenged them, demanded a Christian
doctrine to correct them and saw in the Papacy's rôle as 'mother of the
nations' and guardian of the 'moral force of law and right', the union
'in one person ... of the ... two societies which God had created for the
sanctification of mankind'. This was the 'basis of Christian civilization', and it required the assumption not only that dogma 'freed the
mind' by supplying an 'inheritance of certainty' but also that the monastic life was the 'life of perfection' and the Christian priesthood the
'most democratic of all governments on earth'.

Manning's position, when put summarily, sounds conventional. In
fact it was the strongest statement that was to be made in England – far
stronger than Newman's – of that contempt for the higher mind which
made Tractarianism so subversive. Manning was a great man, with a
great man's simplicity and force, and a great man's capacity to represent the age he lived in. He regarded a high doctrine of papal infallibility as an antidote both to the gentry-style Catholicism by which he was
surrounded and to the residual traces of private judgment that he
discerned in Newman. He supported the Vatican Decrees because
papal infallibility would subvert critical Catholicism as Acton and
Newman were developing it, and because an authoritarian Papacy

alone would succeed in effecting a democratic subversion of the secular influences which Liberal Catholicism wished to appease. Above all, his answer to scientific materialism was the study of St Thomas and Suarez, the fertilization of the intellect by faith and the recognition of God's sovereignty over the will, the intellect and society not in the anarchic ways in which human sovereignty had been recognized by the French Revolution but through the principles of 'order, law, authority, ... social rights and social duty'.

Manning was an anti-Jacobin but he was also a mitred revolutionary. He wanted to blow up the English Establishment and the modern gospel of society, to criticize it by comparing it with a world which had been lost and to draw conclusions from the contrast between 'poor Ireland's ... unending capacity for carrying the Faith throughout the Empire and North America' and the uncertainties which surrounded the Faith in 'Imperial and prosperous England'.

What a history has been the religious history of England for the last three hundred years? [he wrote with a militant nostalgia which Belloc and Waugh ought to have envied] What is its religious state now? What will be its future? The majestic cathedrals of England, the noble abbeys, the churches of ten thousand parishes, the lofty structures of our ancient towns, the sweeter, if humbler, churches in our green hamlets, and in our woodlands, and on our solitary downs show that Faith had penetrated everywhere through the English people, and that the people were profoundly Christian. I have been reading lately the books of piety written here in England some two hundred years before what men call the Reformation, in which, if the tracing of the Spirit of God in the human heart, transcribing itself upon the page, can anywhere be found, it is in the revelations of Divine love and the interior consciousness of the soul which are left to us by our ancestors. Are Englishmen never any more to return to the unity of the Faith? Are we never again to worship at one altar? Are Englishmen to be united in everything but faith, and in faith to be for ever divided?

Throughout his period as Archbishop of Westminster, Manning was the mouthpiece of the view that reunion between the Roman and Anglican Churches was impossible, and that it was only by submission to Rome that Anglican heresy and insularity could be ended. In this respect his position was as unyielding as Ward's. But it was also suffused with a romantic patriotism which, while it could not love England more than it loved Christendom, hoped to love both equally, and to bestow on the 'members of the Anglican body', the 'millions of Dissenters' and the 'noble-hearted poor', that vision of 'Catholic England' which the Reformation had destroyed.

II

THE ASSAULT ON CHRISTIANITY

5

Types of Ethical Earnestness I

'The present anarchy of politics arises from the anarchy of ideas. The ancient faiths are shaken where they are not shattered. The new faith which must replace them is still to come. What Europe wants is a Doctrine which will embrace the whole system of our conceptions, which will satisfactorily answer the questions of Science, Life, and Religion; teaching us our relations to the World, to Duty, and to God.' G. H. Lewes *Comte's Philosophy of the Sciences* 1853 p. 12.

'They who, dissatisfied with this little world of sense, seek to raise their minds to something which the senses are unable to grasp, can hardly fail, on deeper reflection, to perceive how coarse and material is that theological prejudice, which ascribes to such a Power the vulgar functions of a temporal ruler ... and represents him as meddling ... uttering threats, inflicting punishments, bestowing rewards. These are base and grovelling conceptions, the offspring of ignorance and of darkness ... the draff and offal of a bygone age ... well suited ... to those old and barbarous times, when men being unable to refine their ideas, were ... unable to purify their creed. Now ... everything is against them ... The signs of the times are all around, and they who list may read. The handwriting is on the wall; the fiat has gone forth; the ancient empire shall be subverted; the dominion of superstition, already decaying, shall break away, and crumble into dust; and new life being breathed into the confused and chaotic mass, it shall be clearly seen that, from the beginning there has been no discrepancy, no incongruity, no disorder, no interruption, no interference; but that all the events which surround us, even to the furthest limits of the material creation, are but different parts of a single scheme, which is permeated by one glorious principle of universal and undeviating regularity.' H. T. Buckle, *History of Civilisation in England* (1861 vol. ii) 1904 edn vol. iii pp. 484–5.

'Every religion, setting out though it does with the tacit assertion of a mystery, forthwith proceeds to give some solution of this mystery; and so asserts that it is not a mystery passing human comprehension. But an examination of the solutions they severally propound, shows them to be uniformly invalid. The analysis of every possible hypothesis proves, not simply that no hypothesis is sufficient, but that no hypothesis is even thinkable. And thus the mystery which all religions recognise, turns out to be a far more transcendent mystery than any of them suspect – not a relative, but an absolute mystery.

Here, then, is an ultimate religious truth of the highest possible certainty – a truth in which religions in general are at one with each other, and with a philosophy antagonistic to their special dogmas. And this truth, respecting which there is a latent agreement among all mankind from the fetish-worshipper to the most stoical critic of human creeds, must be the one we seek. If Religion and Science are to be reconciled, the basis of reconciliation must be this deepest, widest, and most certain of all facts – that the Power which the Universe manifests to us is utterly inscrutable.' Herbert Spencer *First Principles* 1862 pp. 45–6.

In Part I we have examined the most powerful attempt that has been made in England in the last century and a half to create a coherent Christian intellectuality. There were, of course, other defences of Christianity in the mid-Victorian decades, and there has been a continuous line of Protestant, Roman Catholic, dissenting and Anglican apologetic to which attention will be given in Volume III. Moreover, Tractarianism supplied not only polemic but also a mental cultivation which, in Stubbs, Church, Haddan and C. M. Younge, for example, entered as smoothly and decently into the public mind as anti-Christian opinions have entered into it in the twentieth century. But it was the Tractarians who invented the shock-tactics described in Chapter 1, the Tractarians who followed Burke in identifying a religious crisis more serious than any since the third century, the Tractarians who demanded the counter-revolutionary reconstruction of which Conversion and Ultramontanism were the outcome.

Tractarianism was an announcement that Christianity had lost the intellectual initiative and needed to regain it. But just as the Tractarians began to regain the initiative, new tides of Infidelity began to flow in in the 1840s. These tides – the subject of Part II – are tides which have never really flowed out.

The tides of Infidelity which began to flow into English thought in the 1840s shared with, indeed borrowed from, the Tractarians the idea that a turning-point had been reached, and that reconstruction was necessary in order to deal with it. And just as the Tractarian assault on the eighteenth century was thought of as a preliminary to a Christian reconstruction, so the assault mounted by the thinkers who are to be discussed next was thought of as a preliminary to an anti-Christian reconstruction, in their case as much as in the Tractarian, in response to the beliefs that Protestantism was dying, that Erastianism spelt the death of Christianity and that a new, modern sincerity would be needed if religion was to regain the influence it had had in the Middle Ages.

This assault, like the Tractarian assault, began as a criticism of the defects of existing religion. It became an assault on Christianity, some-times concealed and not always self-confident, but insisting at the very least that moralization was preferable to sanctification and that his-toric Christianity was incompatible with modern knowledge, not only in the form taken by critical historical thought but also in the form which had been made manifest when the intellectual power of science had received practical confirmation from the Industrial Revolution.

In time the assault on Christianity became routine – the conven-tional reassertion of a position which had been won through tears and blood. It was not so in the thinkers discussed in Parts II and III whose enmity to Christianity expanded from generation to generation as new versions were found of the claim that Christianity was dying, and the ethical earnestness which was designed to replace it was replaced by pessimistic illusionlessness.

Many of the thinkers who were most readily attracted by pessimistic illusionlessness were most obviously committed to ethical earnestness even when they pretended not to be. But it is nevertheless the case that in disengaging from Christianity, they claimed to be disengaging at least as much from the thinkers discussed in Part II as these thinkers had disengaged from the eighteenth century.

The desire to assault the eighteenth century, therefore, was by no means confined to counter-revolutionary Christians. Christianity's mid-Victorian enemies felt the same desire – with the difference that they believed, what their assailants denied, that ethical earnestness was its own self-justification, that Christian morality could be retained once Christian belief had been destroyed and that a secular religion was to be found in the proselytising Positivism of which John Stuart Mill was the intellectual advocate.

I

Mill[1] received from his father a thorough grounding in mathematics and the Greek and Latin classics, along with an indoctrination in

---

[1] John Stuart Mill (1806–73). Educ. at home. East India Office 1823–58. Author of *A System of Logic* 2 vols. 1843, *Essays on Some Unsettled Questions of Political Economy* 1844, *Principles of Political Economy* 2 vols. 1848, *On Liberty* 1859, *Thoughts on Parliamentary Reform* 1859, *Dissertations and Discussions* 4 vols. 1859–75, *Consider-ations on Representative Government* 1861, *Utilitarianism* 1863, *Auguste Comte and Positivism* 1865, *An Examination of Sir William Hamilton's Philosophy* 1865, *Inaugural Address at St Andrew's* 1867, *The Subjection of Women* 1869, *Autobiography* 1873, H. Taylor (ed.) *Three Essays on Religion* 1874.

Utilitarianism against which he rebelled during the mental crisis that he described in his *Autobiography*. In the course of this crisis, Mill came to understand that the principle of utility as Bentham and the elder Mill had understood it was incompetent to explain, and was an obstacle to understanding, the romantic sensibility. The crisis had a personal, and probably a sexual, connection. It also had an historic significance in so far as Mill's realization of the importance of poetry and the 'cultivation of the feelings' presented the problem in the terms in which Coleridge and Wordsworth had presented it in the first place.

Mill was heir to the *philosophes* and the Utilitarians; it was by reason of the constructive ambitions of Benthamism and of eighteenth-century and Comtean sociology that he was able to realize the intellectual conquests that he accomplished in *A System of Logic* and *Principles of Political Economy* in the 1840s. But it was his realization of the emotional narrowness of the *philosophes* and the Utilitarians which formed the subject of the vast outpouring of essays that went on throughout his life and made the tensions which had arisen in the course of a complicated intellectual development central to his doctrinal position. This position, though confusing, was not therefore less effective or persuasive. Mill was attractive to the Victorians not in spite of but because of the uneasiness of the conjunctions which he effected and he was able to become a founding father of Victorianism for that reason.

Victorianism was a huge mansion of which the intelligentsia was in only partial occupation. Wealth and social deference, practical energy and inventiveness, sexual and moral respectability, philanthropy and poverty, the Protestantism of the Church of England and the Protestantism of dissent, even Unitarianism and Quakerism, were more central and powerful than some of the opinions discussed in this volume. Yet the Victorian mentality included deep strands of free-thinking deviance which were important not because they were the leading opinions of the 1860s which they were not, but because they were to lay the foundations for the leading opinions of the 1920s.

What is at issue in Parts II and III is the supersession of Church–State Anglicanism and its replacement by something else, and in this respect Mill and his followers were doubly significant because they shared with Ruskin and the Tractarians – and also with Carlyle – the conviction that reconstruction in religion was connected with the reconstruction which had been made necessary by the destruction of the aristocratic polity. This was not on either side an argument in favour of reducing religion to a social policy, though on both sides there were thinkers who came near to doing this. It was an argument, on the contrary, about the seriousness of religion, and the impossibility of maintaining a properly human society without it. The centrality of religion was an important principle of Victorian thought, and all the enemies of Christianity who will appear in this and the next two Parts followed Mill in wishing to find a religion to believe in in place of Christianity.

Mill's doctrine was a doctrine about the future, and he was able to promulgate it because of the view that he took of the past. His past was a living past whose chief feature was the disturbance that western Europe had suffered in the previous three centuries as feudalism had been displaced and the régimes which had displaced it had failed to displace the Catholicism with which it had been associated. It was the failure to supply a system of beliefs suited to the conditions created by science and industrial progress that had made eighteenth-century French society into a 'great lie', and it was the need to undo the lie that had justified both eighteenth-century sociology and the French Revolution. His own task, as Mill understood it, was to provide securer bases for the restoration of belief than either of these had been able to do by themselves.

Though Mill addressed himself to the European, and especially to the French, situation his main address was to England, to the effect which Protestantism had had in differentiating the English character and development from the French and to the spiritual and intellectual aridity which Paley had imposed on the Church of England. He made it plain that the Church of England was incapable of responding to the challenges presented by an uneducated proletariat from one end of the social spectrum and by industrial and landowning philistinism from the other, and that the 'moral and intellectual ascendancy' which had once been 'exercised by priests' should now pass into the hands of 'philosophers'.

This was the central feature of Mill's doctrine as it was explained in *Bentham, Coleridge, Utilitarianism, A System of Logic* Book VI, *Auguste Comte and Positivism,* the *Three Essays on Religion* and *An Examination of Sir William Hamilton's Philosophy,* and it was the combination of Comtean Positivism, predictive sociology, the normative 'Art of Life', the inverse-deductive method appropriate to the Philosophy of History and the principle of utility enlarged to incorporate the moral teaching of a human Jesus which Mill proposed as the basis of the spiritual solidarity of the future.

Mill's religious doctrine was published piecemeal and by implication over more than forty years until *Three Essays on Religion* supplied a posthumous summary which disappointed his more militant admirers. Militant or not, it was Mill who created the mid-Victorian assault and laid down the intellectual principles on which it was to rest – the belief in doubt and self-questioning, the emphasis on thought as a preliminary to action and the consciousness of élitist duty in relation to it, and the unshakeable conviction that the wide diffusion of education alone would be capable of destroying unthinking prejudice, authoritarian and aristocratic mentalities and the Christian supernaturalism which were to be the main targets of the thinkers who will be discussed next.

For these thinkers Mill, though often mistaken and needing to be corrected, was also seminal, and it would be desirable in other circumstances to give an extended account of his attitude to Christianity. This, however, the author has done in an earlier work, and, though he would have put some things differently if that work had been written more recently, it expressed so exactly Mill's significance for our present enquiry that its argument will simply be assumed. The subject of Part II, therefore, will be the assault on Christianity as it was conducted in Mill's shadow by Reade, Morley, Harrison, Stephen, Huxley, Tyndall, Lewes, Spencer and George Eliot.

George Eliot, Spencer and Lewes were more or less contemporaries. George Eliot would probably have married Spencer if he had asked her to, and Lewes if he had not been married already. Though only she and Lewes collaborated to any significant extent, all three shared aims and aspirations. Along with Buckle, Huxley and Tyndall, who were significant contemporaries, they all aimed to subvert existing forms of Christianity.

Where religion was concerned, Huxley and Tyndall were mainly orators and essayists. George Eliot wrote many essays which touched on religion and was a campaigning editor whose novels insinuated her opinions more widely and innocently than the *Westminster Review* could have done. Spencer also wrote many essays but after 1860 conceived of almost everything that he wrote as part of *The Synthetic Philosophy*. Lewes was a genuine polymath, Buckle a brilliant exponent of many of the doctrines they all believed in.

II

Buckle[1] was born two years later than George Eliot and died, young, eighteen years before she did. He published in effect only one book, *History of Civilization in England,* on which he had been working since 1842, freed by wealth from the need for employment and undistracted by domestic ties except with his mother, who criticized his work and with whom he lived until she died in 1859. Once the 800 formidable pages of its first volume were published in 1857, Buckle's reputation was assured. If he had not died at the age of forty, five years later, shortly after the publication of volume ii, *History of Civilization in England* would have had more volumes and he would have had as productive a career as his longer-lived contemporaries.

Buckle was important for two connected reasons. First, because *History of Civilization in England* provided a naturalistic account of the development of society and a justification of naturalistic methods. Second, because Buckle's naturalism was intended to be as subversive of Christianity as Spencer's was.

History of Civilization in England contained a number of separate books. It contained one about the development of English thought since the seventeenth century. There was another about French thought in the same period, a third about Spanish thought, and a long one about Scottish thought. In addition there were equivalents of a separate book about historical thought as an aspect of the 'condition of a people'.

In comparing the development of France, Spain, Scotland and England, Buckle aimed to show that historical events were neither as 'single' nor 'isolated' as 'empirical ... narrative supposed' and to provide reasons for believing that history could be 'raised to the rank of a science'. Freewill and predestination were dismissed; men's actions were said to be 'determined by their antecedents' and 'in ... the same circumstances' 'always' to issue in 'the same results', and a 'philosophic' history to be one that used the conceptions of 'man modifying nature and nature modifying man' to explain the process out of which 'all events sprang'.

In Chapter II, Buckle discussed the influence of 'climate, food, soil' and the 'appearance of nature', concluding that progress in civilization

---

[1] Henry Thomas Buckle (1821–62). Educ. mainly at home. Travelled widely. Accomplished chess player. Author of *History of Civilization in England* 2 vols. 1857–61, H. Taylor (ed.) *Miscellaneous and Posthumous Works* 3 vols. 1872.

involved an increase in human control of nature and that it was because the 'powers of nature' had been 'far greater' outside Europe than inside that Europeans had been better able than others to tame nature for their happiness. This was why the history of non-European countries had had to centre on the 'external world' while the history of European countries centred on 'Man', and why the 'influence of physical laws' which had been a bar to human progress and the most 'fertile source of superstition' in the past would be replaced by the 'increasing influence of mental laws' in the urban life of the future.

This was the point at which Buckle had arrived by the beginning of Chapter IV and subsequent discussion asked whether moral progress or intellectual progress was more essential to the idea of civilization. The answer was that moral agency was static while intellectual agency was progressive, and that the more deeply the answer was considered, the clearer it would become that 'intellectual acquisition' was superior to 'moral feeling' and that 'there was no instance of an ignorant man who, having good intentions and supreme power to enforce them, had not done far more evil than good'.

In retrospect this looks empty and innocuous. It looks less empty and less innocuous once it is seen to have involved a denial that religion had brought any benefits to civilization.

In Chapter V of *History of Civilization*, Buckle worked from the belief that statistical and demographic generalization would show that 'moral principles', 'individual feelings' and 'individual caprice' , which produced 'great aberrations in short periods', corrected and 'balanced themselves out ... over long periods'. This was what he meant by discovering 'the whole of the laws which regulated the progress of civilization', and, while asserting that these laws would eventually be discovered, in *History of Civilization* he assumed only an interim rôle as collector of generalizations

Throughout *History of Civilization* there was patriotic self-congratulation and an insolationist admiration of the uniqueness of English institutions. These, however, though they suffered, also transcended the limitations of Macaulay's self-congratulation, being heuristic conceptions arising from connected assumptions about a nation's life as the subject for historical science.

In justifying these assumptions, Buckle adduced a negative and a positive consideration. The negative consideration was the difficulty that any historian would encounter in writing the whole history of a people even for a short period. The positive consideration was the benefit that would come from studying the history of the *English* people – not only by reason of the 'number' of English 'discoveries', the 'brilliancy' of English 'literature' and the 'success of English arms', but also because in two major respects England's development had been due to 'causes springing out of herself'.

These were that England had been 'insolated from foreign influences' and of all European countries had had the most 'active people'. The English people had developed a 'healthy and natural' civilization in which the 'accumulation and diffusion of knowledge' had been 'interfered with' less than elsewhere by those 'powerful but ... incompetent men' who conducted public affairs and in which, therefore, scientific method could use laboratory conditions to contribute to a 'complete and philosophic' history.

The history Buckle wanted was a radical, or Spencerian, history which would justify the replacement of the hereditary governing classes by the predominance of the 'ablest men'. He wanted particularly to show that 'religion, literature and government' were not the 'prime movers of affairs as many persons supposed', and that those who had exercised leadership through them in the past had obstructed the natural social development which occurred when the 'acquisition and diffusion of knowledge' were unrestricted.

In Buckle knowledge meant 'acquaintance with physical and mental laws' and literature was the form in which a nation's knowledge was registered. Literature was to be judged by the extent to which it contributed to making this acquaintance complete and would not contribute at all if its practitioners were out of touch with the people. Literature, in other words, was not only not an 'illumination of the soul', as Shelley, for example, had supposed, but was also 'of very inferior importance by comparison with the disposition of the people by whom it was to be read'.

Buckle might have denied that he wished to put clamps on the literary imagination or on normal political leadership. But the criticisms he made of a literary education for putting 'too great an interval' between the 'intellectual classes' and the 'practical classes' were intended to subject them to the requirements of social and intellectual solidarity, while his description of the conflict between 'civilization' and the protective, paternalistic spirit not only denied that an age's 'rulers' had been civilization's 'creators' but also seemed to imply that they ought not to be. In conceiving of progressive civilization as subject to popular leadership by 'able thinkers', he dug a Millite or Comtean pit for the clergy as well.

Buckle emphasized that a nation's intellectual condition was prior to its religious condition, that intellectual improvement preceded religious improvement and that 'religious doctrine' had little effect on a people 'unless preceded by intellectual culture'. *History of Civilization* was littered with examples of the 'fraud and hypocrisy' that had arisen during the 'many centuries' when oaths and religious declarations had abounded and 'every government' had thought it its duty to 'encourage religious truth and discourage religious error'. It concluded, nevertheless, that a people's religion could not be diverted permanently by governmental action, that religious principles were 'symptoms' of an age not its cause and that a religion would only take root if the 'minds of men were ripe for its reception'.

Buckle was hostile to aristocracy and Christianity. In this he was on the wave of the future, forging weapons of war, establishing identifications between the 'ablest men and the people' and hacking his way through a jungle as thick and dense as the jungle that Frazer was to hack his way through in a similar cause forty years later.

III

Buckle had nothing to do with George Eliot's activity as a propagandist. Lewes[1] was an accomplished propagandist and as editor of the *Fortnightly Review* contributed as much as she did as editor of the *Westminster Review*.

Lewes came from a theatrical family and was a playwright, theatre critic, naturalist, philosopher, biographer and historian. He was articu-

---

[1] George Henry Lewes (1817–78). Educ. various schools in London, Jersey, Brittany and Greenwich. Worked in notary's and in mercantile offices. Occasional actor 1841–50. Married in 1840 but lived with George Eliot from 1854. Author of *A Biographical History of Philosophy* 4 vols. 1845–6, *The Spanish Drama* 1846, *Ranthorpe* 1847, *Rose, Blanche and Violet* 3 vols. 1848, *The Life of Maximilien Robespierre* 1849, *The Noble Heart* 1850, *Comte's Philosophy of the Sciences* 1853, about ten plays between 1853 and 1866, *The Life and Works of Goethe* 2 vols. 1855, *Sea-Side Studies at Ilfracombe, Tenby, the Scilly Isles and Jersey* 1858, *The Physiology of Common Life* 2 vols. 1859–60, *Studies in Animal Life* 1862, *Aristotle* 1864, *Problems of Life and Mind* 5 vols. 1874–9, *On Actors and the Art of Acting* 1875.

late and self-conscious about the functions he performed, and claimed for literature a vital rôle in drawing up the public mind to the 'excellence' and 'sincerity' of its ideal.

Lewes admired Goethe and had a doctrine about poetic drama as a register of a nation's morality. But his plays and theatre criticism need not detain us. Neither need his novels, nor the naturalistic observations which he published under the titles *Studies in Animal Life* and *Seaside Studies in Ilfracombe, Tenby, The Scilly Isles and Jersey.* For present purposes, his significant works were *The Physiology of Common Life* and *Problems of Life and Mind,* which were published between 1859 and 1879, and *A Biographical History of Philosophy* and *Comte's Philosophy of the Sciences,* which were published between 1845 and 1853.

The Physiology of Common Life described the connections between food, drink, digestion, blood and respiration, the nature of feeling, thinking, sleeping and dreaming, and the 'mysterious' barrier that stood between life and death. Its range of reference, however, was anatomical not philosophical, and stopped deliberately short of the 'creed' whose 'foundations' were sketched in the first two volumes of *Problems of Life and Mind.*

These volumes consisted of 1,000 pages of reflection on problems which Lewes had been considering since his teens – initially by way of Reid, Brown and Dugald Stewart, then through study of the nervous systems of animals, finally in the 1860s as an attempt to make psychology into a science. In defining the conditions under which this might be done, *Problems of Life and Mind* provided an introduction to the Philosophy of Science, a statement about Science's rôle in subverting the 'creeds' of the 'churches', and a quasi-Spencerian attempt to reconcile Science with Religion by ensuring that Religion was 'founded on Science'.

In specifying these aims, Lewes fixed on 'metempirics' as the enemy – not only by reason of the part it had played in sustaining Religion but also by reason of the part it had played in misdirecting Science. 'Metempirics' was a region in which metaphysical problems were 'insoluble', where speculation 'roamed unchecked' and where the crucial problem was to clear up the subjective, deductive mess that had been left by Descartes, Leibniz, Kant, Fichte and Hegel.

Problems of Life and Mind distinguished between the scientific 'laws of sensible phenomena', and the metaphysical 'laws of those laws'. In rejecting simple, positivist assumptionlessness, it emphasized the need for an active ontology, for an abandonment of the 'irrational' search for the 'otherness' of the 'suprasensible', and for the creation of a structure in which all problems could be solved by being conducted within 'empirical limits'.

The distinction between the unknown and the unknowable – as central to Lewes's thought as it was to Spencer's – was pointed principally at the metempirical conceptions which 'twenty centuries' of failure had not prevented even 'great captains of science' being impressed by. *Problems of Life and Mind* gave many instances of the obstructions which metempirics had presented to progress in the particular sciences in the past and fixed on Newton as the supreme exponent of the way in which speculation should be conducted in the future.

Towards the end of Part I of *Problems of Life and Mind,* Lewes specified the absence of philosophy as the 'serious defect in English culture' since the seventeenth century. English philosophy was criticized for producing 'essays, not systems', and in pointing the Spencerian system at it, Lewes provided an up-to-date version of the criticisms of professional science's balkanization of science, the political classes' parochialization of politics and the English distaste for anything 'wearing the aspect of general doctrine', which he had been making from the 1840s onwards.

Goethe and Shakespeare mattered to Lewes as much as Lavoisier and Newton, and it was for this reason that, though science was the modern activity and scientific method the method through which modern knowledge had been acquired, it was as literature that *A Biographical History of Philosophy* and *Comte's Philosophy of the Sciences* had expounded the need to entrench Positivism at the centre of English thought.

In *A Biographical History of Philosophy* volume iv, Lewes had explained the low esteem which the public had come to feel for philosophy on the Continent – in France because of the inadequacy of eclectic historicism, in Germany because of the inadequacy of academic Hegelianism. In reaction he had stated three central principles – that philosophy had to be rescued from the philosophical profession, that non-professional philosophy had been conducted best by the great English philosophers who had written in the wake of Bacon and that Comteanism addressed as the English philosophers had addressed their philosophies to 'thinking men' would be better placed than any other philosophy to respond to the anti-speculative requirements of the English mind. This view was summarized in the dictum that 'Comte was the Bacon of the nineteenth century', by which Lewes meant that contemporary thought and religion were anarchic, that Comte had understood both the 'causes' of anarchy and its 'cure' and that Comteanism alone had the requisite 'generality' without the 'vagueness and ... inapplicability' characteristic of a 'metaphysical' doctrine. This was what Positivism was – the 'greatest work of our century' and a 'mighty landmark in the history of opinion' which supplied a 'sustaining faith' to help men participate in its benefits.

In specifying the benefits, Lewes distinguished between Science as the province of the intellect and morals and Religion as the province of the heart. He pointed out that Positivism demanded an 'insurgence of the emotions against the intellect' and a 'rigorous subordination of the intellect to the heart', and that religion and philosophy would still pose 'deep and urgent questions' even when the political problem had been solved.

The political problem as Lewes understood it was that, though feudalism had disintegrated, nothing had taken its place. The French Revolution had occurred but, as *The Life of Maximilien Robespierre* had shown, had degenerated into tyranny. Communism had been proposed and had attracted widespread attention, but Positivists had to reject Communism because it did not go deep enough. The political problem, indeed, was a religious problem, and a chapter entitled 'The Three Reigning Doctrines' described the unresolved conflict which had been going on in the previous three centuries between the Catholic feudal standpoint embodied in a 'theological' view of Social Science and the negative Protestant standpoint embodied in the 'metaphysical' view of Social Science, and concluded that establishment of the metaphysical view as it had been adopted in 1789 would be as damaging as a reversion to the 'theological' view which it had replaced.

Comte's Philosophy of the Sciences rejected the reactionary Catholicism of Bossuet and De Maistre. But it praised the spiritual independence of the mediaeval Papacy and the 'social genius' of mediaeval Catholicism, and criticized both the 'vague ... theism' which had merged Christianity into 'natural religion' subsequently and Liberalism's attempt to preserve the 'general bases of the pre-revolutionary political system' without the 'spiritual consensus' which had been the 'principal condition of its existence'. The establishment of consensus was declared to be the task of the future, and it was Positivism's destiny to do this by making Order and Progress 'inseparable aspects' of a single principle.

Comte's Philosophy of the Sciences criticized the development of mathematics and the organic and inorganic sciences in the previous two centuries as instances of what the specialized sciences became when isolated from general culture. It was not in the attack on the 'hodmen' whom this process had permitted to masquerade as 'architects', however, that the chief purpose of the book is to be found, but in the description of the scientific sociology which Positivism indicated as the proper resolution of the political problem.

In describing the bases of Comte's sociology in the last third of the book Lewes emphasized that it 'hinged' on the 'fundamental law of evolution' – the fact that human thought went through theological, metaphysical and positive stages of development, and that the task which Comte had specified for the future was to ensure that Positivism would destroy theology and metaphysics as surely as Marx's historicism aimed to destroy all earlier conceptions of economics.

Lewes did not suppose that Positivism would succeed easily or that positivist predominance would be established readily. The 'causes', 'essences', and 'abstract entities' characteristic of theological and metaphysical thought had, nevertheless, to be replaced, and what was needed to replace them was the conception of law not as command but as method – the 'method' which it was science's business to record because it was the method by which Nature travelled towards her destination.

In Lewes's account of the graduation of the sciences, the prospect of establishing a positive method in any particular science diminished the more complicated the science became. The actions of 'men aggregated in masses' were actions of extreme complexity and Comte's achievement was therefore the greater for having shown – what only Montesquieu and Condillac had shown beforehand – that men were governed by laws as 'absolute and rigorous as those governing cosmical processes'.

Comte's conceptions were historical. They distinguished 'dynamics' from 'statics', treated 'absolute' principles as though they were 'relative', and made it their chief business to trace their 'development'. In tracing the development of spiritual consensus from fetishism and polytheism through Catholicism and Protestantism to the Aesthetic, Scientific, Industrial and French Revolutions, Lewes justified the view of the future with which his discussion of Comte's *Cours de Philosophie Positive* concluded.

Like Comte, Lewes avoided simple rejection of Christianity. He claimed to comprehend the significance of all phases of spiritual development, to be leading them all towards a positivist illumination and to see in the 'grand renovation projected by Bacon and Descartes' a way of replacing the 'ascendancy of wealth' by a new class whose authority would depend on the 'voluntary assent of all intelligences' to the doctrines that it would proclaim.

This was a plan for increasing the influence of the 'speculative' over the 'active' life, for recognizing the superiority of the 'speculative' class to the 'active' class and for establishing the predominance of the speculative class in education. A systematization of ethics was to free ethics from 'theological conceptions', and to create for the soul a 'normal consensus similar to that of health for the body', depending neither on 'creed' nor on worship of the 'Supreme Being of the World', as Comte had proposed, but on a 'Religion of the Universe' in which God would be the 'Incarnation of Resistless Activity' and the Universe would proceed in 'abounding power' from Him. It was through this that the speculative classes would unite themselves in sympathy to the lower classes and effect their 'reclamation', this that would persuade all classes to 'implore the necessary protection of that ... spiritual power' which all classes were said at present to dismiss as 'chimerical'.

Lewes's religion was a Comtean derivative. In its positive aspects, it was deeply muddled. Negatively, it was sharp and clear, and demanded as total a subversion of historic Christianity as George Eliot's did.

IV

George Eliot[1] wrote no plays, did no practical science and made no systematic statement of her philosophy. Before she began to write fiction in the late 1850s she aimed at informal literary philosophizing. The work she did between the middle 1840s and the middle 1850s as a translator, book-reviewer, and editor of the *Westminster Review* differed in form, but there was a continuity between the two phases, and in the course of the transition from the one phase to the other, a transposition into art of what had previously been stated didactically.

---

[1] George Eliot (Mary Ann Evans) (1819–80). Educ. at home and in Coventry. Translator (joint) of D. F. Strauss *The Life of Jesus* 3 vols. 1846, of Feuerbach's *The Essence of Christianity* 1854, and of Spinoza's *Ethics* 1856. Author of *Scenes of Clerical Life* 2 vols. 1858, *Adam Bede* 3 vols. 1859, *The Mill on the Floss* 3 vols. 1860, *Silas Marner* 1861, *Romola* 3 vols. 1863, *Felix Holt the Radical* 3 vols. 1866, *The Spanish Gypsy* 1868, *Middlemarch* 4 vols. 1872, *Daniel Deronda* 4 vols. 1876, *Impressions of Theophrastus Such* 1879.

George Eliot had been brought up a Low-Church Anglican and had probably had a Calvinistic Evangelical conversion in her teens. Under the influence of her friends, the Hennells, there had then been a recession. By the time she began to write she had lost her faith in historic Christianity and had symbolized the loss by translating Strauss's *Life of Jesus*. In the 1850s she also translated Spinoza's *Ethics* and Feuerbach's *Essence of Christianity*. Almost everything that she wrote before becoming a novelist was concerned with understanding duty and existence outside the framework of Utilitarianism and Evangelical Christianity.

In London in the early 1850s Lewes and George Eliot belonged to a circle of friends who congregated round John Chapman, the proprietor of the *Westminster Review*. These included R. W. Mackay and F. W. Newman. Mackay and Newman, and also W. R. Greg, were part of George Eliot's intellectual life and contributed to the movement of opinion which she reflected.

Greg was the son of a Lancashire mill-owner. He was born in 1809, was at school under Lant Carpenter, the Unitarian, in Bristol and was then at the University of Edinburgh. After nearly twenty years as a mill-owner and in face of financial difficulty brought on by his obsession with public affairs, he abandoned his mill and became an official. His most important book – *The Creed of Christendom* – was published in 1851.

Mackay was six years older than Greg and was at Winchester, Brasenose College, Oxford, and Lincoln's Inn. After a short period as a lawyer, he gave up the law and devoted himself to German biblical scholarship. Between 1850 and 1863 he published three substantial books – *The Progress of the Intellect as Exemplified in the Religious Development of the Greeks and Hebrews, A Sketch of the Rise and Progress of Christianity* and *The Tübingen School and Its Antecedents*.

Greg was less scholarly than Mackay. But he was more prolific, had a wider range of interests and wrote a great deal about politics and economics. Greg and Mackay were both reputable and produced significant writing. Neither matched the range and fertility of Newman.

Newman was a brother of J. H. Newman and four years his junior. He was a Fellow of Balliol in his twenties but left Oxford when required to subscribe to the Thirty-Nine Articles on the renewal of his Fellowship. After a period as a missionary in Baghdad, he took up teaching, first in Bristol, then at Manchester New College, finally as Professor of Latin at University College, London. In the course of a continuous output which went on until two years from his death at the age of ninety-two in 1897, he published an Arabic dictionary, a Libyan grammar, *First Steps in Etruscan*, *The Higher Trigonometry*, *Essays on Diet*, *Lectures on Logic*, *Lectures on Political Economy* and translations of Horace's *Odes*, Homer's *Iliad* and the speeches of Kossuth. In addition to a discussion of Matthew Arnold's attack on his own view of Homeric translation and a substantial body of writing about the drink problem, neo-Malthusianism, the reform of English institutions and *The Crimes of the House of Habsburg*, he wrote a stream of books about religion of which the most influential were published in 1849 and 1850 under the titles *The Soul* and *Phases of Faith*.

The central works of these thinkers at this time were *The Soul*, *The Progress of the Intellect*, *Phases of Faith*, *The Creed of Christendom*, *The Rise and Progress of Christianity* and Newman's *Essays Towards a Church of the Future as the Organization of Philanthropy*, all of which were published between 1849 and 1854 before Darwinianism had become an issue. Between them they made it clear, at any rate in religion, that Greg, Mackay and Newman had no sympathy for Benthamism even in the hands of George Grote whose agnosticism they otherwise respected, that their chief interest was in the tradition of biblical criticism as Spinoza had initiated it and that their chief aim was to give new twists to Strauss's and Baur's view that since the Bible contained no trace of credal, ecclesiastical or revealed Christianity, Christianity must not be identified with any particular moral system, must not claim sources of knowledge independent of the knowledge which was supplied by science and could only be understood as a human artefact which neither had nor needed divine and miraculous credentials.

Like the Tractarians, these thinkers were responding to the assumption that European Christianity was on the run and that the 'heathenism ... of its town populations' would only be checked by supplying them with a religion that they could understand. But whereas for the Tractarians a religion that could be understood involved the renewal of Church and Creed, *they* believed that it was Church and Creed which were the obstacles to understanding.

Greg, Mackay and – in his later years – Newman thought of themselves as more or less Christian, Mackay in particular treating the Tübingen school as a continuation of mainstream Protestantism. The difficulty in taking them, and George Eliot, at their face value is the difficulty which will be faced in discussing Unitarianism and creedless Christianity in Volume III – that there is nothing distinctively Christian about a Christianity which rejects revelation, proposes a human Jesus and emerges from the earnest subjectivity of the soul.

George Eliot was well aware of the problem presented by historical criticism of the Bible. But her *Westminster Review* articles were by no means confined to the questions she had encountered in translating Strauss, Feuerbach and Spinoza. Though many of the works which she reviewed were historical or didactic, she treated them as contributions to literature, or, like music, as manifestations of Art. In expatiating on the connections between 'the Independence of Art' and 'what was best and noblest in morals', indeed she demanded that Art be allowed 'involuntarily' to 'create its own symbols' and in showing what happened when it failed to, specified Wagner's intellectuality, Kingsley's adoption of the 'parsonic habit', and the premature moralizing which she found offensive in contemporary criticisms of Goethe.

In conceiving of Art as imaginative symbolization, George Eliot was doing nothing unusual. But since she was using it to open up English thought, we may ask what it was that she wished to open it up to. The answer, as she gave it in the course of discussing world literature between Sophocles and Heine, was that English morality should be opened up in order to become the English religion.

In approaching George Eliot's conception of religion, it is necessary to notice the attacks she made on the Reverend John Cumming and the poet Young in the long *Westminster Review* articles that she wrote about them in 1855 and 1857. It was in these articles that she first disclosed the strength of her enmities and implied negatively what it was that a modern religion could offer by way of stimulus and consolation.

To Young, George Eliot's objections were in the first place aesthetic. But in criticizing Young's 'poetic insincerity' she criticized the insincerity of his religion, arguing that his poetry was a failure because of the corrupting view that it took of God.

George Eliot did not suggest that theistic belief could not be embodied in great poetry, since that was what Cowper had done, despite his Calvinism, in *The Task*. What was objectionable in Young was the Anglican balance of 'temporalities and spiritualities', and the odious combination of 'sycophant and psalmist' which had impregnated his life and opinions. In twenty pages of concentrated abuse, Young's character was turned inside-out in order to establish that he had baptized 'egoism as religion', substituted 'interested obedience for sympathetic emotion' and through a 'religious and moral spirit' that was 'low and false' had produced a poetry that was low and false.

Young was an important poet from whom George Eliot had gained pleasure and benefit. Cumming, too, was important. He was a prolific author in his own right, and the editor of the thirty or so volumes of Gibson's *Preservative Against Popery*. As minister of the Scottish National Church in Covent Garden, he provided a suitable target, not only because of his tone but also, George Eliot alleged, because he preached an unctuous, 'bigoted' and egotistical version of the ubiquity of God's presence as Evangelicalism conceived it.

The objections to Cumming, as they appeared in George Eliot's review of his books, were that he dwelt on salvation as a 'scheme' rather than an 'experience', held a rigid belief in the 'annihilation of the impenitent' and was too much at home with the 'external ... polemical ... historical and circumstantial'. Not only did he leave insufficient scope for 'religious rapture' and man's 'tendency towards good', he also ignored the 'criticism and philosophy of the nineteenth century'.

George Eliot assumed that the 'criticism and philosophy of the nineteenth century' made demands which could not be ignored, and that any religion which ignored them deserved to be repudiated. She aimed to elevate morality above 'appetite', to destroy the identification of virtue with prudence and to disclose that capability for the 'love of the good and beautiful in character' which Carlyle had specified as 'the essence of piety'. She rejected 'extrinsic' inducements as subversive of 'true moral judgment', and described the 'impulse of love and justice' as the only ground for moral action. In aiming to eliminate the similarities she discerned between the prevailing 'system of morals' and a 'system of police', she affirmed, as against Kingsley and Balzac, that human action in all ages was 'made up of the most subtly intermixed good and evil'.

George Eliot made a point of distancing herself from what she called 'English unrest', the sense she had of 'each ... trying to get his head above the other'. In its place she proposed a positive morality which would persuade all classes to defer to science and refinement and to find in 'Class Function' a higher means of action than the 'Class Interest' that had governed their actions hitherto. This was part of a 'cause' – the cause of the 'liberal and the just' and was sustained by a rhetoric – the rhetoric of 'virtue', 'trust', 'courage', 'responsibility', the 'common interest' and the 'general good' – along with the 'damaging' effect which followed when 'Ignorance' triumphed over 'Knowledge', 'selfishness' made men aim at 'advantage' over their 'fellows' and 'earnest cultivated minds' were cut off from the 'spiritual wants of the age' by barriers of class, prejudice or sex.

About the condition of women George Eliot was scarcely militant. She recognized the unalterability of the differences between the sexes, and the distinctive character of woman's experience. While praising women's contribution to French literature, she dismissed their contribution to English literature as 'made up of books which could have been better written by men'. Only in one respect was her position militant, though in that respect she was militant both doctrinally and personally.

In the article *Women in France*, which she contributed to the *Westminster Review* in 1854, George Eliot instanced as one cause of the 'intellectual effectiveness of French women' the 'laxity of French opinion and practice with regard to the marriage tie'. She did not deny the effectiveness of the 'conjugal relation' among people who had 'already attained high standards of culture'. But she claimed that 'gallantry and intrigue' were more likely to stimulate women politically and intellectually than 'embroidery and domestic drudgery', and she ended the article with a plea for the 'whole of reality' to be 'laid open to women as well as men', so that women's peculiar experience might assist in a 'marriage of minds which alone could blend all thought and feeling in one lovely rainbow of promise for the harvest of human happiness'.

This line of thinking seemed vague, but was almost certainly more precise than it seemed. By the time she wrote it, George Eliot had been rebuffed by Spencer, whom for a number of years she had been hoping to marry, and, as an unmarried woman in her early thirties, was living with Lewes who had a wife and family of his own from whom he had been unable to obtain a divorce. In the defence that she made of the 'tolerance' which Goethe had shown in *Wilhelm Meister*, in her assertions of the narrowness of the line that divided the morally 'virtuous' from the morally 'vicious' and in the praise that she showered, paradoxically, on *In Memoriam* for being both a 'sanctification of human love' and the 'work of a free human spirit ... amidst a decaying civilization', she was undoubtedly doing what she thought Milton had done in defending polygamy in *Doctrine and Discipline of Divorce* – 'plead' her own cause and reflect her own predicament.

In justifying the erosion of Calvinistic depravity and conventional respectability, George Eliot denied that she was destroying 'faith'. On the contrary, she identified herself with the reaction against the 'want of faith' and organic unity which Lutheran antinomianism had made into the 'disease of the eighteenth century'. Like Mill, Spencer and Lewes, she expected external disinterestedness, 'inward struggle' and the 'deep pathos' induced by the prospect of mortality to provide a more modern conception than 'disbelief' had enabled eighteenth-century thought to conceive of.

As preliminaries to modern belief, George Eliot argued that a personal God, divine Saviour and individual immortality had to be abandoned, 'divine revelation' to be discovered in all ages and nations and the early Christians' interest in the 'special and exceptional' to be replaced by a modern interest in the 'general and invariable'. The 'general and invariable' had been conceptualized in Mill's *System of Logic* and Mill was acclaimed for replacing the '*a posteriori* path' which led only to heaven by an induction 'whence men might see every ... thing on earth'. This was the induction which science could perform, and it was by defending induction that philosophy had a rôle to play in religion where 'deductive reasoning ... kept ... men in the dark' and inductive reasoning encouraged the tolerance characteristic of a 'philosophical culture'.

These were the assumptions which George Eliot brought to consideration of Christianity, and they were central to the chief conclusions that she reached about it – that the master-key to the 'divine revelation' was 'recognition of the presence of undeviating law', that this could be pursued best through the study of science, sociology and ethics, and that it would issue in a 'philosophic' study of mythology and a 'natural history of religion'. In this way, she believed, generic similarities would be established between the early religion of the Jews and all other religions, and the Old Testament contextualized as the 'early ... records' of a 'barbarous tribe' that was on the way from fetishism through polytheism to monotheism. This also was the route by which, 'without', as she claimed, any 'presuppositions' at all, the Bible would be explained on 'purely human grounds' and Jesus shown not only to have contributed 'no new element to ethics' but also to have diminished the value of what he did contribute by 'misconceptions concerning his own mission and the divine government in general' which had been derived from his 'Jewish culture'.

In passing, George Eliot criticized Christianity's egoistic preference for 'asceticism' and 'salvation' over the culture and duties of life on earth. The core of her attack, however, was on Christianity's addiction to dogma, its inability to speak relevantly once science had replaced dogma and its insistence on absorbing human effort in divine effort.

> Fatally powerful as religious systems have been, [went a passage in criticism of Cumming] human nature is stronger and wider than religious systems, and though dogmas may hamper, they cannot absolutely repress its growth: build walls round the living tree as you will, the bricks and mortar have by and by to give way before the slow and sure operation of the sap ... Next to that hatred of the enemies of God which is the principle of persecution, there perhaps has been no perversion more obstructive of true moral development than the substitution of a reference to the glory of God for the direct promptings of the sympathetic feelings ... If ... the glory of God is to be 'the absorbing and the influential aim' in our thoughts and actions, this must tend to neutralize the human sympathies; the stream of feeling will be diverted from its natural current in order to feed an artificial canal. The idea of God is really moral in its influence ... only when God is contemplated as sympathising with the pure elements of human feeling, as possessing infinitely all the attributes which we recognise to be moral in humanity.

'We have long experienced that knowledge is profitable, [went a long passage quoted approvingly from Mackay's *Progress of the Intellect*] we are beginning to find out that it is moral, and shall at last discover it to be religious. Aristotle declared the highest and truest science to be that which is most disinterested; Bacon, treating science as separate from religion, asserted knowledge to be power, and held that truth must be tested by its fruits ... Both assertions may be justified and reconciled by the fact that, while no real knowledge is powerless or fruitless, the fruits differ in refinement and value, the highest being unquestionably those disinterested gratifications which minister to the highest wants of the highest faculties, and ... earn ... for philosophy the title of a divine love, realizing the mysterious longing of the soul, and promoting the accomplishment of its destiny.
> To rise in science as in bliss
> Initiate in the secrets of the skies.'

The opinions that George Eliot expressed in the *Westminster Review* were part of a communal propaganda; if she had produced nothing else, no one would have remembered her. In fact, when she was nearly forty, she began to produce a major *oeuvre* in a mode quite different from the mode she had written in hitherto. The question we have to ask is, were her novels as anti-Christian as her reviews?

In one sense they were not anti-Christian; it is certain that large numbers of her readers read her novels for their story, sentiment and virtue and had no idea that these were being used in the service of an anti-Christian philosophy. This is an argument from consequences and it should carry little weight. What has to be asked is, can her novels have been anything other than the natural history of morals, religion and society for which she had been asking? Were they not a repetition of the success Ruskin had had in 'teaching the truth' not within the covers of 'unsaleable volumes' but through a 'voice' of 'power' which enabled him to 'remould ... life' and become a 'prophet for his generation'?

In making this judgment in 1856, George Eliot may not have understood how seriously Ruskin was taking Christianity, or how committed he remained to reconciling it with Art. It was selectively misleading to say of Ruskin even then that he taught that 'all truth and beauty were to be attained by a humble and faithful study of nature'. On the other hand there can be no doubt that that was what George Eliot thought that Ruskin was doing, and that she carried her self-identification into literature.

The second point that needs to be noticed is that this 'natural history' treated religion as a human invention, not only because that was how the novel had treated it in the past but also because that was how Comte and Spencer had made it desirable to treat it in the future; and to anyone who supposes that this is the natural, or only, way in which to treat religion, it must be replied that this supposition arises from a *parti pris* in relation to which George Eliot straddled problematically. She was moved by other negativities besides the religious one – by an Orwellian desire, for example, to explain that rural society was not as urban Socialism, political economy and Young England had conceived it and would not be reformed without the 'special acquaintance' which came from a 'natural history of social bodies'. But the religious problem was central. It compelled her to think of herself as choosing one rather than the other of the mental worlds by which she was confronted; and it was through the struggle involved in providing a demonstrative enactment of the ubiquity of natural motives and desires that her novels achieved the religious significance that they undoubtedly had.

In the early 1850s George Eliot agreed with Greg, Mackay and Newman, as she had agreed earlier with Hennell, that the Bible did not disclose either a revealed, unique or miraculous Christianity, and that the task of the future was to propose a naturalistic Christianity which would not conflict with modern knowledge. Mackay was more unam-

biguously Protestant than the others, but even he was not far from the
creedless Unitarianism which Newman seems to have arrived at after
various attempts at a creedless Protestantism.

It may be that these thinkers were enemies of revealed, credal and
ecclesiastical Christianity only. But no one who reads them can fail to
sense behind their formal ambivalence an alienation as deep as the
alienation which Mrs Humphrey Ward was to display later from everything that Christianity had ever been or taught. In Spencer a fainter
residue of ambivalence was associated with an even more systematic
negativity.

V

Of all the mid-Victorian attempts to organize knowledge into an encyclopaedia, Spencer's was the most persistent. Spencer[1] succeeded, more
systematically than anyone else, in putting on paper a comprehensive
account of existence and in deducing from it a body of necessary
conclusions about conduct. We may judge the synthesis to have been
synthetic and the conclusions superficial and controvertible, and we
may also judge Spencer's mental energy to have been boring. But the
point about Spencer's thought was that it was expressed, that it was
expressed with force and power and that it dealt with a very wide range
of subject-matter.

In its mature form, from *First Principles* onwards, Spencer's system
encompassed politics and religion, biology, psychology and education,
a universal sociology and legislative descriptions of a system of private
and public ethics. The aim was to provide a comprehensive philosophy
and in the course of providing it, Spencer emerged from the provincial,
Protestant ghetto in which he had been brought up.

When Spencer began his public career in the early 1840s, his main
target had been the English Establishment, and the extent to which its
actions had been corrupted by the 'pecuniary' interests of those who
controlled it, not merely the pecuniary interests involved in employ-

---

[1] Herbert Spencer (1820–1903). Educ. day schools in Derby and Nottingham, railway
engineer 1837–41. Author of *Social Statics* 1851, *The Principles of Psychology* 1855,
Essays Scientific, Political and Speculative 1858–63, *The Art of Education* 1861, *First
Principles* 1862, *The Classification of the Sciences* 1864, *The Principles of Biology*
2 vols. 1864–7, *The Study of Sociology* 1873, *Descriptive Sociology* 1873–81, *The
Principles of Sociology* 3 vols. 1876–96, *The Data of Ethics* 1879, *The Man versus the
State* 1884, *The Principles of Ethics* 1892, *Autobiography* 2 vols. 1904.

ment in the Colonies but also the pecuniary interests involved in benefice in the Church of England. It was as the enemy of interests in this sense that Spencer made his first public profession, and the suspicions associated with this context remained with him throughout his life.

Until he became a writer, Spencer was an engineer. In religion having been brought up by a Methodist father and an Anglican uncle, he identified himself as a Nonconformist. It was in *The Nonconformist* that he first aimed to show that English government and society were oligarchic. It was there, too, that he argued that the oligarchy was not only corrupt but also hostile to freedom.

Freedom was a negative conception; it implied that social organisation would be improved if its constricting Positivism were to be destroyed. It was a radical conception, demanding wholesale transformation and reflecting the mistrust and suspicion and self-righteous intolerance of those who were without, for those who were within, the walls of the Great City. Condemnation was given of mercantilist economic assumptions, aristocratic political assumptions and the religious assumptions which we understand as Church – State Anglicanism, and this was the conglomerate which was given its first trial in the six *Letters on Government* that Spencer wrote for *The Nonconformist* in 1842.

In the 1842 letters Spencer laid it down that governments ought not to build roads or railways, take special care of the nation's health or involve themselves in conducting education, and that they should no more enforce a poor law because 'half of the population' was 'lacking in food and clothing' than they should maintain a 'national religion' because 'the inhabitants of a country were deficient in religious instruction'. It was in rejection of the feudal spirit characteristic of states where war was the norm, of the mercantilist state's monopolistic regulation of commerce and colonies and of the oppression for which the Anglican Establishment had been responsible since 1662 that Spencer sketched the conception of a limited state which had lost the power to wage aggressive war as being one that would free men from the restrictions which a 'tyrannical and selfish legislature' had imposed upon them.

In these writings the reasoning behind the arguments was not really explained; it was not really made clear why 'free men' would operate better in a limited state than servile men in a confessional state, or in what sense working-class enfranchisement could be envisaged once a limited state had been established. What *was* made clear was the nature of the situation Spencer supposed himself to be addressing – the 'open conflict' which was threatening between the 'two great antagonistic elements of social existence'.

In discussing the Rebecca Riots in 1843, Spencer wrote of the conflict between the 'aristocratic spirit' and the 'democratic spirit' as 'cracking' and 'shivering' both the 'tissue of conventionalities' and the 'framework of legal regulations' in which the 'soul of freedom' had hitherto lain 'encaged'. The riots were not, he argued, mere working-class riots. They included a 'large sprinkling of those usually distinguished as the respectable classes' and they mattered because they showed that 'social dissolution' would occur if the 'angered spirit of oppressed democracy' destroyed the 'rotten bonds of national organization' without a new organization being established in its place.

These were the earliest statements of Spencerian principles which, though radical and aggressive, were not expressed systematically. They did not receive systematic expression until the publication of *Social Statics* in 1851.

Social Statics achieved its structure by developing ideas which had been stated embryonically in Spencer's occasional journalism in the 1840s. In one direction it took up the idea that organic nature as well as inorganic nature had its laws, that laws impinged on men socially as well as individually and that the 'whole welfare of mankind depended on a thorough knowledge of social principles and an entire obedience to them'. In another direction it argued that 'infinite variety ... of human character' was essential to the advancement of the human mind, that a 'uniform routine of education' was an impertinence to God and that the prejudices and idiosyncrasies which mankind had developed in the course of time could all contribute to social truth. It was social truth as defined in the Introduction and Part I which underpinned the libertarian blueprint that was sketched in the 300 pages that followed.

The detail of the blueprint was important. What was more important was the assumption of principle from which the detail was alleged to follow.

The assumption of principle was that socialization was inherent in human development and that government was the remedy for the incompleteness of socialization. It was in so far as socialization had not been achieved that government was needed, and the question this raised was, what part had socialization played, and what part ought it to play, in human existence?

In *Social Statics* Spencer distinguished two aspects of social philosophy: what he called *statics* and what he called *dynamics*. *Statics* dealt with the 'equilibrium of a perfect society', *dynamics* with the 'forces by which society advanced towards perfection', the interest in both cases being in the ultimate condition where men would be in perfect harmony with one another. The perfection of harmony provided the standard by which to judge habitual and existing societies, and the 'total disagreement' that Spencer asserted between the doctrines he was promulgating and the institutions among which he lived led him to the perception that 'right principles of action' would become 'practicable' only as man became perfect; 'or rather ... that man would become perfect, just in so far as he was able to obey them'.

Spencer had a structured and analytical, rather than an historical, mind, but historical development was nevertheless central. Whether or not a 'perfect state' might have been established at the beginning of time, the fact was that 'civilization could not possibly have been other than it had been'. The history of the world had happened and was happening, and, since it was going to go on happening in the future, would need time if it was to achieve the equilibrium of perfection that it aimed at.

The equilibrium of perfection – or socialization – was thought of as a condition from which government had disappeared. Government was alleged to decay as civilization advanced, and, with the decay of government, it was said to follow that the development of which each individual person was capable would include recognition of the capability for development of which all other individual persons were capable. The process by which mutual recognition occurred would not necessarily be peaceful, having been marked in the past by the elimination of the morally unfit and the 'extermination' of 'such sections of mankind' as had 'stood in its way'. But, violent and bloody as its operation had been, the law of human history was a progressive and, it seemed to be implied, an inevitable development towards this condition, and the 'conquest of one people over another had been, in the main, the conquest of the social man over the antisocial man; or, strictly speaking, of the more adaptive over the less adaptive'.

This impulse towards socialization was thought of as an assertion of individual purpose or power which aimed generally at 'Human Happiness'. Human happiness, however, was not understood in Utilitarian terms. Paley and Bentham were attacked, first for assuming that government was eternal and building a 'fabric of conclusions' upon its 'assumed permanence'; then for making the greatest happiness of the greatest number the basis of social morality; finally for assuming that mankind was unanimous in its definition of happiness. Government would be dispensed with once the harmony of perfection had been arrived at but since, on the way, 'every epoch and every people' would have 'its own conception of happiness' and every person a 'different balance of desires', the true definition of the greatest happiness of the greatest number would be 'so distant and obscure an undertaking' as to make a 'true philosophy of national life' a task 'far beyond the ability of any finite mind'.

The objection to Utilitarianism, however, was not only that it arrogated to government a priority that government could not properly claim, but also that it arrogated to the 'multitude' a priority which should properly be attributed to the 'component individuals'. In a 'true theory of society', the 'moral law' would originate in the individual's instinct for 'justice' in dealing with other men, and it was this that had become increasingly important as social life had developed and 'Equity, Freedom and Safety' had been attained. A pious passage made the point:

The articles of Magna Charta embodied its protests against oppression, and its demands for a better administration of justice. Serfdom was abolished partly at its suggestion. It encouraged Wickliffe, Huss, Luther, and Knox in their contests with Popery; and by it were Huguenots, Covenanters, Moravians, stimulated to maintain freedom of judgment in the teeth of armed Ecclesiasticism. It dictated Milton's 'Essay on the Liberty of Unlicensed Printing'. It piloted the pilgrim fathers to the new world. It supported the followers of George Fox under fines and imprisonment. And it whispered resistance to the Presbyterian clergy of 1662. In latter days it emitted that tide of feeling which undermined and swept away Catholic disabilities. Through the mouths of anti-slavery orators, it poured out its fire, to the scorching of the selfish, to the melting of the good, to our national purification. It was its heat, too, which warmed our sympathy for the Poles and made boil our indignation against their oppressor. Pent-up accumulations of it, let loose upon a long-standing injustice, generated the effervescence of a reform agitation. Out of its growing flame came those sparks by which Protectionist theories were exploded, and that light which discovered to us the truths of Free-trade. By the passage of its subtle current is that social *electrolysis* effected which classes men into parties – which separates the nation into its positive and negative – its radical and conservative elements. At present it puts on the garb of Anti-State-Church Associations, and shows its presence in manifold societies for the extension of popular power. It builds monuments to political martyrs, agitates for the admission of Jews into Parliament, publishes books on the rights of women, petitions against class-legislation, threatens to rebel against militia conscriptions, refuses to pay church-rates, repeals oppressive debtor acts, laments over the distresses of Italy and thrills with sympathy for the Hungarians. From it, as from a root, spring our aspirations after social rectitude: it blossoms in such expressions as – 'Do as you would be done by', 'Honesty is the best policy', 'Justice before Generosity'; and its fruits are Equity, Freedom, Safety.

In *Social Statics* the moral sense was no more a matter of Art, as in Shaftesbury and his followers, than it was a matter of utility, as in Paley and Bentham. Morality, on the contrary, bore the same relation to a moral system as the 'perception of the primary laws of quantity bore to mathematics'. It was an intellectual function and an acquisition of knowledge that was involved when the 'moral sense originated a moral axiom from which reason might develop a systematic morality', and progress in knowledge was movement from 'unconsciousness of law' to a conviction that law was 'universal and inevitable'. There was an 'inexorable connection' between observance of the law and 'right conduct' – an 'inevitable law of causation' which men had to 'learn and conform to', and any attempt by 'stiff-necked worldly wisdom' to 'benefit by disobedience' would fail.

This, though seeming to suggest the desirability of obedience in a Ruskinian sense, turned out to be a guarantee of individuality. The reason, however, was a temporary one – that men had retained in society, when they no longer needed them, many of the characteristics that had enabled them to adapt themselves to the pre-social conditions in which they had 'sacrificed the welfare of other beings to their own'. The *ultimate* realization of civilization was envisaged as something much more positive – 'an increased sacredness of personal claims and a subordination of whatever limited them' in so far as the socialization, or moralization, of mankind would make this possible.

Spencer dismissed the 'loyalty-producing faculty' as irrelevant to a properly constituted society and a cause of dishonesty, immorality and crime in existing society. In envisaging advance towards the sympathetic beneficence which went with socialized individuation, he emphasized the importance of vegetarianism, temperance reform, the abolition of capital punishment, the improvement of working-class housing, and the prevention of cruelty to animals. In *The Art of Education* he explained why supreme importance was to be attached to education.

The Art of Education began by asserting that the 'harsh ... dogmatic ... discipline' which had been 'natural' in ages of 'political despotism ...

and ... uniformity of belief' when men had 'received their creed ... from an infallible authority' had become anachronistic in face of Protestantism and the Baconian rebellion against the schools. It was in this context that education had had to be 'addressed to the understanding', and for this reason that it had begun to be 'non-coercive'.

A 'non-coercive education' had a number of connected characteristics. It reproduced the 'process of mental evolution' and conformed to the course by which knowledge had been generated 'in the race'. It not only rejected 'teaching by rote'; it also rejected 'teaching by rules', substituting 'principles for rules', and enabling children to 'find things out for themselves' by proceeding from the 'concrete to the abstract', the 'empirical to the natural' and the homogeneous to the heterogeneous. These were the 'Methods of Nature' as they had been discerned by Pestalozzi. They were supposed to make learning 'pleasurable rather than painful', to transcend the 'incurious' Utilitarianism which had no sense of póetry, art, science and philosophy, and to establish in the child's mind a knowledge of that 'law of life' which underlay 'their bodily and mental processes', their daily lives and the conduct of commerce, politics and morals. With the publication of the *Prospectus* for *The Synthetic Philosophy* in 1860 Spencer had made it clear that he aimed to supply an encyclopaedic handbook for this sort of education.

So far we have treated Spencer's writing as though it was concerned solely with terrestrial and sociological considerations. There has been little mention of God and no question about a relationship between God and the world. Yet consideration of this kind was prominent in *Social Statics* where the conception of evil, though a Whig-like emasculation, was seen in its connections with God, and both the faculties that were fundamental to individual freedom and the beneficence which it was the 'office of a scientific morality' to teach were described as 'the established arrangements of divine rule', the 'realization of the Divine Idea', and manifestations of that 'foresight and efficiency of the Divine assumptions', to 'doubt which ... was the true Atheism and Infidelity'. In the course of the amazing output that he achieved in the ten years which followed, Spencer came to represent all the facts that constituted the world of nature, all the activities that constituted the human world, and all the subject-matters that constituted knowledge of these worlds, as though they were autonomous in relation to God and regardless of His existence. In the 1850s one can as certainly see

God disappearing from Spencer's writings as Ruskin claimed to have seen Him disappearing from the Doge's Palace in Venice in the course of the fourteenth century. By the time Spencer was forty in 1860 de-divinization was complete.

About Spencer's mature political doctrine, little needs to be said since the long series of political essays that he wrote between *Over-Legislation* and *The Man versus the State* merely expanded what he had written in 1842. So far as these later essays differed from the letters of 1842, they differed in deploying a developed sociology which identified the democratic franchise as a threat to socialized individuation, 'direct taxation' as an antidote to democratic profligacy and parliamentary and trade union collectivism as the chief obstacles to the transition from the 'authoritarian co-operation' of a 'militant' society to the 'voluntary' co-operation of an 'industrial' society.

The work in which Spencer explained most clearly the claims he made for sociology was a series of lectures that he prepared for delivery in the United States in the early 1870s. In these lectures, and in the book which emerged from them, he explained why sociology was needed and the obstruction that it faced from the prejudices, interests and emotions – what he called the 'automorphism' of the age – which was inseparable from interpretation and yet was always misleading as a guide to it.

In *The Study of Sociology* Spencer was at pains to establish that sociology dealt with actions of 'extreme complexity' and 'transcendent difficulty' and superseded the age's average opinions about the laws according to which life should be lived. Sociology's laws were the laws of, as it were, nature, including human nature. They required study if they were to be understood, and it was the study of the *scientific law of social development according to which life should be lived* which would show what needed to be done, or not done, if man's progress out of barbarism was to go on proceeding towards civilization.

Spencer did not share Marx's or Engels's relentlessness about the relationship between practice and theory. But *The Principles of Sociology* was suffused with the same certainty that they felt about the need to co-operate with the objective evolution which mankind was undergoing and about the principles which sociology would reveal once biases, prejudices and deflections were removed.

In Chapter III of *The Study of Sociology,* fundamental principles were laid out. These were that, just as in all other 'aggregations of living matter', the 'substance of each species of plant or animal' had a 'proclivity towards the structure which that animal or plant presented', so in aggregates of men 'the properties of the units determined the properties of the whole they made up'. Sociology's business was to 'express the relationship between the units and the wholes' with as much definiteness 'as the nature of the phenomena permitted', and fructifying contingency was as important as cause and effect in understanding the necessity of the relations that were involved.

In describing these habits of thought Spencer was both encyclopaedic and transcendent of encyclopaedism. In Logic, Mathematics, Physics, Chemistry, Biology and Psychology, he recognized modern achievements which could supply nutriment to Sociology. But what Sociology needed to take was not the narrowing technical knowledge which made up the subject-matters of these sciences but 'cardinal ideas' which were capable of being absorbed into a 'scientific culture'. It was for their contributions to a 'scientific culture' that Biology and Psychology were singled out as the sciences from which Sociology could learn most, Psychology for its dismissal of books as guarantors of moral education and its belief that moral habits had to be formed by relating action to feeling, Biology for the warning it supplied against the 'injury' that would be done if hindrances were interposed to the 'natural process of elimination by which society purified itself'.

The doctrine that Spencer thought of Biology and Psychology as contributing was what we know as Social Darwinism, with the objections it raised to shielding society's 'weakest members' from their weakness and the 'mentally inferior' from the 'evil results of their inferiority', along with rejection of the 'disciplined improvidence' through which the English had helped the 'dissolute and idle' to 'produce and rear their progeny' while hindering the 'honest and independent' in producing and rearing theirs. Social Darwinism in this form dismissed preaching as an aid to moral improvement, and judged it likely that moral improvement would be achieved when pains and penalties were attached to disregard of the 'requirements of ordinary social life'. While anticipating a millenium in which differences between the sexes would have disappeared, it emphasized that in present conditions women were to be mistrusted for being subservient to 'controlling agencies' like religion, which it was one of the main aims of Sociology to supersede.

VI

The account that Spencer gave of religion in terms of natural causes may be found in two chief places – in the chapter entitled 'The Theological Bias' in *The Study of Sociology* in 1873 and in the section on 'Ecclesiastical Institutions' which constituted Part VI of *The Principles of Sociology* in 1885. In neither place was the position argued: in both places it was assumed that religion was not 'innate' in mankind, as Max Müller was singled out for believing, but had its origins in dreams, ghost-worship and ancestor-worship. Judaism and Christianity were both said to have displayed the 'family likenesses' that were displayed in all other religions and to lack that uniqueness which their protagonists claimed. Priests were said to be indistinguishable from 'rulers' and 'medicine-men', and to be intimately connected with the 'brutal and savage' types of action that arose from war. Ecclesiasticism embodied the 'rule of the dead over the living', discouraged 'criticism and scepticism' and induced not only 'submissiveness' but also an 'extreme development of both political and religious controls'. It was said to be a sign of a developed stage of society that the 'exercise of individual judgment' began to 'deny ecclesiastical authority in general'.

Spencer did not argue against religion: he argued mainly against ecclesiastical religion. He associated the separation of Church and State with the separation of the military functions of priests from the propitiatory, 'industrial societies' based on voluntary co-operation with the death of authoritarian sacerdotalism, and religious independence and a 'reformed ethical creed' with an 'industrial' type of 'life and organization'. He did not deny that ecclesiastical religion had played a part in the earliest stages of social progress and was unlikely to disappear in the immediate future. But he envisaged it as subject to the law of evolution and as having a new function to develop as political institutions became completer, independent churches proliferated with separate 'beliefs and practices' and 'insistence on duty' and 'the conduct of life' became their primary concern and responsibility. He also looked forward to the abandonment of worship, of 'hell and damnation', and of almost all the other characteristics of anthropomorphic Christianity.

These were Spencer's later political, ethical, sociological and religious opinions in which the reasons that were given for hostility to dogmatic Christianity and the new Tory Socialism that was attacked in *The Man versus the State* were the reasons that had been given for hostility to the Tory Anglicanism of 1842, sustained and supported by the more complicated intellectuality which Spencer had established for himself between 1857 and 1862. This was the crucial period in Spencer's intellectual development, and its pivot is to be found in *First Principles*.

When accused of using *First Principles* in order to teach atheism, Spencer replied that he was no more an atheist than Mansel was or Sir William Hamilton had been. In *First Principles*, as in *The Principles of Psychology* which had attracted a similar accusation seven years earlier, nevertheless, he had had much less use for the idea of God than he had had in *Social Statics* in 1851.

From one point of view *The Principles of Psychology* was simply part of *The Synthetic Philosophy*. From another point of view it was a description of the rôle which psychology could play in resolving the 'endless disputes' about 'fundamental questions' which were plaguing the modern world.

In *The Principles of Psychology* Spencer dismissed the distinction between knowing and believing, treated knowledge as being made up simply of 'beliefs' and sought a 'canon' by which belief might be justified. Belief was what was 'taken for granted' in every premise or conclusion, and was 'antecedent to all other facts'. This was said to be true 'universally', and however 'deep' men might 'dig', they would 'never get to anything beyond beliefs ... seeing that the deepest thing ... became a belief' at the moment of its disclosure.

This 'deepest thing' was 'the universal postulate'. It was fundamental to all thought and was 'taken for granted in every act of understanding', and the section entitled 'General Analysis' discussed it in terms of a Realism which harmonized philosophy and common sense, and avoided the illusions of both scepticism and metaphysics.

There is no need to dwell on Spencerian Realism, or the debt that Spencer owed to Hamilton and Mansel. What matters for present purposes is the content of the beliefs – about Evolution and the 'Unknowable' – which were displayed in *First Principles* seven years later.

In the central chapters of *First Principles* the message was that the law of evolution was ubiquitous and that it was the inconceivability of 'lawless phenomena' which distinguished 'modern' from 'ancient' thought. The subject of *The Synthetic Philosophy,* from the 'earliest traceable cosmical changes down to the latest results of civilization', was the advance from the 'indefinite' to the 'definite', the 'homogeneous' to the 'heterogeneous', and the 'incoherent' to the 'coherent'; and this was said to be demonstrable not only, as Spencer recognized that it would have been, by *The First Principles of Inorganic Nature,* if he had written such a work, but also by *The Principles of Biology,* and *The Principles of Morality* (or *of Ethics*) of which *The Data of Ethics* was to have been the preliminary statement. It was with evolution as the law which emerged from all these investigations that Part II of *First Principles* was concerned primarily.

Though the law of evolution in principle was simple, its ramifications were not. The relationship between progress towards definiteness and progress towards heterogeneity was complicated, as was 'Dissolution'. But, even taking into account the complications that were described in Chapter III, the conclusions were emphatic and uncompromising – that Evolution was a change from 'an indefinite, incoherent, homogeneity into a definite coherent heterogeneity' and that this change had been going on in the past and would go on in the future 'among all orders of phenomena that lay within the sphere of observation'.

Chapters III to XVI of *First Principles* need to be read closely if one is to appreciate the complication of Spencer's description of evolution and dissolution. In particular, 'equilibration' needs to be understood as a description of the adaptation of organisms to surroundings if one is to show to what extent Spencer's doctrine was ultimately optimistic. That it was ultimately pessimistic can be shown by reference to the possibility of an 'Ultimate Death' in which 'planets devoid of life' would circle around a 'universe of extinct suns'. But this was conceived of as only a possibility, and of the most ultimate kind: in all earthly and conceivable senses the assumption was that the 'persistence of force', the tendency of organisms to equilibrate and the capacity of the species to adapt itself to new circumstances afforded a basis for anticipating a 'gradual advance towards harmony between man's mental nature and the conditions of his existence' which could end only in the establishment of the 'greatest perfection and most complete happiness'.

In the conclusion to *First Principles,* Spencer made it plain, plainer than in the introduction, that the laws of evolution transcended all the sciences, including the social sciences, and all existing religions. Christianity was not mentioned, but it was rejected by implication, the 'existence of a cause' for which the 'effects' were the laws of evolution being said to be merely a 'datum of consciousness' and 'Being without limits of Time and Space' merely an 'indefinite cognition' which formed the 'necessary basis of men's definite cognition' of Being 'under limits of time and space'. 'Absolute Being' was only a 'datum of ... thought' in relation to which Religion, Philosophy, Science and Common Sense were 'symbols', and it was the twist that this gave to the doctrine of unknowability, when contrasted with Spencer's belief in the knowability of evolution, which made the first hundred or so pages of *First Principles* one of the most significant documents in the mid-Victorian assault on Christianity.

In the introductory sections of *First Principles* it was not suggested that religion was 'supernaturally derived' but neither was religion dismissed out of hand. Spencer avoided simple reductionism, recognized in Coleridgean–Romantic fashion that religion prevented men being absorbed in the 'relative and immediate', and declined to explain it away as Bentham had explained it away in terms of a 'primitive priesthood' inventing 'primitive fictions'. A 'deep-seated' reason was required to account for religion's 'universality', and it was in searching for this that Spencer explained both the nature of religion and its relationship with science.

Spencer claimed to treat religion with 'respect'. He agreed that 'widely-held beliefs' were unlikely to be 'baseless' and that, even if no one religion was 'actually true', all religions might be 'adumbrations of a truth'. He presented science as a 'continuous disclosure' of the 'established order of the Universe' and his own aim as being the discovery of 'some fundamental verity' in which religion and science would 'each find the other its ally'. He emphasized, however, that religion could no more discover this in the specific doctrines of science than science could discover it in the dogmas of Christianity, and that it would only be discovered in an abstract recognition imposed by the 'ultimate fact in human intelligence' that these 'two great realities' were 'constituents of the same kind and responded to different aspects of the same Universe'.

The 'ultimate fact in human intelligence' as *First Principles* explained it was that 'the Power which the Universe manifests to us is utterly inscrutable'. This was what science really meant – that the nature of things was beyond human explanation, that Motion, Matter, Space and Time were 'ultimately incomprehensible', and that 'both ends of the thread of consciousness' were beyond the scientist's grasp. This also was what religion meant, and meant 'essentially' once it was disconnected from dogmas and moral codes. As much in religion as in science, there was an 'ultimate incomprehensibility', and it was from science and religion as merely 'symbols of the actual' rather than as cognitions of it that understanding had to begin.

This was the start of Spencer's attempt at reconciliation, and a great deal followed from it. It followed that symbolic conceptions had not to be mistaken for 'real ones', that theological explanations of 'the mystery of the universe' were misplaced and that the 'positive dogmas' by which 'the mysterious was made unmysterious' were not only misleading but were also disappearing. This was the 'essential change delineated in religious history' – that, though religion had 'obstinately held every outpost long after it was indefensible', it was coming to understand that the claim to know what it could not know was 'irreligious'. Scepticism about its own belief was what had made religion *fear* science in the past, but it was also what guaranteed that science and religion could be reconciled in the future. Religion and science, in fact, were said to be 'correlatives' which would be 'at peace' once science became convinced that its explanations were 'proximate and relative', and religion became convinced that the mystery it contemplated was 'ultimate and absolute'.

Unknowability was described as a 'certainty' to which 'Intelligence' had been progressing 'from the first' and to which it was men's 'duty' to submit themselves in the future. This was the 'religious ... position'; and even if their 'want of culture' had prevented most men being guided by it, Spencer assumed that it could produce sanctions sufficient for action once education had been reconstructed in order to provide them.

Spencer was well aware of the vulnerability of the religion he was proposing and felt obliged to explain why a new religion that had evolved from an old religion which was untrue, could, nevertheless, be judged to be true. He was right to suspect vulnerability where the 'germ' from which all historic religions had grown was 'the truth ... that the power which manifests itself as consciousness is but a differently-conditioned form of the power which manifests itself beyond consciousness' and the 'internal energy which in the experience of the primitive man was always the immediate antecedent of changes

wrought by him' was the 'same energy which, freed from anthropomorphic accompaniments, was now figured as the cause of all external
phenomena'.

In disembarrassing himself of God, Spencer did not deny that theological conservatism had a rôle to play. But the rôle he attributed to it – the
'check' it provided against 'rapid ... advance' in a period of transition
– has really to be understood as a subtle way of eroding historic
Christianity, while being amiably condescending towards it. No doubt
was left that the religion which Spencer envisaged for the future,
though penetrated with a sense of the 'Infinite and Eternal Energy
from which all things proceeded', would deny that any special connection could be established between mankind on the one hand and this
'Infinite and Eternal Energy' on the other.

If we say that [Christianity's] likenesses to the rest [of the world's religions] hide
a transcendent unlikeness, several implications must be recognised. One is that
the Cause to which we can put no limits in Space or Time, and of which our
entire Solar System is a relatively infinitesimal product, took the disguise of a
man for the purpose of covenanting with a shepherd-chief in Syria. Another is
that this Energy, unceasingly manifested everywhere, throughout past, present,
and future, ascribed to himself under this human form, not only the limited
knowledge and limited powers which various passages show Jahveh to have
had, but also moral attributes which we should now think discreditable to a
human being. And a third is that we must suppose an intention even more
repugnant to our moral sense. For if these numerous parallelisms between the
Christian religion and other religions do not prove likeness of origin and
development, then the implication is that a complete simulation of the natural
by the supernatural has been deliberately devised to deceive those who examine
critically what they are taught. Appearances have been arranged for the purpose of misleading sincere inquirers that they may be eternally damned for
seeking the truth. On those who accept this last alternative, no reasonings will
have any effect. Here we finally part company with them by accepting the first.

6

Types of Ethical Earnestness II

'You who have escaped from the religions ... of the world ... into the high-and-dry light of the intellect may deride them; but in so doing you deride accidents of form merely, and fail to touch the immovable basis of the religious sentiment in the nature of man. To yield this sentiment reasonable satisfaction is the problem of problems at the present hour. And grotesque in relation to scientific culture as many of the religions of the world have been and are – dangerous, nay destructive, to the dearest privileges of freemen as some of them undoubtedly have been, and would, if they could, be again – it will be wise to recognize them as the forms of a force, mischievous, if permitted to intrude on the region of *knowledge*, over which it holds no command, but capable of being guided to noble issues in the region of *emotion*, which is its proper and elevated sphere.' John Tyndall *Address Delivered before the British Association Assembled at Belfast* 1874 pp. 60–1.

'The problem which presses for solution is, how, amid the wreck of forms now imminent, to preserve the reverence and loftiness of thought and feeling which in times past found in those forms organic expression. This is not to be done by science only, still less by routine utterances about God and the human soul. From "society", or from aggregates of men in societies, whether "Christian" or otherwise, no voice of guidance as regards this question can possibly come. But if nature have in store a man of the requisite completeness – equivalent, let us say, to Milton and Helmholtz rolled into one – such a man, freed by his own volition from "society", and fed for a time upon the wild honey of the wilderness, might be able to detach religious feeling from its accidents, and restore it to us in a form not out of keeping with the knowledge of the time.' John Tyndall *Fragments of Science* 2nd ed. 1871 pp. vi–vii.

'In spite of prayers for the success of our arms and *Te Deums* for victory, our real faith is in big battalions and keeping our powder dry: in knowledge of the science of warfare; in energy, courage and discipline. In these, as in all other practical affairs, we ... admit that intelligent work is the only acceptable worship; and that, whether there be a Supernature or not, our business is with Nature.' T. H. Huxley *Prologue* (1892) to *Science and Christian Tradition* 1894 p. 38.

What was at issue in Chapter 5 was the idea that science and history were pointing a gun at Christianity, that Christianity had to give way and that the religion of the future would be governed by the liberation which science and history would effect from the restrictions which Christianity had imposed on the thought of the past.

The thinkers who were discussed in Chapter 5 proclaimed their originality and intrepidity, and the need to defy custom in the cause of progress. There was smugness and complacency but there was also an anxious belief that a battle would have to be fought before Truth could be made the preserve of the secular intelligentsia. To the writers who are to be discussed next it seemed that the case had been made, that half the battle had been won and that the new faith could adopt the earnest normality of tone which was at its best in Tyndall and Huxley.

I

Huxley[1] was as close intellectually to Spencer as Spencer was to George Eliot, but his experience was very different. Huxley was a brilliant naturalist who had established himself professionally before he became a publicist, and, by reason of his professional success, became a member of governmental committees and commissions. He received a Civil List pension from a Liberal government and was made a Privy Councillor by Salisbury in 1892; he could almost certainly have

[1] Thomas Henry Huxley (1825–95). Educ. randomly and at Charing Cross Hospital. Assistant Surgeon on H.M.S. *Rattlesnake* 1846–50. Fellow of The Royal Society 1851, Assistant Surgeon, Royal Navy, 1851–4, Lecturer at Royal School of Mines 1854–9, Member of Royal Commissions 1862–8 and 1870–84. Professor at Royal College of Surgeons 1863–9, and at Royal Institution 1863–7, Joint Secretary of Royal Society 1871–94, Inspector of Fisheries 1881–5. Author of *Evidence as to Man's Place in Nature* 1863, *Lectures on the Elements of Comparative Anatomy* 1864, *Lessons in Elementary Physiology* 1866, *An Introduction to the Classification of Animals* 1869, *Lay Sermons* 1870, *Critiques and Addresses* 1873, *A Course of Elementary Instruction in Practical Biology* 1875, *American Addresses* 1877, *Science and Culture* 1881, *Essays on Some Controverted Questions* 1892, *Evolution and Ethics* 1893.

been an M. P. if he had wanted to be. He left behind him an important body of scientific papers and textbooks as well as a large number of essays and books which were central to Victorian public thought. Where the passage of the years turned Spencer into an eccentric recluse who had abandoned engineering too early to have had worthwhile experience of anything except writing, Huxley brought to the discussion of public issues the authority of an Erastian scientist who, though he wrote nothing that was philosophically systematic, commanded as wide an audience and at least as great an authority as Spencer did.

Huxley had been trained as a doctor; it was as a ship's doctor that he collected the zoological observations that made his reputation after the four years he spent on the *Rattlesnake* in Australasia and the Far East in the 1840s. Before 1859 most of his work consisted of technical contributions to the sciences it dealt with. From the Darwinian writer of 1859 he began to command a hearing generally some years before he commanded a hearing as a critic of Christianity. It was not until the 1880s that he gave positive statements of the reasons why Christianity should be replaced by agnosticism.

Huxley's agnosticism, when sketched in the 1860s, had incorporated the doubts about the Old Testament which had been suggested by Lyell, Chambers and Buckland. By the time it became positive, it had been reinforced by Morley's and Stephens's agnosticisms, and by Tyndall's.

II

Tyndall[1] was an important physicist who made major discoveries in magnetism, geology and crystallography, and succeeded Faraday, his mentor, at the Royal Institution. He was a mountaineer as well as a scientist and was author not only of *The Glaciers of the Alps* and *The*

---

[1] John Tyndall (1820–93). Educ. National School in County Carlow. Ordinance Survey of Ireland and then of England; then railway engineer 1839–47. Lecturer at Queenswood College, Hampshire 1847–8 and 1851–4. Student at Marburg and Berlin Universities 1848–51, Professor and Superintendent of Royal Institution 1853–93. Author of *On the Importance of the Study of Physics* 1855, *The Glaciers of the Alps* 1860, *Mountaineering in 1861* 1862, *Heat Considered as a Model of Motion* 1863, *The Constitution of the Universe* 1865, *Sound* 1867, *Natural Philosophy in Easy Lessons* 1869, *Essays on the Use and Limits of the Imagination in Science* 1870, *Fragments of Science for Unscientific People* 1871, *The Forms of Water in Clouds and Rivers, Ice and Glaciers* 1872, *Six Lectures on Light* 1872–73, *Principal Forbes and His Biographers* 1873, *Address Delivered before the British Association Assembled at Belfast* 1874, *Lessons in Electricity* 1875–76, *Fermentation* 1877, *Essays on the Floating Matter of Air* 1881, *Mr Gladstone on Home Rule* 1887, *Perverted Politics* 1887, *New Fragments* 1892.

Forms of Water in Clouds and Rivers, Ice and Glaciers but also of *Mountaineering in 1861* and *Hours of Exercise in the Alps*. Beginning life as a poor Irish boy whose father was both a reading Protestant and a country policeman, he became first a railway engineer, then a teacher and finally a researching scientist. After making a reputation in Germany, he collaborated with Huxley and in the course of the 1850s became a leading English scientist. By the time he made a late marriage to an aristocratic wife who later killed him by accidental poisoning, he had for more than a decade been identified as a leading critic of Christianity.

In his early and middle years Tyndall's politics were Carlylean and radical in the manner of the 1860s. Gladstone's attitude to the Church of Ireland then drove him away from the Liberal Party. He was offered, though he refused, the Conservative candidacy in a Glasgow seat in 1885 and, while professing distaste for the 'mire' of party politics, wrote a handful of party-political articles for Greenwood's *St James's Gazette* in which he attacked both Morley's deference to Gladstone and Gladstone's Imperial record between Majuba and Khartoum. In calling on the 'sturdy Protestantism' of the English people to defend itself against Home Rule, he did not remove the impression that, though a Protestant Irishman in politics, he was a Protestant pantheist in religion.

Tyndall's central statements about religion are to be found in his *Address Delivered before the British Association* in Belfast in 1874 and in the elaborations of it that he published subsequently. By the time of the Belfast address, however, Tyndall had for twenty years been describing Science's place in public doctrine, justifying an increase in its rôle in education and providing cultured laymen with up-to-date accounts of the 'Constitution of Nature' as Science had disclosed it.

Tyndall took a high view of Science and in pursuing a heroic, or romantic, conception of scientific leadership, addressed himself to two connected questions – the question of Science as an investigative and regulative principle, and the question of Nature as the object of Science and the regulative context by which men had to be governed. The outcome was a riveting, as secure as Buckle's or Spencer's, of morals and religion to the rules which Science discovered in Nature.

In Tyndall's popular writings the 'Constitution of Nature' included the nebular hypothesis and the 'lumiferous ether', Helmholtz's Convertibility of Natural Forces and the 'molecular attraction' which 'every particle of matter' had for 'every other'. It included a mechanical conception of heat and light, Haeckel's conception of the protogene as the lowest form of observable life and the idea of the Sun as the source of energy for the living world. Above all, it included Natural Selection, the Ubiquity of Law and the 'rhythm of cause and effect' as the sole explanations of the phenomena of Existence.

Tyndall's popular writings gave an uncontroversial account of the current state of knowledge in the physical, geological and biological sciences. They also drew controversial conclusions about miracle, the primacy of matter over mind and the impossibility of God having created the world.

Tyndall was a materialist and pantheist; he presented life as inseparable from matter and scientific laws as the methods which material nature had used in the course of its own self-creation. It was material nature which was the subject of scientific enquiry, material nature which performed the 'miracles' that science disclosed, material nature which opened up the secrets of existence to the scientific imagination. It was material nature which manifested itself in the 'nebular hypothesis' and the 'lumiferous ether', material nature which had invented molecular attraction and the Convertibility of Natural Forces, material nature in which was to be found Haeckel's protogenes, the mechanical conception of heat and light and the Sun as the source of energy for the living world. It was material nature's 'architectural power' which had created the beauties of nature, Darwinian selection and the spiritual achievements of which human development consisted. And the important point was that 'whatever ... faith might say, ... knowledge showed' that it was material nature which had done these things – the material nature which Wordsworth had described in *Lines Written a Few Miles above Tintern Abbey* and Tyndall in *Mountaineering in 1861* – and not either the person or the providence of God.

In his *Belfast Address*, Tyndall described God's expulsion from inorganic nature by the atomic philosophy and from organic nature by Darwinianism, and emphasized the extent to which Natural Selection had replaced teleology and a 'man-like Artificer'. He singled out Spencer's *Principles of Psychology* as herald of a future in which the mind would be seen as 'the organised register of infinitely numerous experiences received during the ... evolution of that series of organisms through which the human organism had been reached.'

In the *Belfast Address* the progress of science was represented as having begun when 'men of exceptional power' had 'differentiated themselves from the crowd', rejected the 'anthropomorphism' of primitive observation and swept away the 'gods and demons' by whom theory had been obstructed previously. Plato and Socrates were compared unfavourably with Democritus, and Bishop Butler with Lucretius; Aristotle was disparaged as a physicist, and the ascetism, mysticism and authoritarian Scholasticism which Tyndall associated with Christianity's 'menial spirit' adduced as the reason for the 'intellectual immobility' of the Middle Ages. It was not until he reached the point at which Scholasticism had been rejected and ancient atomicism transformed into modern physics that he began to feel confident that scientific materialism had been made impregnable.

Tyndall stated his opinions so confidently that it might seem sufficient to record them and pass on. That, however, would not be sufficient. Tyndall's attitude was ambivalent, dismissive of theology's claim to be a form of knowledge and assertive about the need to replace it by science, but at the same time both so categorical and so sceptical about science as to obscure the contrast that he was drawing.

Tyndall's 'Science' was an oligarchy of scientists who alone had authority in respect of Truth and alone were able to choose their successors. But the most important aspect of scientific thought, and the whole of its moral merit as he saw it, was its method; it was the method, not the content, of science, far less its consequences in terms of amenity of life, which gave science its significance as an instrument of culture.

Tyndall did not undervalue the material conquests which science had made since the seventeenth century. But he was sceptical about the intellectual value of application, and insistent that science's primary impulse must be the uncontaminated inquisitiveness which all men shared, even when they were not all equipped to pursue it.

Tyndall had a lapsed Protestant, or Protestant-Irish, belief in the compatibility between Science and Protestantism, and an accompanying belief in the incompatibility between Science and Catholicism. He dismissed the evasions of Anglicanism, the 'fripperies of ritualism' and the 'verbal quibbles of the Athanasian Creed', while making his main target not Canterbury but Rome, where Jesuitry was holding up science, where Fröhschammer was doing for science what Döllinger was doing for history, and where 'men of iron' were aiming to control both science and speculation.

Tyndall's philosophical position was the Spencerian, or Kantian, position that the human mind was limited and that science shared its limitations. Science needed the imaginative leap which 'lightened the darkness' surrounding the 'world of the senses' and had to 'fashion the ... mysteries' and probe the 'inscrutable'. But it had also to avoid rigidity, and it had, more than anything else, to pursue that loftiness, chastity, courage, reverence and self-renunciation which alone would enable it to follow the argument wherever it might lead.

Tyndall did not write as though there was anything uncertain about the explanations that held sway in the sciences he described. But he was clear that all scientific explanations were reversible, that none was exempt from scrutiny and that 'suspension of judgment', so alien to theological minds, as well as being central to science, should be made central to all other areas of life.

Tyndall did not suppose, as Wells was to suppose in *A Modern Utopia*, that scientists, or intellectuals, should rule. For him on the contrary the task of the future was to proselytize on behalf of a mentality. He expected universities to protect 'the culture of research' from the demands of utility and the teaching profession to inculcate the 'love' and 'earnestness' that were necessary for its propagation, and he claimed for himself the mission of 'extending sympathy' for science to 'intelligent persons' who had no scientific culture. Given these virtuous, and innocent, intentions, the question we have to ask is, in inserting 'science' into public discourse, what did Tyndall mean to say about Christianity?

Tyndall did not exactly attack Christianity. What he attacked was the 'narrowing' of Christianity, the gap that divided it from science, and the attempts it had made to bridge the gap by controlling science. At the same time as Ward was calling on the Papacy to control science, Tyndall was arguing that science had to advance, that Christianity had to retreat and that far less could be known about the nature of existence than Christian theology had imagined. Even if we discount the wanderings in the wilderness of the Carlylean hero described in the second epigraph on p. 141, there can be no doubt that Tyndall attributed to scientific method as dramatic a rôle as Spencer attributed to it in purging religion of its 'accidents'.

Tyndall expressed an earnest respect for religion as the answer to a human need. But he also affirmed the existence of a problem about which, like Newman, he declined to buy 'intellectual peace' at the price of 'intellectual death'. The problem was that, though religion had nothing to contribute to knowledge, its devotees had refused to extricate it from the attempt to make a contribution.

What function, if any, religion was to perform in the culture of the distant future was not made clear. What was made clear was that religion's theological phase was over, and that its next phase would be poetic. It was the poet who would 'keep open the horizons of the emotions', the poet who would prevent the 'shutters' being brought down by 'philosophers and priests', the poet who would 'fill the shores which the recession of the theologic tide had left exposed'. It was poetry that would 'cheer Science with immortal laughter', poetry that would give a 'religious vitalisation' of scientific truth, poetry that would show the way towards that completeness of culture which would be achieved when Shakespeare as well as Newton, Raphael as well as Boyle, and Beethoven, Carlyle, Fichte, Goethe, Wordsworth, Emerson, Kant and Darwin matched 'the inexorable advance of man's understanding in the paths of knowledge' to the 'unquenchable flames of his moral and emotional nature'.

Whatever Tyndall may have thought he was doing, what he was also doing was to create a mentality for a new intelligentsia – a scientific intelligentsia which would have its own subject-matter to complement the subject-matter of classical scholarship and which, by involving itself in literature as well as science, would effect a modern synthesis and give permanent shape to the moral impulse through which, as Tyndall believed, Fichte, Emerson and Carlyle had given him the strength to become a scientist in the first place.

Tyndall was a hard-nosed, Darwinian radical with no more sympathy for aristocratic mentalities or the aristocratic polity than Mill, Ruskin or Newman, and with his full share of the republican virtue which was to come into its own as Liberal Unionism after 1886. In symbolizing the transition in which hostility to Christianity combined with hostility to aristocracy to create a post-Christian normality, he was hardly less significant than Huxley.

III

In his first phase as a publicist, Huxley was involved in the Darwinian argument which issued in the accounts of *The Origin of Species* that he contributed to *The Times* and *Macmillan's Magazine* in 1859 and to the

Westminster Review in 1860, in his book *Evidence as to Man's Place in Nature* which caused religious offence when published in 1863 and in the articles and lectures about the need for public recognition of science which he had begun to deliver in 1854 and collected into volumes entitled *Lay Sermons, Critiques and Addresses, American Addresses* and *Science and Culture* from 1870 onwards.

As a naturalist, Huxley had been brought close to the questions that were raised by *The Origin of Species*; he made himself into one of Darwin's defenders against the attacks that were made on him. As Huxley understood him, Darwin, in destroying teleology, certainly in its Paleyite form, had destroyed what was left of the doctrine of special creation, and in the process had stimulated conflict with 'orthodoxy' or 'official Christianity'. Huxley was critical of 'orthodoxy' for presuming to refute Darwin without the equipment necessary to do so, but in the 1860s he did not attack Christianity itself. It was in rejection of mental Bourbonism rather than of Christianity that he dismissed Old Testament 'cosmogony', defended the 'patient and earnest seekers after Truth' whose lives had been 'embittered by persecution' since Galileo and affirmed that natural phenomena, so far from being explicable by reference to the 'supernatural interposition of the Creator', could only be explained as instances of some 'general law of nature'.

In the 1860s and 1870s, Huxley's tactic was to attack Anglican inadequacy to the point of claiming that the Roman Catholic Church was science's only reputable enemy; even the slogan of a 'scientific Sunday School in every parish' was 'not to be for the purpose of superseding any existing means of teaching the people the things that were good for them'. On the whole, in this phase, Huxley's emphasis was on 'the majesty of fact', the primacy of 'scientific data' based on 'evidence and reasoning' and the impossibility that men of science should recognize a theological reason and morality separate from a scientific reason and morality.

In the course of defending Darwin, Huxley sketched a 'cyclical' view of evolution and of the 'flow of energy' and 'rational order' which 'pervaded the cosmos'. Like Tyndall, he had a Spencerian mistrust of books, a Spencerian view of the continuity between the animal and the human worlds, and a Spencerian belief that it was the better adapted who survived the struggle for existence. While being cautious about ultimate perfectability, he agreed with Spencer about the importance of sociology, about progress towards voluntary co-operation and about female emancipation as a facet of it.

Like Spencer, Huxley made a point of not being a Comtean, giving as his reason not so much Comte's ignorance of science as Comte's wish to replace authoritarian Catholicism by authoritarian Comteanism. Neither was he, at any rate in the 1880s, either a 'modern pessimist' or a devotee of 'modern speculative optimism'. Such restrained optimism as he expressed about human perfectability explained it in terms of 'millions of years of severe training', the inseparability of pain from life and a more extensive use of state power than Spencer envisaged or 'fanatical individualism' encouraged.

In *Administrative Nihilism* Huxley defended the Education Act of 1870 against the criticism that the State had 'no right to do anything but protect its subjects from aggression'. He presented the education of the poor as a preventive of revolution, an antidote to hereditary stratification and an aid to enabling 'capacity to ascend from the lower strata to the higher', asserting that capacity *ought* to occupy the 'higher strata', that incapacity *ought* to descend from the higher to the lower and that education was the best way of ensuring that it would in the absence of coercive machinery for ensuring that it did. In providing for the realization of these principles he replaced the 'dogmatic' view that 'State interference ... must ... do harm' by the positive view that the State was the 'corporate reason of the community' and would perform best when a rule-of-thumb pragmatism pursued the 'middle way' between Individualism on the one hand and Regimentation on the other.

Huxley shared Hobbes's view that civilization was the outcome of man's effort to check the 'struggle for existence'. But he supplemented it with the idea that civilization itself had created a new phase of the struggle as the population grew, competition for resources increased and morality, internalizing itself as 'conscience', destroyed the equilibrium on which it depended. Huxley did not conclude that the diseased, weak, old or deformed should therefore be eliminated. But he left no doubt that whatever men might want, Nature wanted the strongest to survive, that the misery which the masses were experiencing in industrial cities could not be accounted for in terms of vice and idleness and that the social task of the future was to make life tolerable by limiting reproduction.

Huxley criticized Natural Rights theory, defended the 'individual ownership of land' and wrote contemptuously against the *a priorism* of Rousseau and Henry George. While denying that the democratic suffrage provided a 'scientific test of ... good and evil', he agreed that it had to be 'abided by' if anarchy was to be avoided. He added, however, that the competition for 'enjoyments', which was all that civilization retained of the cosmic struggle for 'existence', was well able to place 'wealth and influence' in the hands of those who were 'endowed with the largest share of energy ... industry ... intellectual capacity and ... tenacity of purpose'.

IV

During the middle years of his life, Huxley criticized the ignorance of the value of 'physical science' which infected the minds both of the 'commercial' and of the 'most highly educated and intelligent classes' in England. On the other hand, again like Tyndall, he had a Goethean sense of the relevance of poetry and literature, believed with Carlyle or Ruskin in the interrelatedness of all forms of mental culture and wanted it to be understood that far more had been written about public doctrine in English than the protagonists of classical studies had permitted to be understood. It is only in the most modest way that Huxley can be said to have thought 'science' more important than literature, and it is best to think of him as demanding for science merely a place at the high tables of thought in the same way that Ruskin demanded a place for painting and architecture, Spencer for sociology, Tylor for anthropology, Shaw for the theatre and Lawrence and Ellis for sex.

By science Huxley meant in the first place 'trained and organised common sense' in which, 'as in life', though not as in literature, the 'study of things, not of books' was the source of knowledge, in which 'intelligence' and 'moral energy' predominated over 'brute force' and where the outcome was the 'great ships, railways ... telegraphs, factories and printing-presses' which were fundamental to the 'fabric of modern society'. At the same time he also meant something more significant and even more fundamental – the 'revolution in men's conception of the universe' of which the Royal Society had been the symbol. It was the foundation of the Royal Society which had heralded 'the greatest revolution that the world had ever seen', and in asserting the 'primacy of reason over all provinces of human activity', had 'relegated' ecclesiastical authority 'to its proper place' and insinuated the principles of science into literature, thought, conduct and religion, even when poets and men-of-letters affected to despise it.'

What this meant was that the conduct of life and the progress of thought depended not on religion but on the extent to which men were able to 'learn something of Nature' and come 'partially' to 'obey her', and it was the conception of Nature rewarding the man who obeyed her and punishing the man who did not which led to the conception of a 'liberal education' as the process of learning the rules on which the conduct of life depended.

That man, I think, has had a liberal education who has been so trained in youth that his body is the ready servant of his will, and does with ease and pleasure all the work that, as a mechanism, it is capable of; whose intellect is a clear, cold, logic engine, with all its parts of equal strength, and in smooth working order; ready, like a steam engine, to be turned to any kind of work, and spin the gossamers as well as forge the anchors of the mind; whose mind is stored with a knowledge of the great and fundamental truths of Nature and of the laws of her operations; one who, no stunted ascetic, is full of life and fire, but whose passions are trained to come to heel by a vigorous will, the servant of a tender conscience, who has learned to love all beauty, whether of Nature or of art, to hate all vileness, and to respect others as himself.

Such an one and no other, I conceive, has had a liberal education; for he is, as completely as a man can be, in harmony with Nature. He will make the best of her, and she of him. They will get on together rarely: she as his ever beneficient mother; he as her mouthpiece, her conscious self, her minister and interpreter.

Huxley did not advocate the abolition of literary education, he merely attacked its predominance in the forms which had been bequeathed by the Renaissance. He was clear that the predominance of the classics in middle-class education should be destroyed, that the days of the amateur public schoolboy should be judged to have ended and that there should be expansions in the physical, social and moral sciences and the study of English history and literature. In the education of the poor, he wanted elementary science, English history instead of the 'Jewish history' and 'Syrian geography' that children had had too much of in the past and an attempt to explain the 'reasons' behind the 'moral law', and he made it a merit of this sort of education that it would reconcile its recipients to inequality and enable a 'man of ability' to become 'a great writer or speaker, a statesman, a lawyer, a man of science, painter, sculptor or musician' (though not, apparently, an entrepreneur). These opinions were summarized in a paragraph from a talk on *Technical Education* that Huxley gave in 1877.

The workshop is the only real school for a handicraft. The education which precedes that of the workshop should be entirely devoted to the strengthening of the body, the elevation of the moral faculties, and the cultivation of the intelligence; and, especially, to the imbuing the mind with a broad and clear view of the laws of that natural world with the components of which the handicraftsman will have to deal. And, the earlier the period of life at which the handicraftsman has to enter into actual practice of his craft, the more important is it that he should devote the precious hours of preliminary education to things of the mind, which have no direct and immediate bearing on his branch of industry, though they lie at the foundation of all realities.

Huxley thought of universities as the 'natural outcome and development' of school education. But he did not share Pusey's mistrust of the professorial university and he claimed for it virtues which Pusey claimed for the collegiate university. What Huxley wanted was that universities should stop being finishing-schools for the rich or seminaries for ordination, and should address themselves to the central requirements of modern societies in the way in which the Church had addressed itself to the central requirements of mediaeval society – by cultivating knowledge and developing that openness to talent which had enabled German universities to dominate the 'intellectual world' as Napoleon had dominated the political. Most of all, he wanted universities to be charged with a 'fanaticism for veracity' which was as 'much greater and nobler' than 'much learning' as man's moral nature was 'greater than his intellectual'.

Huxley affected independence of 'dogmatic theology' and party politics. He did not object to the Bible being taught as literature but was vigorously opposed to any interference in education by the partisans of ecclesiastical or theological interests. In party terms in the 1860s and 1870s he was a Liberal; after 1886 he became a Liberal Unionist. But his belief in science included a belief in its incompatibility with the expression of party opinions and he argued on many occasions, most notably when his successor as President of the Royal Society became M. P. for the University of Cambridge in 1887, that science was an autonomous activity whose autonomy had to be maintained scrupulously. It was consciousness of a constituency far wider and more popular than any political constituency which made him speak to one of his audiences of working men of that 'sympathy between the handicrafts men of this country' and its 'men of science' which originated in the fact that men of science 'alone among the so-called learned folk' had a high degree of manual dexterity and were 'brought into contact with tangible facts' in a way that working men were.

V

In the 'Lay Sermon' that he preached in St Martin's Hall on the centenary of the Plague and Great Fire of London in 1866, Huxley argued that religion involved 'consciousness of the limitation of man', that this had been its 'essence' in its primitive forms and 'in the forms furnished by the intellect' as the 'origin of the higher theologies' and that it would continue to be its essence in the future as the area of its authority diminished and science replaced 'fine-spun ecclesiastical cobwebs' by 'worship "for the most part of the silent sort" at the altar of the Unknown'.

These were negative statements with positive implications which were widely perceived and attacked. From Huxley's side the positive implication was a counter-attack, not on religion as such, but on what he claimed were misunderstandings of the nature of knowledge for which religion had been responsible.

Huxley's understanding of the nature of knowledge was expressed best through praise of Hobbes, Berkeley and Kant, through discussion of the 'heroism' with which Descartes had given doubt a place in the scientific conscience and through descriptions of the road which led from the Cartesian transcendence of idealism and materialism to the Humean conclusion that philosophy should be considered in connection with psychology and physiology. The high point of this line of argument was the claim that 'the soul' was a 'mathematical point having place but no extension beyond the limits of the venial body'.

In the 1880s and 1890s Huxley's argument depended on one assumption and one prediction. The assumption was that whatever could not be explained in terms of 'order and natural causation' could not be understood and must be judged to be unknown until certain knowledge made it knowable. The prediction was that the 'immense provinces' which had been added to science's 'realm' in the previous two centuries, would be joined by a 'vastly greater annexation' in the next two as 'phenomena which had not previously been brought under these conceptions' were explained in these terms.

Huxley's earlier polemical writings had been concerned primarily with the impact of science on Christianity as a way of defending science against Christian criticism. They had had an historical component which, however, had not been predominant. In the 1880s, though 'Science' remained a slogan and physical science a source of inconvenient information, *historical* science became more prominent than it had been previously. It was in the rôle of 'expositor' of historical science as it had been absorbed by 'German and Dutch theologians' whose 'tenure of their posts did not depend upon the results to which their inquiries led them' that Huxley defended the 'supremacy of private judgment' against the 'effete and idolatrous sacerdotalism' that the Tractarians had imposed on the Church of England.

In arguing in favour of historical criticism of the Bible, Huxley was not committing himself to the meaning that criticism would disclose. His position on the contrary was agnostic: he contrasted the 'attainment of faith' with the 'ascertainment of truth', hoping merely that the 'rough hand' of historical publicity would refute 'nine-tenths' of the 'metaphysics and ... superstition' which had been 'piled around' the Bible by the 'so-called Christians of later times'.

Huxley's view of the New Testament included doubts whether the Sermon on the Mount was ever preached, whether the Lord's Prayer was ever prayed by Jesus of Nazareth and whether there was any need for supernatural assumptions in explaining Jesus's disappearance from the tomb after the Crucifixion. These doubts were the 'inevitable result' of strict adherence to scientific method by 'historical investigators' and this was said to be a matter not only of superior veracity but also of superior morality as all Churches were blamed for the 'torrent of hypocrisy' which had accompanied the claim that 'disbelief in their ... astonishing creeds ... was a ... moral offence ... indeed a sin ... deserving ... the same future retribution as murder and robbery.'.

Huxley did not deride Christian morality. Neither did he deny that faith had 'power', even in the nineteenth century as the spread of Mormonism had shown. His difficulty was that, in spite of its 'strength' and 'patience', its 'pity for human frailty' and the 'nobility' of its 'moral/ideal', Christianity's historical foundations were being so 'remorselessly destroyed' that there was a manifest incompatibility between organized science in the form it had been given by the Royal Society, and the Roman Cardinals who at the Vatican Council in 1870 'were still at their business of trying to stop the movement of the world.'

In the course of defending himself against attack, Huxley carried the battle into the enemy camp, denying that science was either subversive of morality or had anything to do with the 'bickerings about the unknown' which had been theology's and philosophy's contributions to scepticism. He wrote also as the heir of Tylor, Spencer and Strauss, accepting their accounts of the origins of religion, agreeing with their denials of Christianity's uniqueness, and emphasizing the meaninglessness of belief in the miraculous.

In arguing these positions, Huxley was as condescending as Spencer, recognizing that most men might find it easier to act morally with a theology than without one and agreeing that they would go on 'personifying' their 'intellectual conceptions' even after it was reasonable to do so. From this point of view theology was considered as a 'symbol'. But it was also considered as a human 'fabrication' in which Judaism resembled the religion of the Polynesians and Jesus was a primitive Nazarene who would have regarded the early fathers as 'blasphemous if he could have been made to understand them', while Constantinian Christianity proved that the Galilean, so far from conquering, had in fact been conquered, and the continuity disclosed by the history of theology was that ethics was being disconnected from theology in order to be deduced from the laws of life.

Huxley was fertile in discerning continuities; he was particularly fertile in discerning continuities between Philo of Alexandria and Hamilton's, Mansel's, and Spencer's doctrine of 'incognoscibility', and between the 'ethical purity' of the Jewish prophets and science's attempt to free the 'moral ideal' from the 'stifling embrace' of theology and ritual.

Huxley identified supernatural religion with primitive civilization and its elimination with progress. He dismissed Christian attempts to accommodate science and theology, emphasizing that science could not be compromised, that ecclesiastical Christianity was not compatible with it and that Christians either had to accept scientific culture *tout court* and abandon the 'foregone-conclusion' mode of arguing, or reject scientific culture *tout court* and 'shake Christianity to its foundation'. In all this it became obvious that accommodating, attenuated or liberal Christianity was as objectionable as dogmatic Christianity and that even the replacement of ecclesiastical by scientific theology would not save the 'possessed' Gadarene pigs, the 'talking snake' in the Garden of Eden or the idea that Jesus 'had no human father'. The position was summarized in the claims that the 'evidence' was inadequate to 'prove' either the 'supposed occurrence of miracles' or the 'efficacy of prayer in modifying the course of events', and that the infallibility of the Bible depended on the circular view that it was affirmed by the infallible Church whose 'infallibility' was sustained by belief in the infallibility of the Bible.

By the 1880s, Huxley believed that the Bible had to be abandoned in its supernatural forms and would have a future 'in a democratic age' if it had one at all, either as literature, divorced from 'cosmogonies, demonologies and miraculous interferences' or as a 'Magna Carta of the poor and oppressed'. *Administrative Nihilism* had a vision of the 'blessing' the Established Church could become once it had rid itself of Biblical supernaturalism:

a church in which, week by week, services would be devoted, not to the itera- tion of abstract propositions in theology, but to the setting before men's minds of an ideal of true, just, and pure living; a place in which those who were weary of the burden of daily cares, would find a moment's rest in the contemplation of the higher life which is possible for all, though attained by so few: a place in which the man of strife and of business would have time to think how small, after all, were the rewards he coveted compared with peace and charity.

Huxley was brought up an Evangelical and retained an Evangelical earnestness, even after his Evangelical belief had disappeared. In later life he was conscious of being on the winning side as the 'artillery of the pulpit' ceased to be directed against the doctrine of evolution, as the association between Christianity and the miraculous fell apart 'with continually accelerating velocity' and as the State approached a position of 'non-intervention' in 'religious quarrels'.

These claims reflected relief at having arrived at the central position that Huxley had always wished for. They were a recognition that agnosticism, so far from being merely a 'method', was in process of adopting the rôle which had previously been adopted by theology, and 'in the matter of intellectual veracity' was exerting an 'influence on mankind of which the Churches had shown themselves ... incapable'.

Relatively to myself [went an important passage], I am quite sure that the region of uncertainty – the nebulous country in which words play the part of realities – is far more extensive than I could wish. Materialism and Idealism; Theism and Atheism; the doctrine of the soul and its mortality or immortality – appear in the history of philosophy like the shades of Scandinavian heroes, eternally slaying one another and eternally coming to life again in a metaphysi- cal 'Hifelheim'. It is getting on for twenty-five centuries, at least, since mankind began seriously to give their minds to these topics. Generation after genera- tion, philosophy has been doomed to roll the stone uphill; and, just as all the world swore it was at the top, down it has rolled to the bottom again. All this is written in innumerable books; and he who will toil through them will discover that the stone is just where it was when the work began. Hume saw this; Kant saw it; since their time, more and more eyes have been cleansed of the films which prevented them from seeing it: until now the weight and number of those who refuse to be the prey of verbal mystifications has begun to tell in practical life.

By the 1880s Huxley was pushing at an open door. He found it easy to attack ecclesiasticism once it had become a paradoxical assertion of the need to react defensively to the brisk sneers of free thinkers. He was nevertheless a brisk thinker – far brisker than the thinkers who are to be discussed next.

7

Types of Ethical Earnestness III

'... Turgot was born in Paris on the 10th of May, 1727. He died in 1781. His life covered rather more than half a century, extending, if we may put it a little roughly, over the middle fifty years of the eighteenth century. This middle period marks the exact date of the decisive and immediate preparation for the Revolution ... It was between 1727 and 1781 that the true revolution took place. The events from '89 were only finishing strokes, the final explosion of a fabric under which every yard has been mined, by the long endeavour for half a century of an army of destroyers deliberate and involuntary, direct and oblique, such as the world has never at any other time beheld.' John Morley *Turgot* in *Critical Miscellanies* 2nd Series 1877 p. 137.

'The coarse and realistic criticism of which Voltaire was the consummate master, has done its work. It has driven the defenders of the old faith into the milder and more genial climate of non-natural interpretations, and the historic sense, and a certain elastic relativity of dogma ... The consequence of this ... is that the modern attack, while fully as serious and much more radical, has a certain gravity, decorum, and worthiness of form. No one of any sense or knowledge now thinks the Christian religion had its origin in deliberate imposture. The modern freethinker does not attack it; he explains it. And what is more, he explains it by referring its growth to the better, and not to the worse part of human nature ...

The result of this ... is that we are now awake to the all-important truth that belief in this or that detail of superstition is the result of an irrational state of mind, and flows logically from superstitious premises. We see that it is to begin at the wrong end, to assail the deductions as impossible, instead of sedulously building up a state of mind in which their impossibility would become spontaneously visible.' John Morley *On Compromise* (1874) 1903 edn pp. 150–2.

'Those who have the religious imagination struck by the awful procession of man from the region of impenetrable night, by his incessant struggle with the hardness of the material world, and his sublimer struggle with the hard world of his own egoistic passions ... may indeed have no ecstasy and no terror, no heaven nor hell, in their religion, but they will have abundant moods of reverence, deep-seated gratitude, and sovereign pitifulness ... A man with this faith can have no foul spiritual pride ...; he can have no incentives to that mutilation with which every branch of the church ... has ... afflicted and retarded mankind, ... and he can be plunged into no fatal and paralysing despair by any doctrine of mortal sin ... If religion is our feeling about the highest forces that govern human destiny, then ... the religious sentiment will more and more attach itself to the great unseen host of our fellows who have gone before us and who are to come after. Such a faith is no rag of metaphysic floating in the sunshine of sentimentalism ...'. John Morley *Rousseau* 1873 vol. ii pp. 277–9.

In the last chapter, agnosticism was examined as the conclusion of science. In both Huxley and Tyndall there was an historical and a literary dimension, but in neither case did history and literature supply the primary reason for rejecting Christianity. In this chapter we shall examine two major contemporaries for whom they did.

Tyndall was born in 1820 and Huxley in 1825. Stephen was born in 1832 and Morley in 1838. All four had been brought up as Protestants, and all four made it a main purpose of their lives to expound agnosticism. In examining first Stephen and then Morley, we shall be examining an agnosticism which was not less ambitious because it lacked the authority of experimental science.

I

Stephen[1] was the son of a lawyer who had become a civil servant and in his retirement Regius Professor of Modern History at Cambridge. Stephen was brought up an Evangelical and, after four unsuccessful years at Eton and a short period at King's College, London, was sent to Trinity Hall, Cambridge, where he read Mathematics, spoke at the Union and became an energetic athlete. He then became a Fellow of Trinity Hall, was ordained in the Church of England and turned himself into an energetic mountaineer.

[1] Leslie Stephen (1832–1904). Educ. Eton, King's College, London, and Trinity Hall, Cambridge. Fellow of Trinity Hall 1854–67, clergyman of the Church of England 1855–75. Editor of *Cornhill Magazine* 1871–82, editor of *Dictionary of National Biography* 1882–9. Author of *Sketches from Cambridge* 1865, *The Playground of Europe* 1871, *Essays on Free Thinking and Plain Speaking* 1873, *Hours in a Library* 4 vols, 1874–1907, *History of English Thought in the Eighteenth Century* 2 vols, 1876, *Swift* 1882, *Samuel Johnson* 1878, *Alexander Pope* 1880, *The Science of Ethics* 1882, *Life of Henry Fawcett* 1885, *An Agnostic's Apology* 1893, *The Life of Sir Fitzjames Stephen* 1895, *Social Rights and Duties* 2 vols, 1896, *Studies of a Biographer* 4 vols, 1898–1902, *The English Utilitarians* 3 vols. 1900, ed. *Letters of J. R. Green* 1901, *George Eliot* 1902, *English Literature and Society in the Eighteenth Century* 1904, *Hobbes* 1904.

Until 1864 Stephen was an active Fellow of Trinity Hall, where he taught Mathematics, was closely involved with undergraduates, and wrote mainly about mountaineering. On turning his mind to Mill, Comte and Kant, his religious observances began to cease. Having lost his Fellowship on marriage to Thackeray's daughter in 1867, he renounced his orders just before his wife's death in 1875.

Stephen arrived in London in the middle 1860s with the same purpose that Morley had arrived with a few years earlier. Like Morley, who became a close friend, Stephen had been involved in radical politics, in his case in support of Fawcett, a friend from Trinity Hall, who by then had stood for parliament in both Cambridge and Brighton.

In his early years in London, Stephen wrote for the *Saturday Review*, the *Pall Mall Gazette*, the *Fortnightly Review* and the *Cornhill Magazine* of which he became editor in 1871. In the early 1880s, in company with Sidney Lee, he became the master-mind behind the *Dictionary of National Biography*. Stephen's own biography was written by Maitland; his brother was Fitzjames Stephen, his daughter Virginia Woolf. His second marriage lasted from 1878 until 1895 and was commemorated in *The Mausoleum Book* which he wrote after his wife's death.

Like Huxley, Stephen became a Liberal Unionist in the 1880s and contributed to the secularized celebration of material progress which was to be so important a strand in twentieth-century Conservatism. Moreover, from the late 1860s, also like Huxley, Stephen made a positive position out of theological negation.

The core of Stephen's professional work consisted of encomiums on Clifford and J. R. Green, biographies of Fawcett and Fitzjames Stephen, books about *George Eliot, Pope, Swift, Hobbes* and *Johnson* in the *English Men-of-Letters* series, a three-volume work on *The English Utilitarians* and innumerable magazine articles on literary subjects which were collected together in seven volumes under the titles *Hours in a Library* and *Studies of a Biographer*. When approached in the shadow of the *Dictionary of National Biography*, these works leave an impression of the definitive impregnability and uncontroversial judgment that are necessary in order to establish the foundations of an Academy.

To some extent this impression is correct; the *Dictionary of National Biography*, in particular, has become a national institution. Yet it did for English history what Harrison's *New Calendar of Great Men* was to do in a Comtean mode for the history of the world and, even though conceived of by its publisher rather than by Stephen, takes its place in a propaganda which began to be massive when the campaigning historian disclosed himself in the two volumes of *History of English Thought in the Eighteenth Century* in 1876.

By 1876 Stephen had already sketched a religious position in *Essays on Free Thinking and Plain Speaking* three years earlier. This had had a freshness and vigour indicative of the change of mind that he had undergone since the publication of *Sketches from Cambridge* in 1865. *Essays on Free Thinking and Plain Speaking* signalized the end of Stephen's phase as a don. It moved on a national plane and asked national questions. Most of all, it asked the living question of the 1870s, whether England was any longer a Christian country.

Essays on Free Thinking and Plain Speaking was a statement about the politics of English belief. It dismissed in turn Evangelicalism, ritualism, Ultramontanism and the Anglican assumption that religious formularies should be determined by law. It argued that 'sincerity' was essential, that the problem of belief had to be faced and that there was no stopping-point between believing in Christianity and not believing in it. Supernatural Christianity either was or was not true, and if it was not true, or could not have truth predicated of it, it would be better to face up to the fact that latitudinarianism was merely a disingenuous way of 'slinking out of the orthodox entrenchment into the opposite camp'.

Stephen's rejection was comprehensive, beginning from the claim that 'unsectarian' Christianity was a 'dead' Christianity which 'shirked' the difficulty about Christ without 'meeting' it, and proceeding to the conclusion that the prospect had to be faced of Anglicanism dying as the Church of England split into 'hostile fragments'. In calling for an effort to face the future, Stephen assumed that the crucial conflict would be between the followers of Comte and the follows of mediaeval superstition and that the politico-religious problem was how best to propagate Comteanism among the 'less educated classes ... with the least shock to morality and lofty sentiment'.

In anticipating the supplanting of Christianity, Stephen did not anticipate the supplanting of religion. Religion, on the contrary, was 'indestructible'; he rejected only the 'make-believe' involved when it was a 'substitute for police regulations' or a 'beautiful exercise for the soul'.

What Stephen believed was that a 'new truth' had been proclaimed, that it had to break the 'old mould' and that the Thirty-Nine Articles were 'the product of a series of compromises ... as strange as ... the British Constitution'. He made it clear that 'the old symbols' had 'decayed', the 'temples ... fallen to ruin' and the 'idols ... broken down', and that these facts had to be brought home to a nation which persisted 'prosaically' in assuming that a creed could be believed 'in the same way as a scientific statement'.

In *History of English Thought in the Eighteenth Century*, Stephen's subject was the emergence of a secular culture, free from theological assumptions and controls. English literature was discussed in these terms, the Reformation being seen as a preliminary and the culmination being contemporary literature's abandonment of supernatural Christianity.

History of English Thought in the Eighteenth Century discussed its subject in the shadow of the 'Almighty's retirement behind second causes' and asked 'how order could be preserved when the old sanctions were decaying'. It showed Protestantism acting as a 'screen for rationalism' and 'rationalism expressing itself in terms of Protestantism', and described the Cartesian, Spinozistic and Humean processes by which the 'God of philosophy' had become divorced from the 'God of Christianity'.

Stephen wanted the God of philosophy to prevail; he was averse to the God of Christianity. But his story was complicated and dealt mainly with attempts to marry the two. Behind the expository sympathy that he displayed for the writers he was expounding, his conclusion was that 'Jehovah' could not be equated with 'Nature', that miraculous Christianity could not be reconciled with reason, and that rational Christianity was an illusion arising from the love of compromise which the English had inherited from Locke's *Reasonableness of Christianity* .

In volume i of *History of English Thought in the Eighteenth Century*, the centre of Stephen's story was a paradox – that, except where they had disparaged reason, the advocates of Orthodoxy had expressed 'deist opinions in old-fashioned phraseology' and had objected to Deism only because the Deists were refusing to put 'new wine' into the 'old bottles'. 'Christianity of this kind' went the judgment on one of Christianity's weaker protagonists, was like 'a ship ready for launching, knock out a single bolt, and the whole structure would glide into the deep waters of infidelity'.

Stephen's argument was the Tractarian argument – that the eighteenth-century battle had been a bogus battle, that the 'intellectual' party in the Church of England had been only 'nominally Trinitarian', and that even the defenders of Christianity had shared the assumption of Gibbon and the 'infidel' historians that the Gospels should be placed 'in the same rank as the histories of Tacitus and Thucydides'. At the end of the volume Anglican emptiness was left under sentence of death from Wesley and Paine, Kant and Coleridge, Science and Democracy, and the Romantic and Victorian revivals of religion.

History of English Thought in the Eighteenth Century was a powerful book which dealt at length with all the main eighteenth-century thinkers. It was also the projection of an experience, the exposure of a compromise and an attempt to destroy the edifice of Christian thought.

In deducing an obligation both to pursue truth and to express his 'real opinions' about Christianity, Stephen recognized that a 'terrible ... agony might be involved' and that a decent reserve would be needed in approaching both the 'masses' and the 'weaker brethren' in the faith. No free-thinking book more obviously required a constructive parallel.

The first constructive parallel that Stephen provided was 'literature' through which, in the future, 'men of genius' like Dante and Shakespeare would effect changes in public sentiment, and in relation to which *Hours in a Library, The English Utilitarians* and *Studies of a Biographer* were his major contributions. The second constructive parallel was *An Agnostic's Apology* which was published as a book in 1893. The third was *The Science of Ethics*, which, though published a decade earlier, explained better than *An Agnostic's Apology* the nature and limitations of the sociological doctrine which Stephen wished to substitute for Christianity.

The main aim of *An Agnostic's Apology* was to draw an agnostic conclusion from the Orthodox claim that the unassisted intellect knew nothing about God's nature. In drawing lessons from the victory which Christianity had won over paganism in the Roman Empire, it repeated Mill's belief that 'the man who would abandon the old doctrines' in the nineteenth century had to 'stand alone' as Christians had done in the third century, and that there was as great a difference in the nineteenth century as there had been then between the 'philosophy' of the élite and the need which the masses had for 'religion'.

In explaining which religion would appeal to the 'masses', Stephen became coy and agnostic. He superimposed on the religious crisis a crisis in relations between rich and poor but left it uncertain what sort of creed would speak to it, half-arguing that it could be spoken to best through the 'museums and theatres' which were replacing churches as repositories of public devotion.

An Agnostic's Apology was constructive intellectually but not sociologically. It was only in *The Science of Ethics* that the new religion, the indefeasibility of science and the complexity of the social crisis were connected in order to produce an ethical sociology.

The Science of Ethics explained that there was a gap between ordinary minds and leading minds and between the 'cultivated classes' and 'the mob'. It showed little respect for 'ordinary minds' and the superstitions of the 'vulgar' who 'cared little ... for speculative truth' but expressed equally little doubt that they constituted a danger which could not be ignored. In particular, it argued that duty had to be done and the passions of the poor 'sanctified' even when God, Hell and the devil had been abandoned.

Stephen, while wanting to keep the lower classes quiet, wanted to do this in sincerity and truthfulness and believed that no creed could be important unless the 'faith of the few was ... stimulated by the adhesion of the many'. The question he raised was how 'the many' could be impressed once the 'old husk of dead faith' had been thrown off and men had emerged into the 'blaze of the day' with the 'full use of their limbs'.

In *The Science of Ethics*, Stephen acknowledged debts to Darwin, Hume, Bentham, Lewes, Spencer and the Mills and to the 'doctrine of evolution' in the forms in which it had been adopted by 'modern men of science'. He arrived quickly at the principle that sociology was necessary because the only binding morality was the morality of 'the race'.

Stephen was an eclectic altruist; if he did not dismiss sin, he deprived it of theological terror and discerned in the individual character a natural sympathy from which the morality of the race could be deduced. The individual was the 'product of the race', the race was the 'sum of individuals', and in considering the morality of races, Stephen based himself on what he called the 'most characteristic postulate of modern speculation' – that, since 'the laws ... of society ... could be studied apart from those of the individual atom', the central subject of a scientific ethic was the nature of the 'social tissue'.

In *The Science of Ethics* there was 'constant competition' between 'different parts of the race' and a 'struggle for existence' leading to 'extermination'. But the salient points were that States, Churches and 'industrial bodies' were not ultimate organisms and did not form the 'social tissue', and that the family was the ultimate organism because it depended on basic and primitive 'instincts', 'beyond all comparison the most vitally connected with the happiness of the individual ... and the ... cohesion in virtue of which society became possible'.

In relation to Christianity Stephen was an eroder. In relation to society, he was so far from being an eroder that *The Science of Ethics* blew on dissidence, praised patriotic solidarity and avoided the subversive virtue which had been so strong and insinuating a feature of Mills' sociology.

Stephen was unperceptive about coercion, his interest to a fault being in silent cohesion. He thought of morality as a 'vast induction' whose rules were 'external' to the individual and became his 'internal law' only when his conscience identified duty with the 'public spirit of the race'. But no reader of *The Science of Ethics* can miss the Kiplingesque resistance to naive individualism or the belief that 'in order to be an efficient part of the social organisation ... at a given stage of development', the individual had to acquire 'instincts, qualities or customs' which 'corresponded to the conditions of existence' of the society concerned and summarized 'part of the qualities in virtue of which it had become possible'.

In laying the foundations for morality, Stephen argued that an ontological underpinning was as irrelevant as a theological underpinning. The problem *The Science of Ethics* can scarcely be said to have resolved was the problem which Mill had wrestled with unhappily in *A System of Logic* – whether Utilitarianism could be based on 'propositions about the relations of men to each other' which would be as independent and incontrovertible as the propositions of the physical sciences.

Stephen's answer was that he felt happier giving a 'scientific' account of what had been judged morally right in the past than in deducing moral principles from metaphysical reflection. This tactic was designed, no doubt, to avoid the accusation of arbitrariness. Its effect was to reduce the 'science of ethics' to history, to imply that all thought must be historical, and, in presenting moral opinions as instances of the 'general law of evolution', to achieve an arbitrary conservatism which took past and existing moral systems as the only basis for morality. A passage from the conclusion to *The Science of Ethics* put the position starkly:

It is sometimes said that science cannot provide a new basis of morality: and this is urged as though it were an objection. I at least must thoroughly accept the statement. What science proves, according to me, is precisely that the only basis of morality is the old basis; it shows that one and the same principle has always determined the development of morality, although it has been stated in different phraseology. And, moreover, this principle is not the suggestion of any end distinct from all others. The great forces which govern human conduct are the same that they always have been and always will be. The dread of hunger, thirst, and cold; the desire to gratify the passions; the love of wife and child or friend; sympathy with the sufferings of our neighbours; resentment of injury inflicted upon ourselves – these and such as these are the great forces which govern mankind. When a moralist tries to assign anything else as an ultimate motive, he is getting beyond the world of realities.

Stephen was not much of a philosopher, and *The Science of Ethics* was not well received when it was published. But it expressed a hope, and embodied an aspiration, leading to the belief that, though agnosticism was right, God's existence need not be doubted since for 'modern' men Spinoza's God was 'all reality'.

Stephen's best work was a contribution to the attempt to replace a supernatural by a human morality which was made in the 1870s not only in Sidgwick's *Methods of Ethics* and Bradley's *Ethical Studies*, which abandoned Christianity without discussing it, but also in Morley's *On Compromise* and Reade's *The Martyrdom of Man* which were not so cautious.

Morley was a contemporary of Samuel Butler and Thomas Hardy as well as of Reade. But Butler, though as obviously an enemy of existing types of Christianity as F. W. Newman had been, was ultimately as ambiguous, while Hardy, though pagan by implication, was not explicitly pagan before the 1890s, and did not really commit himself until *The Dynasts* began to be published in 1904.

II

Three years after entering parliament in 1883, Morley[1] was made Irish Secretary in Gladstone's third government. He then became a Gladsto-

---

[1] John Morley (1838–1923). Educ. Cheltenham College and Lincoln College, Oxford. Editor of *Fortnightly Review* 1867–82, M.P. 1883–95 and 1896–1908, Peerage 1908, Liberal Minister 1886, 1892–5 and 1906–14. Author of *Modern Characteristicks* 1865, *Studies in Conduct* 1867, *Edmund Burke* 1867, *Critical Miscellanies* 1871–1908 etc., *Voltaire* 1872, *Rousseau* 2 vols. 1873, *The Struggle for National Education* 1873, *On Compromise* 1874, *Diderot and the Encyclopaedists* 2 vols. 1878, *Burke* 1879, *The Life of Richard Cobden* 2 vols. 1881, *Emerson* 1884, *Walpole* 1889, *Studies in Literature* 1890, *Machiavelli* 1897, *Oliver Cromwell* 1900, *Life of Gladstone* 3 vols. 1903, *Literary Essays* 1906, *Notes on Politics and History* 1913, *Recollections* 2 vols, 1917.

nian, bringing to the service of the cause an unusual combination of vanity, testiness, temper, responsibility, doctrine, dignity and intellectual culture. In the following thirty years he played an important part in maintaining the Ark of one at least of the intellectual Covenants on which Gladstonianism rested. His *Life of Gladstone* sold over a hundred and thirty thousand copies in the decade after it was published in 1903. His resignation from Asquith's Cabinet on the declaration of war in 1914 was a symbolic announcement that Gladstonianism could not cope with the twentieth century.

Morley kept up his literary career after he became a front-bench politician, continuing to edit *English Men of Letters* and breaking new ground with a new series entitled *Twelve English Statesmen* and an edition of Wordsworth's *Complete Poetical Works*. With the exception of *Walpole, Oliver Cromwell*, the *Life of Gladstone*, a new version of *Burke* and the two volumes of *Recollections* that he published in 1917, however, almost everything of importance that he wrote was written during his fifteen-year collaboration with Frederic Harrison which began when he, Morley, succeeded Lewes as editor of the *Fortnightly Review* in 1867.

III

Harrison[1] was seven years older than Morley. Until his marriage he was also a great deal richer, coming from a City family which lived in London and at Sutton Place, Guildford. Harrison's father was a High Churchman. Harrison was at King's College School, London, at the same time as Liddon, and was a sacramental neo-Catholic before becoming an undergraduate and briefly a Fellow of Wadham College,

---

[1] Frederic Harrison (1831–1923). Educ. King's College School, London, and Wadham College, Oxford. Fellow of Wadham 1854–6. Called to bar at Lincoln's Inn 1858, Member of Royal Commission on Trades Unions 1867–9, *Times* Special Correspondent in France 1877, President of English Positivist Committee 1880–1905, Home Rule candidate for London University 1886, London County Council Alderman 1888. Author of *Order and Progress* 1875, translator (joint) of Comte's *System of Positive Polity* 4 vols. 1875–9, *Martial Law in Kabul* 1880, *The Choice of Books* 1886, *Oliver Cromwell* 1888, *New Calendar of Great Men* 1892, *Annals of an Old Manor House* 1893, *The Meaning of History* 1894, *Studies in Early Victorian Literature* 1895, *William the Silent* 1897, *Tennyson, Ruskin, Mill* 1899, *George Washington and Other American Addresses* 1901, *John Ruskin* 1902, *Byzantine History in the Early Middle Ages* 1902, *Theophano* 1904, *Chatham* 1905, *The Philosophy of Common Sense* 1907, *The Creed of a Layman* 1907, *Autobiographic Memoirs* 2 vols. 1911, *Among My Books* 1912, *The Positive Evolution of Religion* 1913, *The German Peril* 1915.

Oxford, where he met Richard Congreve, who at that time was a Fellow of Wadham and an Anglican clergyman.

As an undergraduate Harrison absorbed Mill's *System of Logic* and Spencer's *First Principles*. As a young lawyer in London he read a great deal of science, soaked himself in Comte and asked for and obtained an interview with Comte in Paris. He knew or read Greg, Holyoake, Beesly, J. H. Bridges and Cotter Morison, as well as Lewes, Spencer, George Eliot, F. W. Newman and Mackay. On renewing his acquaintance with Congreve who had by then abandoned the Church of England, he became a Positivist. Though he followed Lafitte rather than Congreve during the rift which occurred in the Positivist Church in the 1870s, he remained a Positivist for the rest of his life and, along with Beesly, Bridges, Congreve and Cotter Morison, was the leading English advocate of the Positivist religion.

Harrison wrote about and helped to translate Comte. He also wrote books about *Cromwell, Chatham*, and *William the Silent*, about *Alfred the Great*, and about *Ruskin*. In *Order and Progress* he probed the 'rottenness and dilapidation of old institutions' and sketched the republican polity of the future in which neither 'personal Authority' nor the 'popular will' would predominate, and the modern statesman would be the 'servant of the people' in the limited sense in which the Pope was the servant of the people. In *The Creed of a Layman* he made one of the clearest statements that English Positivism was to achieve of the need for the anti-Christian assault to transcend the agnosticism, pantheism, atheism and materialism into which it was in danger of falling.

Harrison began public life in 1860 with a *Westminster Review* article in which he attacked *Essays and Reviews*; in the course of his life he made many criticisms of the Erastian disingenuousness of latitudinarianism, the 'world of evasion' which was to be found in the 'advanced theology of Anglican divines' and the absurdity of the belief that Christianity could be defended by combining *profession* of belief with disbelief in the Bible, the Creeds and the Thirty-Nine Articles.

Like Morley, Harrison had a Tractarian sense of the duties of intellectuals and the significance of literature, and made it his own duty to announce the death of Christianity. Where Stephen was vague and Morley contentless about the religion of the future, he specified the nature of the religion that Christianity was to be replaced by.

Harrison expressed a fervent belief in both English patriotism and the unity of mankind, and a fervent disbelief in Imperialism. He identified the Religion of Humanity with the political effort to control industrialism and bring the poor within the framework of the nation. But his Religion of Humanity, so far from being merely political, aimed to provide modern means of sanctifying, or moralizing, the whole of life.

Unlike the latitudinarians, Harrison had no wish to insert new meanings into historic Christian doctrine. His view was that since Christian doctrine had been made anachronistic by science, the religious problem was to address the emotions in a language which did not conflict with science. In the secular versions that he proposed of the Christian doctrines of baptism, confirmation, marriage and death, and in the secular services which were held in Positivist churches under his auspices, he showed how Positivism could supply a wholesale replacement not only of the doctrines but also of the rituals of Christianity.

Harrison reflected, and was consciously indebted to, his High-Church upbringing and to the imaginative structure which he sensed in Tractarianism and Roman Catholicism. He was a High-Church Positivist in exactly the way in which Tyndall was a Protestant Pantheist, and it would be easy to ridicule the evacuation of meaning which accompanied the transition from a dogmatically based Christianity to a dogmatically based Positivism.

Such ridicule would be appropriate if the movement of thought which Harrison embodied had died with his death in 1923. Certainly the Positivist Church, if it had ever been more, had already by then become a relic. But by an irony which is never lacking in the historical process, *The Creed of a Layman* stated with the articulateness of conviction opinions about life, death and the Service of Humanity which, with conviction or without, may be found lurking coyly and unsystematically in the framework of many more twentieth-century minds than would care to be reminded of their provenance.

English Positivism, in the ritualistic and ecclesiastical forms of which Harrison was the advocate, made few converts and deserves little attention. Harrison deserves attention not only because he expressed a mood which has survived, but also because he supported Morley financially during Morley's early years as a journalist, was Morley's intellectual ally in the period of Morley's most impressive output, and helped to make the *Fortnightly Review* the leading organ of political Radicalism and religious reorganization.

Like Harrison's, Morley's political doctrine involved the reconstruction of the whole of life. It was arrived at early and was never entirely abandoned, even when political success had softened the edges of his doctrine, blurred his enmities and emasculated his prose. In early Morley, the edges had been sharp, antagonisms had been strong and enmities had been at the ready. They had been particularly ready to assist at the downfall of aristocracy and Christianity.

When he first appeared as a public figure, Morley admired Cobden and Bright on the one hand, and Huxley, Spencer, Lewes, George Eliot and Mill on the other. During his fifteen years as editor of the *Fortnightly Review* he created a composite position which had mainly tactical affiliations with Nonconformity and aimed to capture, and use, the Liberal party in pursuit of a Comtean revolution.

Morley's mother was a Wesleyan; his father was a doctor of Wesleyan family who attended the parish church as a general practitioner in Blackburn. Morley was at school at Cheltenham and at Lincoln College, Oxford, where, in addition to Mill, Spencer and Comte, he was eventually affected by Darwin. An undistinguished undergraduate career was cut short by a quarrel with his father arising in part from Morley's loss of belief in Christianity and unwillingness to be ordained. After a period of private teaching, he began to earn a living in London as a journalist.

In experiencing a religious crisis in early manhood, Morley followed a pattern that was common in his generation. He was typical in finding in public doctrine a substitute for the religion in which he had been brought up. By the time he arrived in London, journalism had taken the place which might have been taken by ordination.

As a journalist in the 1860s, Morley entertained literary ambitions but regarded journalism and literature as preparations for parliament. We owe the distinction of his political writing to the fact that, though he stood for parliament first when he was thirty, he did not enter parliament until he was forty-five, and passed the intervening years producing a more far-reaching statement of modern Radicalism than he would have produced if he had entered parliament earlier.

In the 1860s Morley's ground was the need to make parliament respond to a 'revived national earnestness'. His argument was that even the most democratic suffrage would be useless unless Whiggery was extirpated and the working classes persuaded to follow Culture's lead in completing the work which the French Revolution had begun.

Morley believed in the Revolution's contemporaneity. He treated it as an 'uprising against the middle ages', as the doom of the class and dynastic system which had preceded it and as an attempt to replace the 'decaying order' of feudalism and Catholicism by a new order which had not yet been established at the point at which he was writing. He assumed that the new order was right and probably irresistible, and he treated Burke's *Reflections* and writings in the 1790s as illegitimate attempts to resist it.

In *Burke* Morley conceded the Terror and recognized that it had been a disaster. But he did not concede Burke's explanation. The Revolution's atrocities had been 'invisible' compared with the atrocities of 'churchmen and kings' and Rousseau could no more be held responsible for the one than Christ could be held responsible for the other. It was the old régime which had failed in sympathy and the Jacobins who represented a movement 'as truly spiritual as that of Catholicism and Calvinism'.·

Morley had Comtean doubts about the 'absolutist' conceptions and traces of 'deductive method' that he found in the *philosophes*. But the 'supremacy of the natural order', the application of 'comparative method' to social institutions and the foundation of 'scientific history and political economy' were acclaimed for establishing the 'modern principle' that 'productive industry' was more important than asceticism or war. The Revolution itself in the eighty years since it had begun was credited with effecting what Cobden was to be credited with in the *Life of Cobden* – the translation of the 'revolutionary watchword of the Fraternity of Peoples' into the 'true Conservatism of modern societies'.

This was a doctrine about history, and Morley made numerous pronouncements about historical method, the contribution which Comte and Mill had made to defining it and his contemporaries' failure to pursue it. In practice, however, these pronouncements were theoretical. So far from achieving the sociological history that they specified, Morley's history was a history of thought which assumed simple connections between the history of the intelligentsia and the history of the masses, and, in tracing the linear course of human development, pursued methods that were as literary as they were scientific.

In identifying himself as a man-of-letters, Morley characterized literature's 'loftier masters', like the 'loftier masters' of 'every other channel of ... aesthetic culture', as 'priests' who created 'ideal ... shapes' out of a 'predominant system and philosophy'. This was the sense in which Shakespeare, Milton and Burke had exemplified feudalism, Protestantism and Whiggism, Byron the 'weariness' of the 'revolutionary' in the most conservative country in the world, and *Sartor Resartus* the 'reverence' and 'earnestness' which England had experienced since Byron's death. It was in the shadow of this Pantheon that Morley exemplified that resistance to the 'dogmatic temper' which was to underpin the religion of the future.

IV

In his first public discussions of religion Morley had shown off his Comtean sense of the importance of 'organization' and a 'common spiritual faith and doctrine'. It was through discussion of Comte that he was led into discussion of De Maistre, Bonald and Chateaubriand, and to the conclusion that, though Comteanism was to be the religion of the future, Ultramontanism had been the only serious religion in the past.

Morley was conscious of a contrast between the Comtean assumption that significant religion meant Catholicism and the English assumption that it meant Protestantism, and he drew the Tractarian conclusion that the Comtean assumption was right. In Protestantism he discerned many attractive features. But whatever he may have said after he became an M. P., in the 1870s he was unflattering, dismissing the Protestant view of God, seeing the Reformation as an 'emancipation' rather than 'an engine of spiritual regeneration' and contrasting it to its disadvantage with Bossuet's 'profound view of the nature of social development'. It was because Catholicism had had what Protestantism was alleged never to have had – a comprehensive conception of the social function of belief – that it was Catholicism which the religion of the future would resemble most, and it was because France was a Catholic country that Rousseau and the *philosophes* had been able to effect the most significant mental transformation since the fall of the Roman Empire.

Morley sneered at the 'paraphernalia' of 'dogma and mystery', and at Christianity's failure to make 'brotherhood' universal. He assumed that Christianity had been relevant to an age that was past, had been most relevant to the backwardness of Byzantium and had rendered its greatest service, as Turgot had ironically observed, to natural religion.

Morley disliked 'effeminacy and pedantry' while inserting a feminist element into the loathing of the 'man-of-the-world' which he had borrowed from Newman. He was against the 'mimetic rites' of Tractarianism, the 'romping heroics' of 'muscular Christianity' and the 'monstrous flood of sour cant' which had emerged from Puritanism and

Evangelicalism. Latitudinarianism, however, he disliked even more, preferring George Eliot's decision to 'do without opium', denying that 'honest doubt had more faith than all your creeds' and finding in 'rational certainty' a 'narrow' land from which to view the 'vast order' that 'stretched out unknown before it'.

Morley believed that 'good natures' displayed sympathy 'extremely early' and could be led readily to subvert the aristocracy of sex as well as the aristocracy of birth. This was the task of the Religion of Humanity and it indicated the task of the 'modern instructor' – to teach the 'voiceless ... unnumbered millions' to think for themselves about a universe from which the Gods had departed.

Morley assumed that eighteenth-century society had needed a new religion and that Voltaire, Diderot and Rousseau had done more than the Jesuits to provide it. To the question, what relevance had this for England, his answer was given in *On Compromise* and *The Struggle for National Education*.

The Struggle for National Education was a statement of the brittle and mistrustful Radicalism of which Joseph Chamberlain had become leader in the course of the 1868 parliament. In instancing Forster, Gladstone and the Education Act of 1870 as proof of the Liberal Party's conservatism, it explained why the Church of England needed to be dethroned.

Morley's reasons for wishing to dethrone the Church of England were the reasons he supposed the *philosophes* had had for wishing to dethrone the Church in France – that 'the tendencies of civilization' demanded it, that ecclesiastical predominance in an Erastian régime destroyed freedom while state predominance destroyed spirituality and that refusal to recognize the principle of 'the free church in the free state' obstructed that exercise of responsibility which was characteristic of a modern mentality.

In *The Struggle for National Education*, Morley adopted the Nonconformist as well as the Comtean version of 'the free church in the free state'. There was a tension between the two, however, and he left the impression of using a Nonconformist principle to replace Nonconformity by 'secular integrity'. This was what Morley stood for in the 1870s – the demand to stand up and be counted against Christianity, and his position, as it was explained in *On Compromise*, depended on the assumption that in some respects the Gladstonian Liberal Party was as much its enemy as the Conservative Party and the Church of England.

On Compromise was a work of responsible Radicalism, teaching that conscience should assist at the march which progress would make into the future, while incorporating both the Burkean and the Comtean antipathy to violent revolution. It recognized that conscience needed the interposition of time and the preparation of opinion if it was to be effective, and that a struggle was going on in which Rousseau, the *philosophes*, the Ultramontanes and the Tractarians had been on the right side, and 'men of the world', 'practical men' and the 'political spirit' had been on the wrong side.

The 'political spirit' was an historical phenomenon, a patriotic conception and a term of abuse. Morley associated it with the 'lack of imagination', 'robust ... sense' and mistrust of 'theory' characteristic of the English mind in the past, along with the sluggishness, philistinism and 'accommodation with error' that the English were displaying in the present. He represented it as a mentality which feared 'enquiry', 'economised' with Truth and encouraged the 'enlightened classes' to profess beliefs which they had ceased to believe in because they judged them 'useful' for 'less fortunate people'. The political spirit, indeed, was a threat, and *On Compromise* explained that the 'House of Commons view of life' could 'never be useful', that relations between the enlightened classes and the mass of the people should be conducted without guile and that the only remedy for a religious 'void' was for 'honest and fearless' men to march 'with firm step and erect front' on the way to standing up to be counted.

What those who stood up had to be counted against in *On Compromise* was not only Christian dogma but also the 'triumph of the political method in things spiritual'. In this respect, Morley argued, there were no half-way houses and failure to adopt categorical positions would involve a 'futile' intrusion of Anglican fudging into an area where fudging was inappropriate.

Morley aimed to destroy orthodox Christianity, but claimed for the new religion that he was propagating as close a relationship to Christianity as Christianity had had to Judaism. In drawing parallels with the rôle played by the 'Christianizing Jew' in the development of the 'moral and spiritual truth that lay hidden in the primitive Church', he denied that he was 'reconciling the irreconcileable' or turning the dogmas of the Church into 'good friends' of 'history and criticism'. His point was that patience in dealing with dogma would create a state of mind in which dogma's impossibility would become 'spontaneously

visible' and 'even those who held fast to Christianity' would admit that
the Christianity of the future would have to do without it.

Morley's religion, as he explained it in the 1870s, was a religion of
sincerity. But he was as sensitive as Stephen to the dangers of sincerity,
and did his best to allay fears that it might lead to revolution. There
was, he wrote, 'no instance in history ... of ... mere opinion making a
breach in the essential constitution of a community so long as the
political position was stable and the economic and nutritive conditions
sound,' and it was safe, therefore, he implied, for 'unbelievers and
doubters' to 'speak out' since Christianity could perfectly well be
replaced while property and dividends were preserved. One passage is
typical of many that appeared in Morley's writing in the 1870s.

What is this smile of the world [he asked in Chapter IV of *On Compromise*] to
win which we are bidden to sacrifice our moral manhood; this frown of the
world, whose terrors are more awful than the withering up of truth and the
slow going out of light within the souls of us? Consider the triviality of life and
conversation and purpose, in the bulk of those whose approval is held out for
our prize and the mark of our high calling. Measure, if you can, the empire
over them of prejudice unadulterated by a single element of rationality, and
weigh, if you can, the huge burden of custom, unrelieved by a single leavening
particle of fresh thought. Ponder the share which selfishness and love of ease
have in the vitality and the maintenance of the opinions that we are forbidden
to dispute. Then how pitiful a thing seems the approval or disapproval of these
creatures of the conventions of the hour, as one figures the merciless vastness
of the universe of matter sweeping us headlong through viewless space; as one
hears the wail of misery that is for ever ascending to the deaf gods; as one
counts the little tale of the years that separate us from eternal silence. In the
light of these things, a man should surely dare to live his small span of life with
little heed of the common speech upon him or his life, only caring that his days
may be full of reality, and his conversation of truth-speaking and wholeness.

On Compromise was a significant book and Morley a significant thinker
who played as important a rôle as Gladstone in keeping Liberalism out of
the hands of philistine dissent. Neither *On Compromise* nor the *Fortnightly Review* made as significant or far-reaching an attack, however, as
Reade made on the nature, claims and truth of Christianity.

V

Reade was born in 1838, was at Oxford in the late 1850s and, after
leaving without a degree, wrote two novels and a history of the Druids.

Like Samuel Butler he was much affected by *The Origin of Species* and made his first journey to Africa in 1862 on a Darwinian investigation. Having qualified as a doctor on his return to England, he spent most of the rest of his short life travelling in Africa. By the time of his death in 1875 he had written a couple more novels, a couple more scientific-travel books, and a book about the Ashanti Campaign of 1873 which he had covered as Correspondent for *The Times*.

Most of Reade's books were unsuccessful and are of no great importance, even *See-Saw* – a novel about Protestantism and Roman Catholicism – being eminently neglectable. What should not be neglected are *The Outcast* and *The Martyrdom of Man*.

The Outcast was a novel in the form of fourteen letters. It began with a young man of the landed classes committing suicide as a result of the doubt and despair he had acquired about God, first from Malthus and Darwin, then from the death of his young wife. The main letters discussed the letter-writer's own life, the effect of Lyell's *Principles of Geology* in disengaging him from the priesthood twenty years earlier and the loss of faith, cultural dilapidation and anger against God he had experienced when his own wife had died subsequently. The concluding letters recorded what Reade wished to say about the impossibility of knowing anything about God except through the 'natural laws which governed the earth'.

The Outcast was written when Reade was dying, and was published after his death. It was narrow and subjective, and its ethical earnestness reeked. In *The Martyrdom of Man* three years earlier, he had given one of the most explicit accounts that were to be given in nineteenth-century England of the damage which Christianity had done to the progress of the world.

The Martyrdom of Man was divided into four chapters – entitled 'War', 'Religion', 'Liberty' and 'Intellect' – and illustrated by examples from most of the world and most periods of world-history. Its doctrine was at once Malthusian, Comtean and Darwinian, and acknowledged a list of authorities which reads like a roll-call of Christianity's assailants. For three-quarters of the way, its subject was the place of 'Negroland or Inner Africa' in Universal History and the naturalistic explanation through which Universal History was to be understood. Religion appeared as a form of poetry, a guide to government and a continuation of war by other means. Its origins were found in 'dreams' and 'indigestion', in savage social organization and in a servile courtiership which was 'by no means inviting ... to the ... European mind'.

The 'number and arrangement' of the gods of the past were explained in terms of the conditions in which they had been conceived and their 'moral dispositions' in terms of the people by whom they had been created, and wherever an 'intellectual and learned' class had been differentiated from an 'illiterate and degraded' one, two religions were said to have emerged – or two versions of the same religion – a 'creed' for the 'ordinary man' to place his 'deluded faith' in and a 'suspension of doubt and judgment' for 'minds of the highest order'.

In the main chapters of *The Martyrdom of Man* Reade contextualized Moses and Jesus, explaining Moses in terms of a conflict between Egyptian and Bedouin culture and Jesus as a 'man of the people' who had taken the part of the 'outcast and oppressed' and had condemned 'all the rich and almost all the learned' to 'eternal torture'. Though it was not the case that Jesus had 'ceased to wash' and had 'skipped about ... like a goat' on receiving his mission, he had resembled the prophets who had done this and, though as superior to them as Newton was to Ptolemy, had shared the 'hallucination' of supposing himself 'appointed to prepare the world ... for God's kingdom ... on earth'.

In describing the rise and development of Christianity, Reade employed the Darwinian idea of 'natural selection' preparing Europe for the 'one-God species of belief'. Early Christianity was described as an 'heroic age' in which Christians had been 'missionaries' who 'believed much' and whose lives had been 'beautified' by 'sympathy and love' and Constantine as the Nero of the Bosphorus who had made Christianity into a 'concubine' of the State and a 'creature of the crown' and at the Council of Nicea had given episcopal ignorance the opportunity to define 'that which had never existed.'

About the impact of Islam on Africa, Reade was more sympathetic than about the impact of Christianity on Europe. But his Mahomet was as problematical as his Jesus and ultimately as ambiguous, the prophetic purity of his early teaching being submerged in an 'inordinate self-conceit' and his 'gospel of the sword' being the agency by which slavery had been brought to Africa.

In the chapter entitled 'Intellect', Reade gave an account of the material Utopia that would be established by electricity, synthetic food-production and the conquest of space, and of the abolition of slavery as an incident in the 'rebellion against authority' which had begun in the Middle Ages and would culminate in the abolition of the 'tyranny of religious creeds' in the Utopia of the future.

The Utopia that Reade envisaged was primarily a material Utopia based on obedience to Nature's laws. But it was also a moral Utopia in which, for the first time, men would 'worship the Divinity that lay within them' and 'obey the Laws that were written in their hearts'.

As to whether Christianity's destruction was necessary in the interests of morality, Reade made three points – that the 'great laws of morality' were perennial, that the 'Christian conception of God' was immoral and that the 'destruction of Christianity' was therefore 'essential to civilization'. In answer to the question which Morley and Stephen asked – whether it was right to inflict the pain which would be inflicted by 'publishing the truth' about Christianity – he replied that Christianity was true only for 'uneducated people', was 'not in accordance with the cultivated mind' and was 'inadvertently adverse to morals' because it was 'adverse to intellectual freedom.

The Martyrdom of Man chased Christianity down every alley that it was to be found in. It identified 'animal heat' as 'solar heat', replaced God by the disintegrating Sun, and saw in the Sun's creation of life a 'glorious ... narrative' fit for scientists to discover and 'poets to portray'. It absorbed geology's destruction of Genesis and the cruelty of Darwinian Nature, and in explaining God as an 'ideal of man's mind', found theology's garrulousness about the origins of existence infinitely inferior to science's silence. In scientific observation of Nature it found a proper occupation for the 'imagination and the reason' and a 'unity of plan' in which 'moral' as well as 'physical' phenomena were 'subject to laws as invariable as those which regulated the rising and the setting of the sun'.

In treating Christianity as a 'scientific' question, Reade made three accusations – that a personal God was an impossibility, that Darwinian Nature could not have been the work of a benevolent God and that the Christian God who had created men for his own good, and permitted them to suffer pain, grief and disease, could not possibly have been a God of Love. Not only was 'Jesus a man' and the 'Old Testament miracles as insignificant as the Homeric miracles', but since man's soul was mortal and heaven and hell did not exist, worship of Jesus's God was 'idolatry', prayer 'useless' and Christianity's 'Syrian Book' a 'fetish of ink and paper'.

For Reade as for Mill the future was the crux, and about the future Reade's agnosticism was as unagnostic as Mill's. Not only were the European Gods destined to become as irelevant as the Gods of Olympus and the Nile, but the new religion which would expel them would stand as high above Christianity as Christianity had stood above the idolatry of Rome. 'In matters of religion', Reade wrote, 'there should be no deceit', and he used the 'clearest language he was able to command'. Christianity taught that 'reason ... be sacrificed upon the altar', that worship be given to a 'hideous image of dirt and blood' and that 'intolerable pride' and 'lickspittle humility' be made the basis of morality. The new religion would replace fear by love, connect the 'desire to do good' to the 'instinct of the human race' and 'unite ... the whole world' into a 'heavenly Commune in which ... men would give up all for mankind'. ·

I think you will admit [went one archetypal passage from *The Outcast*] that one may cease to believe in a Personal God and in the Immortality of the Soul, and yet not cease to be a good and even a religious man ... and that ... indeed, the ... Religion of Unselfishness for those who are able to embrace it, is far more ennobling than any religion which holds out the hope of celestial rewards.

We teach that the soul is immortal, [went a similar passage from *The Martyrdom of Man*] that there is a future life ... and ... that there is a Heaven in the ages far away; but not for us single corpuscles, not for us dots of animated jelly, but for the One of whom we are the elements, and who, though we perish, never dies, but ... by the united efforts of single molecules called men, or of those cell-groups called nations, is raised towards the Divine power which he will finally attain ... We teach that there is a God, but not a God of the anthropoid variety, not a God who is gratified by compliments ... and whose attributes can be catalogued by theologians. God is so great that he cannot be defined by us ... and ... does not deign to have personal relations with ... us ... Those who desire to worship their Creator must worship him through mankind ... To do that which deserves to be written, to write that which deserves to be read, to tend the sick, to comfort the sorrowful, to animate the weary, to keep the temple of the body pure, to cherish the divinity within us, to be faithful to the intellect, to educate those powers which have been entrusted to our charge and to employ them in the service of humanity, that is ... the only true religion.

The Martyrdom of Man was as ill-received on publication as *The Science of Ethics*, but went through many editions in the years that followed. If it was arrested more clearly than less powerful books at the opinions of the milieu from which it emerged, that does not make it the less remarkable. Reade caught an argument and a mood – the argument and mood of the 1870s – drove them through an immense subject-matter and achieved a certainty and coherence which stands comparison with the certainty and coherence of *On Compromise, First*

Principles and Buckle's *History of Civilization*. In doing so he made the sharpest statement yet made of the assumptions from which the next generation of Christianity's assailants was to disengage itself completely.

III

THE ASSAULT ON CHRISTIANITY IN THE TWENTIETH CENTURY

8

The Revision of Ethical Earnestness I

'Anthropologists have shown us what this Pagan Man really is. From the West Coast of Africa to the Pacific Isles ... he meets us, with the old gaiety, the old crowns of flowers, the night-long dances, the phallus-bearing processions, the untroubled vices. We feel, no doubt, a charm in his simple and instinctive life, in the quick laughter and equally quick tears, the directness of action, the un-hesitating response of sympathy. We must all of us have wished from time to time that our friends were more like Polynesians; especially those of us who live in University towns. And I think, in a certain limited sense, the Greeks probably were so. But in the main ... the Greek and the Pagan are direct opposites. That instinctive Pagan has a strangely weak hold on life. He is all beset with terror and blind cruelty and helplessness. The Pagan Man is really the unregenerate human animal, and Hellenism is a collective name for the very forces which, at the time under discussion, strove for his regeneration. Yet ... one of the most characteristic things about Hellenism is that, though itself the opposite of savagery, it had savagery always near it. The peculiar and essential value of Greek civilization lies not so much in the great height which it ultimately attained, as in the wonderful spiritual effort by which it reached and sustained that height.' Gilbert Murray *The Rise of the Greek Epic* 1907 p. 9.

'No doubt the higher moral effort of man in every nation will, for the great majority, express itself in the traditional religious conventions of that nation. Moral idealism in England will be for the most part Protestant, in Austria Catholic, in Turkey Moslem, in China Confucian or Buddhist. But in the more civilized communities, as in ancient Greece, there has always been a minority who ... have felt ... that the traditional frame of dogmas current about them did not present the exclusive truth, the necessary truth, or even any exact truth at all about the ultimate mysteries, and have tried to keep their sense of the duty of man towards his neighbour and his own highest powers clear of the confusing and sometimes perverting mythology on which it is traditionally said to be based.' Gilbert Murray *Stoic, Christian and Humanist* 1940 pp. 12–13.

'The problem of living a Christian life in an unChristian world is one with which the Churches have been familiar ever since they came into being. There is a similar problem facing the Liberal living in an illiberal world.' Gilbert Murray *Liberality and Civilization* 1938 p. 74.

In Part II we have examined the structure of thought at which Christianity's assailants had arrived by the 1880s and the use they made of the ubiquity of law and the impossibility of divine intervention in the regularity of Nature. We have seen Science being presented as the reflector of law through the investigation of Nature and historical criticism as a proof that Christianity lacked divine credentials. We have seen Christ converted into a man, Christianity demoted to being one religion among many and Christian theology presented as an anachronistic obstruction to evolution and the progress of knowledge. We have discussed the expectation that Christian morality could be retained without Christian theology and that naturalistic or subjective sanctions for morality could be made available once supernatural sanctions had been abandoned. And we have seen it affirmed that the abandonment of Christianity would not be allowed to liberate the poor and uneducated from the obedience into which they were alleged to have been inducted by Christian terror.

The thought that we have examined in Part II was in no way contemptible. It took seriously the challenge of history and science and responded intelligently to them. It declined to coerce them and called for elasticity in reacting to them. If it was not without its own style of Darwinian illusionlessness, its chief defect was the assumption that fanaticism and irrationality could be overcome by converting religion into poetry or a social doctrine, and by permitting ethical earnestness to carry humanity towards a problemless future. The thinkers we are about to discuss were as anti-Christian as the thinkers we have discussed so far and worked as hard as they did to provide a new doctrine to replace the doctrine which had been supplied by Christianity. But they wished it to be understood that doctrinal reconstruction would be more problematical than these thinkers had suspected, that the savage and primitive would be more persistent and irrationality more endemic than ethical earnestness had imagined and that more deliberate remedies would be needed if the subversion of Christianity was not to result in the subversion of society.

These shifts in opinion coincided with fear of working-class intentions under a democratic franchise and of the emasculation of culture which might arise from universal education, and with the attacks which historical and socialist economics were making on the finality of Political Economy. They produced the sexual and sociological postures which we know as decadence and the recessions from liberal or rational optimism which were represented by Nietzsche, Wagner, Schopenhauer, William James, Ibsen and Freud. In the thinkers who are to be discussed in Chapters 9 and 10, these cut so deep as to cause a landslide. In Frazer and Murray, who form the central subjects of this chapter, they produced mainly mule-like reassertions.

I

Murray[1] was of Irish, Welsh and Scottish extraction, and was born in Australia. His father – an Irish Roman Catholic with a second, Protestant, wife – was a landowning settler who had become rich, had narrowly avoided bankruptcy and, though an important politician, had died poor when Murray was seven. After early schooling in Australia, Murray moved with his mother to England where, like Mansel before him, he was at Merchant Taylors' and St John's College, Oxford. After a short period as a Fellow of New College, Oxford, he was appointed to the Chair of Greek at Glasgow at the of twenty-three. Twenty years later, in 1908, he was appointed to the Chair of Greek at Oxford which he retained until his retirement at the age of seventy in 1936.

In Glasgow and Oxford Murray found small but ready-made audi-

---

[1] Gilbert Murray (1866–1957). Educ. Merchant Taylors and St John's College, Oxford. Fellow of New College, Oxford, 1888–9 and 1905–8. Professor of Greek at Glasgow 1889–99, Regius Professor of Greek at Oxford 1908–36, Chairman of Executive of League of Nations Union 1923–38. Author of *A History of Ancient Greek Literature* 1897, *Carlyon Sahib* 1900, translations of Euripides, Sophocles, Aeschylus, Menander and Aristophanes 1902–56, *The Rise of the Greek Epic* 1907, *Four Stages of Greek Religion* 1912, *Euripides and His Age* 1913, *The Foreign Policy of Sir Edward Grey* 1915, *Faith, War and Policy* 1917, *Essays and Addresses* 1921, *Problems of Foreign Policy* 1921, *Five Stages of Greek Religion* 1925, *The Classical Tradition in Poetry* 1927, *The Ordeal of This Generation* 1929, ed. *The Oxford Book of Greek Verse* 1930, *Aristophanes* 1933, *Liberality and Civilization* 1938, *Stoic, Christian and Humanist* 1940, *Aeschylus* 1940, *Greek Studies* 1946, *From the League to the UN* 1946, *Hellenism and the Modern World* 1953, J. Smith and J. A. Toynbee (ed.) *Gilbert Murray: An Unfinished Autobiography* 1960.

ences. Elsewhere he created audiences for himself, through the publication and performance of his translations of Greek plays and through
books about Greek literature and religion and English and European
politics. Until well into his seventies he made a significant impact on
English thought and opinion and reflected important aspects of it. It
was only at the end of a writing life which went on until he was eighty-
nine that his Hellenism, Comteanism and post-Gladstonian Liberalism
became beleaguered relics in the unsympathetic world which had been
created by Lloyd George, T. S. Eliot, D. H. Lawrence, Stalin, Hitler
and Nasser.

Murray was a cricketer, tennis-player and mountaineer and shared
the late-Victorian devotion to physical exercise. He was neither
properly English nor Victorian middle class; his marriage to the
eldest daughter of the ninth Earl of Carlisle and the Earl's radical
teetotal wife just before he went to Glasgow, accentuated a commitment to radical causes which would probably have been expressed
at length whether he had married into an eccentric radical family or
not.

As a young man, Murray identified himself with Morley and Joseph
Chamberlain before 1886 and with Morley and Gladstone thereafter.
Having opposed British involvement in the Boer War, he supported the
1914 war and worked for H. A. L. Fisher, a colleague from New College, when Fisher became Minister of Education in the Lloyd George
government. From 1918 to 1923 Murray was Asquithean parliamentary candidate for the University of Oxford, being defeated on each
occasion by Oman and Lord Hugh Cecil. From 1918 onwards, along
with Lord Robert Cecil, he was one of the leading protagonists of the
League of Nations and the League of Nations Union, transcending in
their service the disappointment he was not alone in experiencing at the
Liberal Party's collapse in 1924.

II

Among Murray's earliest political writings was a contribution to the
volume entitled *Liberalism and the Empire* which he edited with Hammond and Hirst in 1900. Though he thought of standing for parliament
at this time, he decided against it, his interests up to 1914 being primarily literary, theatrical and academic. From 1914 onwards he spent two
and a half decades in intensive political activity as the earliest of the
essays that made up *Faith, War and Policy* were followed by *The*

Foreign Policy of Sir Edward Grey, Problems of Foreign Policy, The Ordeal of This Generation and *Liberality and Civilization*. In helping to capture the 1914 war for Liberalism, in analysing the damage that the war had done and in proposing remedies against recurrence, Murray converted the Liberal Party position, of which the events of 1918–24 had deprived him, into a supra-party position which he called *Liberality*.

For Murray the 1914 war was an evil; he repeated about it some of the ideas that he had expressed about the Boer War. In 1914, however, these ideas were directed against Prussian militarism rather than against British Imperialism, their premise being that the German people were not to blame and that Britain had taken the 'path of duty' against the 'force, fraud ... ruthlessness ... terrorism and mendacity' which were attributed to the Prussian government.

Murray was not only a radical, he was also a Democrat. In so far as the war had produced 'heroism' and 'self-sacrifice' and diminished class hatred, it confirmed his belief in Democracy. In so far as it had induced jingoistic hatred and the 'herd instinct', he judged it necessary to create instruments of 'conscious control' to prevent it recurring. In the 'fraternity of public right' advocated by Condorcet and the 'English Liberal statesmen of the nineteenth century' and the legitimist reaction in favour of a 'Concert pledged to make collective war upon the peacebreakers' in 1815, he supposed himself to have found instruments suitable for the purpose.

Murray had written about the possibility of a League of Nations in the course of opposing the Boer War. In time his conception of the League broadened. As the hopes of the 1920s became the fears of the 1930s, the League became the symbol of his judgment of Western society and civilization.

In sketching a politics for 'civilization', Murray was not always perceptive. He played down the Communist threat and predicted, just before the rural terror in Russia, that Russia must 'sooner or later settle down into a system of peasant proprietors'. On the other hand, in some respects he was as reactionary as Churchill, lamenting the 'degradation of political conduct' which had occurred since 1914 and calling for an attempt to get back to the standards of Macaulay, Cobden, Mill, Salisbury, Gladstone and Peel. Until Hitler began to loom, he aimed to show that the League of Nations could be used in the service of the British Empire, that it might prevent a war of the 'yellow, brown, red and black' races against the 'white or Christian' races and that this combination of uses could be justified by the fact that the machinery of world government was in the hands of 'those nations or groups of nations who were ... the least unworthy' to hold it. In *The Ordeal of This Generation* these positions were recommended to 'the young'.

The Ordeal of This Generation was a curious example of late-evolutionary thinking. It recognized fighting and killing as 'fundamental facts of life' and the 'soldier' and the 'fighting races' as making a deeper appeal to 'human instincts' than the merchant. But it stigmatized the romantic admiration for war as a hangover from primitive mentalities, argued that all civilized men practised an amount of discipline which was 'more than the moral equivalent' of the discipline required by war and concluded that the moral justification of the League was the encouragement it would give to the sort of 'ideal act of sacrifice' through which the soldier had become a 'hero' in the past.

Between the wars, Murray became self-consciously Victorian. He praised the Victorians for having been creative rather than critical and for having had an 'ideal dream of revolution'. He attacked the 'dirt ... and sensuality' which were obsessing 'modern writers' and discovered in the world about him a widespread pandering to the lowest taste in newspapers, the cinema, wireless, advertising, education and business. The reconstruction he envisaged was very different from the reconstruction envisaged by Strachey, Eliot, Huxley, Lawrence and the younger generations of post-Victorian rebels, reactionaries and Catholicizers by whom he felt himself threatened in the 1920s.

The Ordeal of This Generation, among other things, was a contribution to the electoral situation of 1929. *Liberality and Civilization* was an attempt to build up resistance to Hitler and Neville Chamberlain.

Liberality and Civilization expressed better than anything else that Murray wrote the quality and content of his politics. It situated itself at a 'crisis of civilization', was addressed to conditions in which the threat to 'conscious control' had become acute and proposed a way of thinking which could make conscious control effective.

What *Liberality* was, was 'the thing for the lack of which European civilization was perishing'. It was something that Gladstone had looked for, and for which Europeans in all countries were longing. It included 'freedom'. But it was not the same as 'democracy' or 'individualism' and its Spanish origin was played down in favour of a Roman origin 'derived from the Greek'. Liberality on this view indeed was 'not a doctrine'. It entertained variety of thought and discussion and appealed to the authorities and 'the multitude' alike to 'beseech themselves' that they 'might be mistaken'. Liberality was the enemy of fanaticism, injustice, falsehood, bad faith and persecution and, since it had also been the driving force behind Raphael, Newton, Einstein, Aeschylus and Shakespeare, it followed, Murray claimed, that Europe had 'lost liberality' because it had 'so largely lost the main elements of civilization' and had lost these because it had 'failed in liberality'.

In *Liberality and Civilization* the contemporary enemies were Marxism, Mussolini and the Japanese, with nationalism and economic autarky following, with Conservatism being criticized rather mildly and with the Russian Revolution being justified by the intolerable nature of the Tsarist régime and the tolerable nature of Bolshevik diplomacy since. Imperialism was bracketed with Nazism, and there were commitments to a European federation and a World State. Liberality's 'nineteenth-century social conscience' and 'ever-widening range of imaginative sympathy' was contrasted with the violence and illiberality that were attributed to the heirs of the Great War in general, to Hitler's 'uneducated' replication of Prussianism in particular and to the arrogance shown by the white and advanced races towards the coloured and the backward.

Murray was to go on about the United Nations long after Hitler and Mussolini had destroyed the League of Nations, repeating in his essays of the 1940s and 1950s the conceptions that he had propagated between the wars and underlining, as his eighties wore on, what had been obvious by 1939 – that he was an elegant survivor from an age which had passed.

The writings of Murray's old age were indubitably senile. They contained, nevertheless, as well as a litany of complaint, expressions of hope about the modern world, as was made clear during the talks that he broadcast on British and French radio at the age of eighty-seven under the by then almost unbearable title *Hellenism and the Modern World*.

III

The Hellenism that Murray inherited was contractable or not according to the needs of its users. By and large it had aimed to reconcile Greek thought with Christianity. In Frazer's case it had done the opposite.

Frazer[1] lived to be eighty-seven: Robertson Smith died when Frazer was forty. But it was in 'gratitude and admiration to ... his friend' – more properly his intellectual mentor – that Volume I of *The Golden Bough* was dedicated in 1890, and it is necessary if we are to understand Frazer's work, to do so in the light of *The Religion of the Semites, The Prophets of Israel, The Old Testament and the Jewish Church* and the *Lectures and Essays* of the 1880s in which Robertson Smith followed Kuenen in laying the foundations for historical treatment of the Old Testament as it was to be conducted in England in the next generation.[2]

Robertson Smith was the son of a minister in the Scottish Free Church. After a successful undergraduate career as a mathematician and theologian, he was appointed on ordination to the Chair of Hebrew and Old Testament Studies at Aberdeen at the age of twenty-four. Before he was thirty he had become a member of the committee that was to produce the Revised Version of the Bible and would have become a leading luminary of the Free Church if he had not ceased to exercise his ministry on being delated for heresy in the 1870s. On being tried for heresy, he withdrew from Aberdeen and was editor of *Encyclopaedia Britannica* until appointed first to the Chair of Arabic in Cambridge and then to the Cambridge University Librarianship.

Robertson Smith did not leave the Free Church; he was buried by its ministers when he died in 1894. But he was important as a symbol of the Mill-like right to think freely about the Bible, and because he approached the Old Testament in the light of the universal religion of which Tylor had systematized the existence.

---

[1] James George Frazer (1854–1941). Educ. Glasgow University and Trinity College, Cambridge, Fellow of Trinity College, Cambridge 1879–1941. Editor of *C Sallusti Crispi Catalina et Jugurtha* 1884, author of *Totemism* 1887, *The Golden Bough* 2 vols. 1890, 3 vols. 1900, 12 vols. 1911–36, *Passages of the Bible Chosen for Their Literary Beauty and Interest* 1895, ed. and translation of Pausanias *Description of Greece* 6 vols. 1898, *Lectures on the Early History of Kingship* 1905, *The Scope of Social Anthropology* 1908, *Psyche's Task* 1909, *Totemism and Exogamy* 4 vols. 1910, ed. *The Letters of William Cowper* 2 vols, 1912, *The Belief in Immortality and the Worship of the Dead* 3 vols. 1913–24, ed. *Essays of Joseph Addison* 2 vols. 1915, *Folklore in the Old Testament* 3 vols. 1918–19, *Sir Roger de Coverley* 1920, *The Worship of Nature* 1926, *The Gorgon's Head* 1927, *Publii Ovidii Nasonis Fastorum Libri Sex* 5 vols. 1929, *Myths of the Origin of Fire* 1930, *The Growth of Plato's Ideal Theory* 1930, *Garnered Sheaves* 1931, *The Fear of the Dead in Primitive Religion* 3 vols. 1933–6, *Condorcet on the Progress of the Human Mind* 1933, *Creation and Evolution in Primitive Cosmogonies* 1935, *Totemica* 1937, with Lady Frazer *Pasha and Pom* 1937.

[2] For Robertson Smith see Volume III.

IV

Tylor[1] was born of a Quaker family in the same year as Stephen, and more than twenty years earlier than Frazer. He was educated at a Quaker school in north London and worked in his father's brass foundry until travel following on illness introduced him to a rich American ethnologist whom he accompanied to Mexico in 1856. His first book – *Anahuac or Mexico and the Mexicans* – was published in 1861 and was followed by *Researches into the Early History of Mankind, Primitive Culture* and *Anthropology*. In 1883 he was appointed to the first Readership and in 1896 became the first Professor of Social Anthropology at Oxford. He received a knighthood from Asquith in 1912.

Tylor's anthropology resembled Buckle's history in being a science which aimed to apply to human nature the methods which had previously been applied to inorganic nature. In the three seminal works which he published between 1865 and 1881, he sketched the content of the science and, as an unbeneficed propagandist without academic expectation, presented it as dealing not only with primitive life and culture but also with the continuities which linked them to civilization.

Like Buckle, Tylor affirmed that human conduct was governed by laws 'as definite as those which governed the rest of nature' and that a 'philosophy of history' was needed in order both to explain them and to direct conduct in the future. But he was inhibited by Buckle's 'haste' and, while holding up Buckle's ideal of a history of the whole lives of tribes and nations, confined himself in practice to a history of culture.

In confining himself in this way, Tylor claimed to be seeking the laws by which cultural evolution had been governed. This was the way in which he treated the diffusion of culture, the decline of civilization and the irreversibility of progress in the practical arts. It was also the way in which he treated racial characteristics, statistical regularities and similarities between cultures and Whately's and De Maistre's criticisms of Gibbon's 'progressive-theory of civilization'; not, that is to say, as dogmatic truths, like the truths of theology, but as subjects for critical investigation, like Tyndall's laws of science.

In elucidating his own view of the laws of cultural evolution, Tylor

---

[1] Edward Burnett Tylor (1832–1917). Educ. Grove School, Tottenham. Reader and then Professor of Social Anthropology at Oxford 1883–1909. Author of *Anahuac or Mexico and the Mexicans* 1861, *Researches into the Early History of Mankind* 1865, *Primitive Culture* 2 vols. 1871, *Anthropology* 1881.

was guided by three ideas – the idea of the chief difference between savage and educated men being the latter's ability to relate cause to effect and separate subjective from objective impressions; the idea of advanced cultures incorporating ritual and linguistic 'survivals' which the progress of science had deprived of the 'matter-of-fact' meaning that they had had originally; and the idea of primitive mentalities needing to be understood not as missionaries, philistines and Utilitarians understood them in terms of a motiveless depravity but as 'practical' reactions issuing in 'reasonable thought' about the world as primitive ignorance understood it. All three ideas were applied to culture generally, to religion in particular and in tracing the 'intellectual clues' which connected the 'thoughts and principles of modern Christianity ... to the very origins of civilization'.

Tylor did not disparage religion. But he treated it as a branch of culture and subjected it to the evolutionary chronology to which he subjected the rest of culture. His chronology was Comtean, presented the challenge of the future as arising from a Comtean conception of the past and showed how much less adequate contemporary religion was at relating itself to modern knowledge than primitive religion 'at its stage of development' had been at relating itself to primitive knowledge.

Tylor inherited a developed subject-matter and found in it a securer basis for anthropology than was to be found in the philosophies of Huxley and Spencer. At the same time he gave a twist to his inheritance even when most insistent that he was not doing so, and, in connecting magic, mythology, poetry and Christianity to one another, was as much part of the inductive, anti-transcendentalist, anti-theological, free-thinking mentality of the 1870s as Huxley and Spencer were.

Tylor wrote at length about magic, witchcraft and the occult. He found in them 'pernicious delusions', 'a great philosophic–religious doctrine' and evidence of the identity between the 'laws of the mind ... in the time of the cave-dwellers' and the 'laws of the mind ... in the time of the builders of sheet-iron houses'.

In exploring the nature of the human imagination as it appeared in mythology, Tylor was the advocate of a conjunction between a comparative method which examined similarities between cultures and an historical method which discovered the meanings which myths had had 'for the times they belonged to'. His conclusion was that the 'wild metaphor' of the savage had to be understood as poetry and that a shared belief in the 'reality of ideas' linked the modern poet to the 'uncultured ... mind ... in the mythologic stage of thought'.

Tylor was a prophet of science and recognized a methodological incompatibility between science and poetry. But he emphasized that the poet 'contemplated the same natural world as the man of science', was as much excited by poetry as Tyndall was and shared Tyndall's enthusiasm for its attempt to 'render difficult thought easy ... by referring the being and movement of the world to the personal life ... which its hearers ... felt within themselves'. This was what linked poetry to myth and rescued myth from being 'motiveless fancy', and it was also why the 'shapers and transmitters of poetic legend', in 'moulding ... ancestral ... heirlooms of thought and word', were displaying not only the 'operations of their own minds' but also the 'arts ... manners ... philosophy and religion of their ... times'.

Tylor's view of myth was that it was the 'history of its authors, not of its subjects' and recorded the lives 'not of superhuman heroes but of poetic nations'. What rôle then, did he attribute to religion?

In *Primitive Culture* the religion of primitive men was 'Animism' and in approaching it, Tylor insisted that it was not to be understood in the terms in which modern minds, and particularly modern Christian minds, understood religion. In order to understand Animism, 'narrow definitions' had to be avoided; it had to be understood that a religion could be a religion even if it was disconnected from ethics and morality, had no belief in God or eternal judgment and did not practise the rites and worship which were to be found in the advanced religions of the world. The 'minimum definition' of religion was 'belief in Spiritual Beings' and Tylor described this as being present 'among all low races with whom ... modern investigation ... had attained to an intimate acquaintance'.

Animism, as Tylor handled it, was much more than an innocent historical fact. It was not only the root from which all subsequent religions had grown in 'unbroken continuity' from the 'lowest scale of humanity' up to 'high modern culture', it also disclosed the 'fundamental religious condition of mankind', provided the 'groundwork of the Philosophy of Religion' and reduced to insignificance the divisions which had separated the 'great religions of the world' into 'intolerant and hostile sects'.

In exploring the links which bound the savage to the 'modern professor' and the 'fetish-worshipper' to the 'civilized Christian', Tylor showed how 'spirits' had become gods, how prayer had been directed at them and how the primitive conception of the soul had developed into the doctrines of transmigration, immortality, future retribution and a bodily resurrection. In the process of exploration an even tone did not obscure a polemical purpose.

In presenting primitive religion's compatibility with the world as savage ignorance had understood it, Tylor not only argued that harmony had been lost subsequently but also that it was necessary to restore it. He made it plain that, however advanced it might be, a 'theory of animation' which imputed human characteristics to nature was incompatible with a scientific knowledge of nature. Natural science had replaced 'independent voluntary action' by 'systematic law', and anthropology, in exposing Christianity's animistic and anthropomorphic origin, had challenged the 'scientific student of theology' and the thinking classes generally to bring Christianity into as close a harmony with modern knowledge as primitive religion had been in harmony with primitive knowledge.

Tylor criticized Protestantism's subservience to dead theologies and Anglicanism's and Roman Catholicism's anachronistic acquiescence in 'sacerdotal usurpations', and he drew attention to the command which Reason was taking over 'hereditary belief' both within Christianity and in the positivistic secularism which was superseding it. But he was neither especially complacent nor especially optimistic about the prospects for modern thought. He was as much aware of modern credulity as of modern scepticism and gained little comfort from the thought of 'traditionalists and commentators' rigidifying anthropology after him. He had, nevertheless, a simple aim – to 'make known ... the tenure of opinions in the public mind', to distinguish 'what was received on its own direct evidence ... from ... what was ... time-honoured superstition ... reshaped to modern ends' and, in employing anthropology as a 'reformer's science', to establish for the future the 'painful' preliminaries necessary to ensure the victory of truth over 'ancestral belief'. In all these respects Frazer was his follower.

V

Many thinkers besides Tylor and Robertson Smith were lodged in the framework of Frazer's mind. But apart from Tylor it was Robertson Smith to whom Frazer looked chiefly and we may properly treat the

fifty enormous volumes of Frazer's writings as expressions and system-
izations of the insights which the shortness of Robertson Smith's life
and perhaps his residually Christian profession had prevented him
elaborating and systematizing for himself.

Like many of his contemporaries, Frazer abandoned the orthodoxy
of his (Presbyterian) upbringing, while being far slower to abandon
religion. Frazer 'dared neither confirm nor deny the existence of God',
but insisted that religion must be wrestled with even when Christianity
had gone. No struggle could have been more impressive so long as the
fundamental premise was granted. Nothing could have been better
calculated to destroy Christianity once the fundamental premise was
abandoned, as in subsequent generations it was, and, unless it be
Sidgwick, no thinker better than Frazer represents the universal aspiration that remained and the anxious seeking for a reconstructed future
that persisted when an academic mode of thought had replaced the
'sacred associations' of historic Christianity.

Frazer was the son of a well-to-do Glasgow chemist. He was brought
up in Glasgow, and was an undergraduate at Glasgow University
where he studied Greek, Latin, Mathematics, Physics, Logic, Metaphysics and English Literature. He was then sent to Trinity College,
Cambridge, rather than to Oxford, because his father mistrusted Tractarianism. Having become a Fellow of Trinity in 1879 after a disserta-
tion which defended Plato's demolition of the philosophy of experience, he remained a Fellow until his death in 1941. In company with
Sidgwick, who was sixteen years older, of James Ward, who was eleven
years older, of McTaggart, who was twelve years younger, of Russell,
who was eighteen years younger, and of Housman after Housman's
arrival in Cambridge in 1911, he was part of a pagan element in the
Trinity ethos.

Housman's paganism was not argued; it was merely assumed. Ward
had begun life as a Congregationalist minister and found the process of
disengagement searing and distressing; as a philosopher, he did not
discuss Christianity in its own terms but made exuberant claims on
behalf of philosophy and psychology in its stead. Sidgwick wrestled
publicly with Christianity in some of his essays in the 1860s and 1870s,
but thereafter discussed it usually by implication; its absence is note-
worthy from *Philosophy Its Scope and Relations* and its virtual absence
elsewhere not compensated for by a few guarded words in *Methods of
Ethics*. Even McTaggart's brilliant statement of the inseparability of
dogma from religion in *Some Dogmas of Religion* was the work of an

Hegelian atheist who merely conformed to the observances of the Church of England and gave as little consideration to the content of Christian dogma as Ward and Sidgwick did. Among these thinkers, Frazer's distaste for Christianity was not unusual.

Frazer's first published work was a contribution to an edition of Sallust's *Catiline and Jugurtha* which was to be followed later by editions of Pausanias's *Description of Greece* and Ovid's *Fasti*. At the same time he read Tylor and began writing about anthropology. With the publication of *Totemism* in 1887 when he was thirty-three and of the two-volume edition of *The Golden Bough* three years later, the anthropological side of his life-work had been established.

Frazer was not a field worker; he synthesized the observations of others. His thought underwent development, especially about totemism, the fire festivals and the difference between magic and religion. But few problems troubled its surface once the surface had been laid with the second edition of *The Golden Bough* in 1900.

During half a century as an author, Frazer wrote about a great many subjects. There were sentimentalities about Cambridge and Truth. There was a sketch of a 'League of the West' on a federal basis with a federal flag and a celebration of Condorcet as the 'shadow of night' fell upon Europe in 1933. There was a Venizelist demonstration in 1917 and recurrent praise of France, the Anglo-French alliance and English and French chivalry. If Frazer had written about religion as he wrote about the eighteenth century, 'gathering flowers ... in the wide garden of English literature', he would have deserved little attention. His view of religion, however, deserves the closest attention as the subject-matter of Social Anthropology.

Frazer was not the first occupant of a university post in Social Anthropology. But, apart from Tylor, he was its most distinguished. In his obituary notice of Robertson Smith in 1894, in the inaugural lecture that he delivered in Liverpool in 1908 and in the Gifford Lectures of 1911/12, he explained the part which the subject would play in the public doctrine of the future.

The subject-matter of Social Anthropology was 'the general laws which had regulated human history in the past' and 'might be expected to regulate it in the future'. These 'coincided ... to a certain extent' with sociology or the philosophy of history and assumed as Tylor had assumed that 'civilization had always and everywhere evolved out of savagery'. In discussing them, Frazer's attitude to religion differed markedly from his attitude to politics.

About politics, Frazer's first work had been *The Golden Bough* which, from one standpoint, was an account of the nature of kingship in a primitive community. That, too, was the subject of *Psyche's Task* which drew attention to the roots that modern secular societies had in primitive superstition. Moreover, *Psyche's Task* was concerned not with the demolition of primitive beliefs and institutions but with describing the valuable rôle that superstition had played in political and social development by supplying 'multitudes' with a 'wrong motive' for the right action that issued in sexual and social morality.

In *Psyche's Task*, as in *The Golden Bough*, Frazer was respectful of humanity's history but unwilling to believe in linear progress. The conception of the 'moral code' as the work of 'the whole people' was used as 'material for a future science of comparative ethics' while the defence of cannibalism and the 'mutilation of dead enemies', the refusal to condemn witch-hunting and human sacrifice and the descriptive explanations of the killing of the King of the Wood 'in the full bloom of divine manhood' were deductions en route from factual observation of the variety of ethical codes to the normative conclusion that the 'principles of right and wrong' could no longer be thought 'immutable'.

Frazer had little to say about advanced forms of social and political organization. He dwelt on the merit that *The Golden Bough* discovered in the 'public profession of magic' and the predominance of the magician – that it 'shifted the balance of power from the many to the one', created a 'monarchy' where previously there had been gerontic oligarchy and had a tendency to place the 'control of affairs in the hands of the ablest man'.

Frazer was as critical as Toynbee of the judgment of the mere multitude and as much committed to the primacy of High Politics. In no modern English writer is there a firmer affirmation of the importance of the 'wily intriguer' to good government or of the essential part played by the 'ruthless victor' in man's emergence from savagery to civilization. Nowhere more than in *The Golden Bough* was the celebration of the despotism of talent more whole-hearted, the conflict between 'talent' and 'tradition' more obvious or the reluctance to entrust power to the people made more manifest. Throughout Frazer's life, indeed, he assumed that thinkers who advanced knowledge were more important than 'statesmen and legislators' and that thought and knowledge alone went deep enough to control the volcano that lay beneath civilization.

These intimations of the fragility of civilization and the contrast between the 'avowed creed' of the 'enlightened minority' and the 'stationary' creed of the 'mass of mankind' were the common-places of a generation which looked to university faculties to destroy the 'ranters' and 'sophists' who had deceived the 'ignorant multitude' in the past. They were central also to the justification of natural theology which Frazer held out in relating his own interests to Lord Gifford's will in the Gifford Lectures of 1911/12.

In his introductory lecture Frazer identified himself by reference to the prevailing climate of opinion. He was not, he explained, speaking 'dogmatically' since 'hardly anyone' now believed that the dogmas of even a 'natural' theology were true. *Philosophical* 'enquiry' on the other hand *was* 'appropriate' since the 'opinions of educated and thoughtful men ... were ... unsettled, ... and conflicting'. Being, however, as he claimed, incompetent to reach philosophical conclusions himself, Frazer offered his lectures as a 'history' of natural theology in which the most striking feature would be the 'close analogies' it would dislose between the 'barbarous superstitions of ignorant savages' and the doctrines which had been 'accepted with implicit faith' in the traditional versions of the advanced religions.

Frazer admitted that doctrines could not be 'refuted' by historical description. But he emphasized that historical enquiry could weaken faith and that the 'comparative method' suggested a 'melancholy' duty to 'strike at the foundations' of the beliefs on which 'the hopes and aspirations of humanity' had hitherto rested. Neither in *The Golden Bough* nor anywhere else did he deny himself the virtue which came from undertaking the duty.

To the question whether study of primitive religion could be thought to be relevant to the study of the great religions, Frazer had three answers. First, that the religious opinions of even the 'educated and enlightened portion of mankind' had been 'handed down' by 'tradition' and could best be understood 'in their origins' at an 'exceedingly low level of culture'. Second, that historical treatment would disclose the 'genetic development of culture' and a 'graduated scale' on which 'all the known peoples of the world' would be placed 'according to their degree of civilisation'. Third, that an understanding of the primitive religion out of which the great religions had emerged would underline the similarities between religions and expose beliefs and practices that had acquired the sanctity of acceptance to a relativistic analysis which would undermine their indefeasability. It was not just because 'the study of inorganic chemistry' preceded that of 'organic chemistry' that Frazer wanted analysis of the savage mind to precede analysis of the 'more complex phenomena of civilized beliefs', but because an analysis of the savage mind would show that the complexities of the great religions were based on the same misconceptions that were to be found in primitive religions. Neither need there be any doubt that the association of traditional Christianity with the primitive was designed to shatter the 'old structures' and 'build up' the 'fairer and more enduring' structures that would succeed them.

In pursuing these aims, Frazer displayed a Spencerian disdain for books by comparison with 'word of mouth' and a Spencerian conviction of the historic importance of the 'mass of people who did not read books'. He left the impression of respecting peasant beliefs, of admiring the 'crude and barbarous philosophy' which peasants had invented to deal with their 'everyday needs' and of regarding these as a real religion which went deeper than the great religions and had been resistant not only to Christianity but also to the mental culture of the Roman Empire.

Frazer despised superstition, especially peasant superstition, and looked forward to education and the urban masses acting as its solvent. In treating peasant religion as embodying the 'genuine beliefs and customs of the folk', however, he supposed himself to be going as deep as Freud and to be describing features so fundamental to human character that the endeavour to elevate, or eliminate, them would turn out to be little more than an aspiration.

In the 1880s Frazer had committed himself to a belief in the importance of totemism in the origination of religion, and in the first edition of *The Golden Bough* had explained religion as a way of acquiring material benefits by erroneous observation of the course of nature. It was not until the late 1890s, and most notably in the second edition of *The Golden Bough*, under the influence of Jevons, that he drew a distinction between religion on the one hand and magic and science on the other.

This distinction seemed flattering to religion in so far as religion arose from an understanding that what had been 'taken for causes' in the early stages of development were 'not causes' and could not produce the requisite manipulation of nature. In other ways, the distinction was even less flattering to religion than the initial identification. For whereas the first edition of *The Golden Bough* had given religion a central rôle in human history, the second treated it as merely an interlude between magic and science – an outcome of the erroneous belief that the world was moved by 'superhuman' beings who acted on 'impulses and motives like man's'. It was 'in so far as religion assumed the world to be directed by conscious agents' who might be 'turned from their purposes by persuasion' that it was in 'fundamental antagonism' to both science and magic, and it was because science and magic shared the belief that the 'processes of nature' were 'rigid and inalienable in their operation' that the line of advance from magic to science was a better line of advance than the line which led to prayer, sacrifice and sacerdotalism.

Frazer had an historical mind: it was no accident that Macaulay was quoted on p. 1 of *The Golden Bough* as well as Turner, or that one aspect of its message was that the mind of Classical Antiquity could not comprehend the 'strange rule' of the Arician priesthood. It was through historical analysis of what the human mind had been before Classical Antiquity had begun and of what it was now, where high civilization had not intruded, that Frazer's account of religion was most persuasive.

As Frazer explained it, religion involved a 'propitiation or conciliation of powers' which were 'superior to Man' and were believed to 'control the course of natural and human life'. Religion on this view was often strange, bloody and superstitious, but there was no suggestion that it was idealistic. Frazer's view was that primitive religion was a materialistic system with a physical soul, sensuous modes of thought and a practical object – the ensuring of the food supply – which made it a reflection of the surrounding 'social system' in the way in which the religious 'conservatism' of the Egyptians reflected natural regularities in the Nile Delta.

Frazer faced the problem presented by the 'beings, real or imaginary' whom the religious imagination had 'clothed with the attributes of humanity', and gave due weight to the part played by plants, animals and inanimate objects in a complex relationship. His conception of religion generally and of Christianity in particular, however, was reductionist in exactly the ways in which Spencer's had been.

Frazer's view of Christianity was that it had originated 'like Buddhism' in 'essentially ethical reforms' which had been occasioned by Christ's ethical loftiness and had been propagated by the 'inflexible Protestantism' of the early missionaries. At the same time he viewed Christianity's conquest of the world as involving the 'supple policy, easy tolerance and comprehensive charity' of the 'shrewd ecclesiastics' who had 'relaxed' the 'too rigid principles' of the early Church. Moreover, throughout *The Golden Bough*, Catholicism was merely primitive religion with the doctrine of asceticism superimposed. Innumerable passages of concealed polemic pointed out that the rites and beliefs which Christians regarded as Christian were not so, and that many of them were merely hangovers from Tylor's primitive religion. Gibbonian irony explained Catholicism's 'divergence' from primitive Christianity as a response to human weakness and to the damage which 'poverty and celibacy' would have done if the 'vast majority of mankind' had not 'refused to purchase a chance of saving their souls with the certainty of extinguishing the species'.

As well as being an Evolutionist, Frazer was a Hellenist. He believed that books should be written 'in the language of polished society' rather than in the 'uncouth jargon of the schools' and that the study of Greek was the 'best preparation for a general study of man'. He was an agnostic and as brutal as Morley or Stephen about the Arnoldian endeavour to preserve God by emptying him of his traditional content. His view was that 'God' meant what it had meant to the savage and that the main task of study and thought in his generation was to destroy the 'venerable walls' of traditional societies in order to prepare the way for an eventual reconstruction.

Frazer was an enemy of Christianity and a protagonist of progress who wanted science to succeed and the principles of the Greek Enlightenment to prevail. He did not, however, always expect them to, in part because peasant religion might be more durable than Enlightenment, in part because 'science' might be supplanted by 'some totally different way' of 'looking at nature'. Two typical passages reflect illusionlessness, uncertainty and an insecure intellectual hope.

The rites still practised by the peasantry at opposite ends of Europe, [went a passage in *Spirits of the Corn and of the Wild* in 1912] no doubt date from an extremely early age in the history of agriculture. They are probably far older than Christianity, older even than those highly developed forms of Greek religion with which ancient writers and artists have made us familiar, but which have been for so many centuries a thing of the past. Thus it happens that, while the fine flower of the religious consciousness in myth, ritual, and art is fleeting and evanescent, its simpler forms are comparatively stable and permanent, being rooted deep in those principles of common minds which bid fair to outlive all the splendid but transient creations of genius. It may be that the elaborate theologies, the solemn rites, the stately temples, which now attract the reverence or the wonder of mankind, are destined themselves to pass away like 'all Olympus' faded hierarchy' and that simple folk will still cherish the simple faiths of their nameless and dateless forefathers, will still believe in witches and fairies, in ghosts and hobgoblins, will still mumble the old spells and make the old magic passes, when the muezzin shall have ceased to call the faithful to prayer from the minarets of St. Sophia, and when the worshippers shall gather no more in the long-drawn aisles of Notre Dame and under the dome of St. Peter's.

The truth seems to be that to this day [went the preface to *Balder the Beautiful*] the peasant remains a pagan and savage at heart: his civilization is merely a thin veneer which the hard knocks of life soon abrade, exposing the solid core of paganism and savagery below. The danger created by a bottomless layer of ignorance and superstition under the crust of civilized society is lessened, not only by the natural torpidity and inertia of the bucolic mind, but also by the progressive decrease of the rural as compared with the urban population in modern states; for I believe it will be found that the artisans who congregate in towns are far less retentive of primitive modes of thought than their rustic brethren. In every age cities have been the centres and as it were the lighthouses from which ideas radiate into the surrounding darkness, kindled by the friction of mind with mind in the crowded haunts of men; and it is natural that at these beacons of intellectual light all should partake in some measure of the general illumination.

Frazer was influential as an anthropologist, as a reminder of savagery and in delineating an attitude towards religion. What, we have to ask next, did Murray do to this line of thinking?

VI

In an article that he wrote in 1928 about Theopompus, the Greek historian, Murray contrasted the Tolstoyan belief that 'nothing matters except the soul' with the belief which he attributed to most practitioners of historical writing that history's proper subject was 'the struggle for life and the doings of those who come to the front in that struggle'. Statesmen, he asserted, had to be judged by 'public social values' and the 'established tradition of public social life' in the forms that it took in *The Times* and the House of Commons and had taken in

Plutarch would not easily be superseded. All he offered, therefore, was a warning – that the 'label never tells the truth', that 'the spirit' could rebel and that the 'rebellion' and the 'tradition' against which it rebelled were Greek.

Murray's first book was published in 1897, a little while before illness had compelled him to resign the Glasgow Chair. *A History of Ancient Greek Literature* was a 400-page survey of its subject from the pre-Homeric period to Julian the Apostate. Much of its discussion, particularly in the Homeric section, was about the process of composition rather than about the significance of the literature. There was, however, a strong sense, as there had been in his Glasgow Inaugural Lecture eight years earlier, of the 'religious freedom ... genuineness of culture and humanity ... and reasoned daring of social and political ideals' through which almost all the major Athenian writers had appealed to nineteenth-century readers 'more intimately' even than 'our own eighteenth-century writers' had done.

What Liberality was to Murray's conception of modern politics, Hellenism was to his conception of Greece, and in considering Greek literature, he faced up to the problem of religion as Comte, Tylor, Robertson Smith and Frazer had faced up to it before him and as Bury, H. M. Chadwick, Farnell, Cornford and Jane Harrison were to face up to it in his lifetime.

As an undergraduate Murray had fed on Mill, Swinburne, Lang, Nietzsche and Wilamowitz-Möllendorf, and was well aware of the difficulties which rational thought was supposed to have encountered in emerging from primitive barbarity. But whereas Frazer, for example, recorded only the rise of rational thought, Murray also recorded the decline which had occurred when the world 'flung itself' on a system of 'authoritative revelation'. This was how Christianity appeared in *Ancient Greek Literature*, and the history that Murray predicated was one in which Christianity had stamped 'free enquiry as a sin' and 'acknowledged no truth outside itself'.

'Hellenism' in Murray resembled the 'revolution' in Morley in being a movement from the past which presented a challenge in the present. *The Rise of the Greek Epic, Four Stages of Greek Religion, Euripides and His Age, Essays and Addresses, Stoic Christian and Humanist* and the allied essays and books that Murray published between 1907 and 1940 listed the lessons and morals of which the challenge consisted.

In *The Rise of the Greek Epic*, Murray considered the 'growth of Greek poetry ... as the embodiment of a force making for the progress of the human race'. 'Service to the community' was the yardstick by which poetry was measured, and one of the main aims of the book was to evaluate the service which the Greek epic had rendered to it.

At the beginning of *The Rise of the Greek Epic*, Murray took off from three statements – that Hellenism was not an 'easy-going, half-animal form of life', that the Greeks were not a 'gay, unconscious, hedonistic race ... untroubled by conscience, ideals or duties' and that the only reason why anyone had ever supposed that they were was the Christian need to build up Christianity by making the Greeks the 'type of what the natural man would be without Christianity'. Murray emphasized that the 'Pagan Man' of Christian apologetic was not Greek, that the Greeks were the 'chief representatives of high civilization outside modern Christendom' and that Hellenism was the 'collective name' for the 'wonderful spiritual effort' with which they had striven for Pagan Man's 'regeneration'. 'Greek civilization rose from the swampy level of the neighbouring people', went the central formulation, 'and the jungle grew thick and close ... around it.' The 'barriers' between civilization and barbarism had been 'very weak' and the totemism, cannibalism, slavery, human sacrifice, subjection of women and 'unchastity' in the 'relations of the sexes' which were endemic in Greek life were 'remnants ... of the ... primeval slime' which Hellenism had been trying to get rid of.

In *The Rise of the Greek Epic*, Murray explained what was known about Aegean civilization and the invasions it had suffered from the Aryan Zeus-worshippers who had brought the basis of the Greek language with them from the North. He also described the emergence of the polis and the success it had had in superimposing worship of itself on the forms of worship which had preceded it.

Murray was well aware of the 'narrowness' of the polis even at its best, and of the criticism it received from Plato and others. But he was interested less in the defects of the polis once it had become established, than in the part played by Homer in elevating it in the first place. The hero was 'Homer', or rather the poets who constituted 'Homer' and the 'regeneration' for which they had been responsible after 'tribal custom and religion' had been undermined. Parallels were drawn between the Homeric invention of Hellenism and the conversion of semitic paganism into Jewish monotheism as Robertson Smith had interpreted it, and between the expurgation to which the Old Testament had been subjected after Deuteronomy and the expurgation to which the saga literature had been subjected by Homer.

In *Four Stages of Greek Religion* Chapters I and II, there was a Frazerian attempt at empathy with primitive religion. The prevailing contrast, however, both there and in *The Rise of the Greek Epic*, was between the 'terror' and 'beast-like elements of humanity' character-istic of 'customary' morality and religion and the 'lightening of clouds' that occurred whenever Hellenism had succeeded in 'taming' them.

What Murray reported the Homeric poems, and particularly the *Iliad*, as doing, was to play down incest, eschew torture, sweep away sodomy and human sacrifice, impose a 'chivalrous' spirit on war and achieve the 'remarkable' intellectual feat of extirpating beings who were part-men and part-gods. They did this, he argued, through a 'traditional' book dependent on a living faith which issued in an 'inspiring' history and by addressing themselves to 'men gathered from ... kindred cities' who wished to hear it 'in public gatherings ... worshipping their common gods'. In effecting this liberal clean-up, the Homeric poems were said to have replaced the 'myths and beliefs ... of the conquered races' by a conquering, aristocratic and 'race ideal'. This was the beginning of Hellenism, and it had needed only the adoption of *The Iliad* as the staple item in Athenian education for Greece to have found herself a book which was as important as the Bible had been to the Jews.

Murray's Athens was peopled with contemporaries, Euripides in parti-cular being a liberal martyr who appealed to 'young people', criticized 'the Herd' and shared 'the same doubts and largely the same ideals as ourselves'. In 'no period in the world's history, not even the opening of the French Revolution', had the prospect of the human race seemed so brilliant as to 'the highest minds of Eastern Greece' in the early fifth century, and the revolution which these 'highest minds' had begun in 'ideals of freedom, law, progress, truth, beauty, knowledge, virtue, humanity and religion' was as important to Murray as the eighteenth-century revolution had been to Morley.

The Greek revolution was important not only because it had aimed at liberation from Orthodoxy but also because 'the instincts of the herd' had 'turned and trampled upon it'. Fifth-century Greece, in other words, had been a scene of tension between common minds and higher minds which had passed through tension to crisis as Aristides and Anaxagoras were banished and 'thoughtful men' withdrew from 'public life'. The 'superstitions', 'cruelties' and narrow-minded conservatism of the mass of the Athenian people were connected with the 'brutality and superstition' of the French peasantry after 1789, and the Enlightened attempt to convert France with Greek poetry's attempt to convert phallic rituals into comedy and the ritual killing of the Corn God into tragedy.

Murray was a devotee of the unconscious, but it was the Frazerian rather than the Freudian unconscious that he was devoted to. Consequently, he discerned in the vegetation and phallic rituals not a perennial satisfaction of human needs but a primitive phase which the higher mind had transcended. In almost all his works, the higher minds were to be found testifying to the existence of 'other values ... beyond the obvious values of physical life' and the opportunity these gave to 'conquer death ... and the alien forces among which ... man's spirit ... had its being'.

In *Euripides and His Age, Aeschylus, Aristophanes* and *The Classical Tradition in Poetry*, Murray showed how Greek poetry had created a doctrine which had divided the educated from the mass of the Athenian people. In *Four Stages of Greek Religion, The Conception of Another Life, The Stoic Philosophy* and *Pagan Religion and Philosophy at the Time of Christ*, he followed its fortunes as even the educated capitulated to Obscurantism and Superstition.

VII

Four Stages of Greek Religion, when published under that title in 1912, was a very short book. Without the chapter on 'The Great Schools', which was added after the title was changed in the second edition, it dealt with pre-Olympian and Olympian religion, with the failure of nerve involved in Hellenistic religion and with 'The Last Protest' which consisted mainly of a translation of a fourth-century contribution to the Emperor Julian's revival of paganism. Though the chronological range was long, the book was dominated by the moral, despite the denial that a moral was being taught. The moral was that religion had only once been on the right lines 'for a few generations' in fifth-century

Athens, that the 'effort had been too great for the average world' and that there had thereafter been only degrees of darkness as 'asceticism, mysticism, pessimism, ... ecstasy, suffering and martyrdom' had come to be associated in Christianity and all the religions of the late Roman Empire with 'indifference to the welfare of the State', 'contempt for the world' and the soul's 'conversion' to 'God'.

Murray was guarded in his dismissals, writing as though mankind had not yet decided between the ideal of 'the good citizen' who lived in the world and the ideal of the saint who rejected it, and leaving open the possibility that the Hellenistic age had been merely a *'preparatio evangelica'* involving a 'softening of human pride' after everything that had gone before. The conclusions, on the other hand, were unambiguous – that Hellenistic religion was a facet of the collapse of 'Greco-Roman civilization' and that Hellenistic asceticism and superstition were reversions to primitive religion, like the reversions which Liberality was to face in the 1930s in Europe.

The good side of the Hellenistic age as Murray presented it was that it was an age in which the 'schools of Greece' were 'Hellenizing' the world. The bad side was that that Hellenization then was no more effective than the Hellenization of the fifth century had been and had been overwhelmed by the vulgarizing transition which had occurred when 'ignorant ... Levantine congregations' invented 'gods begetting children of mortal mothers' and St Paul was willing to be laughed at in Athens for preaching the 'uprising of corpses' and the 'resurrection of the dead'.

If one were to put it simply, one would say that Murray's Hellenism was the Comtean or Frazerian recognition that religion retreats as science advances. But Murray's opinions, though not subtle, were not simple, and it would not only be wrong to suggest that his chief aim was to replace religion by science, it would be far more to the point to suggest that his chief aim was to replace Christianity by uplift. He certainly wrote about science in a friendly fashion. But his conception of science was academic, even monastic, had as little to do with the Industrial Revolution as Keble's conception of poetry, and in that respect supplied merely a rationalistic version of the Romantic or High-Church disdain for commerce which he exposed eloquently and pharasaically in *Religio Grammatici*.

Like Morley's, Murray's view of literature was full of the language of religion. In poetry he found a 'secret' religion and a 'common worship' and in literature generally an element of 'revelation'. Neither literature nor religion was ever 'exactly true', being the 'guess' that went before 'scientific knowledge'. But both dealt with 'the things which men most longed to know', and it followed that the 'emotional value' of literature was likely to be as intense as the emotional value of religion.

All this, though applicable in principle to all literature, was not applied to Christian literature, or indeed to any literature at all except Greek literature. *Religio Grammatici* described only the 'philosophic temper ... gentle judgment ... and interest in knowledge and beauty' with which classical studies opened up means of escape from the 'events and environments of the moment', seeing in this, however, a perennial philosophy which it was criticism's business to convert into 'living thought and feeling'. This was why philology was inadequate and textual emendation only a preliminary, why literature and criticism were the vehicles of an 'Eternal Spirit' and why the 'Eternal Spirit' involved was the 'spirit of man' not God, and could not operate until dogma had given way to the Intellect's 'search for Truth' through philosophy.

Murray did not wish to say that 'all the religions that had existed in the world were false'. He recognized that men had to have 'some ... relation towards the ... mysterious'. But faith, when turned into 'intellectual' belief, was 'false', and the disconnection of moral good from 'supernatural rewards and punishments' was especially necessary in a world which no longer believed in 'Sin, Judgment, Heaven and Hell'.

Four Stages of Greek Religion was an historical book and confined itself to expounding the nature and fate of historic Hellenism. *What is Permanent in Positivism* took up the story in the modern world, presented Positivism as the continuation of Hellenism and, while accepting almost everything that mattered in Comte's sociology (except its view of sex and Democracy), invoked Freud's help in dismissing views that conflicted with Comte's view of religion.

Murray's religion had been defined in Athens before it was refined by Comte, and had acquired a gallery of heroes from Euripides, St Francis, Shelley, Tolstoy, Condorcet, Acton and Kropotkin to world-historical contemporaries like Gandhi, Masaryk and Smuts. It was dedicated not just to truth, but especially to the truth that, though every society needed an 'inherited conglomeration of ... taboos and dogmas', none of them had 'the slightest chance of being ... true or sensible'. It built on this, denied Christianity's uniqueness and authority and concluded that not only the Christian God but any God was an 'intrinsically human conception' inspired by an 'inordinate human conceit'.

Murray had an odd life. He seems, intellectually, to have married his mother-in-law as well as his wife, to have been at times a verbal fantasist, and to have had little real sympathy for the twentieth century. He was both a cradle Catholic and a death-bed one, though in neither case, apparently, of his own volition, and in between was a relentless enemy of all conventional religion. Nevertheless, he set up as a religious teacher and, as heir to a long line of Hellenists who had done the same, did not spare religions that he disliked. In the case of so influential and representative a thinker, one hesitates to pass judgment. But if judgment is to be passed, can it be other than that his religion involved as nonsensical a pretension as Lawrence's phallic religion and differed from Lawrence's chiefly in drawing Victorian curtains across the parts that Lawrence wished to expose?

9

The Revision of Ethical Earnestness II

'The leading principle of the Utopian religion is the repudiation of the doctrine of original sin: the Utopians hold that man, on the whole, is good. That is their cardinal belief. Man has pride and conscience ... he has remorse and sorrow in his being. How can one think of him as bad? He is religious; religion is as natural to him as lust and anger, less intense, indeed, but coming with a wide-sweeping inevitableness ... And in Utopia they understand this, or, at least, the *Samurai* do, clearly. They accept Religion as they accept Thirst, as something inseparably in the mysterious rhythms of life.' H. G. Wells *A Modern Utopia* 1905 (Nelson Popular Editions of Notable Books n. d.) pp. 288–9.

'Our supreme business in life – not as we made it, but as it was made for us when the world began – is to carry and to pass on as we received it, or better, the sacred lamp of organic being that we bear within us. Science and morals are subservient to the reproductive activity; that is why they are so imperative. The rest is what we will, play, art, consolation – in one word religion. If religion is not science or morals, it is the sum of the unfettered expansive impulses of our being ... the stretching forth of our hands towards the illimitable. It is an intuition of the final deliverance, a half-way house on the road to that City which we name mysteriously Death.' Henry Havelock Ellis, *The New Spirit* 1890 (Modern Library edition) pp. 291–2.

'Our statesmen must get a religion by hook or crook; and as we are committed to Adult Suffrage it must be a religion capable of vulgarization. The thought first put into words by the Mills when they said 'there is no God; but this is a family secret', and long held unspoken by aristocratic statesmen and diplomatists, will not serve now ... The driving force of an undeluded popular consent is indispensible, and will be impossible until the statesman can appeal to the vital instincts of the people in terms of a common religion.' G. B. Shaw *Back to Methuselah* (1921) in *Prefaces by G. B.Shaw* 1934 p. 516.

In Frazer and Murray there were undercurrents of doubt about ethical earnestness but basically both remained within its ambit. The writers who appear in this chapter and the next were moving out of its ambit, were more conscious of its defects and were more willing to reject it, especially in discussing sex.

In twentieth-century English literature sex has become a major preoccupation and in some respects has extended the intellectual liberation for which the Victorian advocates of rational responsibility had been arguing. In other respects it has had a contrary effect – providing new reasons for rejecting Christianity by undermining the concept of rational responsibility. In this chapter and the next we shall examine the ways in which pessimism, sex and irrationality sustained the assault on Christianity as it was conducted by Russell, Lawrence, Maugham, Ellis, Shaw and Wells.

I

Wells's[1] earliest writings consisted of lightweight journalism, essays about drama and literature and historical and text-book versions of

---

[1] Herbert George Wells (1866–1946). Educ. Commercial School and Normal School of Science, South Kensington. Apprentice in pharmacy and drapery shops. School teacher 1883–mid–1890s. Author of *Text Book of Biology* 2 vols. 1893, *Honours Physiography* 1893, *Select Conversations with an Uncle* 1895, *The Time Machine* 1895, *The Island of Dr Moreau* 1896, *The Invisible Man* 1897, *The War of the Worlds* 1898, *Love and Mr Lewisham* 1900, *The First Man in the Moon* 1901, *The Discovery of the Future* 1902, *Mankind in the Making* 1903, *The Food of the Gods* 1904, *A Modern Utopia* 1905, *Kipps* 1905, *Socialism and the Family* 1906, *The So-Called Science of Sociology* 1907, *Tono-Bungay* 1908, *New Worlds for Old* 1908, *First and Last Things* 1908, *Ann Veronica* 1909, *The History of Mr Polly* 1910, *The New Machiavelli* 1911, *Marriage* 1912, *An Englishman Looks at the World* 1914, *The Peace of the World* 1915, *Bealby* 1915, *The Research Magnificent* 1915, *What is Coming* 1916, *Mr Britling Sees It Through* 1916, *The Soul of a Bishop* 1917, *God the Invisible King* 1917, *The Outline of History* 1920, *The Salvaging of Civilization* 1921, *A Short History of the World* 1922, *Mr Belloc Objects to the Outline of History* 1926, *The World of William Clissold* 3 vols. 1926, *The Open Conspiracy* 1928, *The Autocracy of Mr Parham* 1930, *The Work, Wealth and*

Huxleyite science. It was in expansion of Huxleyism that Wells began to write science-fiction and in expansion of science-fiction that detachment from the existing world was turned into the critical mind 'ignorant of our history and traditions coming ... from another planet ... to the earth' in order to contemplate its defects.

Wells's first doctrinal books sketched a social philosophy based on the principle that life was a 'succession of births'. *Mankind in the Making* in particular proposed concern for the 'newcomers' as a necessary antidote to the 'pursuit of private interests', and provided for the 'graceless children' of the poor a eugenic care, financial support and common accent and language that would give them access to the central heritage of the nation.

Wells was heterosexual and highly sexed; from an early age sex played a large part in his life and experience. His didactic works expressed distinctive sentiments about love, marriage and the rôle of women in life, presenting sex as the 'cardinal problem' and describing the 'shy jealousy' through which the 'lovable ... being of childhood' was turned into the sexual adult. In providing for proper sexual instruction and public discussion in adolescence, they pursued a middle way between 'license' and 'accepted righteousness', insisting that 'lasciviousness' was a 'leprosy of the soul', 'wisdom' more important than 'rules' and the 'true antiseptic' a 'touch of the heroic in the heart and the imagination'.

Mankind in the Making enabled Wells to announce criticisms of Democracy, of Mill and Gladstone, and of the British system's denial of the 'principle of promotion from the ranks'. It praised the working-class at the expense of the suburban and upper-middle-class home, advocated a system of 'honours and privileges' to reward 'sound living and service' and disparaged the semitic plutocracy in the language of the republicanism of the 1870s.

Like Shaw's, Wells's Socialism was connected with 'national efficiency' and 'commonsense'. In *The Great State* it was also connected with liberty.

The Great State was a 9,000-word essay about the contrast between a 'traditional and customary' type of human association which had

Happiness of Mankind 2 vols. 1932, *The Shape of Things to Come* 1933, *Experiment in Autobiography* 2 vols. 1934, *The Anatomy of Frustration* 1936, *Travels of a Republican Radical in Search of Hot Water* 1939, *The Fate of Homo Sapiens* 1939, *The Rights of Man* 1940, *The Outlook for Homo Sapiens* 1942, *Mind at the End of Its Tether* 1945.

been the 'lot of the enormous majority of human beings' since the Neolithic Age, and the 'abnormal and surplus' ways of living created by the 'minority'. It was a 'minority' which had created usury and debt, built roads and markets and invented law, literature, arts, science, philosophy and religion, and Socialism was an attempt to mediate between 'Normal Social Life' and the forces which were challenging it.

Wells was not a Luddite: he was as much against 'hens, cows and dung' as against the 'servitude of women'. But neither was he in favour of Fabian regimentation of the poor. In doing doctrinally for the society of the future what 'normal societies' had done without doctrine in the past, he claimed to be seeking a 'more spacious social order' to which 'free personal initiative' would have been restored by the 'voluntary nobility' that he described in the chapter entitled 'The Samurai' in *A Modern Utopia*.

The Samurai were to be men of 'imagination' and Comtean spirituality, for whom literature would do what the Bible had done for the Jews, and whose political function would be to play a campaigning rôle against distinctions of class, race, nation and colour. At the same time Wells's conception was physical, including women as well as men, requiring careful planning of health, dress and procreation, and assuming that the Samurai, being 'chaste' rather than 'celibate', would avoid that mistrust of the 'physical and emotional instincts' for which monasticism had been responsible in the past.

Wells shared the radical determination to destroy the power of the hereditary aristocracy. But he dodged the practical question, implying that the Samurai would bring 'constructive brotherhood' to anyone who might want it while making it obvious that the order was not only to be self-selecting but would also supply the only administrators, public officials and voters. In discussing relations between stability and progress, privacy and homogeneity, and individuality and social cohesion, he no more avoided the contradictions of freedom than Mill had.

II

In justifying his politics, Wells claimed that mankind had 'struck ... its ... camp' and was 'out upon the roads', and that existing society had to be replaced by something better. The future was of fundamental significance, the difference between legal or submissive and legislative or creative minds being the difference between 'retrospective' thought which deduced 'rules of conduct' dogmatically from 'the past' and thought which treated morality as something to be 'designed, foreseen and ... attained in the future'. The future, indeed, was said to be 'fixed and determined' and a possible object of knowledge, and 'the laws of social and political development' to be as capable as the 'laws of chemical combination' of ensuring that 'chance impulse and individual will and happening' would be eliminated.

This emphasis on prophecy and prediction was connected with a view of 'great men' as 'symbols and instruments' of the 'forces' that 'lay behind them', and of Socialism as having the sort of consonance with the forces of the future that great men had had with the forces of the past.

In relating Socialism to fundamental forces, Wells dismissed trades unions as 'arresting and delaying organizations' which 'the wider movement of modern civilization was against'. He assumed that working-class and lower-middle-class interests coincided, and that the lower-middle-classes had no interests in common with the plutocracy or governing aristocracy. From that point of view Wells's politics was a response to the realization that the level of ability in government was 'a scandal', that industry needed to be reorganized and that revolution would put an end to the 'slack, extravagant life ... of the last three or four decades' unless Socialism did so first. In *The New Machiavelli* this was presented as a response to problems which all thinking men recognized equally.

The New Machiavelli was an argument in favour of divorce, a commination against sexual censoriousness and an anti-Liberal tract. Its chief target was the Liberal mentality and its chief implication that the Liberal Party was either effete and absurd, or the instrument of mindless manufacturers. It bristled with doctrine, but its sneers at the Webbs and Keir Hardie, its praise of Balfour (i.e. Evesham) and its hero's conversion to Conservatism did not mean that Wells had become a Conservative. What Wells wished to suggest was that, since Liberalism was doomed and the Webbs an irrelevance, mindless Toryism might be converted into the sensitive aristocracy of which Mill had dreamt. This was the point of *The New Machiavelli* – that a thinking aristocracy, and even the servile lower-middle classes, might be persuaded to adopt the programme which the Samurai had adopted in *A Modern Utopia*.

The New Machiavelli was a political novel – the only fully political novel that Wells wrote. It gave a trans-party twist to *Tono-Bungay's* dissection of commercial greed and to the novels of lower-middle-class life out of which Wells's second reputation had been made. For the origin of the gloom Wells was to purvey between the wars, it is necessary to return to his first reputation, as a writer of science-fiction.

Wells's earliest novels had been pessimistic and eschatological, and put question-marks against all kinds of optimism. If *The War of the Worlds* and *The Island of Dr Moreau* are to be taken seriously, they must be understood as warnings of the fragility of civilization and the dangers that would come from the application of physics to war and biology to life. From 1914 onwards Wells was obsessively pessimistic about the world's future.

Wells supported the 1914 war not as a war against the German people but as an attempt to resist the 'dynastic ambition' and 'national ... greed' which were the fruits of 'fifty years of basely conceived ... education'. He identified Socialism with the war effort, criticized conscientious objectors, 'genteel Whigs' and those products of the university system who had been unable to make a proper contribution, and in attacking both the 'rich curs' who profited from the 'West End' and the 'labour curs' who were obstructive on the Clyde, spoke on behalf of the 'young and untried ... of thirty and under who were now in such multitudes thinking over life and their seniors in the trenches'.

The preferences which Wells attributed to the 'young and untried' included the establishment of 'love' and the disestablishment of the 'home' and the replacement of literary and forensic by a scientific, higher education leading to replacement of the 'ungenerous' leadership typical of existing respectability by a new style of leadership which would be more in sympathy with the Britain of the 'factories' and 'the new armies'.

Towards the end of the war, Wells began to be optimistic about international relations, discovering in the prohibitive cost of modern warfare a guarantee of Great Power preponderance and 'organised world control', and deducing from the Russian Revolution and the American declaration of war the prospect of secret diplomacy being superseded. Optimism did not survive the arrival of Hitler. Though Wells went on believing right up to his death that civilization would be destroyed unless a World State was established, he seems eventually to have believed that working-class political consciousness had become an obstacle to establishing it.

Wells's politics, especially his later politics, were impatient and self-important. They were governed, nevertheless, by a coherent view of the rôle that thought should play in the world's future.

III

Between 1902 and 1945 Wells wrote millions of words about thought's rôle in dissolving 'custom and tradition' and about the part which 'book-sellers ... news-vendors ... circulating libraries ... post offices ... free public libraries' and the endowment of authors should play in creating a 'better intelligence and ... heart' for mankind. 'In this matter', he insisted, books were not only 'a quiet counsellor and ... safer than a ... priest' but could also achieve 'supreme' influence by displacing the influence of the 'elected governing bodies' which did the work of contemporary society.

We who write are trying to save our world in a lack of better saviours, to change this mental tumult into an order of understanding and intention in which great things may grow. The thought of a community is the life of that community and if the collective thought of a community is disconnected and fragmentary, then the community is collectively vain and weak ... Though that community have cities such as the world has never seen before, fleets and hosts and glories, though it count its soldiers by the army corps and its children by the million, yet if it hold not to the reality of thought and formulated will beneath these outward things, it will pass, and all its glories will pass, like smoke before the wind, like mist beneath the sun; it will become at last only one more vague and fading dream upon the scroll of time, a heap of mounds and pointless history, even as are Babylon and Nineveh.

Readers who took from Wells a political, social and sexual doctrine disconnected from religion, may be excused for annexing him, as they annexed Ruskin, to the belief that religion was irrelevant. As in Ruskin's case, so in Wells's, readers who made this assumption would have been mistaken. Like Ruskin, Wells was obsessed by religion.

In Wells's earliest novels, the eschatological theme showed up the credulity and ordinariness of contemporary suburban life. This, however, was the continuation of a prevailing genre which Wells had not invented. Neither did these works discuss religion. By the time Wells began writing futuristic utopias, religion had become significant. In *Anticipations, A Modern Utopia* and the first version of *First and Last Things*, it was given a rôle. During the 1914 war, it became central.

Wells dismissed Christianity. But he left the impression of recoiling from dismissiveness and of wishing to extract as much as a humanistic religion could extract safely. What he claimed to want was relief from logic and classification and provision of an area of activity in which men could operate freely and responsibly, uninhibited by the 'utilitarian' and 'material' or the 'cocksure ... exactitude' of Comte and Spencer. His slogan was that the 'direction of conduct followed ... from belief' and that 'beliefs', so far from being 'proven facts', were forms of 'artistic expression' involving 'arbitrary assumptions' which men 'imposed' upon the universe pragmatically and experimentally in the hope that they would correspond with something 'real'.

Having asserted this perfunctorily at the the beginning of *First and Last Things,* Wells spent the rest of the book giving it a content. In both the 1908 and the expanded wartime editions, the content began with the 'Act of Faith' that 'life' was 'ordered' and 'co-ordinated', and proceeded to the experience Wells remembered, from 'the silence of the night and ... rare lonely moments', of 'communion' with 'something greater' than himself.

Wells's conception of God was expressed most clearly in *God the Invisible King.* There he affirmed that there was a 'living God' quite different from the 'triune God' of the Nicene Creed. This was the 'God of the Heart' who was not separated from men by 'reverence' or omnipotence and would not be obscured by 'dogma'. It was a God, moreover, who was neither magical and providential nor the 'bickering monopolist' whom Colenso had attacked. The 'God of the Future' on the contrary was a 'finite ... spirit' which 'existed or strove to exist in every human soul', working 'in ... and through men' and giving them 'courage, generosity ... thought and will'.

Wells aimed to transcend the 'hunting for a cosmic mortgage' that he associated with Naturalism and Utilitarianism. He rejected personal immortality by reason of its 'egoistical encumbrances' while absorbing the individual personality into the 'Being of the Species' and the Eternal ... Being of all things'. In explaining in what sense he held 'all religions' to be 'in measure true', he praised Mohammedanism, dismissed Hinduism and the 'transmigration of souls' and explained that, though *any* religion could be said to be true which worked for those who 'lived' by it, no existing religion worked for him.

Wells wrote approvingly of the idea of 'sorrow and atonement' and agreed that a 'religious system' as 'many-faced and enduring' as Christianity must have been 'saturated with truth'. But he found Christian theology 'over-defined and excessively personified', and Christ's 'incomprehensible sinlessness' an 'image of virtue' so 'terrible' as to have made 'fellowship with men' impossible.

Wells wrote as one who had been through the 'conviction of sin' and the 'darkness of despair'. But he believed in a 'scheme' which 'passed his understanding' and enabled believers to achieve salvation by 'shaping' their thoughts and actions according to it. In 'individuals' as merely 'experiments of the species', and in 'nations, states and races' as 'bubbles' upon its blood, he found perceptions strong enough for this purpose.

In explaining his religion, Wells claimed to be not only 'vague and mystical' but also 'mystical and arbitrary'. That 'things moved to Power and Beauty' he rightly described as 'rhapsodical and incomprehensible', while the idea of the 'whole living creation ... walking in the sleep of instinct and individualised illusion' was not much improved when 'man rose out of it' and 'began to perceive his larger soul ... and collective, synthetic purpose'. Indeed, if this meant anything at all, it meant that religion issued, as Wells explained it, not in churches or 'religious institutions' but in 'socialisation of existing state organisations' and the creation of a 'world state'.

In the second edition of *First and Last Things,* Wells quoted Creighton's dictum that 'the church' was 'mankind knowing and fulfilling its destiny' and attached to it the rider that 'the church so explained' was coterminous with 'human thought'. It was the 'whole body of human thought' of which Wells was thinking when he argued that 'we moderns ... are children of the Catholic Church' and that that Church could become 'something greater than Christianity' if it would accept the authority of 'morally-impassioned ... writers and speakers' for whom 'reformation and reconstruction' would be the task of the future.

This was said to be a task for 'men of goodwill'. It was said to be especially the task of Socialists who wanted a Church through which they could 'feel and think collectively', serving God's kingdom on earth, 'propagating the idea of it, establishing the method of it, and incorporating all that one did into its growing reality'.

Modern religion [went a conclusion] is a process of truth, guided by the divinity in men. It needs no other guidance and no protection. It needs nothing but freedom, free speech and honest statement ... It comes as the dawn comes, through whatever clouds and mists may be here or whatever smoke and curtains may be there. It comes as the day comes to the ships that put out to sea. It is the kingdom of God at hand.

This was Wells's religion in 1917; it did not change much subsequently. *The Salvaging of Civilization* laid out the need for a new 'Bible' or 'Bible of Civilization' as Comenius had conceived it. *The Open Conspiracy* saw in a new religion and a 'new kind of psychology', the chance to 'subordinate self' and assimilate 'whatever was digestible' in traditional Socialism. In *A Short History of the World, The Work, Wealth and Happiness of Mankind* and innumerable other works of social prophecy that Wells published in the 1920s, 1930s, and 1940s, religion's rôle was described encyclopaedically and with provision for an educational discipline, the main aim of which was to transform the world on this side of the grave.

Four of Wells's novels were masterly; he had an enormous influence both inside the Labour movement and outside it. But he need not be taken too seriously. He would deserve to be taken a good deal more seriously if a solemn normality of tone had been made acceptable by the cynical tone that we find in Shaw.

IV

As a musical critic and dramatist, Shaw[1] became a significant figure in the 1890s. As a public prophet, he came into his own with the arrival of the Labour Party in the State between 1920 and 1950. By the time of his death in the latter year at the age of ninety-four, he had for long been enthroned next to the Coles, the Webbs, Tawney, Russell, Wells and Priestley as one of the high priests of English Socialism.

Shaw was more readable than Cole, more prolific than the Webbs, more wide-ranging than Tawney, more Socialist than Russell, more

---

[1] George Bernard Shaw (1856–1950). Educ. Wesley Connexional School, Dublin. In Estate Agent's office 1871–6, then Cashier. Moved to London 1876. Author of *Cashel Byron's Profession* 1886, *An Unsocial Socialist* 1887, ed. and contributor to *Fabian Essays* 1889, *The Quintessence of Ibsenism* 1891, *Widowers' Houses* 1893, *Arms and the Man* 1894, *The Sanity of Art* 1895, *The Perfect Wagnerite* 1898, *Plays Pleasant and Plays Unpleasant* 2 vols. 1898, *Fabianism and the Empire* 1900, *Three Plays for Puritans* 1901, *Man and Superman* 1903, *John Bull's Other Island* 1904, *The Common Sense of Municipal Trading* 1904, *Major Barbara* 1905, *The Doctor's Dilemma* 1906, *Pygmalion* 1912, *Androcles and the Lion* 1913, *Heartbreak House* 1920, *Back to Methuselah* 1921, *St Joan* 1924, *Do We Agree* 1928, *The Intelligent Woman's Guide to Socialism and Capitalism* 1928 etc., *Everybody's Political What's What* 1944.

insolent than Wells, more subtle than Priestley and more cynical than any of them. In his later years he became a bore, windbag and licensed clown, approaching Socialism by devious and often silly routes. Through all his silliness and deviousness he conveyed the impression that Socialism was rooted in illusionlessness. If we are to understand socialist illusionlessness in Shaw's sense, and the intensity of conviction that it masked, we must examine Shaw between the early 1880s and the early 1920s, when Wagnerism, Ibsenism, Nietszcheanism, Butlerism, Eugenicism, Feminism and anti-Vivisectionism all helped him to invent one of the oddest of English mythologies.

Shaw was a versatile writer, except in poetry, but he had, through all the variety of genres in which he wrote, a similar tone and manner, along with a Ruskinian belief in the interconnectedness of all public statement. His very earliest writings lacked power, but even they were statements of doctrine, and if we begin with his doctrine about politics, it should not be supposed that he thought politics more fundamental than anything else.

Shaw was one of the earliest members of the Fabian Society, wrote some of its literature and was one of its most important managers and speakers. Fabianism, as he never tired of explaining, meant a gradual revolution. But it also meant, as he also never tired of explaining, a total revolution. It did not mean, as Social Democracy has come to mean, a flabby, central position with which it would be difficult to argue even if one wanted to. In the 1880s, Fabianism and Social Democracy involved as fundamental an assault as Marxism, and Shaw and the Fabians rejected Marxism only because a Marxist strategy would fail to achieve the revolution that it aimed at. The conflict with impractical Marxism ran right through Shaw's writings, reaching its climax with the diagnosis he gave in the 1930s of the failure of the Russian Revolution of 1917 on the grounds that it had neglected to take 'special care' of 'the managers' and had abolished 'private property' and 'private enterprise' before full employment could be achieved 'without checking productivity'.

In the 1930s, Shaw's tone about the Russian Revolution was self-consciously unsentimental, excusing the assassination of the Tsar as 'the most merciful regicide in history', justifying the Tcheka for 'bringing home a sense of responsibility to public functionaries' and praising Stalin's purges and victory over Trotsky as a 'triumph of common sense'. In discussing forced collectivization he left the impression that almost anything that Stalin did could be justified by the overriding duty to replace capitalism by Communism.

Shaw's Stalinism, his affectation of callousness and his rejection of Liberalism, were connected with the assumption that 'our civilisation' needed to be 'saved'. In this respect Shaw was a Cassandra. He believed that West European capitalism lacked intellectual foundations and was breaking down. He judged Fascism to be 'better than Liberalism' and praised it for training citizens to take the 'corporate view of themselves'. He despised the 'rottenness' of bourgeois and parliamentary institutions, the imitations of the *Forsyte Saga* that ran through English 'secondary education' and the failure of English universities to come to grips with the 'heterodox and controversial works of the moment'. An envenomed passage at the beginning of an unpublished work written after a visit to the Soviet Union in 1931 in the company of Lady Astor put the general case, while discussing Wells's *Outline of History,* in the form of a comment on Gladstone.

Mr H. G. Wells understated the case [went this passage] when he complained that Gladstone, a typical product of public school and university education, was grossly ignorant. If he had been, his natural mental power and character would have enabled him to learn easily all that he needed to know. But he began his political life with every corner of his mind so carefully stuffed with pernicious rubbish: tribal superstitions imposed on him as religion; glorifications of piracy, brigandage, slave-trading, and murder disguised as history; excuses for robbery, idleness, and mad pride labelled as political economy; and dishonest slacking and shirking of social duty idolized as liberty, that when he became Chancellor of the Exchequer, he declared that England's prosperity was increasing by leaps and bounds when it was in fact a feebly palliated hell for nine-tenths of the population, whilst the rest were wasting the plunder of the poor in digging their graves with their teeth, not having been taught even how to feed and clothe themselves healthily. A grossly ignorant person would have been a far safer leader of the nation; for he (or she) might have done the right thing by accident or sheer naiveté, whereas though Gladstone never said to himself 'Evil, be thou my good', yet having been carefully trained by his upbringing and schooling to mistake evil for good, his condition came to the same thing in an incurable form. That is why our Cabinets, consisting of men of unchallenged respectability and often of the best intentions, are in effect Cabinets of scoundrels, and why our bishops, who always have a saint or two among them as well as a blackguard or two, are at best in the position of chaplains to a pirate fleet. The corruption of a predatory society cannot be cured by reforms within that form of society: it is fundamental; and the remedy is the revolutionary one of a complete substitution of systematically enforced honesty for systematically encouraged predacity.

Shaw intended his dismissal of Liberalism to be cynically realistic, to avoid the 'taint' of 'self-sacrifice' and to prevent Fabianism being mistaken for a way of 'exhorting the working classes not to do anything rash'. It connected his politics in the 1930s with his politics in the 1880s, when Political Economy had ratified anarchy, when the division between 'self-regarding' and 'other-regarding' activities had been a 'decaying superstition' and when the 'theory of liberty' had been a 'cast-off garment of eighteenth-century sociology' made irrelevant and absurd by the 'interdependence' of individuals that had been brought about by the 'minute division of labour in modern communities'.

In the course of an active political life, Shaw declared himself about many questions of policy. From an early stage he favoured the abolition of the House of Lords and sex and property qualifications in voting, and the institution of public payment for M. P.s, Councillors and candidates for parliament. He favoured expansion of both central and local government. He was a well-known anti-vivisectionist, teetotaller and vegetarian; he treated the medical profession with the mistrust that was due to the modern successor of the mediaeval clergy. He argued at different times in favour both of a properly co-ordinated Imperial bureaucracy and a properly constituted League of Nations. About Ireland he wrote prolifically. He opposed the partition of Persia and Grey's continental diplomacy before the First World War, and the ostracization of Germany after it. He waged a running battle against the persecution of conscientious objectors and the vindictive nature of the prison system. He welcomed wartime collectivization in the 1914 war, while pointing out that it had been a military collectivization rather than a socialist one, and sneered at the 'reactionary' politicians who had led Labour in the war and were in office in the 1920s. In proscribing poverty as a threat to élitist and managerial life, he expressed a massive disdain for the mental capacity of the poor as it had been developed by the Education Acts of 1870 and 1902 and the Northcliffe and Rothermere newspapers. Since he died in 1950, before the British spy-ring had become public property, we have been spared his opinion of it. If it cannot be established that he was amongst those who taught Philby, Burgess and Maclean what Blunt claimed to have been taught by Forster in the 1930s, there can be no doubt about the liberating effect which he had on the loyalties of the earnest literate young between the wars.

To list the causes which Shaw came to support either on his own account or as a member of the Fabian Society, may be unduly to compress the flavour of his public personality. This combined moral commitment with a coat-trailing fluency which to some extent was a natural endowment, to some extent a doctrinal necessity and to some extent an Irish response both to the indestructability of the system he was attacking and to the muddled nature of the progressive movements of the 1880s.

In the 1880s and 1890s Shaw wrote anti-Marxist articles about economic theory. But the main facts from which he began, the main assumptions he wished to assert, were the facts and assumptions which Marxists shared with Fabians and Social Democrats – that capitalism had disconnected 'law' from 'honesty' as outward respectability concealed from the 'pious Christian', 'model husband and father' and 'benefactor of the poor', the fact that he was a 'parasite on the commonwealth' who 'consumed a great deal' and 'produced nothing ... felt nothing, knew nothing, believed nothing and did nothing' except what was done by 'all the rest'.

In this analysis there were two axioms – that the system of production was 'due solely to the labour of man working upon the material of nature', and that the distribution of property was a form of institutionalized theft through which 'the landlord and the capitalist enjoyed the labour of others'. The conclusions which followed were that poverty would destroy the Commonwealth if allowed to continue, and that existing methods were inducing a 'gambling spirit' at variance with the spirit of Socialism.

Socialism was the principle that 'each man should replace what he consumes', that 'none should profit at his fellows' expense' and that 'men should honestly labour for those who labour for them'. The 'exhibition of personal graces by certain classes of the community' was an insufficient return for the property which they 'took from other classes', and voluntary work in amelioration of poverty was damaging to the 'slaves' it was designed to assist. Slavery had begun when the first 'landless proletarian' renounced the 'fruits of his labour' and the 'right to think for himself', and the proletariat's 'filthiness, ugliness and dishonesty' would go on 'poisoning ... the lives ... of the propertied and educated classes' until those classes gave up the 'surplus value' they extracted from the nation's wealth, and averted the 'bloodshed' that would be caused if the 'capitalist parliament' refused to transfer control of 'the police and soldiery' to the working classes. These were the circumstances to which Socialism was a response and it was

Socialism's duty to show, what 'our hearts' had 'known all along', that the 'respectability of today' was an 'inversion'. It was only when 'every man's property and liberty' had become the 'property and liberty' of the State, with no 'theoretic limit' on the State's 'right' to treat the individual as 'merely its tenant and delegate', that rent would be transferred to 'the whole people' and the people turned from 'beasts of burden' into 'men'.

These were the 'sacred imperatives' which Shaw preached throughout England in the 1880s and 1890s. They were represented as continuations of the Factory Acts, the Income Tax and the reconstructed political economy of Mill, George, Jevons and Cairnes. They were also impregnated with Marx, who was treated as a great prophet, like Jesus or Mohammed, and who continued to attract respect and admiration, not only during Shaw's flirtation with Hyndman, but also after he had settled down to being the anti-Marxist Fabian who played Wickstead against Marx's economics and Lassalle against Marx's politics.

Shaw was against immediate, violent revolution but he did not argue that gradual, or Fabian, methods were preferable morally. What he argued was that the failure of Chartism and the Commune had made it necessary to devise new methods of proceeding if common objectives were to be achieved. It was because Trades Unionism had failed as completely as Chartism, and in the light of Marx's failure as a political organizer, that Lassalle was acclaimed as the inventor of Social Democracy.

At all periods in his life, Shaw expressed deep contempt for the 'phalanx of fools' involved in parliamentary politics which repelled 'men of character and ability' who wanted to do more than 'organize the labour of the masses for the benefit of the classes'. Lassalle was praised for his refusal to capitulate, for the success he had had in retaining the independence of the innovator and for the crowning glory of 1862 when he had had the 'routine politicians' by the nose and had 'forced his way into politics from the study instead of creeping into them through the caucus'. This was marked out as the beginning of Fabianism, and Lassalle as the author of the first formulation of the Fabian aim of creating an independent working-class party dedicated to the 'overthrow of the middle class' not only in respect of financial organization and power but also in respect of the 'God ... Church ... code of manners ... family institutions ... and standards of glory ... honour and womanliness' which the middle class 'held sacred'.

V

In *The Perfect Wagnerite,* Shaw wrote of European music since Mozart that it was 'the most fascinating and miraculous art in the world', going deeper then poetry and achieving in the symphony a record of the 'vicissitudes of the soul' which was beyond poetry's capability. Similarly, in the 'Author's Apology' that he wrote for the collected edition of his theatre criticism in 1907, he acclaimed the 'apostolic succession' from 'Eschylus' to himself for being as 'serious and as continually inspired as ... the apostolic succession of the Christian Church'. The impertinence did not conceal the seriousness of the conclusions – that 'bad theatres were as mischievous as bad schools or churches', that London should take its 'conscience' and 'brains' with it when it went to the theatre, and that not only was art the 'most efficacious instrument of moral propaganda' but also that 'dramatic art' was raised above 'imposture and pleasure-hunting' by the 'vision' which the dramatist had in the 'magic glass of his art-work'.

It is evident from Shaw's novels, and from his musical, dramatic and literary criticism, that he did not think of himself as an ordinary practitioner of these activites. Even in his earliest works, there were wide claims and implications, and, just as his Socialism avoided being a bag of merely political tricks in the shadow of Marx and Lassalle, so novel-writing was dropped and criticism became something else as it began to discuss Ibsen, Wagner and Nietzsche. *The Quintessence of Ibsenism* became religious when Ibsen proved drama's right to 'scriptural rank' and 'modern ... literature and music' formed a 'Bible far surpassing in importance ... the Hebrew Bible that had served ... so long'.

At the time at which Shaw persuaded theatre managers to perform his plays, he began to publish the texts of the plays together with specially written prefaces. The earliest prefaces were concerned with theatrical censorship and the intellectual weakness of dramatic criticism in London in the 1890s, and with the connected question of the London theatre audience's ignorance of economics and hypocrisy about sex, and its inability to connect sex, Socialism, prostitution and poverty. The preface and conclusion to *Man and Superman* in 1903 made it clear that these problems were facets of the problem of religion.

Shaw stated repeatedly that a modern society, indeed 'any empire or political organisation', needed a 'religion'. But he also stated that 'the great modern religion' would not be ecclesiastical, and would be only in the most controversial sense Christian.

Shaw's view of Christianity was coloured by two fundamental contrasts – the contrast between real Christianity and historic Christianity on the one hand, and the contrast between real Christianity and the world of established respectability which Socialists wanted to abolish on the other. It was because historic Christianity had become inseparable from capitalist respectability that it was insupportable politically; it was because it had become inseparable from a false philosophy and metaphysic that it had become insupportable intellectually. Whether, in establishing the real nature of Christianity, as Shaw supposed himself to have done in the preface to *Androcles and the Lion*, he thought of himself as providing a jocular version of his inherited Protestantism is a question to which more than one answer may be given. But it is certain that he was obsessed by religion, wished to make something out of Christianity and knew, like Huxley, that he had to gut it of its historic characteristics if he was to do so.

In doing this, Shaw was at pains to establish that Christ had not been either the 'gentle' Jesus of modern invention or an 'English curate' of the 'comedy type'. The most important fact about Shaw's Christ was that, at a certain point in his life, he had come to 'believe himself to be God' and had been crucified after a 'straightforward' trial on the reasonable ground that he had uttered the blasphemy of 'claiming' to be God, displaying 'physical fortitude' in asserting his claim but dying incontestably for blasphemy, and not for the subversive 'social and political opinions' he had expressed in the process. In putting himself right, as he claimed, with 'respectable society', Shaw emphasized that he made no defence of 'such persons as Savonarola and John of Leyden' and, if he had been in Pilate's shoes, would have recognized as plainly as Pilate the need to suppress attacks on the existing social order by people with 'no knowledge of government ... acting on the very dangerous delusion that the end of the world was at hand'.

Christ, in other words, was not to be taken seriously as God. He was, however, to be taken seriously as the propagator of a 'doctrine' about 'political and social practice' which could certainly have got the world out of its 'misery' if it had been followed in the spirit of a 'modern practical statesman'. The doctrine had not been 'peculiar to

Christ' and would have evolved if Christ had never lived. But the 'imagination of mankind' had 'picked' Christ 'out' and 'attributed all the Christian doctrines to him' and since he had got hold of the 'right end of the stick' where Barabbas, for all his 'victories ... empires ... money ... moralities ... churches ... constitutions' and fraudulent conversion of the Cross, had got hold of the wrong end, it followed that modern men would need to inform themselves if they were to use Christ's teaching to solve the world's problems.

In the preface to *Androcles and the Lion,* Shaw emphasized the 'obsolescence' which had overtaken the Bible since 1860 and the freedom this had brought in interpreting it. He also emphasized that the Bible was not a modern book, that it would not 'do to read ... it ... with a mind formed only for the reception of ... a biography of Goethe' and that it had to be approached as a contribution to the 'history of human imagination'.

About religion, Shaw made three assumptions – that it was what occurred when the 'open mind' lost its openness, that it had supplied the basis for all public action in the past and that it had been maintained by a small percentage of mankind whose concern for their own and other peoples' souls had everywhere developed in the same way through all its changes of 'name, form, fashion and taste'.

This common religion was 'Salvationism' – the belief that super-natural beings controlled those aspects of the universe which men did not control and that flattery and sacrifices were needed in order to propitiate them, in socially undivisive ways while society retained a measure of primitive solidarity, in divisive ways when the attack on inequality made religious reformers demand 'gratuitous' methods of salvation for the poor. It was by this route that Shaw accounted for the idea of a 'redeemer ... compounding for the sins of the world', of justification by faith 'abolishing the charge for admission into heaven' and of Christ as enemy of Barabbas and advocate of a religion which 'put the economic question first'.

This was the main point of the preface to *Androcles and the Lion* – that until he began talking about his divinity, Christ had been a 'civilized' and 'cultivated' person who happened to prefer a 'bohemian' life to the 'routine of wealth, respectability and orthodoxy' and whose 'thoroughly Marxist' religion had made him very like Shaw once Pauline theology and the 'medieval and methodist will-to-believe' had been abandoned.

Shaw can scarcely have believed that Christ was a 'first-rate' political economist, biologist and psychologist who understood, as well as evolutionists understood, that 'we are gods, though we die like men'. He is much more likely to have believed that 'if civilization' was to be 'saved', it would be because 'the Life Force ... could not be beaten by any failure'.

In order to understand the Life Force it is necessary to notice the long attack which Shaw made in 1895 on Max Nordau's book *Degeneration,* in which Nordau had criticized 'modern works of art' for being 'symptoms of the nervous exhaustion of the race by overwork'. In the course of defending Impressionism, Wagnerism and Ibsenism, and the innovations which they had introduced, *The Sanity of Art* related the duties of the artist to the fact that 'laws, religious creeds and systems of ethics' had tended historically to encourage a slavish division between those who did, and those who did not, have the time to think deeply about them.

Shaw was an enemy of the Aesthetes and of university culture, declined to be over-awed by professionalization and dismissed the human quality of artists and writers who, as 'anyone who was in touch with them' knew, had adopted their professions because they were 'incapable of steady work and regular habits'. On the other hand, he wanted art and literature to be made accessible to the 'unskilled' and 'untaught'. For the 'great artist' he claimed the 'privileges of religion' and a capacity to 'sweep the world clear of lies' by extirpating 'baseness, cruelty ... superficiality and vulgarity' and adding a 'fresh extension of sense to the heritage of the race'. In theorizing the struggle that this entailed, he gave *The Sanity of Art, The Perfect Wagnerite* and *The Quintessence of Ibsenism* a standing as religious polemic.

The innovation that was advocated in *The Quintessence of Ibsenism* was negative; the main line of Shaw's positive argument appeared only fragmentarily there and in *The Perfect Wagnerite*. In *Man and Superman* and *Back to Methuselah* it was systematized when the antipathy to idealism which had been praised in Ibsen, despite Ibsen's 'deep sympathy' with his idealist characters, was converted into the doctrine of Creative Evolution.

In structure, *The Quintessence of Ibsenism* was a discussion of Ibsen's works in chronological order. In essence, it was an approving assessment of Ibsen's insistence on the damage that was done to civilization by idealisms – the corrupt idealism which cloaked capitalistic corruption, the constricting idealism that had emerged from the dark side of the Protestantism in which Ibsen had been brought up and the Voltairean idealism which, on 'renouncing supernatural revelation', had fallen into the same trap as its Christian enemy. Ibsen was the 'crustiest, grimmest hero since Beethoven'. He no more approved of the 'syllogism-worship' that underpinned Spencerianism, vivisectionism, vaccination and the Contagious Diseases Act than he approved of male-dominated romantic marriage, and he had not only shown why the 'age of reason' was as irrelevant as the 'age of faith' but had also established that Schopenhauer's invention of the will-to-live was the most important turning-point in modern thought.

Shaw rejected Schopenhauer's pessimism. But he also showed Schopenhauer undercutting pessimism and leading the way through the Ibsenite 'repudiation of any customary duty ... that conflicted with ... freedom' to Lassalle's 'godless' insistence on the need to adapt 'economic and political institutions' to the poor man's 'wish to eat and drink ... his share of the product of his labour'.

In describing Lassalle as a 'self-worshipper', Shaw intended 'no reproach ... for ... self-worship ... was the last step in the evolution of the conception of duty'.

Duty arose at first, a gloomy tyranny, out of man's helplessness, his self-mistrust, in a word, his abstract fear. He personified all that he abstractly feared as God, and straightway became the slave of his duty to God. He imposed that slavery fiercely on his children, threatening them with hell, and punishing them for their attempts to be happy. When, becoming bolder, he ceased to fear everything, and dared to love something, this duty of his to what he feared evolved into a sense of duty to what he loved. Sometimes he again personified what he loved as God; and the God of Wrath became the God of Love: sometimes he at once became a humanitarian, an altruist, acknowledging only his duty to his neighbour. This stage was correlative to the rationalist stage in the evolution of philosophy and the capitalist phase in the evolution of industry. But in it the emancipated slave of God fell under the dominion of Society, which, having just reached a phase in which all the love was ground out of it by the competitive struggle for money, remorselessly crushed him until, in due course of the further growth of his courage, a sense at last arose in him of his duty to himself. And when this sense is fully grown the tyranny of duty perishes; for now the man's God is his own humanity; and he, self-satisfied at last, ceases to be selfish. The evangelist of this last step must therefore preach the repudiation of duty. This, to the unprepared ... is indeed the wanton masterpiece of paradox ... But why not? God Almighty was once the most sacred of our conceptions; and he had to be denied. Then Reason became the Infallible Pope, only to be deposed in turn. Is Duty more sacred than God or Reason?

Towards the end of *The Quintessence of Ibsenism* Shaw suggested that Ibsen's 'attack on morality', so far from being a sympton of the 'extinction of religion', was a symptom of its 'revival'. 'Religions' began in 'revolt against morality', he argued, and perished when 'morality conquered them'. This was why Ibsen had been kinder to the man who 'went his own way as a rake and a drunkard' than to the man who was 'respectable because he dare not be otherwise'. It was also the reason why conduct had to 'justify itself by its effect' rather than by 'conformity' to a 'rule' or the 'letter'.

On a number of occasions, Shaw complained that critics had assumed that he had picked up Creative Evolution from Schopenhauer, Nietzsche, Ibsen and Wagner when in fact he had picked it up from Samuel Butler. He may well have picked it up from Butler, but had only himself to blame for leaving a contrary impression. It is certainly the case that his next approach to philosophical statement after *The Quintessence of Ibsenism* was *The Perfect Wagnerite*.

The main part of *The Perfect Wagnerite* considered the 'modern' conflict between the lust for capital on the one hand and Godhead, Law and the 'creative, life-pursuing activities' on the other. Alberic's 'Plutonic power' was shown threatening the Gods with destruction in the way in which capitalism had threatened the Church with destruction; *The Ring* as a whole was presented as an announcement through the theatre of a conflict in the world between the 'infirmity' of the Gods or the Church and an 'order of Heroes' whose 'strength and integrity' would be such that even the Gods and the Church would obey them.

In discussing *The Ring,* Shaw drew attention to an inconsistency between the original conception which Wagner had had after 1848 and *The Ring* as he completed it in the 1870s. Shaw despised Wagner's interest in 'love', preferred the socio-religious and economic allegory which formed the substance of *Rheingold, Siegfried* and *The Valkyries,* and felt the same reserve about *Götterdämmerung* that he had felt about the Progressive Movement when he had encountered it in London in the 1880s

Shaw's reserve raised the question 'Why Wagner Changed His Mind'. In 1898 he found the explanation in the transition *The Ring* had suffered from being a 'philosophic music-drama' or 'symbol of the world as Wagner had observed it' into being a 'didactic opera' in which 'Love' was the 'solvent' of human problems. In 1913 the explanation was found in the emergence of Bismarck, the failure of the Siegfrieds of 1848 and Wagner's unFabian inability to anticipate the process by which the class struggle would work itself out in practice.

What Shaw admired in Wagner's original *Siegfried* was less the 'hero' whom the Gods recognized as their superior than the 'type of healthy man' whose 'confidence in his own impulses' had raised him above 'sickliness of conscience'. *Siegfried* had shown that both 'the grace of God' and 'the Age of Reason' could be replaced by the 'unfettered action of Humanity ... doing what it liked' because the 'joy of life' led it to like doing what was necessary 'for the good of the race'. No 'individual Siegfried', however, could transcend the obstacles which 'the weakness of mobs' presented to 'the few who governed' and, since 'the majority of men in Europe' had 'no business to be alive', 'no serious progress' would be made towards Siegfried's Fabian, neo-Protestant anarchism until an 'earnest' and 'scientific' effort had been made to breed a 'race of men in whom the life-giving impulses predominated'.

In *The Perfect Wagnerite* Shaw's view was that *The Ring's* pessimism led backwards to Lohengrinizing, that *Parsifal* was a hopeless invention and that vigilance and skill would be needed if *The Ring* was to give out the right message. The right message was that reason was subordinate to the will, that 'man ... was higher than the Gods' and that 'Life' was a 'tireless power ... growing from within and ... driving ... onwards and upwards ... to ever higher forms of organization'.

By the beginning of the twentieth century, Shaw had theorized his cynicism, given illusionlessness a content and demanded the replacement of both supernatural and rationalistic religion. What he had not done was to explain the details of the positive doctrine which was to replace them. The only detailed explanations that were to be given were given in *St Joan*, *Man and Superman* and *Back to Methuselah*.

In the preface to *St Joan* Shaw affirmed the inevitability of intolerance and persecution, while drawing attention to the damage they could do to the 'originality' which lurked beneath the surface of orthodox societies. He restated Wells's vision of the Roman Catholic Church becoming 'something greater than Christianity' if it would defer to the 'morally impassioned writers and speakers' whom Wells preferred to its existing clergy. He pushed Wells's argument to the conclusion that Roman Catholicism would play no part in modern culture until it disengaged itself from the 'spiritual needs ... of the poor and ignorant', interested itself in the heresies that arose when the Holy Ghost flashed 'with unerring aim' through the saints and prophets of 'free thought' and came to terms with the prospects and possibilities suggested by the evolutionary resolve of *Back to Methuselah.*

Back to Methuselah was written in the shadow of the 1914 war which it explained as the outcome of 'cinema-fed romanticism' and political neo-Darwinism. It made it clear that civilization had been put at risk, that religion would have to rescue it and that the only possible religion was eugenic.

In the preface and *The Revolutionist's Handbook* that Shaw had attached to *Man and Superman* in 1903, the eugenic problem had been approached through women's 'initiative' in 'sex transactions', the failure of aristocratic and 'plutocratic in-breeding' and the defects of Democracy. It was because the 'Yahoo' would 'wreck the Commonwealth ... by his vote', and because 'selective breeding' alone could eliminate the Yahoo, that Socialism was said to require the separation of 'mating' from 'marriage' and a systematic 'improvement of human livestock'.

Man and Superman was a eugenicist tract which provided for a Government Department, Chartered Company or Private Society to carry out a policy. It was abrupt, dogmatic and naive. Only really in *Back to Methuselah* did Shaw expose such intellectual structure as his religion had, once objective morality, transcendental superstition and the 'romance of miracles and paradises and torture chambers' had been removed.

An important aspect of the preface to *Back to Methuselah* was its attack on Darwinianism not only as a cause of the 1914 war but also as an attempt to remove Mind from the universe. Shaw did not attack Darwin as much as he attacked Darwin's followers. But he attacked both, and, in doing so, aimed to show that it was Lamarckian Evolution which was vital to the future of civilization.

The reasons Shaw gave for looking back to Lamarck were that Lamarck had seen evolution as a 'mystical process' which depended on the proposition that 'living organisms changed because they wanted to'. Shaw described the transition from willing to instinctive performance, the hereditary character of its transmission and the higher intellectual achievements that were its outcome. Schopenhauer was brought into play for his 'metaphysical' sense of the 'will-to-live', Nietzsche for conceiving 'power over self' as the objective of the 'Will to Power' and Butler for 'leading us back when we were dancing to damnation' on the idea that the 'world could make itself without design, purpose, skill, intelligence or ... life'. In this context Darwinianism was a 'hideous fatalism' which treated Nature as a 'casual aggregation of dead matter' and debarred 'beauty, intelligence ... honour, aspiration ... imagination, metaphysics, poetry, conscience and decency' from consideration'.

Darwinianism was said, thus, to have marked the breakdown of cosmopolitan Liberalism which in its turn was treated as opening up the prospect of a breakdown of civilization. Shaw did not argue that it would be easy to save civilization, since Nature 'held no brief for the human experiment' and would 'try another experiment' if 'Man' did not 'serve'. What he argued was that, if civilization was to be saved, Man had to 'save ... it himself'. The question was how, and, in giving his answer, Shaw placed a heavy burden on art, drama and music. It was through the acts of symbolic realization of which they were capable that the religion of the future would be propagated and it was only when propagation had occurred that civilization would be saved as it came to be understood that the highest triumph of the will was the 'self-controlled man ... dominating and regulating his appetites and fixing the duration of human life ... at three hundred or three thousand' as readily as at the three score and ten years at which he had fixed it on opportunist grounds hitherto.

Except as a contribution to the revival of the English theatre and the renaissance of English music, Shaw's religion was empty. If it conceptualized a transition from the religion of the Church to the religion of the library, the theatre and the concert-hall, that was a real transition at which to have assisted, and was quite as important as the parallel transition from the religious leader as priest to the religious leader as social worker. The difficulty about it was that for all his pretence at avoiding sentimentality, Shaw did not avoid it. Certainly Socialism as self-willing, aesthetic humanitarianism has had a long run under many forms in the twentieth century. But if the ideal type that Shaw was projecting was merely the rebarbative product of a 'homopathic education' which questioned and dismissed all previously established moralities and opinions, then Superman was a pious delusion, rendered respectable only by its capricious flirtations with illusionlessness. Among all the modern English substitutes for Christianity, Methuselah, reborn as radical, rebarbative, perpetual youth, is by a long way the least persuasive.

Like Wells, Shaw associated Socialism with female emancipation. Shaw, however, though he registered the advanced sexual opinions of the 1880s and used stage characters to prognosticate about the feminity of the future, did not make sex his primary theme. In Havelock Ellis, sex was the primary theme.

VI

Ellis[1] was the son of a ship's captain, was brought up as an Evangelical, and was trained as a doctor. Having been an inadequate medical student, he never practised as a doctor; instead he became a writer and, after participating in progressive and socialist politics in the 1880s in London, acquired a leading reputation as protagonist of a distinctive view of relations between sex, science, literature, morality, religion and public policy.

Ellis was a voluminous writer of both books and essays; he was also a powerful and subtle one. There was nothing simple about his mentality or about the ways in which he related his interests to one another. He needed to write in order to live; his writing reflected the fact. But it was also creative, claiming for sexual activity the sort of rôle that Ruskin had claimed for literature, painting and architecture.

In all of Ellis's writings literary and scientific interests went hand in hand. His first published books were editions of Elizabethan dramatists in the *Mermaid* series of which he was editor and a volume entitled

---

[1] Henry Havelock Ellis (1859–1939). Educ. schools in Merton and Mitcham. School teacher in Australia 1875–9, medical student 1881–9. Author of *The New Spirit* 1890, *The Criminal* 1890, *The Nationalisation of Health* 1892, *Man and Woman* 1894, with J. A. Symonds *Das Kontrare Geschlechtsgeful* 1896, *Sexual Inversion* 1897, *Affirmations* 1898, *The Evolution of Modesty* 1899 (i.e. the eventual volume i of *Studies in the Psychology of Sex* 7 vols. 1897–1928), *The Nineteenth Century* 1900, *A Study of British Genius* 1904, *The Soul of Spain* 1908, *The Problem of Race Regeneration* 1911, *The World of Dreams* 1911, *The Task of Social Hygiene* 1912, *Impressions and Comments* 3 vols. 1914–24, *Essays in Wartime* 1916, *The Philosophy of Conflict* 1919, *Little Essays of Love and Virtue* 1922, *The Dance of Life* 1923, *More Essays of Love and Virtue* 1931, *Views and Reviews* 2 vols. 1932, *My Confessional* 1934, *Questions of Our Day* 1936, *My Life* 1940.

Man and Woman in a *Contemporary Science* series which for a time he also edited. He wrote about Spain and about Australia as the 'sun-drenched' civilization of the future. For a few months in 1886 he was the *Westminster Review*'s theological reviewer. Throughout his life he wrote prolifically about English and European literature, and about the Russian, French and German mentalities. Even his major 'scientific' work, *Studies in the Psychology of Sex*, was impregnated with literary references and conceptions.

Ellis's sexual writings were connected first of all with his interest in women and the difficulty he experienced in finding or providing sexual satisfaction, his sexual pamphlet, *Women and Marriage*, of 1888 following articles he had written on that subject in the previous seven years. They arose, secondly, from an interest in crime and disease, from the part which a socialist State might play in dealing with them and from a Galtonian endeavour to use eugenic methods to regenerate the race. *The Criminal* included a social analysis and policy for crime and *The Nationalisation of Health* a social analysis and policy for medicine. *A Study of British Genius, The Task of Social Hygiene, The Problem of Race Regeneration, Essays in Wartime* and *The Philosophy of Conflict* were some of the works in which Ellis explained why eugenicists were right, why birth-control was desirable if genius was to do its work and why the 'very existence' of the 'feeble-minded' was a 'dead weight on the race' and 'depreciated the quality of a people'.

By the middle 1890s Ellis had become interested in psychosomatic differences between the sexes. In the knowledge that his wife was a lesbian, he had persuaded J. A. Symonds to collaborate in a book about *Sexual Inversion* and, when Symonds's procurer and executor raised difficulty in the course of publication in German after Symonds's death, published his own contribution as the provisional volume i of *Studies in the Psychology of Sex* by itself. It was only with the publication of *The Evolution of Modesty* as the definitive volume i in 1899 that he established the line of argument which was to carry him through the four further volumes that were published by 1910.

These were the years in which *The Golden Bough* was being completed, and the parallel between the two works was close. Both were contributions to anthropological sociology; both were limited in their ideas once the initial ideas had been expressed; in both the method was to illustrate by example. Ellis's mind was the looser but

Studies in the Psychology of Sex was as powerful a monument to liberal scholarship and demanded as total a liberation from superstition as *The Golden Bough.*

Ellis did not originate his view of sexual activity; he was the heir to a long-standing literature about clinical practice. Moreover, though it was Krafft-Ebing rather than Freud who appeared most in volume i, *Studies in the Psychology of Sex* coincided with the translation of Freud's writings into English and was overtaken by them. Yet Ellis's range of reference was wider than Freud's, while being addressed far more than Freud's was to English problems. Along with Russell and Lawrence, Ellis considered problems which in an English context were so fundamental that it came to seem doubtful whether religion could stand up to the sexual and psycho-analytical revaluation that was effected in the 1920s.

In the 1890s, Ellis set the tone that he was to maintain subsequently. He was then, he claimed, concerned to cast aside 'prejudice', to 'reason clearly concerning the nature and causes of things' and to 'get at the facts' through the only 'key' that could 'open the door: the key of sincerity'. Sex was the 'central problem of life' but sexual 'secrecy' was the enemy of sincerity and it was as attempts to destroy inhibitions against sincerity that *The Evolution of Modesty, Man and Woman* and *Sexual Inversion* achieved their definitive rôle in the body of his work.

The main chapters of *Man and Woman* described the physical, emotional and intellectual capabilities of its subjects, entering into considerable detail about the male and female bodies and the nature of female menstruation, and emphasizing that there were irremoveable differences between the naturalness of women and the artificiality of men. Male pre-eminence in religion, art and intellectual activity and woman's confinement to the home, the brothel and the witches' coven were treated as historically located and therefore transitory phenomena, while men's insistence on treating women as objects to 'play with or worship' but not work with was held responsible for the 'attractive' but 'complex' personalities which women might abandon once prevailing norms were altered.

Throughout *Studies in the Psychology of Sex* Ellis emphasized the presence of deviance behind the chaste, exclusive heterosexuality of contemporary norms. In the auto-eroticism of volume i, in the sexual inversion of volume ii and in the psychic conditions and performances described in volumes iii to v, deviance came into its own. The descriptions that were given of sadism, masochism, fetishism, self-stimulation and sexual hysteria, and the connections that were asserted between religiosity and female stress, and pain, courtship, love, masturbation and Christianity, presented such impressive evidence of the prevalence of deviance that male-dominated norms and the Christian rules of sexual purity were made to seem inadequate responses to it.

Ellis's explanatory works were not, and did not pretend to be, explanatory merely. They were relativistic in their assumptions and used the diversity of moral norms that was observable in the history of civilization to effect as fundamental an undermining of existing norms as Tylor and Frazer had used the history of primitive practice to effect in *Primitive Culture* and *The Golden Bough*. Where Tylor and Frazer were interested in the higher thought rather than in practical conclusions, however, Ellis drew many practical conclusions.

What Ellis assumed was the importance of birth-control, contraception and 'puericulture' to the 'regeneration of the race'. What he argued for was the tenderness of love, the 'sacredness of motherhood' and the centrality of the child, a sane attitude to nakedness, breast-feeding and sexual instruction, and the removal of the horror with which venereal disease had been approached in the past. Prostitution, though undemocratic, was declared to be the 'buttress of our formal marriage system', the difference between the woman who 'sold herself in prostitution' and the woman who 'sold herself in ... a ... marriage that was ... sanctified by law and religion' being only a difference in the 'price and duration of the contract'. The aims of marriage were defined as erotic and parental, and its means as eugenic selectivity and 'mutual love'. These were said to be the only legitimate means and it followed that the 'Christian-ascetic' and 'contractual ... property' bases of existing marriage should give way to a 'sexual love ... so deep' as to make it impossible for a man to have intercourse with a woman in its absence.

Ellis did not pretend that the remoulding of marriage would be easy or that public opinion was ready to accept it. 'More than half of sexual intercourse' in modern Europe, however, took place 'outside marriage' and it was necessary, therefore, he argued, to have a 'French Revolution in the home' and a 'new theory of the family' to shake the 'ancient structure' of the 'husband's ... throne'.

In advocating the legalization of abortion, the proliferation of divorce and the establishment of 'trial marriage' as a preliminary to conventional marriage, Ellis was not aiming to licence promiscuity. On the contrary he was the moralist of the new sexuality, justifying it in terms of 'liberty and sincerity' and the independence which women had acquired through the progress of civilization, and arguing that skill and effort would be needed if the coital requirements of men were to be adjusted to the more complicated requirements of women.

What Ellis hoped for from sexual revolution was partly a change in the female character – a reduction in the dissimulation which men had forced on women in the past. It was much more a heightening of humanity as investigation of the 'hormones' of the 'ductless glands' established that sexuality, so far from being an appetitive response to external stimuli, was a 'complex mechanism' operating at 'inner foci' to produce the most 'mighty force' in the body. A religious passage made the point:

Sexual activity ... is not merely a bald propagative act, nor ... merely the relief of distended vessels. It is something more even than the foundation of great social institutions. It is the function by which all the finer activities of the organism ... may be developed and satisfied. Nothing, it has been said, is so serious as lust – to use the beautiful term which has been degraded into the expression of the lowest forms of sensual pleasure – and we have now to add that nothing is so full of play as love. Play is primarily the instinctive work of the brain, but it is brain activity united in the subtlest way to bodily activity ... Lovers in their play ... are thus moving amongst the highest human activities, alike of the body and of the soul ... passing to each other the sacramental chalice of that wine which imparts the deepest joy that man and woman can know ... subtly weaving the invisible cords that bind husband and wife together more truly and more firmly than the priest of any church. And if in the end ... they attain the climax of free and complete union, then their human play has become one with that divine play of creation in which old poets fabled that, out of the dust of the ground and in his own image, some God of Chaos once created Man.

VII

In adolescence Ellis renounced Christianity and started to write a book about *The Foundations of Religion*. Since, moreover, *Studies in the Psychology of Sex* referred admiringly to the interest which the Catholic Church had taken in both 'normal and abnormal sexuality', he was well aware that his sexual revolution would involve the replacement of Christianity by the new religion he believed was being established as literature converted Christianity's 'child of sin' into the 'naturally social animal' of modern thought.

Ellis did not treat literature as art. Music and painting were art, but literature was 'closer to life' and 'recorded ... manifestations of psychic aptitude and artistic impulse'. In the half century that followed his *Westminster Review* article on *The Novels of Thomas Hardy* in 1883 and his *Time* article on *The Present Position of English Criticism* two years later, he produced an enormous body of literary reflection.

In his sexual writings Ellis was radical and innovatory. Elsewhere he was neither, tending rather to blanket revolutionary claims in a rhetoric of 'balanced harmony'. As a Socialist he identified Liberalism with a narrowly optimistic view of human nature and a capitalistic 'righteousness' which demanded that the weakest should 'go to the wall'. As a Galtonian, he hated the 'degenerate' but fertile classes which had no part to play in the 'delicate mechanism of modern civilization' and connected eugenics not only with a programme of domestic reconstruction but also with the programme of international reconstruction that was sketched in *The Task of Social Hygiene*.

Ellis's doctrine was addressed to England and praised the 'heroism' which had kept English literature in touch with the 'facts of life' between Chaucer and Fielding. It described the replacement of literary by commercial heroism subsequently, the subjugation of literature to the 'atmosphere of the drawing-room' and the destruction, notwithstanding, of Britain's commercial supremacy in his own lifetime. For the future it looked forward to Britain becoming 'a sacred shrine' which would make up in the production of 'visions' and 'ideals' for what it had lost in Imperial greatness.

For some English authors – Hardy, for example, Shelley, Cowley, Milton, Landor, Browning, Shaw, Conrad, Wells and Ben Jonson – Ellis expressed a high regard; for Shakespeare his regard was limitless. On the whole, however, his heroes were not English, *Affirmations* and *The New Spirit* arguing that English thought was sunk in Victorian self-congratulation.

In looking to the future Ellis emphasized the importance and reasonableness of the scientific, democratic and sexual revolutions. He was especially concerned to disconnect the sexual revolution from Swiftian Rabelaisianism, and to underline the types of virtue that he found in Zola, Casanova and Walt Whitman.

Ellis recognized that Whitman's soul was not what it might have been, that Casanova's *Memoirs* contained only one view of human nature and that Zola was 'encamped' at the 'periphery' of the senses. Whitman, nevertheless, was presented as 'one of the very greatest emotional forces of modern times', Zola as having a 'tragic intensity of ... vision' which had brought the sexual, digestive and 'modern material' worlds into literature and Casanova's 'sincerity' and 'earthiness' as providing an 'unashamed ... presentation of a certain human type in its most complete development'.

In *Casanova* Ellis praised his subject's sexual attentiveness and the 'moral quality' which had enabled him to love many women while breaking few hearts. Casanova was said to have been heroically 'natural' in the 'abnormal' way in which Spinoza and St Bernard had been natural. Whitman's homosexuality was also praised, Whitman being said to have been disembarrassed of Christianity's disgust, to have denied that a 'loved one's body' could be 'impure or unclean' and to have achieved a physical conception of comradeship that went deeper than duty or religion. Whitman was compared with St Francis – the 'monk of nature' who had been 'sinner' as well as 'saint', had accepted Christianity 'because it was there but was not of it' and had followed Jesus not Paul in embracing 'all men' in his love.

In *The New Spirit* and *Affirmations*, Ellis affirmed the importance of a new attitude towards sexual and bodily functions and a systematic attempt to make morality responsive to human needs. In both works the discussion of morality was overshadowed by the historic presence of Christianity and the breadth and variety of the forms that religion had taken outside Christianity. Through the praise of science that formed the theme of *Diderot*, through the liberation that was praised in *Heine* and through the animus that *Ibsen* brought to bear on conventional Protestantism, Ellis proclaimed himself the heir of the Reformation and the French Revolution, and lined himself up behind Lessing, Goethe, Rousseau, Thoreau, Wagner, Darwin, Tolstoy and Nietzsche.

When *Nietzsche* was published as an article in 1895, Ellis claimed to be introducing the English public to a writer who, having 'stood at the ... summit of modern culture', had made the 'most determined effort ever made to destroy its morals'. Ellis had no more illusions about the nature of Nietzsche's sexual personality than he had about his own. But he contrasted Christianity's horror with Nietzsche's joy and praised the post-Wagnerian interlude when Nietzsche had liberated himself from 'every law save that of sincerity'.

The Nietzsche Ellis admired was the Nietzsche of 1876–82 who spoke better of Pilate than of Jesus and in the battle between the

'Classic' and the 'Christian' spirit was not on Christianity's side. This Nietzsche was less genial than Renan and less conscious than Pater of the 'germ of Christianity in things pagan', and had driven a horse and cart through George Eliot's, Mill's and Spencer's attempts to preserve Christian morality 'while denying Christian theology'. In his best phase Nietzsche had been a 'mole ... undermining ... two thousand years of European morality', disparaging the 'dread of pain' that 'modern morality' had retained from Christianity, and, by speaking 'out of the mouth of his own wound', achieving a status as the 'Pascal of Paganism'.

Ellis wished to replace the 'negative' virtue which Europe had come to admire by a 'positive' virtue in which wickedness and disease would play a part, and pity and God's grace would play none. Every man had to 'shed his own blood', 'feel his own pain' and become 'his own saviour', and it was for these reasons that there could only have been 'one Christian ... who had died on the Cross'.

What *Nietzsche* and also *Huysmans* said, was said negatively in the course of rejecting Christian dogmatism, mediaeval nostalgia and the plebeian Utilitarianism which Ellis attributed to the English. In *Tolstoy* he tried positively to absorb historic Christianity into a post-Christian naturalism.

Tolstoy described the division between the 'official Russia' of Peter the Great and the 'genuine Russian spirit' as it had been expressed in the Russian novel. In discussing Gogol, Turgenev, Dostoevsky and above all Tolstoy, it alleged an identity between 'Russian ordinary life' and the 'religious movement' which was manifesting itself even as Ellis wrote in 1890 in the characteristically Russian instincts of 'Communism, fraternity and sexual freedom'.

Ellis's essay on *Tolstoy* acquired significance from the fact that like St Francis, Tolstoy had been a sinner, claimed, indeed, when young, to have committed any 'crime or vice' that presented itself to him, and, after a change of mind in his early twenties, had achieved an understanding of death, the interdependence of the generations and the nature of God to which Ellis attached the highest importance. It was from the conception of God as being 'known by living' that Ellis's Tolstoyanism established connections between art, religion, social duty and the 'violence and misery of the world'.

Ellis praised Tolstoy's realism and populism, and his post-Whig realization that the 'respectable and well-to-do' were the 'direct causes' of the misery of the poor. Tolstoy was adduced as a reason why

244 *The Assault on Christianity in the Twentieth Century*

philanthropy should be abandoned, Christianity disengaged from contemporary oppression and Christian faith understood to be so 'lunatic' that only the minimum version could be accepted. In the course of defining the limits of acceptability, Jesus's teaching was declared to have had much in common with primitive religion and the other great religions of the world, and with men of 'power and sweetness' like Leonardo da Vinci, Napoleon, Darwin and Shakespeare to whom Einstein, Joyce and Croce, among others, were added in *The Dance of Life* in 1923.

The Dance of Life began by establishing that it was a book in the sense in which the Bible had been a book – that it offered a 'revelation' of something latent within the writer's 'soul' which was 'ultimately the soul of mankind'. It also established that life was an Art, not a matter of laws and commandments, that recognition of this would restore the unity which Christian, scientific and moralistic dogmatism had destroyed and that there was no division of essence between the 'restless fertility' of the 'scientific imagination' and literature's record of the 'footfalls' of the 'human spirit' in its 'great adventure across the universe'. It was in the context of a 'Chinese' understanding of life that Art was presented as the 'reality of morality', the 'moulding force of culture' and the 'whole stream of action' which was 'poured' through the nervous current ... of a man or an animal'.

In the chapter on '*The Art of Thinking*' Ellis made two seminal points, that Art – the ironic Art embodied in Plato's Socrates and the Jesus of the Gospels – resolved the conflicts of philosophy, and that the reason why supreme scientists were 'recognisably artists' was because their 'curiosity' had the same roots as 'sexual curiosity'. This was why Leonardo was the highest human type – at once 'man, woman and child', 'engineer ... and painter' and why he was to be admired for treating 'every problem in painting as a problem in physics' and 'every problem in physics' as a problem for the artist. This also was why Art was of fundamental significance for religion.

In Ellis's writing religion had a distinctive connotation. It did not mean duty, neither did it mean creed. On the contrary, it meant something wider and deeper – that 'enlarged diastole of the soul', which Ellis described as mysticism. Mysticism included science as well as religion, and one of the objects of *The Dance of Life* was to show that harmonious satisfaction of the religious and scientific impulses might be attained 'in the modern world' by an 'ordinary balanced person in whom both impulses strove for satisfaction'. After describing his own religious history and conversion, Ellis affirmed that 'the Kingdom of Heaven' was 'within one' and that 'conversion' involved merely an 'adjustment of psychic elements to each other' enabling the 'psychic organism or soul' to 'revolve truly on its own axis ... and ... become one with the universe'.

This was Ellis's positive position but it entailed its opposite – the disjunction which he alleged between mystical and conventional religion. Not only, on this view, was 'morality' outside the sphere of the 'mystic' but a 'religious man', like Jesus, was 'not necessarily a moral man'. The religious or mystical impulse, on the contrary, was a 'natural impulse' like the 'scientific impulse' which, since it had 'no transcendent objective truth' to conform to and no objective morality to sustain, performed a 'spiritual', almost 'psychological', function as each man created truths for himself.

This was fundamental. Ellis attacked the 'ghouls of the Church' but, so far from attacking religion, emphasized its importance. For 'morality' he claimed the regulative function that historic Christianity had claimed for itself, conceiving of it as a free, élitist invention which supplied guidance and leadership to the mass of men who responded naturally to the leadership-principle and assumed that duty was to be found in 'blind obedience to words of command'.

In contrasting the élite with the masses Ellis, though an élitist, was not a simple élitist. He wrote approvingly of the advance-guard's 'moral freedom' but disapprovingly of 'prancing philosophers who flaunted their moral theories before the world'. While appreciating both the 'moral unity' of primitive ages and the 'psychic differentiation' that had occurred since, he argued obscurely that men were still 'not far removed from the savage', and that their 'only valid rule' was a 'creative impulse' issuing in a 'traditional ... way of living based on real motor instincts which would blend ... reason and the manifold needs of personality'.

The Dance of Life sketched a position; it also specified enemies and a pedigree of support. The enemies included Kantian duty, the principle of utility, quantitative demography, social statistics and 'ambitious moral reformers' when these were 'rule-regulated', like the Jewish prophets. The pedigree culminated in Shaftesbury who alone had understood the connection between beauty and morality and alone had identified the 'sphere of instinct' as part of the 'sphere of art' to which 'aesthetic criteria had to be applied'.

This was Ellis's view of morality and he was conscious of the need to defend it against the accusation of being flippant or hedonistic. Through the darkness that he drew attention to in Chapter VI, he supplied a rebuke to Victorian optimism.

In our human world [it went] the precision of mechanism is for ever impossible. The indefiniteness of morality is a part of its necessary imperfection. There is not only room in morality for the high aspiration, the courageous decision, the tonic thrill of the muscles of the soul, but we have to admit also sacrifice and pain. The lesser good, our own or that of others, is merged in a larger good, and that cannot be without some rending of the heart. So all moral action, however in the end it may be justified by its harmony and balance, is in the making cruel and in a sense even immoral. Therein lies the final justification of the aesthetic conception of morality. It opens a wider perspective and reveals loftier standpoints; it shows how the seeming loss is part of an ultimate gain, so restoring that harmony and beauty which the unintelligent partisans of a hard and barren duty so often destroy for ever. 'Art,' as Paulhan declares, 'is often more moral than morality itself.' Or, as Jules de Gaultier holds, 'art is in a certain sense the only morality which life admits.' In so far as we can infuse it with the spirit and method of art, we have transformed morality into something beyond morality; it has become the complete embodiment of the Dance of Life.

Ellis was deficient in wit and humour, lacked Shaw's Irish showmanship and lent himself readily to presentation as a lubricious, or dirty old, thinker. He was neither. Ellis was an intense, serious thinker, like almost all the subjects of Parts II and III – a crusader who, since he was able to build on an existing body of truths, felt no need to ridicule his enemies. He was a bore, though less of a bore in socio-religious matters than Forster, say, or Auden. He embodied, nevertheless, an aspiration which infiltrated itself into the English public mind in the 1920s and in the hands of Russell and Lawrence supplied the basis for a major assault on sexual reticence.

10

The Revision of Ethical Earnestness III

'With our present industrial technique we can, if we choose, provide a tolerable subsistence for everybody. We could also secure that the world's population should be stationary if we were not prevented by the political influence of Churches which prefer war, pestilence and famine to contraception. The knowledge exists by which universal happiness can be secured; the chief obstacle to its utilization for that purpose is the teaching of religion. Religion prevents our children from having a rational education; religion prevents us from removing the fundamental causes of war; religion prevents us from teaching the ethic of scientific co-operation in place of the old fierce doctrines of sin and punishment. It is possible that mankind is on the threshold of a golden age; but, if so, it will be necessary first to slay the dragon that guards the door, and this dragon is religion.' Bertrand Russell *Has Religion Made A Useful Contribution to Civilization?* 1930 pp. 29–30.

'There must be manifestations. We *must* change back to the vision of the living cosmos; we *must*. The oldest Pan is in us, and he will not be denied. In cold blood and in hot blood both, we must make the change. That is how man is made. I accept the *must* from the oldest Pan in my soul, and from the newest *me*. Once a man gathers his whole soul together and arrives at a conclusion, the time of alternatives has gone. I *must*. No more than that. I *am* the First Man of Quetzalcoatl. I am Quetzalcoatl himself, if you like. A manifestation, as well as a man. I accept myself entire, and proceed to make destiny ... What else can I do?' D. H. Lawrence *The Plumed Serpent* 1926 p. 338.

'D'you remember how Jesus was led into the wilderness and fasted forty days? Then, when he was a-hungered, the devil came to him and said: If thou be the son of God, command that these stones be made bread. But Jesus resisted the temptation. Then the devil set him on a pinnacle of the temple and said to him: If thou be the son of God, cast thyself down ... But again Jesus resisted. Then the devil took him into a high mountain and showed him the kingdoms of the world ... But Jesus said: Get thee hence, Satan. That's the end of the story according to the good simple Matthew. But it wasn't. The devil was sly and he came to Jesus once more and said: If thou wilt accept shame and disgrace, scourging, a crown of thorns and death on the cross, thou shalt save the human race, for greater love hath no man than this, that a man lay down his life for his friends. Jesus fell. The devil laughed till his sides ached, for he knew the evil men would commit in the name of their redeemer.' W. Somerset Maugham *The Razor's Edge* 1944 (1963 edn) p. 209.

Throughout Part III the main theme remains what it was in Part II – the doubts about Christianity and the assault which has been made on it in England since 1840. But just as in Part II the main theme was developed in the shadow of the ethical earnestness which occupied the vacuum left by the abandonment of Christianity, so Part III develops in the shadow of the pessimistic illusionlessness which began after 1870 to edge ethical earnestness off the stage.

Not all the thinkers who are discussed in Part III were devotees of pessimistic illusionlessness or drew consistent conclusions from it. But all of them to some extent renounced liberal optimism – not only the thinkers who were examined in the last two chapters but also the three thinkers we shall examine next.

The thinkers who are to be examined in this chapter were unusually prolific and their writings commanded unusually wide attention. Maugham and Russell were older than Lawrence and were established authors before he began publishing. But by 1914 all three were established and all three had come into their own by the end of the 1920s. Maugham, Lawrence and Russell will be considered in that order.

I

Maugham[1] was born in 1874. At the age of twelve he was orphaned and was put in the care of an uncle who was an Anglican clergyman. Maugham was brought up by his uncle and his uncle's wife and was educated at King's School, Canterbury before becoming a medical

---

[1] William Somerset Maugham (1874–1965). Educ. King's School, Canterbury, and Heidelberg University. Medical student at St Thomas's Hospital 1892–5. Author of *Liza of Lambeth* 1897, *The Making of a Saint* 1898, *Orientations* 1899, *The Hero* 1901, *Mrs Cradock* 1902, *A Man of Honour* 1903, *The Merry-go-round* 1904, *The Land of the Blessed Virgin* 1905, *The Bishop's Apron* 1906, *Lady Frederick* 1907, *The Explorer* 1908, *The Magician* 1908, *Jack Straw* 1908, *Mrs Dot* 1908, *Penelope* 1909, *Smith* 1909, *Grace* 1910, *Loaves and Fishes* 1911, *The Land of Promise* 1913, *Of Human Bondage* 1915, *Caroline* 1916, *Our Betters* 1917, *Love in a Cottage* 1918, *Caesar's Wife* 1919, *Home and Beauty* 1919, *The Moon and Sixpence* 1919, *The Unknown* 1920, *The Circle* 1921, *The Trembling of a Leaf* 1921, *East of Suez* 1922, *On a Chinese Screen* 1922, *The Camel's Back* 1923, *The Painted Veil* 1925, *The Casuarina Tree* 1926, *The Constant Wife* 1926, *The Letter* 1927, *Ashenden* 1928, *The Sacred Flame* 1928, *Cakes and Ale* 1930, *The Breadwinner* 1930, *The Gentleman in the Parlour* 1930, *Six Stories* 1931, *The Narrow Corner* 1932, *For Services Rendered* 1932, *Sheppey* 1933, *Ah King* 1933, *Don Fernando* 1935, *Theatre* 1937, *The Summing-Up* 1938, *Christmas Holiday* 1939, *Books and You* 1940, *France at War* 1940, *Strictly Personal* 1941, *Up at the Villa* 1941, *The Razor's Edge* 1944, *Catalina* 1948, *Great Novelists and Their Novels* 1948, *A Writer's Notebook* 1949, *The Vagrant Mood* 1952, *Points of View* 1958.

student in London. At the age of twenty-three he began a career as a writer.

Maugham was one of the most self-conscious and professional of English writers, with an output which was prodigious in a variety of forms. In the decade after he began publishing in 1897, he wrote a travel book and half a dozen novels. For the next quarter of a century he was a leading London dramatist. From the end of the 1914 war he was a best-selling writer of novels and short stories. He went on writing successful books in his seventies and eighties. At his death at the age of ninety-one in 1965, he had not ceased to be a best-selling writer. He still has not ceased to be.

In later life Maugham claimed that his only aim was to please and amuse. The claim was absurd. Though Maugham was dedicated to Art and disciplined by its requirements, he knew what he thought, edged his readers towards it and in doing so covered a very great deal of ground.

Except in discussing his life as a spy, Maugham on the whole avoided politics. Yet he can be found expressing political opinions, from the pro-Boer opinions of *The Hero* in·1901 through the euthanasic opinions of *The Sacred Flame* in 1928 to the anti-war opinions of *For Services Rendered* in 1932, while in praising the Labour Party of the 1940s for disposing of inequality and unemployment, he lined up behind Churchill and Bevin as symbols of the patriotic war to which Labour had contributed. Maugham no more liked the consequences of his Radicalism than Churchill liked the consquences of *his*, but it is probable that Maugham's Radicalism resembled Churchill's, or just possibly Beaverbrook's, more than it resembled anyone else's.

Maugham had an appalling stammer, was extremely ugly, and was a probably instinctual homosexual. After affairs with both men and women in his early life, he had an unhappy marriage. From his early forties he had affairs and then lived with first one male secretary and then another. In this respect he presents a problem more peculiar even than the problem presented by Anthony Blunt. For whereas Blunt wrote in a manner which sustained the doctrine to which he was committed in his secret life, so that his doctrine about Art was consistent with the doctrine which sustained his life as a spy, Maugham felt obliged to conceal his life and experience in so far as the public he was addressing would not like an authorial personality which had what it judged to be deviant sexual peculiarities. Maugham professed the belief that for the real writer the whole of his own life and experience was the subject. In practice, however he was better placed to display his religion than his sexuality, since the lending libraries for which he wrote between the wars were less sensitive about Christianity than about homosexuality which, except in *Theatre, Don Fernando* and *Ten Novels and Their Authors*, he did not treat as something that literature should deal with even in the age of Freud and Ellis.

Maugham's treatment of sex was coloured by a pessimistic cynicism about relations between men and women which would doubtless have been as cynical and pessimistic if he had dealt with relations between men. Except in *Of Human Bondage* he connected sex with boredom and disappointment, or with violence, suicide and death. *Liza of Lambeth, The Hero, A Bad Example, The Narrow Corner, His Excellency, Rain, The Painted Veil, Up at the Villa* and *The Colonel's Lady* were only some of the works in which sex was treated in this way.

In his second phase as a novelist – after the First World War – Maugham used as his background the settings he encountered as a traveller, playwright and socially accomplished man of letters. In his earliest fiction he had used the more conventional backgrounds he had observed as a child in Kent and as a medical student in London.

In *Liza of Lambeth* the background was the philistine social solidarity of the slums. In *The Hero* it was the philistine social solidarity of an English village. In both cases the message was that there was an unavoidable conflict between social solidarity and individual self-fulfilment. But whereas *Liza of Lambeth* made the point in a secular setting, *The Hero* made it in an Anglican setting.

The subject of *The Hero* was the return to civilian life of a young officer – James Parsons – whose father had been court-martialled some years earlier for losing his unit in an Indian frontier ambush, and who himself had won the Victoria Cross in South Africa for rescuing a wounded fellow-officer who was then killed during the rescue by Boer gun-fire. The theme was the relationship between Parsons, his parents, his boyhood fiancée and the busybodies by whom they were surrounded. Dismissive accounts were given of the fiancée's high-minded philanthropy, of military and public-school snobbery, and of the idea that Marie Corelli was a Christian intellectual. The novel ended in operatic misery, with Parsons committing suicide because he could neither marry the woman he loved nor satisfy his parents' and the villagers' wishes by marrying the fiancée whom he had come to hate.

There were also edifying conclusions – that parental love could be ruthless and stultifying, that marriage without love was prostitution and that the free individual should follow passion alone in deciding to whom to be married.

The Hero was as unsavoury a book as *Liza of Lambeth*. The fiancée was bossy and insensitive, the parents 'cruel in their ... kindness' and the village characters, including the vicar, morally and intellectually despicable. Even the valour which had won Parsons the Victoria Cross turned out to have been idle since the wounded officer would not have been killed if he had not been rescued, while the ease with which the officer's parents recovered from his death did not suggest that his life had been very important. The conception of the 'gentleman' was dismissed not only in itself but also in its connection with Christianity, and it was stated emphatically that, though Christian respectability denied 'passion', passion would not be denied since Nature had 'no sense of decency' and no respect for the 'proprieties'.

The Hero, whatever else it was, was an anti-Christian tract, connecting Christian 'ignorance' with 'prejudice' and 'illiteracy', inventing Christian characters who regarded the body as 'indecent', and contrasting them to their disadvantage with the hero who, as a natural man, regarded soul and body as 'indissoluble'. There was a Darwinian, or Huxleyite, diminution of Christian pity and priggishness, a Mill-like dismissal of death and a pagan respect for suicide as the remedy for difficulties when they became intolerable.

Maugham had a Wellsian sense of the importance of books and used his own books to make statements of his doctrine. If his books are read as doctrine, his novels and short stories will be seen to have pointed a liberated sexuality at the constraints of sexual respectability, and *A Writer's Notebook*, *The Summing-Up*, *The Vagrant Mood* and *Points of View* to have provided didactic versions of the post-Christian syncretism which *The Painted Veil* and *The Razor's Edge* had extracted from *Of Human Bondage*.

Maugham had had a Christian upbringing both at home and at school. But from the time he began writing he rejected Christianity, because of its hatred of passion, its belief in eternal punishment and the cruelty and self-deception which had been occasioned by its egoism about the soul. From this point onwards he was an agnostic for whom science was the 'consoler and healer of troubles' and religious altruism an obstruction to evolution and for whom religion's use, if it had a use, was to be a non-proselytising, non-missionary aid to morality. These opinions (without the emphasis on science) were given definitive expression in *Of Human Bondage* when it was published in 1915, and it was evident then and later that Maugham disliked both the wartime revival of religion and Shaw's and Wells's attempts to cash in on it.

Maugham was well aware of the view that Englishmen with the religious instinct who 'in former days would have taken Orders' now 'gave all or part of their time to writing'. In his case, however, the war served merely to confirm an 'instinctive disbelief'. He not only rededicated himself to Art, as *The Moon and Sixpence* most obviously proclaimed, but also proclaimed the artist's liberation from all sense of social responsibility. It was not until 1925 that Maugham began even marginally to do what Shaw and Wells had tried to do ten years earlier.

In his first twenty years as a novelist, Maugham had written eight books and a number of short stories in which religion played a part. In these he conveyed an aversion to Puritanism, a regard for self-fulfilment and the belief that life without self-fulfilment was a life without value. The post-Trollopian twists of *The Bishop's Apron*, the fraudulence of the Tractarian in *Of Human Bondage*, the concupiscence of the missionary in *Rain*, the mixture of sacred and secular in *The Making of a Saint*, and the 'opulence' and 'ease' of Andalusian Catholicism in *The Land of the Blessed Virgin*, all implied a contrast between Anglicanism's mean hostility to self-fulfilment and Catholicism's magnificent hostility.

Maugham was respectful of Buddhism, Hinduism and ordered Catholicism whether in the China of *The Painted Veil*, the Spain of *Don Fernando* or the India and Burma of *The Gentleman in the Parlour*, *The Saint* and *A Writer's Notebook*. He expressed high regard for the sanctity which occured when worldly ties were renounced and 'peace' became the object of life, and presented mysticism as a real experience which, though detached from conventional, and detachable from all, religion, was capable of answering man's needs and feelings as he understood them.

Like Wells, Maugham claimed to have had 'a shattering' experience of 'communion with the universe'. From the miracle of *Faith* in 1899 to the miracles of *Catalina* in 1948, he interested himself in ecstasy and illumination, even when leaving it uncertain whether his interest was sincere or satirical. There can be no doubt about the sincerity of his interest in the bearers of truth and heroes of sanctity who are to be found scattered about his pages.

Maugham's bearers of truth were a job-lot – Waddington in *The Painted Veil*, Nicholls and Saunders in *The Narrow Corner*, Souzanne Rouviez and Sophie Macdonald in *The Razor's Edge*, for example. His heroes of sanctity were not very much better.

Maugham's heroes of sanctity were not priests. Their common denominator was an uncompromising illusionlessness, a belief in the superiority of mystical over puritanical religion and a summons to a spiritual quest which transcended the materialism of Kensington and Chicago. If none of them rose above caricature, all together left the impression, through all of Maugham's irony, that Maugham's ideal was the sort of spiritual pin-up which Durrell supplied in *The Razor's Edge* in succession to the sexual pin-up which Carey had supplied in *Of Human Bondage*.

Durrell was wetter than Carey, less plausible, except probably physically to Maugham, and less interesting. But he embodied a contrast with the worldliness that he fled from and a positive claim to spiritual integrity as Maugham had decided to understand it.

The background to *The Razor's Edge* was provided by an American family whose central members were Templeton, an arrivé art-dealer who had become a Roman Catholic, his ruthless and insensitive niece and her Chicago financier-husband who, together with his father, was destroyed by the 1929 slump. The husband and the niece were caricatures, Templeton better than a caricature, of American types. Durrell as hero was used as a contrast to both the niece whom he refused to marry and to the cliché-ridden joviality of the average 'good fellow' whom she married instead. The central theme was the religious Odyssey that Durrell underwent after being rescued from death by a fellow-pilot who had been killed during the rescue in the First World War.

Like Buchan's Arbuthnot, Maugham's Durrell was a decent member of western civilization who had made his way to the East and achieved a certain intimacy with it, and had picked up along with its languages the 'strange lore' that it taught about the nature of existence and the qualities which constitute moral goodness. The account of moral goodness was further elaborated through one of the male, and two of the central female, characters. Templeton, in spite of being an essentially ridiculous figure, was vouched for by a Catholic bishop as a man whose 'defects were of the surface'. Souzanne Rouviez and Sophie Macdonald were vouched for by Durrell who had lived with both, the former being the embodiment of natural sexuality and of prostitution as a profession, the latter being the 'modest, high-minded, idealistic child ... whose voice had trembled with tears when she read out an ode of Keats' in Durrell's presence when young, and who had achieved a 'tragic nobility' when the simultaneous deaths of her husband and child turned her into a drunken slut who had her throat cut for her pains.

Maugham disliked conventional respectability, was as averse as Newman to 'evangelical depravity' and was as tolerant as Greene of sins which flowed from the goodness of heart. His treatment of Christianity led through a Catholic condescension towards conventional Protestantism into a Hindu condescension towards mystical Catholicism.

The Razor's Edge was a secular narrative into which Maugham's views of Christianity were inserted in two stages – through the account that he gave of Durrell's meditations on Plotinus, Boehme, Eckhart, Ruysbroek and the 'blessedness of union with God' in Christianity, and through the account that he gave of Durrell's experience of yogis, ashrams and meditation in Hinduism. Hinduism was contrasted with Christianity, the significance of the contrast being that, though Durrell was a 'religious man' who had been separated from Christian faith and belief by the 'thickness of a cigarette paper', he had not wanted to believe in God and would not have found religious satisfaction at all if the Hindu gods had not shown him that a 'God who could be understood' was not a God.

The Hinduism that Durrell encountered in India was a higher mysticism which enabled Hindus to believe and practise their religion 'not half-heartedly, nor with reservation and unease' as Christianity was believed and practised in England, but 'with every fibre of their being' as Christianity had been believed and practised in Europe in the Middle Ages. Maugham's cynical ambivalence was everywhere apparent in *The Razor's Edge*, and we need not identify him with Durrell. But neither need we disregard the identification. Durrell's rejection of acquisitiveness, his detachment from conventional effort and achievement and the freedom from 'selfhood ... and sense' that he found in Hindu 'tranquillity' were important aspects of his thirst for religion. They were also aspects of Maugham's philosophy, and it is not too much to see in Durrell's philosophy of 'loafing' the vindication of a type of knowledge which, though incomprehensible to philistines, was something which Maugham expected Anglo-Saxon readers to be interested in during the revival of religion which was occurring at the height of the Second World War when *The Razor's Edge* was published in exactly the way in which Shaw and Wells had expected Anglo-Saxon readers to be interested in *their* religious opinions during the revival of religion which occurred at the height of the First World War.

It would be painful to look more closely at Maugham's beliefs. Readers who read Chapter 6 of *The Razor's Edge*, Chapters 63–77 of *The Summing-Up* and the last seventy pages of *A Writer's Notebook*, however, will find consideration being given to the transmigration of souls as the solution of the problem of evil, to communion between the self and the universal as the 'outcome of meditation' and to meditation as the natural conclusion to an active life; and that the disjunction between the 'Absolute of the Metaphysician' and the 'God of the Christian' was not paralleled in Maugham's mind by any similar disjunction between the Absolute of the Metaphysician and the Absolute of the Hindu.

Maugham disliked the humourlessness, intolerance and 'ungentlemanly demand for praise and worship' which he attributed to the Judaeo-Christian God and expounded the leading doctrines of Hinduism and Buddhism in order to diminish Him. But he was also critical of Hinduism and Buddhism even when most earnestly explaining them – Atman and Brahman, for example, though easier to believe in than the individual soul, being merely 'pleasing fancies' and the Hindu argument in favour of immortality being as 'alluring' but 'unconvincing' as a 'house agent's advertisement in a daily paper'.

Maugham was self-conscious and self-moved and, not least in his continuous duplicity about himself, a deliberate writer who had read some theology and philosophy and had thought seriously about it. Even if the outcome was a commonplace refurbishing of Spinoza, Schopenhauer and Russell, his skill as a writer made it as serviceable and interesting as most of the other writers discussed in this book. And, indeed, if life really does have 'no meaning' and mystical ecstasy 'no objectivity' and if 'God' really is so 'mysterious' a conception as to be irrelevant to conduct, then it may well be the case that philosophies can only express the 'temperaments' of philosophers, that 'courage' in face of mortality is as beautiful as the 'beauty of art' and that courage of this sort really is the 'only refuge' from 'pessimism and despair'.

Readers may judge that the account given here of Maugham's religion has emphasized an aspect of Maugham's life which Maugham thought marginal. Readers who do this would be mistaken. Pessimism when young, fear of death when old, and a cosmic selfishness throughout, made Maugham suppose that his religion was to be taken very seriously indeed, not only as literature but also as a response to literature's audience. If the religion that he sketched between 1925 and 1954 was woolly and latitudinarian, it was not less so than the pagan religion which Lawrence sketched between 1914 and 1930.

II

By 1914 Lawrence[1] had published three novels, some poems, a play and a number of short stories; he had given up schoolteaching because of illness, and had eloped with and married the German wife of a professor at Nottingham University where he had himself done a teacher-training course some years earlier.

After their elopement Lawrence moved with his wife from cottage to cottage, in Germany, England, Italy and elsewhere, living on the charity of friends and irregular payments from publishers, and succeeding at the same time in achieving doctrinal explicitness not only about class and sex, which provided the subject-matter of his fiction, but also about literature and religion. In *Twilight in Italy* and *Sea and Sardinia* a doctrine was implied, as also in the description of high-class homosexual mendicancy which formed the introduction to Magnus's *Memoirs of the Foreign Legion. Study of Thomas Hardy, The Crown, Education of the People, The Reality of Peace, Movements in European History, Psychoanalysis and the Unconscious, Fantasia of the Uncon-*

---

[1] David Herbert Lawrence (1885–1930). Educ. Nottingham High School and Nottingham University, school teacher 1905–11. Author of *The White Peacock* 1911, *The Trespasser* 1912, *Love Poems* 1913, *Sons and Lovers* 1913, *The Widowing of Mrs Holroyd* 1914, *The Prussian Officer* 1914, *The Rainbow* 1915, *Twilight in Italy* 1916, *Amores* 1916, *New Poems* 1918, *Bay* 1919, *Touch and Go* 1920, *Women in Love* 1920, *The Lost Girl* 1920, *Movements in European History* 1921, *Psychoanalysis and the Unconscious* 1921, *Sea and Sardinia* 1921, *Aaron's Rod* 1922, *Fantasia of the Unconscious* 1922, *England My England* 1922, *Studies in Classic American Literature* 1923, *Kangaroo* 1923, Introduction to *Memoirs of the Foreign Legion* 1924, *St Mawr* 1925, *Reflections on the Death of a Porcupine* 1925, *The Plumed Serpent* 1926, *Mornings in Mexico* 1927, *The Woman Who Rode Away* 1928, *Lady Chatterley's Lover* 1928, *Collected Poems* 2 vols. 1928, *The Virgin and the Gypsy* 1930, *Apocalypse* 1931, *Etruscan Places* 1932, E. D. McDonald (ed.) *Pheonix* 1936, F. W. Roberts and H. T. Moore (ed.) *Pheonix II* 1968.

scious, Studies in Classic American Literaturre, Reflections on the Death of a Porcupine, Mornings in Mexico, Etruscan Places and *Apocalypse* achieved doctrinal explicitness in the course of sketching the post-Christian religion with which Lawrence was still wrestling when he died in Venice at the age of forty-four in 1930.

Before the 1914 war, Lawrence had expressed a commonplace contempt for upper-class life, for democratic electioneering and for England's 'sourness' and 'despair'. On eloping, moreover, he had begun to feel that his wife's upbringing made it necessary that they should both 'fall into the intelligent, as it were, upper class' wherever they might live in the future. It was not until he began to be lionized by Keynes, Russell, Lady Ottoline Morrell and Lady Cynthia Asquith in 1915, however, that he expressed a practical interest in politics.

Lawrence was self-conscious about the social superiority he believed himself to have acquired from his mother, who had married beneath her, and by reason of the connection of which he was acutely aware between his mendicant rôle as a man of genius and the Midlands self-respect about money to which he had as little right as Magnus. Even when claiming to be a 'democrat in politics' or by moving happily in all classes to have transcended all of them, he was unashamedly 'aristocratic' and became more so in face of working-class support for the war.

To the war Lawrence expressed two sorts of objection: on the one hand, a personal objection to the intrusion that it represented in his life and privacy which increased as *The Rainbow* was suppressed, as publishers became reluctant to handle his work and as the 'ignominy' and 'humiliation' of a medical examination in connection with conscription for military service came into view; on the other hand, the public objection that the war was a 'mechanical stupidity' which was turning the 'sensitive' into 'crippled beings' who would 'burden our sick society' when peace returned. Though later for a time Germany was perceived to have been apprenticed to Satan, Lawrence had at first no sense of an enemy, only of the war as a 'disaster' which he hoped might soon be ended. When the war simply went on, he became a defeatist, arguing that 'senile Europe' had provoked Germany to destruction, that the British Empire should be handed over if that would bring the war to an end and that the 'external evil of Prussian rule' might be beneficial if it helped to check the moral collapse of civilization. The first signs he showed of hope about the future began when the killing achieved a gigantic scale in 1915 and the 'whiteness of the ghost legions' became unavoidable.

In making his judgment on wartime England, Lawrence's view was that every man was 'bent on his own private fulfilment', that the conception of 'the whole', as Plato and the Middle Ages had envisaged it, had been submerged in a 'paucity and materialism of mental consciousness' and that the conception of the whole would only be restored by 'smashing the frame' of existing thought and society and making detailed plans for social and political reconstruction. These were the identifications of friendship which, however, did not last, except with Lady Cynthia Asquith. Lawrence had never liked Keynes and came to dislike him intensely. With Lady Ottoline Morrell, relations ended with the account that he gave of her in *Women in Love*. With Russell, relations became difficult as soon as Lawrence read *Principles of Social Reconstruction*.

Lawrence criticized Russell for 'hatred of flesh and blood', 'falsity and cruelty of will' and 'invincible respectability'. Lawrence did not believe in 'democratic control'; neither did he share Russell's belief in 'the people'. It was 'wrong' he argued 'to give power into the hands of the working class' however right it might be to love them physically, and since a revolution was 'inevitable during the next ten years', it was essential to ensure that if 'Capital' was overthrown, it would not be 'Labour' that overthrew it. In the course of half-baked preparations for political action he came to the conclusion that dictatorship, in which the 'highest understandings' dictated for the 'lower understandings', was the only way of avoiding a 'bourgeois' Republic.

In contemplating direct political action, in establishing *The Signature* and a Cornish Utopia and in co-operating with Middleton Murry and Katharine Mansfield, Lawrence had his eye on politicians, including, especially, Balfour. Thereafter political engagement receded along with his friendship with Lady Ottoline Morrell. The 'aristocrats' were soon seen to have betrayed the 'vital principles of life', the people to be 'purposeless' and 'aimless' and not only the Lloyd Georges but also the Balfours to be 'canailles'. By 1917 Lawrence had begun to 'spit' on 'England's government and armies', was unwilling to 'sink with a ship he did not belong to' and, while the world 'slid in horror down to the bottomless pit', planned to 'save himself' and 'if possible' become 'happy' by going to America.

To a large extent Lawrence preserved these prejudices subsequently, retaining from his period of political engagement a deep hatred of the poor, of the envy and mediocrity of the 'middling masses' and of the 'destructiveness' which the modern oligarchy of antinomian martyrs had inherited from Christianity, and committing himself increasingly to an authoritarian legitimacy in which obedience was fundamental and kings, 'whether elected or not', would be responsible solely to God. Though he made many statements of such positions in the 1920s, his desire for revolution assumed in fact that he had retired from politics in order to prepare for the revolutions in psychology and religion which he had been reaching for in his pre-war writings.

Between 1912 and 1914 Lawrence had arrived rather uncertainly at theoretical preliminaries. He had identified himself as a Georgian poet, had praised the joy and eagerness of Masefield, Drinkwater, de la Mare and Brooke, and had associated *Georgian Poetry* with the idea that God could be served best by taking one's 'whole, passionate, spiritual and physical love' to the woman who 'loved one in return'. It was in these years that he picked up the beliefs that 'starvation of the flesh' was the 'modern weakness', that 'sitting tight on the crater of one's passions and emotions' was 'killing ... England' and that Puritanism had to be replaced by a sexuality which rejected asceticism and did not hate the body.

About sexual conduct, Lawrence had strong views. He was anti-homosexual, as he showed most notably after his visit to Russell in Cambridge in 1915 and in the efforts that he made to convert David Garnett to heterosexuality. If there were traces of homosexuality in himself, as there were, the judgment must be that he was sexually obsessive and transposed the heterosexual norm into a very high key indeed.

The essence of Lawrence's sexual doctrine was that sex was not enough by itself, and that, in order to achieve love, there had to be encounter with another person. This was what he meant by the higher sexuality which manifested itself in the 'suffering' involved in the 'journey towards another soul' and when the 'sex group of chords' became ... the 'great harmonies' of the 'sinless' religion which was to be found in the unconscious.

Lawrence believed that conscious life was a 'masquerade of death' and that men who refused to submit to the unconscious would be destroyed. There was, as *The Golden Bough* reminded him in 1915, 'another seat of consciousness than the brain and the nerve consciousness' – a 'blood consciousness' whose 'underground roots' alone made men capable of growth. In *Study of Thomas Hardy* he established that 'living' was not the same as 'working', that the vanity and mortality of effort contained in the phoenix and the poppy were not less necessary to growth than practical work and effort and that 'work' and 'all effort for public good' should be merely means to self-fulfilment. It was acquisitiveness and the modern belief in 'riches' as a means to 'freedom' which stood in the way of self-fulfilment, and an 'eternity of pure leisure', he claimed, would open itself up if, instead of being obsessed in this way, men would work a few hours a day and devote the rest of the day to 'producing themselves'.

Study of Thomas Hardy described these 'selves', Hardy's preferences being characterized, approvingly, as aristocratic and individualist and kings as having been heroic in the past because, where other men had been under the compulsion to 'do', they had had the opportunity of 'being' and had been better able therefore to disregard oppressive sexual conventions.

In *Study of Thomas Hardy* the 'sexual act' was the 'centre' of a man's life. But to go to a woman to 'heal oneself' was mean-minded and as self-regarding as sodomy or masturbation. The reason for 'going to a woman' was not only to 'know oneself' but also to know her. This was what love was – an exploration 'upon the coasts of the unknown'. It was because ordinary Englishmen of the educated class went to women as a form of self-masturbation that 'freedom of the soul' was unknown in England, and it was only when a 'constructive, synthetic metaphysical process' had replaced the analytic introspection which Lawrence associated with Renaissance and contemporary English homosexuality that decay would be halted, love established and 'consummation' achieved.

'Consummation' was not described fully in *Study of Thomas Hardy*. It was described obscurely in *The Crown*, and obliquely in *The Quest for Peace*. It was given its first lucid expression in *Psychoanalysis and the Unconscious* and *Fantasia of the Unconscious* where the chief aim was to subvert rationalism and moral idealism, and reverse the Freudian insistence on bringing the content of the unconscious into consciousness.

Lawrence accepted Freud's subversion of sexual conventions. But he criticized Freudian therapy and rejected the Freudian unconscious for undermining moral spontaneity and erecting a new obstacle to the discovery of 'the true unconscious where life bubbled up, prior to any mentality'. Men, he insisted, were not 'masters of their fate' and the attempt to pretend that they were had been responsible for the shrieking agony which modern moralism had made of 'love and unselfishness'. The argument, if that is the right word, is to be found at the end of Chapter 2 of *Psychoanalysis and the Unconscious.*

What we must needs do is to try to trace still further the habits of the true unconscious, and by mental recognition of these habits break the limits which we have imposed on the movement of the unconscious. For the whole point about the true unconscious is that it is all the time moving forward, beyond the range of its own fixed laws or habits. It is no good trying to superimpose an ideal nature upon the unconscious. We have to try to recognize the true nature and then leave the unconscious itself to prompt new movement and new being – the creative progress.

What we are suffering from now is the restriction of the unconscious within certain ideal limits. The more we force the ideal the more we rupture the true movement. Once we can admit the known, but incomprehensible, presence of the integral unconscious; once we can trace it home in ourselves and follow its first revealed movements; once we know how it habitually unfolds itself; once we can scientifically determine its laws and processes in ourselves: then at last we can begin to live from the spontaneous initial prompting, instead of from the dead machine-principles of ideas and ideals. There is a whole science of the creative unconscious, the unconscious in its law-abiding activities. And of this science we do not even know the first term. Yes, when we know that the unconscious appears by creation, as a new individual reality in every newly-fertilized germ-cell, then we know the very first item of the new science. But it needs a super-scientific grace before we can admit this first new item of knowledge. It means that science abandons its intellectualistic position and embraces the old religious faculty. But it does not thereby become less scientific, it only becomes at last complete in knowledge.

In laying out the need for a science of the unconscious and an education based upon it, *Psychoanalysis and the Unconscious* and *Fantasia of the Unconscious* were vague and sketchy. Even *Education of the People* was largely declamatory. If a serious content is to be extracted from Lawrence's psychological and religious writings, it will be found in the view that religion had been right about the 'causeless' nature of individuality and had something significant to say both about modern science and about modern life.

As a student Lawrence underwent a recession from the Nonconformity in which he had been brought up; but he did not reject religion altogether. His position almost always was that 'religion was a most comforting companion', that it 'linked' mankind to 'an eternity' and that conceptions of 'life', 'blood' and 'the flesh' which were 'wider than the intellect' were to be associated with a commitment to art as the outcome of its yearning'. At no subsequent point in his life did he recede from the opinion he expressed in 1914 that he was 'primarily ... a passionately religious man' whose 'novels had to be written' from the 'depths of his religious experience'.

Lawrence's experience included recollections of the Christian images with which he had grown up, a Ruskinian sense of Christianity's physical presence in the landscape and an historical appreciation of the Age of Faith before the Reformation. His interest in Nature (St Francis's, or any other), however, was little different from Ellis's, his interest in Christianity's presence was much the same as the interest which Frazer had displayed in *The Golden Bough*, while the contrast that he drew between paganism's subjectivity and Christianity's objectivity was more attenuated even than the attenuated Christianity achieved by Middleton Murry in the early 1920s.

In *Landmarks in European History*, Lawrence described the 'beauty and gentleness' of Jesus, the 'innocent love' of the early Christians and Christianity's rôle in 'keeping hope alive' during the Dark Ages. But he also described the Renaissance as the 'most wonderful' century in European history, Savonarola as a reversion to the 'old methods of ... violence and ... horror' and the Reformation as establishing for 'individual men and women' the sort of freedom which any lapsed Protestant might have claimed for it – freedom, that is to say, to believe 'as their souls prompted them', to act 'as their hearts desired' and to become the 'beautiful, flexible' human beings in which it was freedom's nature to issue.

Lawrence's view of the past differentiated itself from average Protestantism by its scepticism about liberty, its antipathy to Democracy, and traces of an Arnoldian regard for mediaeval Christianity. But his mediaevalism nowhere transcended nostalgia; most of it was indistinguishable from the Comtean doctrine that mediaeval Catholicism, though suitable to its time and mentality, had become anachronistic when the Christian epoch came to an end.

Lawrence discerned two epochs in the past – the epoch of 'the Law ... the Father ... and Nature', of which Plato, Dante and Raphael had been the culmination, and the epoch of 'Love ... the Son ... and Knowledge', which had culminated in Sue Bridehead, Dostoevsky's

Idiot, Turner's later painting, Debussy's music and Symbolist poetry. These epochs were not, however, at odds with one another, and he saw the task of the future as being to effect a reconciliation by means of the complementarity which existed between woman as embodiment of law and conservatism and man as the embodiment of love and change. On this view God was a symbol of what was 'missing according to aspiration', and it was the impossibility of 'obtaining complete satisfaction ... at all times' which made it necessary to have a God – an 'unrealised component' which would reveal what a man or woman 'lacked and yearned for' in their living.

In woman, [went the approach to the central dictum] man finds his root and establishment: in man, woman finds her exfoliation and florescence.

Man and woman are roughly the embodiment of Love and the Law, [went the dictum] they are the two complementary parts.

In the body, [went the dictum's development] they are most alike ... Starting from the connection, almost unification, of the genitals, and travelling towards the feelings and the mind, there becomes ever a greater difference ... between the two ... till at last ... the two are ... one again ... and ... any pure utterance is a perfect unity ... united by the Holy Spirit.

In *Study of Thomas Hardy*, *Fantasia of the Unconscious* and *The Reality of Peace*, Lawrence illustrated his meaning through the mixtures of male and female characteristics that he found in writers and painters between Job and Swinburne. In *Mornings in Mexico* he illustrated it through the religion that he thought he had seen among the Mexican Indians, and in *Etruscan Places* through the evidence which phallic architecture supplied of the sinless religion which he had already found in the post-Freudian Unconscious.

What Lawrence wrote in these writings was that 'suppression' and 'power-mania' were endemic in western Rationalism and that they could be neutralized best by new versions of the 'Prophets and Kings' who had 'shone like morning' and 'blazed like Gods' in the 'old physical world' which had not yet been deadened by intellectuality. What he meant was that religion should not be 'deadened by morals', that ethical earnestness was a mark of death and that it was only by understanding the process of death which infected the living dead of the modern world that death could be transcended.

Sappho leaped off into the sea of death. But this is easy. Who dares leap off from the old world into the inception of the new? Who dares give himself to the tide of living peace? Many have gone in the tide of death. Who dares leap into the tide of new life? Who dares to perish from the old static entity, lend himself to the unresolved wonder? Who dares have done with his old self? Who dares have done with himself, and with all the rest of the old-established world; who dares have done with his own righteousness; who dares have done with humanity? It is time to have done with all these, and be given to the unknown which will come to pass.

Of all the religions discussed in this book Lawrence's was the most unrelievedly naturalistic and, even at its least sexual, the most heavily impregnated with physical love. Lawrence's conception of love may have had Christian overtones or recollections, as Patmore's had, and it is possible theoretically to conceive of a Lawrentian Christianity which infused the objectivity of love into the subjectivity of materialistic anthropocentricism. Lawrence did not arrive at such a position, and there is little reason to believe that he would have done so if he had lived longer. If one reads what he wrote, the religious significance of his writings will be found not in hints of conclusions that did not materialize but in the intensity of his negations, and in the fusion between the sexual and psychological loves and antagonisms which constituted the subject of almost all his fiction and the religious reconstruction which constituted the main theme of *The Plumed Serpent*.

The Plumed Serpent dealt with religion as subjectivity on the one hand and as public ritual and doctrine on the other. In putting flesh on the bones which Lawrence had displayed didactically elsewhere, it saw religion through the eyes of an American Irishwoman who had become sexually involved with the leader of an insurrectionary attempt to replace Mexican Catholicism by the religion of Quetzalcoatl.

In *The Plumed Serpent* Quetzalcoatlism appeared in two forms – as an historic type of Mexican Gallicanism which was ultimately reconcilable with Roman Catholicism, and as a sexual pantheism in which the blood of individuals was offered up to the 'great blood-being' of the tribe or nation and the 'white man's ... mental-spiritual consciousness' was fused with the 'old blood and vertebrate consciousness' which was to be found among Mexican Indians. And it was the violence and horror involved, and the energy that fusion released, which were represented as making Mexico 'thrill' with the 'new thing' that Quetzalcoatl had brought.

This 'new thing' in fact was an old thing – the 'supreme phallic mystery ... of the primeval world'. It was embodied principally in the 'power of the will' displayed by the man-gods, Ramon and Cipriano, who were the leaders of the revolution, but it was also embodied in the 'undying Pan faces' of their followers in whose 'glinting eyes' the 'power was limitless' and whose

ancient demonic gift ... rose like a ... pliant column ... between heaven and earth ... Save the Unknown God pours His spirit over my head and fire into my heart, and sends His power like a fountain of oil into my belly and his lightning like a hot spring into my loins ... I am nothing [went one of the liturgical professions of the 'strange, dumb ... heirs of Montezuma'] ... and save I take the wine of my spirit and the red of my heart, the strength of my belly and the power of my loins, and mingle them all together and kindle them to the Morning Star, I betray my body, I betray my soul, I betray my spirit and my God.

Lawrence may have meant to distance himself from Quetzalcoatlism; but if he did, he was remarkably unsuccessful. The impression left by *The Plumed Serpent*, and especially by its conclusion, is that it was as much a translation into fantasy of the principles of Lawrence's religious psychology as *The Ball and The Cross* and *The Innocence* and *The Wisdom of Father Brown* were of Chesterton's *Orthodoxy*.

Like Frazer, Lawrence had a feeling for the primitive and preferred primitive to modern forms of religion. Like Spencer's God his God was unknown, but it was darker than Spencer's, just as his 'soul' was more spontaneous and unconscious than Freud's. Lawrence had little time for Christian morality, even less for Christian charity and equality and none at all for Christianity's ambivalence about sexual satisfaction. He believed in the moral virtue of sexual discovery, in the naturalness of anger and retribution and in natural vitality as the guarantee of the superiority of superior people. As surely as Mill, he expected inferior people to obey superior people.

Whether the political reconstruction which Lawrence envisaged in the 1920s involved anything more than recognition of the need for obedience and objectivity without any substantive content for obedience to discern objectivity in, is something which the material does not enable us to decide. What it does enable us to decide is that Lawrence's Christianizing tendency was negligible, that his didactic writings superseded Christianity in the same way that George Eliot's and F. W. Newman's had done and that his mingling of Christian with non-Christian language and symbols contributed as surely as Yeats's to converting them into something else.

Lawrence's fiction on the whole was inexplicit and may be considered appropriately, alongside George Eliot's fiction, in connection with the post-Christian consensus. The conclusion to which we are led by consideration of his didactic writings is that, though right to regard himself as a 'passionately religious man', he succumbed to a connected difficulty – that in an age of uncertain religion, it is only too easy for a passionately religious man to make a fool of himself.

After his death, Lawrence's standing as a thinker became and remained so high that his writings are still a major landmark in English thought. In this respect at least Russell was his equal.

III

When Russell's[1] book, *The Problems of Philosophy*, was published in the Home University Library in 1912, Russell was forty. He was the celebrated author, with A. N. Whitehead, of *Principia Mathematica* volume i and had also published *An Essay on the Foundations of Geometry* and *The Principles of Mathematics*. *The Foundations of Geometry*, *The Principles of Mathematics* and *Principia Mathematica* were technical works, comprehensive essays in establishing the content of a new

[1] Bertrand Russell (1872–1970). Educ. at home and at Trinity College, Cambridge. Fellow of Trinity College 1895–1902. Author of *German Social Democracy* 1896, *An Essay on the Foundations of Geometry* 1897, *A Critical Exposition of the Philosophy of Leibniz* 1900, *The Principles of Mathematics* 1903, *Philosophical Essays* 1910, with A. N. Whitehead *Principia Mathematica* 3 vols. 1910–13, *The Problems of Philosophy* 1912, *Our Knowledge of the External World* 1914, *The Philosophy of Bergson* 1914, *Justice in Wartime* 1915, *Principles of Social Reconstruction* 1916, *Political Ideals* 1917, *Mysticism and Logic* 1918, *Roads to Freedom* 1918, *Introduction to Mathematical Philosophy* 1919, *The Practice and Theory of Bolshevism* 1920, *The Analysis of Mind* 1921, *The Problem of China* 1922, *A Free Man's Worship* 1923, *The Prospects of Industrial Civilization* 1923, *Icarus or the Future of Science* 1924, *What I Believe* 1925, *On Education* 1926, *The Analysis of Matter* 1927, *An Outline of Philosophy* 1927, *Why I Am Not a Christian* 1927, *Sceptical Essays* 1928, *Marriage and Morals* 1929, *The Conquest of Happiness* 1930, *Has Religion Made A Useful Contribution to Civilization?* 1930, *The Scientific Outlook* 1931, *Education and the Social Order* 1932, *Freedom and Organisation 1814–1914* 1934, *In Praise of Idleness* 1935, *Religion and Science* 1935, *Power: A New Social Analysis* 1938, *An Enquiry into Meaning and Truth* 1940, *A History of Western Philosophy* 1945, *Human Knowledge: Its Scope and Limits* 1948, *Authority and the Individual* 1949, *Unpopular Essays* 1950, *New Hopes for a Changing World* 1951, *The Impact of Science on Society* 1952, *Satan in the Suburbs* 1953, *Human Society in Ethics and Politics* 1954, *Portraits from Memory* 1956, *My Philosophical Development* 1959, *The Autobiography of Bertrand Russell* 3 vols. 1967–9, *War Crimes in Vietnam* 1967.

subject – the revolutionary mathematics of Boole, Cantor and Peano which had done more, Russell claimed, to advance understanding of the subject than had been done 'in the whole period from Aristotle to Leibniz'. This was the revolution which had established that 'logic' is the essence of mathematics, and Russell's fame and intellectual superiority would have been assured if he had turned his attention to nothing else.

When he first set up as a philosopher, Russell was not only an expositor of the new mathematics, but was also a missionary for the 'new philosophic logic' which he suggested would open 'as great an epoch in pure philosophy' as the 'immediate past' had been in mathematics. This claim was made with the greatest emphasis and at a very early stage in Russell's life. It provided the basis for his earliest excursions into the public realm as his attention was turned to *Mathematics and the Metaphysicians*, *The Place of Science in a Liberal Education*, *Mysticism and Logic* and *On Scientific Method in Philosophy*. The high achievements of this phase of thinking were published between 1910 and 1914 as *Philosophical Essays*, *The Problems of Philosophy* and *Our Knowledge of the External World*.

In making logic the essence of philosophy, Russell was reacting against Hegelianism, Pragmatism and Evolution, indeed against the whole of Classical Metaphysics which had been vitiated by self-assertion on the part of the philosophers concerned or by an inappropriate desire to provide comfort or consolation. Self-assertion, comfort and consolation had to be abandoned, as had 'guidance in moral perplexity', and what Russell admired in mathematical logic as the basis of a new philosophy was what he admired in all science – the sweeping away of mystery and timidity and the entry into a 'region of absolute necessity' which was 'independent of mankind', did not regard men's 'desires, tastes and interests' as affording a key to the understanding of the world and supplied those who pursued it with satisfactions that were 'more massive than any epic poem'.

Though Russell had other aims than his main one in considering philosophical method in the first phase of his life, his main aim then was to free philosophy from domination by 'religious and ethical ideas' and to pursue knowledge which was 'so certain that no reasonable man could doubt it'. This in its turn involved criticism not only of the 'principles employed' in 'science' and 'daily life' but also of the mystical intuitions which had hampered comprehension of reality in the past. It involved the 'methodical doubt' that Descartes had desiderated leading to an accurate evaluation of sense-perception, the subversion of which was treated as one of the most objectionable achievements of Classical Metaphysics.

In defending sense-perception, Russell did not deny that 'philosophical propositions were both *a priori* and true independently of such facts as could be discovered by the senses'. It was Logical Atomism's presupposition that there were 'general propositions which might be asserted of each individual thing' even though it was not the case, as idealists had argued, that 'all the things there were' formed a separate whole in addition.

Russell did not present the new logic as an immediate solution to philosophy's problems, its initial effect being, on the contrary, to 'diminish very greatly the extent of what was thought to be known'. Moreover, the construction of a 'repertory of abstractly tenable hypotheses' demanded 'patience and modesty' and the rejection of classical philosophy's desire to rethink the universe. All that was needed, nevertheless, to 'secure for philosophy in the near future an achievement surpassing all that had hitherto been accomplished' by philosophers in the past, was 'the creation of a school of men with scientific training and philosophical interests, unhampered by tradition ... and not misled by the literary methods of those who copied the ancients in all except their methods'.

These claims formed the basis for all of Russell's subsequent philosophical writing from *Introduction to Mathematical Philosophy* through *The Analysis of Mind* and *The Analysis of Matter* to the comprehensive statements embodied in *An Outline of Philosophy, An Enquiry into Meaning and Truth* and *Human Knowledge, Its Scope and Limits*, which were all attempts to deliver goods ordered before 1914 and supplied by a philosopher who had suffered a transforming experience from 1914 onwards.

The transforming experience of 1914 was the war. Where previously Russell had been a distinguished but recherché thinker, whose chief entry into public life had been as an advocate of free love, free trade and the rights of women, he now became a rebarbative public figure who had discovered that England was not a liberal country, and that the jingoism of the average Englishman was matched by the jingoism of the average Frenchman, German, Austrian and Russian. It was jingoism, prejudice, mass opinion and the herd spirit, and the difficulties Russell experienced personally in and out of prison as an opponent of the war, that turned his pre-war Radicalism into the progressive, anarchistic pessimism that he was to profess for the remainder of his life.

Russell's pre-war doctrine cannot properly be described as optimistic, though it included a faith in the prospects of science which the use made of science in war then went a long way towards destroying. Russell did not cease to believe in the desirability of the scientific outlook after 1914, but his advocacy came to be coloured by the fear that science would destroy mankind. In early Russell there had been cosmic detachment, and also cosmic gloom. There had, however, been no political gloom. It was not until he came to see how the human race could destroy itself that he experienced his share of the gloom which the war inflicted on his generation of English Liberals.

When Russell first considered social life – in *German Social Democracy* in 1896 – he had been concerned with the connection between theory and practice in German Marxism and with the obligation he attributed to the ruling classes in Germany to respond to the demands of humanity. Humanity involved Socialism, but Russell did not suggest that the socialization of Germany would be easy. Moreover, he did not treat Socialism as though it was above criticism. The Labour Theory of Value was rejected, along with a number of other arguments central to Marxist economics. There was, however, no mistaking the general approval that Russell gave or the admiration that he felt for the 'support' which was given 'in the midst of the most wretched conditions' to the more intelligent German 'working men and women' by belief in the 'advent of the Socialist State' and the conviction that 'the diminution and final extinction of the capitalist class' was an 'inevitable decree of fate'.

By the time he was twenty-four, Russell had acquired an advanced political position. In the following eighteen years, he acquired fringe experience of English political life as an incongruous member of the Co-Efficients, as a Radical candidate for parliament and as a supporter of the Suffragette movement. From the winter of 1914 his already existing demand for the reconstruction of philosophy was matched by an equally comprehensive demand for the reconstruction of life.

Between 1914 and 1930 Russell made a series of statements about the society of the future which between them constituted the main part of his contribution to the social aspect of public doctrine. Though the applications of the doctrine varied later as Fascism, Nazism and Soviet–American predominance obtruded, everything of moral and political consequence had already been established by the time he wrote *The Conquest of Happiness* in 1930.

Of the sociological works of these years, *On Education* dealt with education and *Marriage and Morals* with marriage. *The Practice and Theory of Bolshevism* described a visit to Russia, *The Problem of China* was the result of a period of teaching in China. All four dealt with their subjects in face of the need to find something for men to believe in and be moved by in the world that had been created by the Industrial Revolution.

Russell's view of human sociability was post-individualistic. While aiming to restore true individuality, it emphasized the importance of impulse and passion and the isolated individual's dependence upon 'the whole life of the community'. It emphasized that impulse and passion were indestructible, that the 'life of impulse' would need to be changed as much as the 'life of conscious thought' and that a life governed by 'purposes and desires' was likely to 'exhaust vitality'. 'Only passion' could 'control passion', only a 'contrary impulse' could check an 'impulse', and the social problem arose because of the need to establish mentalities and institutions which would provide 'outlets' for the 'impulses' that men had spontaneously.

Russell did not claim to impose suitable structures from outside: he claimed, on the contrary, to be demanding external changes which would minister to human impulses and lead them in socially desirable directions. He asserted that instinct was malleable and, in contributing to malleability, claimed to be superseding existing beliefs and institutions which were themselves both inhibiting vitality and moulding human impulses in evil directions rather than good ones.

These twin desires – to mould impulses and respect vitality – were not necessarily compatible. They were expressed, nevertheless, in all Russell's sociological writing, along with expressions of his awareness of their incompatibility. Even, therefore, when his doctrine was most legislative, it was also sceptical of legislation, and left the impression of wanting to reform or control the world without the inconveniences that are inseparable from control or reformation.

In setting up the conflict for which his doctrine was to provide the resolution, Russell dismissed existing life by contrast with the sort of life that desirable mentalities might create. He dismissed it comprehensively, because it depended on tradition, force and authority, and denied growth, curiosity, constructiveness, love and the joy of life.

In thus type-casting existing life, Russell wrote from the outside, as he was to do repeatedly in the next fifty years, judging it as it was lived and experienced by the poor, the rich, the dweller in the suburban street, the politician, the busy businessman and the jingoistic professor, and implying that the acceptance of tradition and authority and the prevalence of hope and fear were inhibiting growth, thwarting creativity and condemning men to a living death arising from a 'failure to live generously out of the warmth of the heart and ... the living vision of the spirit'.

The rhetoric of growth, joy, love and liking as the basis for reconstruction formed the core of Russell's work, not only between 1914 and 1930 but through all the successes and disappointments that events were to bring forth afterwards. They were pursued at length and with passion in the contrasts that he drew between European and Chinese mentalities and in the welcome that he gave to, and the doubts that he expressed about, the Russian Revolution. Most of all they were pursued in the contrast that he drew between *creativity* on the one hand and *possessiveness* on the other.

Like *acquisitiveness* in Tawney, *possessiveness* in Russell was the villain of the piece, the type of impulse that divided men and women from one another by substituting conflict and hatred for joy and light. Whereas the possessive impulses aimed to 'acquire or retain something' which could not 'be shared' with other human beings, creative impulses aimed at 'bringing into the world some valuable thing' in which there could be no private property and where, therefore, there could be mutual co-operation. Creativity had as its characteristic mode the pursuit of knowledge, art and goodness; it was associated with the intelligentsia; and Russell's praise of it implied the possibility of generalizing the intelligentsia's values to the whole of life. For, whereas creativity was said to produce the best sort of life that was open to men, possessiveness was said to produce the worst, inhibiting growth, joy, love and liking, and making existing life in the Western world the desert that Russell supposed it had become.

In *Principles of Social Reconstruction* the demand to replace possessiveness by creativity was applied to Property, Education, Marriage and Church Establishments, and to the State in its relations with other States. It was suggested that in all these areas fundamental changes would be needed if social life was to become an embodiment of the 'living spirit'.

Russell's starting-point was war and the damage that war had done to relations between the citizen and the State, and he was an advocate of extensions of state power. But he was also an advocate of restrictions on State power – through a syndicalist encouragement of associations, co-operatives and local government, and through international co-operation leading to world government.

Russell identified nationalism as the cause of war. But he assumed a close connection between the belligerent character of nation-states and the capitalistic organization of land and capital, and asserted that warlike impulses would not be curbed unless 'international co-operation' was supplemented by measures in restraint of capitalism.

Though he was clear that all property rights should be open to expropriation, Russell did not advocate the abolition of private property. He saw no reason to abolish 'private capitalistic enterprise' so long as capitalism was curbed, and he listed not only 'scientific' and 'literary' men and the 'working classes' but also 'shopkeepers, manufacturers and merchants' among those who, by contrast with the landed classes, were the people who had made England 'of any account in the world'. He anticipated danger from the 'huge technical organizations' that modern industry needed, and concluded that 'the monarchical organization of industry must be swept away' by co-operatives, trades unionism and 'industrial democracy'.

Between 1917 and 1923 Russell wrestled with the problems presented by incompatibilities between a number of variables. He assumed that 'the Labour movement was morally irresistible', that existing institutions were restrictive and that state power should be used in order to reform them. But he discerned 'pitfalls' in Fabian Socialism and 'inconvenience' in both Marxism and syndicalism, and saw no point in replacing economic decisions in favour of capitalists with log-rolling on behalf of 'sections of the wage-earning classes'.

Nor were Russell's doubts reduced by the Russian Revolution and the visit that he paid to the Soviet Union in 1920. The revolution, it is true, was the greatest event since 1789 for which the Bolsheviks deserved 'gratitude and admiration'. But 'rough and dangerous' methods had been employed, there had been insufficient preparation in the 'opinions and feelings of ordinary men and women' and the reason why Bolshevism had to be criticized was that its new world order was insufficiently respectful of the 'free spirit of man'.

This was what *The Practice and Theory of Bolshevism* taught. It taught that Bolshevists were 'industrialists in all their aims' and were performing the 'necessary' task of introducing 'American efficiency among a lazy and undisciplined population'. It taught also, however, that the Bolshevik régime was a party dictatorship, that its Polish and Asiatic wars had made nationalists out of international Communists and that it was in a state of acute tension with rural Russia. On this stage Trotsky was a jingoistic orator who induced in a Moscow audience that he addressed in Russell's presence in 1920 the same sort of response that London audiences had given to jingoistic orators in the autumn of 1914.

Russell found Lenin 'grim' – an 'intellectual autocrat' who wanted Arthur Henderson to become Prime Minister of England because 'nothing of importance would be done' and 'organized labour ... would ... turn to revolution'. But it was Lenin, with his honesty, courage and orthodoxy who for Russell epitomized the revolution, and who, if the choice became unavoidable, was more likely than anyone else to sacrifice Russia to it. It was an interview with Lenin which convinced Russell that 'love of liberty' was 'incompatible with wholehearted belief in a panacea for human ills'.

His sight of the Bolshevik revolution did not turn Russell against Communism. Nor did it stop him believing that Bolshevik methods were unavoidable in backward countries. In *The Problem of China*, he asked whether Communism was suitable for China.

Russell recognized that in certain respects European civilization was superior to Chinese; no amount of loathing for capitalism could diminish his regard for European science. But he was at pains to establish that Europeans were not 'missionaries of a superior civilization', that they had no right to exploit the Chinese as an 'inferior race' and that where Western society was acquisitive and aggressive, China had produced a character which was 'quiet', 'dignified', 'tolerant', 'urbane' and 'courteous', and felt a proper respect for its Confucian, examination-based, governing intelligentsia.

Russell was not advocating a static conservatism, China's problem being to modernize without capitulating to Western vices. In the 1911 revolution he saw analogies with the 1688 revolution in England, and among an older generation of Westernized Chinese replicas of Mill and Darwin. But the main argument was that the inhabitants of China were 'at the present time ... happier on the average, than the inhabitants of Europe taken as a whole', that Young China, having 'thrown over the prejudices' in which it had been brought up after 1911, had become 'genuinely free in its thought' and that a nation in which private liberty and trading and a 'very weak state' were the norm would give no encouragement to Bolshevism.

The chief thing that Russell acquired from his visits to Russia and China was a sense of the problems which confronted any society that experienced the change of life which Europe had experienced since 1750, and a deep conviction that 'the Bolshevik commissary and the American trust magnate' resembled each other in attaching undue importance to 'mechanism for its own sake'. Russell denied that the 'mechanistic conception of society was inevitable' and described the problem of the future as the adjustment of mechanical organization to minister to individual 'freedom and happiness'.

In all this Russell was conscious chiefly of difficulty, and in particular of the difficulty that the use of state power to effect the necessary revolution might replace a capitalistic society based on authority by a communistic society based on authority. He believed that 'democracy' had to perform a critical operation on 'customary beliefs and opinions' and to develop that 'distinctive individuality' which, though 'loved' by the artist, was needed by all men if they were to achieve the 'full dignity which was native to human beings'. This sort of transformation had, it is true, to be effected by state action, and, in underdeveloped countries by a Bolshevik 'oligarchy of believers'. But state action was to be self-liquidating since not only were existing policies and politicians parasitic on something more fundamental, i.e. the capitalistic organization of society, but the politics that Russell was advocating were parasitic on the fundamental changes in mentalities that he regarded as essential for the conquest of happiness in the future.

Russell's politics were as utopian as the politics he had criticized in *German Social Democracy*; they demanded a transformation in the atmosphere surrounding all aspects of life. They demanded more than anything else a transformation in education and marriage as prerequisites to all other sorts of transformation.

IV

In describing the damage that had been done to creativity by 'snobdom', Russell attacked both the financial constraints that 'snobdom' was alleged to have imposed on middle-class fecundity and the authoritative and competitive modes that it had imposed on education. In both areas *Principles of Social Reconstruction* had demanded a liberation of creativeness: by ensuring that 'neither the law nor public opinion should concern itself with the private relations of men and women, except where the children were concerned', and by developing a recognition on the part of teachers that 'there was something sacred, indefinable, individual and strangely precious' in children – a growing principle of life, an 'embodied fragment of the dumb striving of the world'.

On Education and *Marriage and Morals* gave extended attention to the 'limitation of families' that had come to be practised in Western Europe not only by career women but also by the middle classes, by skilled artisans and by working-class boys who rose 'by means of scholarships' into the professional classes. They dwelt on the relative increase that had occurred amongst the 'very poor', the 'shiftless and drunken' and the 'feeble-minded', and among 'those sections of the population which still actively believed in the Catholic religion', and concluded that 'shiftlessness, feeble-mindedness, stupidity and superstition' were on the increase, that 'prudence, energy, intellect and enlightenment' were in retreat and that the cost of bringing up children should not be borne by the State where the parents were unsuitable.

Russell was against sexual 'license'. But there was, he insisted, nothing 'sinful about sex' and, since sexual intercourse apart from love had 'little value', the marriage laws should cease to be either guarantors of morality or preventers of fornication. It was by 'separating love from children and a common life' that the existing law prevented men and women achieving 'the full measure of possible development', and it was in order to diminish prostitution that *Marriage and Morals* argued in favour of unfaithfulness within marriage, the 'liberties' which contraceptives had made possible and abandonment of the idea that divorce should be thought of as a punishment for adultery.

It is unnecessary to examine the details of Russell's view of marriage, the sexual peculiarities that may have produced it or the expectations he entertained from the replacement of the husband's authority by a Mountbattenesque liberty between the partners. What was important was the similarity he implied between reconstruction in marriage and reconstruction in education.

Russell's view of past sexual education was that it had imposed taboos on nakedness, kept children in ignorance of their sexual natures and perpetuated the fears and reticences which had been established by the 'weary asceticism' of late Antiquity. His view of past education generally was that it had made children credulous of teachers and ruthless towards each other, and that these defects would only be removed through the reconstruction which he sketched in *Principles of Social Reconstruction, The Prospects of Industrial Civilization, On Education* and *Education and the Social Order.*

In all this Russell professed to be incorporating the lessons of psychology. But he no more swallowed Freud whole than he had swallowed Marx whole. Though anxious to destroy inhibitions and repressions, he emphasized the *difficulty* of education, and the hard work that was involved in acquiring it. He also recognized that authority was inseparable from teaching and that pupils had in some respects to accept what they were told.

At the end of Part I of *On Education*, Russell wrote that 'one generation of fearless women could transform the world by bringing into it a generation of fearless children'. He did little to pursue this idea, tending by and large to be dismissive of parents as embodiments of conventional mentalities and looking to teachers, and in England to the National Union of Teachers, for the effort that would be needed if children were to achieve that 'constructive doubt' which was an essential feature of a fully human civilization.

As an educational propagandist Russell took a broad view of the the social significance not only of school education but also of universities. He wanted English universities to become institutions of learning rather than finishing-schools for gentlemen, and he continued the Huxleyite emphasis on the importance of opening them to the talents. On the other hand, while recognizing that Democracy lacked instinctive sympathy for the 'life of the mind', he argued that it might show more sympathy than plutocratic capitalism had shown and that 'learned bodies' might find it advantageous to become dependent on 'public money' since an 'educated' Democracy might well be persuaded to support projects which 'captains of industry' would be 'unable to appreciate'. The way to prevent any dangerous opposition between universities and the Labour movement was in any case for university teachers to show that they were not all 'hangers on of the rich' and for some of them to 'devote their energies to helping Labour in its struggle'.

In demanding inculcation of qualities that he regarded as the outcome of a properly conducted education, Russell listed obstacles that stood in the way of achieving them. At various points in his work he listed respectability, good form and capitalistic, patriotic, class, state and imperialistic sentiment. He also listed religion.

V

Almost everything that Russell wrote about religion, he wrote in the shadow of the assumption that a proper evaluation of science would lead to a proper evaluation of religion and a diminution of many of the claims that had been made on its behalf by its protagonists in the past.

By science Russell meant not only knowledge that had been established beyond reasonable doubt but also the critical process that established it. It was the systematic assertion of the possibilities of critical science that he pointed at the claims which Christianity had made on behalf of religion.

The claims that Russell made on behalf of science were made in two separate ways – as an enquiry into the nature of knowledge and as an enquiry into the place of science in life, and the second enquiry depended on the first. In this sense one may say that it was Russell's theory of knowledge that eroded religion. But in another more fundamental sense, it was his description of the 'scientific attitude' which produced the profoundest grounds for thinking that religion should be abandoned. It was the *scientific* attitude of which religion was the enemy and to the protection of which Russell devoted himself from *German Social Democracy* onwards.

In *German Social Democracy* the threat had been faced in the form of German Marxism. Both Russell's praise and his criticisms of German Marxism stemmed from its character as belief, from the fact that, so far from being based on a 'mere economic theory', it was a 'religion' which appealed to men's whole 'emotional nature' and inspired its supporters with 'unshakeable confidence in the ultimate victory of their cause'. This was regarded as a good thing in so far as it brought hope to the poor and oppressed but as a bad thing in so far as it obstructed science and understanding.

In arguing that religion obstructed science and understanding, Russell did not at first deny that religion was desirable. Until *Principles of Social Reconstruction* he emphasized the need for a dogmaless religion to replace Christianity. In both *Principles of Social Reconstruction* and *The Prospects of Industrial Civilization* his view was that dogmatic religion was about to die. This then merged into the view that all religion was evil.

The more important of Russell's grandfathers was Lord John Russell, the Whig Prime Minister who was a Protestant Anglican. Russell's parents, on the other hand, were free thinkers. Both had died before he was six and, though they had made provision for him to be brought up as a free thinker, the Courts forbade this, and Russell was brought up as a Christian. Russell in his turn in adolescence developed doubts about Christianity, and, as an undergraduate, abandoned it altogether. He did not, however, abandon religion. Even the abandonment of Hegelianism, under G. E. Moore's influence in about 1900, so far from carrying with it the rejection of religion, made the designation of a culturally suitable religion an important aspect of his intellectual activity.

What Russell claimed to be conscious of in *German Social Democracy* and thereafter was the prevailing lack of belief, and the need for the social system to be such that the people could 'believe in' the assumptions on which it was based. He argued that the existing system did not command 'authority' in the sense in which the mediaeval Church had commanded it, and would go on failing to command it unless existing assumptions were transformed.

Russell dismissed Christianity from two different points of view. He dismissed it for being an ecclesiastical religion in which endowment had put the Church into bondage to dogma. He dismissed it for being a persecuting religion which cared more for dogma than for truth, and, by emphasizing Hell, sin and God's wrath and ignoring God's responsibility for evil, had made cruelty its central feature.

Russell described Christian asceticism, virginity and sexual reticence as producing conditions in which 'almost every adult in a Christian community' was 'more or less diseased nervously'. He attacked 'personal immortality' as a licence to immorality on earth and denied that men needed 'allies in the sky'. 'God' being an 'unworthy conception derived from the oriental despotisms', he dismissed the Christian illusion that 'the universe was controlled by a Being' who shared men's 'tastes and prejudices' and had arranged 'cosmic evolution' to minister to their pleasure.

Like Huxley, Russell treated Roman Catholicism as Christianity's 'effective representative'. He made much of Catholic intolerance and compared its psychological 'certainty as to God's tastes and opinions' with the psychological certainty that he associated with lynching. In disparaging Christ by comparison with Buddha and Socrates, he argued that Christianity had not only not made men virtuous but, 'when organised into churches, had been ... the principal enemy of moral progress in the world'.

Russell's preoccupation with Christianity was at its strongest between 1900 and 1930. Thereafter he found other targets to attack and other threats to resist in the course of defending 'intellectual freedom'. There can be no doubt, however, that the aim in this earlier period was not so much to replace religion by 'intellectual freedom' as to establish a compatibility between 'intellectual freedom', the intelligentsia-values of *Principles of Social Reconstruction* and the 'religion' that had been described in *The Free Man's Worship* and *The Essence of Religion*.

The Free Man's Worship and *The Essence of Religion* asserted that the universe was as science described it, that it was neither good nor made for man's convenience and that men's bodies were subservient 'to the tyranny of outside forces'. 'The life of man, viewed outwardly, was but a small thing in comparison with the forces of nature', and in relation to this the only sane reaction was 'passive renunciation', abandonment of the 'struggle for private happiness' and the illusionless contemplation which liberated the mind from death by accepting death and working within its confines. This provided the foundation of an eloquent, pessimistic humanism which recognized that 'individual life' could not be preserved 'beyond the grave', that humanity would eventually be extinguished with the death of the solar system and that Christian hope should be replaced by an 'unyielding despair' lightened only when 'a sense of infinity broke through from some greater world beyond the existing world'.

In *The Essence of Religion* this sense of infinity was specified as a 'form of self-surrender', where 'all personal will ceased' and where the 'soul' felt itself 'in passive submission to the universe'. Russell was emphatic that 'surrender' and the 'sense of infinity' were not 'in ... essence' dependent upon belief in God and that the worship he was describing was a worship of existence which so enlarged the bounds of the thinking self as to make it embrace *with love* whatever of good or evil might come before it.

In thus reducing religion to its essentials, Russell claimed a great deal for its operation. Whatever deflation it directed at Christianity and the 'consolations' of Idealistic philosophy, *The Essence of Religion* left no doubt that there were large areas of feeling which were religion's proper concern. Not only was Russell not religion's single-minded enemy at this time, in *Principles of Social Reconstruction* three years later he showed how necessary religion was to the renovation of life that he was in the process of demanding.

What Russell had demanded in *The Essence of Religion* was respect for 'infinity' and an attempt to live life in its shadow as Christian lives had been lived in the shadow of Christ. In *Principles of Social Reconstruction* another principle was fundamental – the distinction between 'the life of the mind' and 'the life of the spirit', and between science as the outcome of the former and religion as the outcome of the latter. Both were said to be saturated with impersonality, but it was impersonal *thought* which formed the focus for the life of the mind, and impersonal *feeling* which formed the focus for the life of the spirit. It was because mind was negative in relation to instinct that it needed support from spirit; it was the part that spirit could play in controlling instinct and mind which gave religion its function.

In *Principles of Social Reconstruction*, religion's function was to replace the mediaeval synthesis which Christianity had established by the 'new growth' effected by the Renaissance and Reformation, the Industrial and Scientific Revolutions and the Feminist Revolution of the twentieth century, and what Russell claimed for this was that it would replace 'fear and submission' by 'hope and initiative', prevent men 'slipping negatively' through life as they had in the past, and address itself to the modern problems which arose from the art, intellect and government that Christ had ignored in peasant Palestine. Above all, he claimed, the 'new growth' would establish that the world was men's world and that not only 'the power' but also the 'glory would be men's ... if they had courage and insight to create them'.

The religious life that we must seek will not be one of occasional solemnity and superstitious prohibitions, it will not be sad or ascetic, it will concern itself little with rules of conduct. It will be inspired by a vision of what human life may be, and will be happy with the joy of creation, living in a large free world of initiative and hope. It will love mankind, not for what they are to the outward eye, but for what imagination shows that they have it in them to become. It will not readily condemn, but it will give praise to positive achievement rather than negative sinlessness, to the joy of life, the quick affection, the creative insight, by which the world may grow young and beautiful and filled with vigour.

Russell left no reason to suppose that he saw how rhetoric was to become reality. There were rancorous calls for 'us, the old' to come out of the living death which had made the 1914 war and to live 'by truth and love' in face of 'loneliness and obloquy'. Science was said to be the 'beginning' of a 'new ... life' for all mankind, and 'men of science' to be the 'happiest of intelligent men in the modern world' since they had 'less difficulty than any others in finding an outlet for creativeness'. In the main, however, Russell's religion was negative – a demand for a language and posture to complete the already existing disjunction from Christianity.

Between 1930 and 1969 Russell discovered new versions of the threat which Christianity had presented to intellectual freedom in the past, and became almost amiable towards liberal Christianity in face of Nazi and Stalinist totalitarianism and American nuclear power. Russell was not, in these years, exactly in retreat. But one of his central targets was now the 'scientific outlook' which, when reduced to a 'technique' by 'experts, governments and large firms', presented a threat to freedom and civilization and, if allowed to operate earlier, would have tried as hard as the Church had tried to suppress the minority culture without which Copernicus, Galileo and Darwin would never have emerged.

Once the outlines of his position had been established, Russell left a sense of continual replay. *A History of Western Philosophy* and *Freedom and Organisation* organized the past in order to convey a familiar message. *Human Society in Ethics and Politics* welcomed the 'decay of dogmatic belief', contrasted the world of science with the world of imagination and dismissed 'Stalin's language' for being 'full of reminiscences of the theological seminary in which he had received his training'. It was said to be 'peculiarly odious' that 'the principles of the Sermon on the Mount' should be adapted with a view for making atom bombs more effective'.

In the earliest stages of his life, Russell's socio-political doctrines, though intimately connected with his religion, were seldom in harmony with it. It was only really in the shadow of 1914 that harmony was established as religious illusionlessness in face of the universe was equated with democratic courage in face of war, and the Bolsheviks, the rank-and-file Japanese and the 'common soldier in Western Europe' were said to have equalled the courage of their commanders. This Russell acclaimed as an irreversible transformation which had converted courage from an aristocratic into a common virtue and, for the first time in history, had opened the way to abolishing that division between 'leaders and followers' which was the chief obstacle to the 'realization of democracy'.

The realization of Democracy was a political conception. But it was also an ethical conception with a religious basis – a demand for the rejection of timidity, servility and superstition and a proclamation of the hope that men would be able to live courageously together once religious authority and the aristocratic mentality had been destroyed, and it had come to be understood that courage was needed to live in an unencouraging universe.

This was a Whig hope modified by Darwinian pessimism and destined to be used as a critical instrument against all the authoritarianisms that were to offend against Russell's conception of liberty. It may be captured best in two formulations that Russell gave of it in 1925 and 1927.

Religion, [he wrote in *What I Believe*] since it has its source in terror, has dignified certain kinds of fear, and made people think them not disgraceful. In this it has done mankind a great disservice: *all* fear is bad. I believe that when I die I shall rot, and nothing of my ego will survive. I am not young, and I love life. But I should scorn to shiver with terror at the thought of annihilation. Happiness is none the less true happiness because it must come to an end, nor do thought and love lose their value because they are not everlasting. Many a man has borne himself proudly on the scaffold: surely the same pride should teach us to think truly about man's place in the world. Even if the open windows of science at first make us shiver after the cosy indoor warmth of traditional humanising myths, in the end the fresh air brings vigour, and the great spaces have a splendour of their own.

We want [he wrote in *Why I Am Not A Christian*] to stand upon our own feet and look fair and square at the world – its good facts, its bad facts, its beauties and its ugliness; see the world as it is, and be not afraid of it. Conquer the world by intelligence, and not merely by being slavishly subdued by the terror that comes from it ... When you hear people in church debasing themselves and saying that they are miserable sinners, and all the rest of it, it seems contemptible and not worthy of self-respecting human beings. We ought to stand up and look the world frankly in the face. We ought to make the best we can of the world, and if it is not so good as we wish, after all it will still be better than what these others have made of it in all these ages. A good world needs knowledge, kindliness and courage: it does not need a regretful hankering after the past, or a fettering of the free intelligence by words uttered long ago by ignorant men. It needs a fearless outlook and a free intelligence. It needs hope for the future, not looking back all the time towards a past that is dead, which we trust will be far surpassed by the future that our intelligence can create.

Russell had many talents but seems at times fluent and superficial, and one feels in considering his religion that adversity might have heightened his awareness of difficulty. He remains, nevertheless, the nearest that the assault described in Part III of this book has come to finding a universal prophet.

IV

ASSAULTS ON THE ASSAILANTS

11

Literature and the Counter-Revolution I

'Every religion ... which has ever influenced great masses of mankind ... is mainly a result of pure democratic action ... Whilst nowhere is the power of the few – of the very few – more conspicuous than in the domain of religion, nowhere is the power of the many more conspicuous also. No religion has ever grown, become established, and influenced the lives of men unless its doctrines and ... spirit have appealed to those wants of the heart and soul which have been shared, to a degree approximately equal, by all members of the communities, nations or races amongst whom the religion in question has become established.' W. H. Mallock *Aristocracy and Evolution* 1898 p. 225.

'It has been said that the part which democracy plays in the development of religion is shown us by the Church of Rome with greater distinctness than it is by any other great communion of believers; and the reason is that no other great communion of believers shows us with so much precision the part played by an aristocracy, and thus leaves the part played by democracy with so sharply defined a frontier ... The Roman Catholic religion, regarded as a body of doctrines which have actually influenced the spiritual lives of men, is a magnified picture, projected, as it were, upon the sky, of those secret but common elements of the human mind and heart, in virtue of which all men are supposed to be equal before God, and which unite the faithful into one class, instead of graduating them into many.' W. H. Mallock *Aristocracy and Evolution* 1898 pp. 228–9.

'Certain facts of history relating to religion may or may not be capable of "verification" to the multitude; but the dogmas which are the substance of a religion, can only be really apprehended – assuming them to be real and apprehensible – by the exceedingly few to whom the highest powers of contemplation, which are usually the accompaniments of equally extraordinary virtues, are accorded. The mass of mankind must receive and hold these things as they daily receive and hold a thousand other things – laws, customs, traditions, the grounds of common moralities, etc. – by faith; their real apprehension in such matters extending for the most part only to the discernment of the reasonableness of so receiving and holding them.' Coventry Patmore *Principle in Art* 1889 (1890 edn) p. 11.

In Part I of this work we examined the Ruskinian and Tractarian attacks on the eighteenth century and the demand for a Christian counter-revolution. In Part II we examined the mid-Victorian, and in Part III the post-Victorian, assaults on Christianity and on the idea of a Christian counter-revolution. It remains now to explain why, where we might have examined the post-Christian normality which followed, we shall examine instead the fate of the Christian counter-revolution since the Tractarians.

The salient feature of the post-Christian writing of the past fifty years has been the entrenchment of the assumption, which was expressed by White at the end of *Mark Rutherford's Autobiography*, by Pearson in *The Ethics of Free Thought* and by Julian Huxley in *The Humanist Frame*, that the Christian argument has been closed and need not be re-opened. This is what has deprived post-Christian writing of its bite and sting, and made it the conventional embodiment of an established opinion. The salient feature of the writing we are about to discuss has been the demand to re-open the argument, to put Christianity under the spotlight and to establish that the work which the Tractarians had begun has not been brought to a conclusion. This is what has given the Christian counter-revolution its bite and sting, despite manifest defects of depth and tone, and as religious polemic has made its literature superior to the literature of the post-Christian consensus which we propose for the moment to ignore.

The post-Christian position has a long pedigree. But whereas its earlier exponents provided articulated systematizations of the conflict between Christianity and Infidelity in the manner of the proselytizers who have been discussed in Parts II and III, there has since the 1930s been as complete a recession in articulateness among the enemies of Christianity, including the Marxist enemies, as there has been in the desire for conflict. No anti-Christian thinker with the authority and suggestiveness of the thinkers discussed in Parts II and III has begun writing about religion in England since 1930, and anti- and post-

Christian hypotheses, where they have become established, have been established, or insinuated, so silently and smoothly as to make them suitable subjects for the second part of Volume III.

Volume III, Part II, will describe the most effective response of modern thought to the challenge presented by Christianity. Modern thought – really modern thought – however, is obtuse about Christianity. It is because of its obtuseness, its silence and its refusal to accept the challenge that the remainder of this volume will discuss not the 'Post-Christian Consensus' which is the institutionalization of this obtuseness, but literary or critical Catholicism which, despite high aims and ambitions and a wish to insert itself into the fabric of English life and thought, has not achieved the institutionalized impregnability on which a predominating religion depends.

Since 1840, English Christianity, dissenting as well as Anglican, has been well supplied with modern assumptions of which Westcott, Lightfoot and Hort laid the bases in one mode, and Whately and Thomas Arnold, Jowett and Stanley, and Caird, Gore, Green, Creighton, Inge, Henson and the two Temples laid the bases in another. These modes of thinking, which will be discussed in Volume III, incorporated many of the messages that were delivered by the Tractarians. But they did so in acute awareness of the consensual restraints imposed by the climate of academic and educated lay opinion, and avoided both the aggression and way-out spiritual antinomianism, and the reactionary hostility to modern mentalities, which was the Tractarian legacy to literary Catholicism.

Literary Catholicism is a very different matter from the Tractarianism it succeeded. Though some of the Tractarians were romantic Luddites, they had fresh memories of a Christian establishment and a confessional state and thought of themselves, however resentfully, as heirs to a central political tradition. Many of the Roman Catholics we are about to discuss presented Christianity in a European, or Ultramontane, framework, criticized the modern world by reference to the mediaeval or used the idea of a Christian society to disparage the society in which they lived. Even when surrounded with landed or aristocratic influences, they were a long way from identifying themselves with English political establishments and provoked a deliberate breach with Anglicanism, particularly of the bourgeois, public-school, Evangelical and Kiplingesque varieties. Marxism was not more hostile, or critical of industrial society (leaving aside Mallock), and it would not be incredible if it were true that while one son of an Anglican bishop (Hollis of Taunton) became a Roman Catholic, another son became a successful Russian spy.

Moreover, the Roman Catholics who appear in this Part, though hoping for a Christian restoration, were also in retreat, even when they did not wish to be. Few of them were able to say what they wanted to say without obliqueness, paradox or contortion. They all believed that it would be difficult to defend Christianity against modern mentalities and that unusual arguments would have to be employed if defence was to be effective. Certainly Patmore's arguments were unusual.

I

In the autobiography that he began to write on Gerard Manley Hopkins's insistence at the age of sixty-five, Patmore[1] explained that, after receiving a minimal religious education as a child, he had come first to the realization of God and then to a belief in the Incarnation in the course of considering the possibility of composing a poetic tragedy when he was fifteen. 'The idea', he added, 'not only of a loving and governing God' but also of a God 'who was ... Man and capable of affording to men the most intimate communion with Himself', once conceived of as a reality, became 'what it has ever since remained ... the only reality seriously worth caring for.'

It is impossible to verify Patmore's account of his conversion to Christianity in the late 1830s. What is certain is that his conversion to Roman Catholicism in Rome in 1864 became the occasion for a bitter attack on many aspects of modern thought.

Like Newman's and Manning's, Patmore's father had been virtually bankrupted and Patmore, having lived prosperously until he was twenty, had become an unprosperous member of the staff of the British Museum. His marriage to the daughter of a Congregationalist minister then produced six children, the domesticity which was recorded in *The Angel in the House*, and a *modus vivendi* between Patmore's own

---

[1] Coventry Patmore (1823–96). Educ. at home. Printed Books Department of British Museum 1846–64. Author of *Poems* 1844, *Tamerton Church-Tower* 1853, *The Angel in the House* 1854–6, *Faithful for Ever* 1860, *The Unknown Eros* 1877, *Amelia* 1878, *Poems* 4 vols. 1879, with M. C. Patmore translation of *St Bernard on the Love of God* 1881, *How I Managed and Improved My Estate* 1886, *Hastings, Lewes, Rye and the Sussex Marshes* 1887, *Principle in Art* 1889, *Religio Poetae* 1893, *The Rod, the Root and the Flower* 1895, F. Page (ed.) *Courage in Politics 1885–1896* 1921.

hankering after a cultivated High Anglicanism and his wife's Protestant antipathy towards Rome. It was not until his wife's death in 1862 that Patmore was free to become a Roman Catholic, and not until his marriage to a second, wealthier, wife who having nearly married Manning after the death of Manning's wife had recently been converted by him, that the fastidious landed reactionary of the 1880s and 1890s became a marital and financial possibility.

In his first phase as an author forty years earlier, Patmore had been a friend of Ruskin, Tennyson, Browning and Carlyle, had shared Coleridge's view of poetry and had written about its rôle in relation to Christianity what Ruskin and Lindsay were writing at the same time about the rôle of painting and architecture. In putting Tennyson into this framework and praising Tennyson's Christian sensibility at Carlyle's and Emerson's expense, Patmore misunderstood him no more than Ruskin misunderstood Turner.

On emerging from the decade of rural seclusion which followed his conversion and second marriage, Patmore lost touch with his friends, developed doubts about Tennyson as a person and drew out the ambiguities that he had begun to discern in Tennyson's religion in the 1850s. He also began to pursue the implications of the view he had taken then about the arts as 'conveyors of aliment to the soul', about Protestantism's failure to encourage the arts since the Reformation and about the fact that contemporary Anglo-Saxon literature was as 'pagan' as it was possible for a literature produced in the 'atmosphere of Christian influences' to be.

In his Anglican phase Patmore was an enemy of didacticism since didacticism was an enemy of 'suggestiveness'. Poetry, nevertheless, was conceived of as the 'most philosophical of all writing' and the poet's and the novelist's responsibility as being 'scarcely inferior to that of the preacher'. Not Beauty, as pagan art had imagined, but Reality was art's proper subject, and the artist whose energies were 'absorbed in ... expressing ... the light ... which had been vouchsafed to him' was 'as truly employed' in God's service as he who 'occupied himself ... in expressing the Christian spirit by charities'.

In the 1850s Patmore acknowledged complementary debts to the liberation from sensationalism which German thought had effected since 1790, and to the genius that he discerned in Shakespeare, Milton and Wordsworth. It was not until he had become a Roman Catholic and declared himself a political reactionary that his conception of literature achieved the Christian content that it was to be given thirty years later.

Until middle age Patmore was a Palmerstonian Liberal with sufficient political engagement to have played a part in founding the Volunteer movement. His only serious political statements, on the other hand, consisted of articles which Frederick Greenwood – a long-standing, and also ex-Palmerstonian, friend – commissioned him to write for the *St James's Gazette* in the 1880s.

Patmore claimed to have understood from a comparatively early stage in his life that Gladstone was going to be the 'Danton' of an English Revolution. This, at any rate, was his argument in the 1880s when 'for the first time in English history' party divisions coincided with the division between the 'silly' and the 'sensible' and the 'frantic ambition of one bad man' was bringing about 'fifty or a hundred years sooner than it need have done' the disintegration of English nationality and the liquidation of English public life.

In face of Gladstone, Patmore's argument was that political health depended on liberty, and that the 'despotism of the multitude' was as lethal as the despotism of an 'irresponsible emperor'. Democracy hated distinction, the poor were as 'vicious' as the rich, and this combination of evils was destroying the self-transcendence which a healthy public life could give to those who wanted it. So long as these evils obtained, as Patmore implied that they would for a long time to come, so long would popular education supply an 'indulgence of individual vices', an 'advancement of individual covetousness' and a lowering, tyrannical or Mill-like attempt to subject everyone to common influences.

Patmore's target in the *St James's Gazette* was not only 'Liberalism' but also the 'frightened' Conservatism which had abandoned the calls of 'honour and patriotism'. 'Honour and patriotism' was what the Conservative Party ought to be standing for, and it was because he had shown courage in standing for the opposite that Gladstone had become as popular as Boulanger and achieved an amount of power which the drunkenness of the poor alone would prevent him using to their advantage. That a writer like Walt Whitman, moreover, should have 'attained to be thought a distinguished poet' was held to 'more than justify ... the forecast ... of a future ... dominated by the ... loudness ... profanity ... verbiage ... and inhuman humanitarianism' which Patmore regarded as the consummation of Democracy.

In Patmore's account of Democracy there were elements of de Tocqueville, hints that an aristocracy might be on the way in America, and the hope that even in England 'distinction' might be re-established after Gladstonian democracy had brought itself to a violent end. For the short term, there was pessimism about philanthropy, a hatred of the 'press' and a revulsion against that 'feminine' or 'sentimental' element which was impregnating all aspects of English public life.

In criticizing the literature, as in criticizing the politics, of the 1880s and 1890s, Patmore specified his enemy. This was described variously as the 'sensitive or feminine school of criticism' and the preference for 'lawlessness, self-assertion, oddity and inorganic polish' which, having modelled itself on the 'violent and ... vicious excitements' characteristic of French life and literature, was now seeping down from the governing classes into middle-class literature in England. In rejecting it, along with the perversions of the Aesthetes, Patmore adduced Lessing, Goethe, Hegel, Aristotle and Coleridge to support the principle that 'bad morality' was 'bad art'.

With Coleridge and Goethe, Patmore had the usual difficulty about their personal conduct; writing before *Tess* and *Jude*, he managed to make Hardy sound like Jane Austen. However, Godwin, Blake, Keats, Clough, Swinburne and D. G. Rossetti were censured and the Shelleyite doctrine of love – the 'most powerful moral solvent which the literature of our country had produced' – condemned as the work of a 'beautiful, effeminate and arrogant boy'. Positive vettings were given to Shakespeare, Sir Thomas Browne, Goldsmith and Burns, and also to Wolner, William Barnes, Robert Bridges, Francis Thompson, Gerard Manley Hopkins, Aubrey de Vere and Mrs Meynell, whose 'literary manners' had imposed upon her 'inferiors' a 'moral compulsion' such as Patmore discerned in few of her contemporaries.

In *Principle in Art*, Patmore explained the difference between contemporary criticism and the criticism of the future which was destined, by injecting a masculine element into the predominant femininity, to end the liberated self-indulgence with which even its most distinguished practitioners were alleged to be conducting it. *Principle in Art* conceptualized poetry as 'rejoicing in' and being 'completed' by law and 'scientific' criticism and developed the accounts which Coleridge and Newman had given of the relationship between poetry, knowledge and the 'mass of mankind'.

Patmore seems not to have been oppressed by the contrast he drew between the many who received their beliefs and traditions 'by faith', and the 'exceedingly few' who alone possessed the 'highest powers of contemplation'. He treated the contrast as necessary if criticism was to do its work and, in describing the significance of this work, distinguished 'Understanding' from that 'properly human knowledge' which apprehended the 'truth of life'. 'Apprehension' was the work of 'genius' and 'intellect', displayed itself in style as much as in doctrine and required from those who had it an unbending sincerity in expressing it. Though saints, statesmen and poets had all had it in the past, however, it had now become so rare that the poet – the 'ideal genius' of the modern world – alone could do anything to restore it.

In *Principle in Art*, Patmore gave a brief account of the features which constituted poetry's ideal content. Along with many technical points, he made it obvious that poetry was 'holy' and 'religious'.

During thirty years as a Roman Catholic, Patmore mistrusted priests and shared none of the Tractarian interest in the university as an instrument of clerical domination. His interest was in sanctity, in seers and prophets, and in the reality of the Christian experience. In *Religio Poetae* and *The Rod, The Root and The Flower*, he did for contemporary religion what *Principle in Art* had done for poetry, explaining what he despised about it and what he hoped for from the sort of Christianity that he wished to replace it with.

As an advocate of Christianity, Patmore attacked the 'levity' and 'melancholy' of the Aesthetes, the 'carelessness and indifference' of the agnostics and the 'congenital' blindness which prevented 'rational democrats' recognizing 'spiritual realities' when they saw them. Sexual equality was criticized for being heretical, and toleration for being ambiguous, in relation to truth. Macaulay, Bacon, Grote, Spencer, Huxley, Morley, Mill, Emerson, Benjamin Franklin and George Washington were named as symptoms of error, along with the Protestant 'fear of God' and the sexual Manicheeism which had infected the Roman as well as the Protestant Churches since the Reformation.

Patmore despised Wagner, dismissed Manning's 'atheism' and came to dislike the 'immorality' of Goethe's 'self-culture'. On the other hand, he admired Gibbon's anti-clericalism, Schopenhauer's 'Catholic ... atheism' and the Buddhist doctrine of the 'abnegation of self'. 'Ninety-nine hundredths' of what Swedenborg had written was 'in perfect harmony with the Catholic faith', and the Catholicism that Patmore proposed for the future owed as much to him and to Coleridge as to orthodox Christianity.

In an article in the *British Quarterly Review* in 1849, Patmore had looked forward to the rise of a new devotional Art based on a true 'catholicity far other than that which had its centre in the Vatican'. In the 1890s, he believed that poetic insight had been the religion of 'nearly all religious people' in the nineteenth century, that it was so by reason of a 'calculus' as 'special' as Newton's calculus and that there was room for a poem to explain what modern Catholicism had forgotten – that there was a 'passionate humanity ... at the core of all the doctrines of the Catholic Church'.

Religio Poetae identified poetic insight as the 'real apprehension' which had been described in *Principle in Art* and the means by which Christianity might appeal to the 'natural instincts and feelings'. In explaining why he had written it, Patmore added that, though he was only doing what Coleridge had intended to do before he died, he was well aware of the objections to Coleridgean Romanticism and aimed principally to give it the Catholic structure which was to be found in St Augustine, St Thomas Aquinas, St Bernard, St François de Sales, St Teresa and St John of the Cross who had had more 'poetic insight' than 'all the poets of the past two thousand years' put together.

This was the basis for the 'New Dispensation' which, however, was to depend on dogma. Dogma was the 'key' of which the soul was the 'lock', and without dogma the soul could neither 'believe its own ... instincts' nor approach the real Christianity at which they hinted – an unpleasant religion which was unintelligible to most souls, had to be communicated in myths and enigmas and needed the 'reticence' and 'reserve' with which the Church had habitually surrounded it in the past.

Patmore did not explain in what sense Christianity was unpleasant, or why unpleasantness justified reticence and reserve. He did explain, however, that Christianity had nothing to do with social progress and a lot to do with 'minding one's own business' and that it differed from the natural sciences by reason of its dependence on the 'spiritual senses' which hardly existed among the 'mass' of mankind. The cultivation of these senses was 'painful' and 'repugnant to nature', and could not begin until love had replaced fear as man's dominant motive. Love was the beginning of wisdom, and the 'celestial secrets' which it revealed were far more significant than the 'life's labour' of the 'herd of good people' who busied themselves with 'much service' when they ought to have been sitting 'attentive ... at the feet of Truth'.

The central feature of the new phase of Christianity was, therefore, to be a science of love as free of subjectivity as Orthodoxy and the Natural Sciences, as dependent as these had been on 'obedience' and self-sacrifice and as publicly demonstrable as *The Angel in the House*, which Patmore had conceived of as a central work of Victorian literature when it was published in the 1850s. Not only was the 'incomprehensible happiness of love between the sexes' to be founded on the 'voluntary honour' which 'manly nature' paid to the 'weaker vessel', but the 'ideal womanhood' which every woman – the Virgin Mary preeminently – was able to 'represent' to 'some man' was to become the 'light and joy of the universe', and whenever a 'lover said and meant that he had been "made immortal by a kiss" he stated an unexaggerated truth since eternity ... was but the sum, simultaneity, explanation and transfiguration of all our pure experiences in time'.

The analogy between divine love and human love, and between 'the intimacies' of sex and marriage and the 'intimacies' of God's relations with his elect, was one of the major routes by which Patmore tried to insert Catholicism into public discussion. It was in some ways an austere and in other ways an accommodating route, and if it sounds suspiciously like the route that Lawrence was to follow thirty years later, with Christian love in place of phallic Etruscanism, that may merely be to say that Patmore's religion, though reactionary and uncompromising in intention, was as private and literary as Lawrence's was.

Patmore lacked Manning's authority and Newman's intellectual power, and failed to make his religion as attractive as his poetry. He has been considered here not because his justification of Christianity was persuasive but because it was suffused with a contempt for modern thought and, through the almost wilful deliberateness of its failure, exposed the difficulties which even Mallock's superior sophistication and acceptance of industrial society were incapable of overcoming.

II

Many of the thinkers who were discussed in Parts I–III were unenthusiastic about the accumulation of wealth and in their hearts were enemies of large-scale industry. Mallock[1] suffered none of these inhibitions. Mallock was the protagonist of industrial society and along with Salisbury is the best answer to the accusation that in modern England the assault on Infidelity has been connected with hostility to economic expansion.

Mallock was a man-of-letters; apart from a short period as a Conservative parliamentary candidate in Scotland, he regarded literature and the provision of 'facts and principles for politicians' as the forms of action of which he was capable. His novels, with their liberating doctrine about love and marriage, on the whole were unsuccessful. So was much of his theoretical polemic, only *The New Republic* and *A Critical Examination of Socialism* having really survived. He deserves attention, nevertheless, as a critic of Socialism and as the exponent of a considered conception of the relations that ought to obtain between literature, politics, religion and life.

In Mallock's earliest writings, there was virtually nothing about politics. *Every Man His Own Poet*, *The New Republic*, *The New Paul and Virginia*, *Lucretius*, *Is Life Worth Living?*, the *Poems* of 1880 and *A Romance of the Nineteenth Century* – all published before he was thirty-five – dealt with literature, religion, love, art and the manners of London society. It was not until after the General Election of 1880 that Mallock wrote about politics and not until the publication of *Social Equality* as a book in 1882 that he made a substantial contribution to the attack which he, Courthorpe, Greenwood and Austin were to develop on the new Radicalism of the 1880s.

---

[1] William Hurrell Mallock (1849–1923). Educ. at home and at Balliol College, Oxford. Converted to Roman Catholicism on death bed. Author of *Everyman His Own Poet* 1872, *The New Republic* 2 vols. 1877, *Lucretius* 1878, *The New Paul and Virginia* 1878, *Is Life Worth Living?* 1879, *Poems* 1880, *A Romance of the Nineteenth Century* 2 vols. 1881, *Social Equality* 1882, *Atheism and the Value of Life* 1884, *Property and Progress* 1884, *The Landlords and National Income* 1884, *The Old Order Changes* 3 vols. 1886, *In an Enchanted Island* 1889, *A Human Document* 3 vols. 1892, *Labour and the Popular Welfare* 1893, *The Heart of Life* 3 vols. 1895, *Studies of Contemporary Superstition* 1895, *Classes and Masses* 1896, *Aristocracy and Evolution* 1898, *The Individualist* 1899, *Doctrine and Doctrinal Disruption* 1900, *Lucretius on Life and Death* 1900, *The Fiscal Dispute Made Easy* 1903, *Religion as a Credible Doctrine* 1903, *The Veil of the Temple* 1904, *The Reconstruction of Belief* 1905, *A Critical Examination of Socialism* 1907, *An Immortal Soul* 1908, *The Nation as a Business Firm* 1910, *Social Reform* 1914, *The Limits of Pure Democracy* 1918, *Capital War and Wages* 1918, *Memoirs of Life and Literature* 1920.

Mallock was well aware of the distaste felt for the 'academic politician' by 'men who approached politics from the practical side'. But with all the deference that was due to the practitioner, he insisted that 'there *were* crises when the general truths of the thinker may have instant ... effect on the conduct of men of action' and that in Britain in the 1880s there were 'general truths with regard to human nature and civilization which ... once fully recognised by politicians and the public, would make each of our moderate parties better understand the other and prevent our extreme parties being listened to any longer by anyone'.

What this meant was that Britain faced a 'social catastrophe', and that this would revolutionize the distribution of property and subject 'every existing arrangement of a household, every existing style of furniture, and all existing habits, manners, modes of thought or amusements' to the sort of transformation that was desiderated by the 'continental democrat'.

In outlining a philosophy of resistance, Mallock sketched the need for an alliance between the landed classes on the one hand and Big Business, the middle classes and suburban villadom on the other. He argued that Chamberlainite Radicalism was the cause of a class and that the class it represented was a wealthy minority which, 'having no definite idea' of its 'own social position ... and duty', aped the aristocracy at the same time as it attacked it, and ignored the truth that the poor could not be made 'impatient of rank' without being made 'envious of riches'.

Mallock's positive doctrine began from the assumption that democratic theory provided an imperfect account of political power. In *Social Equality*, in the numerous political articles that he wrote between 1880 and 1885 and in almost all of his later works, he argued that political systems were necessarily oligarchic, that modern systems were not less oligarchic than ancient systems and that they would go on being so however much democratic theory, or agitation, might assume that they would not be. Modern thought was supplementing equality of political rights with 'equality in the conditions of private life and ... material circumstances', and it was in scrutinizing modern thought in this sense that Mallock asked two fundamental questions: 'Why', as he put it in November 1880, 'should the many toil for and obey the few?' why should they put up with conditions in which the few, 'without manual labour, commanded at will the manual labour of the many' and 'the many whose labour was commanded ... never themselves tasted any of its ... choicer fruits?'.

Mallock affected to believe that rational explanation of social facts might succeed in 'averting the catastrophe' which threatened. He shared the Fabian belief in the importance of thought, and aimed his own thought in as 'truly a scientific spirit' as Shaw and the Webbs claimed to aim theirs, at those 'shadows of feeling' in the public mind which were 'dividing the world' into two hostile parties, the one denying and the other asserting 'certain social propositions' without any basis in 'scientific knowledge'.

Of Conservative thought and rhetoric, Mallock was as critical as of Radical thought and rhetoric. Property was on the defensive, he argued, and the 'millions who had least cause to be tender with it' would no longer equate attacks on it with 'theft'. Socialism, indeed, had turned theft from being a 'sin' into being a restoration of violated right, and what the defence of property needed was a scientific refutation – the 'missing science' which would replace the 'pseudo-science of modern democracy'.

The key proposition of the 'pseudo-science of modern democracy' was that 'the majority' would benefit from the 'equalization of property'. The key propositions of the 'missing science' would be that inequality of property which was the 'cause of civilization' was also the 'cause of plenty', and ought therefore to be respected by 'the many' as well as by the 'few'. The new science had to proclaim these truths in the light of the fact that Adam Smith had not understood them, that men now were 'as much in the dark ... with regard to social problems as they were before Hume's day with regard to economic problems' and that property might be put into a 'new state of security' if it could be proved that its enemies were either 'quacks' or 'criminals'.

In sketching the contours of the 'missing science' Mallock was conscious of contextual challenges and opportunities. He was friendlier to Buckle and Spencer than to Proudhon and Marx, and in associating Bright with Proudhon and Chamberlain with Marx, hoped to concentrate Liberal as well as Conservative minds around the truth of the future – that the redistribution of wealth was a 'scientific impossibility'.

Mallock's 'science' was meant to be realistic rather than cynical and to supply hope rather than disappointment for the poor. It was a matter of induction not preference, he argued, that 'labour was not the ultimate cause of wealth', that the 'rise ... and maintenance of civilization' had been caused by the 'desire for ... inequality' and that 'any social changes that tended to abolish inequality' would 'tend also to destroy ... civilization'. These were 'facts' which science could establish, and it followed that the distance between rich and poor would not be diminished 'until the world collapsed in barbarism ... and reduced the rich to poverty'.

In distinguishing poverty from misery, Mallock was at his craftiest, arguing that it was 'misery that was miserable, not inequality', that the 'sufferings of the poor' were not caused by their 'having little as compared with the rich' but by their 'having little as compared with the simplest demands of human nature', and that not only had 'the bulk of human unhappiness' nothing to do with the 'existence of social inequalities' but also 'that there was not the least reason to despair ... because these inequalities could never be done away with'. For the future he held out the hope that 'wealth ... culture ... wisdom and ... philanthropy' which were now 'forced unwillingly ... to regard the cause of the poor with suspicion' would align themselves on the side of the poor once the intellectual battle had been won.

In *Social Equality*, Mallock explained why it was that inequality had played a dominant rôle in material progress in the past. Whether in discussing primitive military systems based on plunder, ancient civilizations based on slavery or the discipline which modern industry exercised through wages, he contrasted the meagre achievements produced by the desire for ease and subsistence which was the normal motive of most of mankind with the 'monuments of progress from the walls of Babylon to the streets of Chicago' which had been created when ambition drove 'the few' to 'get wealth out of the labour of men who had no desire to produce it'. The entrepreneurs who had broken up ease by discovering America, creating science and developing modern industry were said to have been doing what had been done by the Pharoahs when they had broken up ease in Egypt; for

whenever in any society the production of wealth had begun, there had always been present either overt physical force, which had made some men slaves, or certain social arrangements which had made some men free labourers ... and ... every civilization that had ever existed in the world had been begun against the will of the majority of the human beings concerned in it ... When modern democrats looked back at the past and declared that the history of it was one long history of oppression, they were simply bearing witness to the truth of this fact ... that civilization in every case had been begun by a minority ... whose motive was solely its own advancement.

This belief in the dependence of the many on the few, of the masses on the classes and of the poor on the rich, and in the damage that inequality would do to both civilization and the happiness of the poor, remained the basis of Mallock's political doctrine in the forty years that followed the publication of *Social Equality*. In all the political works that he wrote in this period, these were the basic principles to which only *Aristocracy and Evolution* added anything substantial.

Aristocracy and Evolution did four important things. It applied the criticism which *Social Equality* had made of 'aggregation' in Buckle and Spencer to the work of Kidd, Shaw and Sidney Webb. It presented social science as the transference to the 'problems of civilization and society' of the evolutionary conceptions which had reorganized physics and biology. It turned evolutionary relativism against the demand which Socialism, historical economics, and democratic theory had made for the subversion of the existing distribution of property. And it differentiated the 'survivors in the Darwinian struggle for existence' whose 'fitness' consisted in what they accomplished for themselves or their dependants from the great men who gave leadership in wealth-production where the struggle for existence took place between 'members of a minority ... in which the majority played no part as antagonists whatever'.

In describing this minority, Mallock insisted that they were unlikely to be Arnoldian mortalists, Carlylean heroes or men of scholarship, culture and wit. They were likely, on the contrary, to be men of 'exceptional narrowness' and to require as a precondition of their operation the prospect of a high level of personal position, possessions, pleasures or other advantages by way of inducement and reward.

This was Mallock's justification of inequality and of the 'indefeasible rights ... of the few' – that the production of commodities was beneficial, that it was by the 'ability of the few' that the 'labour of the many was multiplied' and that the 'ability of the few' could have this effect only, as Marx had implied, when it met with the labourer in an open market which was regulated by wages. Mallock described his argument as 'aristocratic', and so in a sense it was, even when it provided for social mobility through education and the redistribution of wealth which occurred in the course of normal economic activity. But it was also 'democratic' in so far as the production of commodities under capitalism responded to popular demand in ways which could be made undemocratic only by the advent of 'socialism and slavery'.

Mallock's sociology was a call to understand that working-class agitation was a threat, that neither prejudice nor sentimentality would be strong enough to resist it and that a calculating rationality about human action was the essential prerequisite to resistance. Having understood this, we ask, then, how was this related to Mallock's understanding of Christianity?

In a chapter entitled 'The Qualities of the Ordinary as Opposed to the Great Man' which appeared in Book III of *Aristocracy and Evolution*, Mallock explained that, though economic progress was desirable, economic activity was not 'the whole of life', and that there was a difference between man as producer of commodities and 'man as a moral being, moving in a circle of prescribed duties'. Earlier in the book he had argued that, though the development of religion had owed a great deal to 'exceptional individuals' like Christ, Buddha and Mohammed, not only religion but also family life were spheres in which a 'pure, spontaneous and unadulterated democracy' could operate as it had done in all the historic religions including, pre-eminently, Roman Catholicism which, so far from being a 'structure ... imposed ... by the misguided ingenuity of priests ... on a credulous and passive laity', consisted of 'beliefs' which 'ordinary believers' had imposed on their priests. It was religious Democracy in this sense that Mallock wished to establish in place of the 'democratic consummation' that he had denounced in *Social Equality* and the purpose of this section is to lay out the reasoning which led him to this conclusion.

Mallock's early religious writing took the form of a running attack on intellectual error as it was to be found in the authors who had dominated English thought and literature in the thirty years before he began writing. Not only was his initial work negative but a great deal of his subsequent work was as well, and it is necessary to examine his negativity before sketching the 'Catholicism' that he described in *Doctrine and Doctrinal Disruption*, *Religion as a Credible Doctrine* and *The Reconstruction of Belief*.

Like Chesterton, and like Butterfield half a century later, Mallock wanted to bring assumptions into the open in order to allow Christian assumptions to get to work amongst them. He had a Ruskinian breadth, an awareness of the implications of literature and a nostalgia about the rôle which poetry had played until the middle of the century as register of the nation's 'thoughts and feelings'.

Of the writers whom Mallock considered in detail during his first decade as a critic, only Ruskin and Tennyson escaped condemnation, Ruskin because he had stood out against deterioration, Tennyson because, as a survivor from a less odious age, he was 'in spiritual retirement' and now merely 'submitted' to contemporary thought where previously he had been its 'exponent'. Mallock admired Tennyson as the 'mirror of his age', but he did not admire the age which Tennyson mirrored, and it was only because what had followed was worse that he made as much as he could of the Tennysonian mixture of 'love, friendship, domesticity, patriotism, cosmopolitanism, and undogmatic Christianity'.

What had arrived since Tennyson was young was not only Arnold, Pater and Jowett, whom Mallock disposed of in *The New Republic*, but also Positivism and atheism. Their arrival was an event 'without parallel in the experience of humanity', and in describing its manifestations in Fitzgerald and *The Rubaiyat of Omar Khayyam* and in Spencer, Buckle, Seeley, George Eliot, Clifford, Mill, Huxley, Harrison, Stephen and Tyndall, Mallock uncovered a 'rot' that threatened to become ubiquitous.

The 'rot' consisted of the beliefs that immortality was an illusion, that each man was 'as much alone as if he were the only conscious thing in the universe' and that there was 'no-one' to 'enquire into' and 'judge' his 'inward thoughts'. These were the bases of 'positivism' as it appeared in the writers Mallock was discussing, and his first criticism was that, though a religion, because 'religion in greater or less proportion lurked everywhere', it was de-religionizing life because a Godless determinism had lowered men's estimate of their individuality, and made them think of themselves as a 'uniform mass ... which ... moved ... like a modern army whose alternative lines of march had been mapped out beforehand'.

Mallock accused the Positivists of subverting conscience and subordinating it to the passions. But because many of the Positivists were morally blameless and oblivious of temptation, the battle he envisaged was less a battle with depravity than with the dullness and listlessness for which he expected Positivism to become responsible.

The battle was to be a battle to the death, and Mallock rejected Newman's vision of a future where 'faith' and 'positivism' would fight an endless battle which neither side would win. The question he asked was, given that there was going to be this sort of battle, had Christianity any chance of winning it? His answer was that 'dogmatic' or 'Catholic' Christianity could win because lives lived in its shadow had a vigour and tension which lives lived in the shadow of the religion of humanity lacked.

In the long review that he wrote of *The History of Robert Elsmere* after it had become a best-seller, Mallock criticized Mrs Humphrey Ward for emasculating Christianity by rejecting the miraculous and supernatural. The 'large part of orthodox and traditional Christianity' which was concerned with 'practical life and character' had survived her attentions, he agreed, but it had survived as a 'psychological fact' rather than a 'theological doctrine'. To the question whether the 'psychological fact' could 'honestly appropriate' Christ's name while abandoning his theology, his answer was that the 'Christianity of the heart' could not be detached from the 'Christianity of the intellect' without a 'spiritual fraud' involving the reduction of Christ to being 'merely one saint amongst many in the great calendar of humanity'. 'The Christians praised a certain type of character', went the central criticism, 'because Christ embodied it. Mrs Ward praises Christ because he embodied a certain type of character', but unless miracles had happened and Christ was God, her opinion was merely a 'personal predilection', like the predilection which had been imposed on English Christianity by 'middle-class nonconformity, with its hatred of culture and obsession with riches, and its stock set of moral judgments about matters' which were 'in complete contradiction to the letter of Christ's teaching'.

This was a variant of Arnold's criticism. But Mallock went further than Arnold had gone, treated non-theological as well as Nonconformist Christianity as an arrested fossil and took development 'under the guidance of the Holy Spirit' as seriously as Newman had taken it. Beside the grandeur and variety of Christian development as Newman had conceived it, he found it easy to dismiss non-theological and Nonconformist Christianity as enslaved to a 'half-educated ... Syrian moralist' whose words in their literal sense were 'wholly unsuitable to advancing material civilization'.

In the course of criticizing Anglican reactions to Darwinianism in the 1860s, Huxley had developed the idea that Roman Catholicism was science's only effective enemy. In *Doctrine and Doctrinal Disruption*, Mallock repaid the compliment, arguing that Roman Catholicism alone among modern versions of Christianity resembled science, and alone could supply as authoritative reasons for believing in miracle and immortality as science claimed to supply for rejecting them. Mallock did not question science's authority as a form of knowledge; he argued simply that religion was an area in which it had no authority, that an authority was needed to do for religion what science did for knowledge and that the Church of England had failed to supply one.

Doctrine and Doctrinal Disruption was occasioned by the judgment which Archbishop Temple had given against the Reservation of the Sacraments in July 1899. Mallock treated the judgment as significant because of the uncertainty it disclosed about the authoritative definition of doctrine in the Church of England and he pointed out, with *Lux Mundi* in mind, that all sections of Anglican opinion, from Halifax and Gore at one end to Wace and Henson at the other, had abandoned those 'divines of the sixteenth century whose doctrines the English law imposed on them' and had adopted instead the doctrines of modern scientific criticism which had indicated neither on what authority the Bible could be accepted as a 'sacred literature' nor how its inspired parts could be differentiated from its human parts.

Mallock argued that the Roman doctrine of Infallibility was the sole guarantee of Christian truth, and especially of the truths which Mrs Humphrey Ward was trying to deny, that the development to which it could subject doctrine would point the way to a 'really scientific theory' capable of harmonizing Christ's teaching with the 'universal processes of nature' and that the functions which the 'infallible Church' had performed in absorbing classical learning in the Middle Ages would become even more important now that

the rains and floods of criticism had descended and beaten on the whole doctrinal edifice, washing away the sands on which Protestant thought rested it … It was only now, when men found themselves planted by modern knowledge in a new world unknown to the theologians and the apologists of the past, that, desiring still to retain the heritage of their ancient faith, they realised the full necessity for the guidance of a living teacher, whose authority was not indeed opposed to that of science, but was independent of it, and though not contradicting anything which science demonstrated, was able to assure them of the truth of events and things which scientific evidence alone could not even render probable.

Doctrine and Doctrinal Disruption assumed not only that the Church of England lacked the infallibility which was needed to define dogmas but also that Roman infallibility alone could use the 'philosophy of Darwin, Spencer and Huxley' which 'many people regarded as destined to complete its downfall' in justification of its authority. Chapter XI contained a far-fetched Spencerian contrast between Protestantism as the 'undifferentiated protoplasm' which formed 'the lowest grade of living things' and the Roman Church as a 'higher biological organism' whose memory reached back to the beginnings of the Christian dispensation.

The defence of Roman Catholicism as the 'closest analogy to modern science' and a system which Gibbon had agreed was 'no more absurd or incredible' than Protestantism, was a *tour de force* that was not to be repeated. While *The Veil of the Temple* presented Christianity as a subject of natural concern to educated men, Mallock's last three books about religion began from the belief that it was much more difficult than Catholic apologetic had supposed to supply proper proofs of the main Christian dogmas.

In attempting to supply proofs, Mallock started from the assumption that the conflict between science and religion was no longer a conflict between a 'materialistic' and a 'spiritualistic' philosophy. It was now, he argued, a conflict between a 'monistic' and a 'dualistic' philosophy which centered round the questions whether the universe consisted of 'one order of things or two' and whether 'universal substance' as science conceived it was made or even permeated by God. After discussing the inroads which physics, psychology, physiology and biology had made on Christian theology, his conclusions were that the 'actual facts of the universe as science ... was ... revealing them' left no room for the 'great primary doctrine which ... lay at the root of everything that we mean by religion ... and civilization' and that it was necessary in these circumstances to find ways of reconnecting science to that 'entire conception of existence which alone for the mass of mankind had invested life with value'.

In pursuing this aim, Mallock recognized that science existed and would not go away, and that some of its assumptions had to be accepted. But just as his sociology counter-attacked with the fact of inequality and built a defence around the assertion of its ubiquity, so in religion he accepted science's autonomy in areas where its knowledge was demonstrable while asserting the existence of areas in which it was not. In doing this, his chief instrument was the 'practical synthesis of contradictories'.

In developing this principle, Mallock made two connected points – that 'simultaneous assent' to 'contradictory propositions' was to be found 'at the bottom of all knowledge' and that religious knowledge and scientific knowledge in that crucial respect resembled one another.

The 'ether' as Haeckel had explained it, for example, had 'got rid of the mystery of physical action at a distance' only by proposing a 'system of expansion and contraction' which was 'more mysterious still', and the difficulties this presented to the monist were said to be 'practically one and the same' as the difficulties inherent in the 'theistic conception of God'. Both were instances of the principle that 'whatever conception men may form of the nature and origin of the universe ... they find that a fact in which they are compelled to believe, contains, when they analyse it, an implication which they are unable to think', and that 'if all the facts of the universe as science and observation revealed them ... united in showing that the primary doctrines of religion ... were superfluous as hypotheses, they could still hope to discover facts which would justify them in arriving at a contrary conclusion'.

In describing a 'good God and a free will' as unthinkable, therefore, Mallock did not mean to imply that any alternative conception was *more* thinkable. His position was simply that space, time and eternity were as unthinkable logically as God and free will, and that reason was as powerless to supply the initial validation of science as it was to supply the initial validation of religion. To the question, how then could religion be validated, his answer centred on the principle that God and immortality supplied 'logical and practical completeness' to that 'moral and spiritual life' of which individual freedom was the 'foundation', that the 'whole meaning of life so far as religion was concerned depended on the ... individual' and that evolutionary science's subordination of the individual to the 'type' had made it incapable of accounting for religion. It was in this sense that Mallock imposed on contemporary Catholicism a duty to provide a reasonable version of the unreasonable resistance which it had provided to Copernicus's and Galileo's diminutions of anthropocentricism, and for this reason that, since 'progress or evolution' could have 'no significance ... unless the individual had some personal destiny beyond that of being sacrificed to a purpose in which he was not himself included ..., some system of doctrine equivalent in its effects to the doctrine of theistic religion ... was ... absolutely essential to a higher civilization'.

This was Mallock's justification of religion – that belief in the 'growing accord of human nature ... with some reality ... akin to and above it' was an 'act of common sense and of will' which, though resting neither on scientific observation nor on reason, was as 'essential to civilization as a sound nervous system'. It was this capability which was being lost in the modern world, and the 'active and bracing' rôle which a 'believer's nature' could play in 'creating the truth which it affirmed' that Mallock's apologetic was designed to defend

not only on the grounds that it ministered to and interpreted the special aspirations and emotions which men commonly called religion and which in their more urgent form were confined to a small minority but also on the grounds that it was essential to and implied in the entire development and exercise of the higher human faculties generally'.

In *Religion as a Credible Doctrine*, Mallock described the mass of mankind as attesting by its 'love ... blood ... tears ... joys ... sorrows and prayers' to that moral and religious reality which he wished to restore to the centre of life and thought. This was not an attempt to flatter the big battalions, and neither was it designed to be pliant. It was designed to offend the liberal-minded, to establish the difficult connection between popular and dogmatic Christianity and to supply yet another statement of the Tractarian hope that dogmatic Christianity could become the religion of the masses.

Mallock presents a problem. He was not a Roman Catholic until his deathbed, if he became one then. On the other hand he was intensely critical of the Church of England and showed little sympathy for its difficulties. Why in these circumstances he did not become a Roman Catholic earlier, and whether there was a connection between his failure to do so and his sexual and marital doctrines and experience, is a question to which there seems to be no answer. The ultimate judgment on his apologetic must be that, despite his high talent and skill, his contribution to the Christian counter-revolution was ultimately insubstantial. The same must be said about the talented apologists whom we are to consider in the next chapter.

12

Literature and the Counter-Revolution II

'We may say broadly that free thought is the best of all the safeguards against freedom. Managed in a modern style the emancipation of the slave's mind is the best way of preventing the emancipation of the slave. Teach him to worry about whether he wants to be free, and he will not free himself ... The man we see every day – the worker in Mr Gradgrind's factory, the little clerk in Mr Gradgrind's office – he is too mentally worried to believe in freedom. He is kept quiet with revolutionary literature. He is calmed and kept in his place by a constant succession of wild philosophies. He is Marxian one day, a Nietzscheite the next day, a Superman (probably) the next day; and a slave every day. The only thing that remains after all the philosophies is the factory. The only man who gains by all the philosophies is Gradgrind. It would be worth his while to keep his commercial helotry supplied with sceptical literature. And now I come to think of it, of course, Gradgrind is famous for giving libraries.' G. K. Chesterton *Orthodoxy* (1908) 1961 edn p. 106.

'There was sadness and decay, of course, in Hanoi, as there couldn't help being in a city emptied of all the well-to-do. For such as I there was sadness in the mere lack of relaxation: nothing in the cinemas but propaganda films, the only restaurants prohibitive in price, no café in which to while away the hours watching people pass. But the peasant doesn't miss the café, the restaurant, the French or the American film – he's never had them. Perhaps even the endless compulsory lectures and political meetings, the hours of physical training, are better entertainment than he has ever known.

We talk so glibly of the threat to the individual, but the anonymous peasant has never been treated so like an individual before. Unless a priest, no one before the Commissar has approached him, has troubled to ask him questions, or spent time in teaching him. There is something in Communism besides the politics.' Graham Greene, *The Man as Pure as Lucifer* (1955) in *Collected Essays* 1969 (Penguin edn 1970) pp. 302–3.

'The existence of God was once a premiss, in the sense that belief in God belonged to the framework of thought and belief which was common to the society of the time ... This is hardly the case today. Talk about God is a realm of discourse which cannot be taken for granted ... For some people at any rate, it is, so to speak, a foreign language, an alien tongue. And if the concept of God has once come to be regarded as a superfluous hypothesis or as a projection characteristic of a past culture, the only way in which it can recover reality and relevance is through a man's personal rediscovery of God as a reality, by belief in God issuing from his own experience of his world.' Rev. F. C. Copleston S. J. *Christianity without Belief in God* (n.d.) reprinted in *Philosophers and Philosophies* 1976 p. 73.

The counter-revolutionary mentality described at the beginning of the last chapter had about a dozen main pillars of whom Waugh appeared in Volume I. Waugh was a critic not only of English religion but also of the English obsession with politics and English self-congratulation about the parliamentary system. Among the others R.M. Benson, R.A. Knox, D'Arcy, Martindale and Copleston had only marginal political components. The political component was radical in Belloc, Chesterton, Dawson and Greene and when used in the service of the Conservative Party, as by Hollis, reflected the squirearchical anti-establishmentarianism which had been transmitted from Disraeli by Wyndham and adopted by Macmillan who, long before he became a politician, had thought of becoming a Roman Catholic.

In pointing the way through conversion to re-Christianization, the counter-revolutionary mentality has aimed to blow up the entrenched complacencies of the nineteenth and twentieth centuries in much the way in which the Tractarians had aimed to blow up the entrenched complacencies of the eighteenth, and this has been so whether the politics involved have been the reactionary Toryism of Waugh or the reactionary Liberalism of Jerrold. If the present chapter had been longer, it would have discussed Jerrold, Benson, D'Arcy, Martindale, Knox and Hollis – D'Arcy and Martindale for their presence and apologetic, Knox for his satire and *Enthusiasm*, Jerrold, Benson and Hollis for their novels of ideas and a handful of living Roman Catholic thinkers, convert and otherwise, for the ease, range and flexibility of their journalism. As things are, Copleston, Dawson, Greene, Belloc and Chesterton will represent the rest.

I

In treating Chesterton[1] in a primarily negative rôle as an enemy of the assailants of Christianity, one is responding to a central theme in his writing and a major preoccupation in his public life which, both before and after his conversion to Roman Catholicism, displayed a pressing desire to defend Christianity by diminishing the self-congratulation of all the contemporary creeds which claimed to have superseded it.

Chesterton's conversion was of first consequence for himself, but it is not of first consequence for this book. Chesterton had been a 'Catholic' from an early stage and would probably have become a Roman Catholic at least ten years before he did if it had not been for his wife who, having played a part in making him an *Anglo*-Catholic, was hesitant about the transition to *Roman* Catholicism. Moreover, Chesterton was more interested in doctrinal than in ecclesiastical questions and attached far greater importance to defining a position than to developing its practical implications. The Roman Catholic phase contained some of his finest writing, but it did not contain much that was new in principle even about Roman Catholicism, and almost everything that he wrote about religion and politics in the last fourteen years of his life

[1] Gilbert Keith Chesterton (1874–1936). Educ. St Paul's School. Editor of *New Witness* 1916–23 and *G. K.s Weekly* 1925–36. Converted to Roman Catholicism 1922. Author of *Greybeards at Play* 1900, *The Wild Knight* 1900, *The Defendant* 1901, *Twelve Types* 1902, *Thomas Carlyle* 1902, *Robert Louis Stevenson* 1902, *Tolstoy* 1903, *Charles Dickens* 1903, *Robert Browning* 1903, *Tennyson* 1903, *Thackeray* 1903, *G. F. Watts* 1904, *The Napoleon of Notting Hill* 1904, *Heretics* 1905, *The Club of Queer Trades* 1905, *Charles Dickens* 1906 *Tennyson as an Intellectual Force* 1906, *All Things Considered* 1908, *The Man Who Was Thursday* 1908, *Orthodoxy* 1908, *The Ball and the Cross* 1909, *George Bernard Shaw* 1909, *Tremendous Trifles* 1909, *Five Types* 1910, *What's Wrong with the World* 1910, *William Blake* 1910, *The Ballad of the White Horse* 1911, *The Innocence of Father Brown* 1911, *Appreciations and Criticisms of the Work of Charles Dickens* 1911, *Man Alive* 1912, *The Victorian Age in Literature* 1913, *The Flying Inn* 1914, *The Wisdom of Father Brown* 1914, *The Barbarism of Berlin* 1914, *Letters to an Old Garibaldian* 1915, *The Crimes of England* 1915, *Poems* 1915, *Divorce versus Democracy* 1916, *A Short History of England* 1917, *Utopia of Usurers* 1917, *Irish Impressions* 1919, *The New Jerusalem* 1920, *The Superstition of Divorce* 1920, *Eugenics and Other Evils* 1922, *The Man Who Knew Too Much* 1922, *What I Saw in America* 1922, *St Francis of Assisi* 1923, *The Superstitions of the Sceptic* 1925, *The Everlasting Man* 1925, *William Cobbett* 1925, *The Outline of Sanity* 1926, *The Catholic Church and Conversion* 1926, *The Incredulity of Father Brown* 1926, *The Return of Don Quixote* 1927, *The Secret of Father Brown* 1927, *Robert Louis Stevenson* 1927, *Generally Speaking* 1928, *The Thing* 1929, *The Resurrection of Rome* 1930, *Chaucer* 1932, *St Thomas Aquinas* 1933, *The Well and the Shallows* 1935, *The Scandal of Father Brown* 1935, *As I was Saying* 1936, *Autobiography* 1936.

had already been implied or stated in reaction to the situation from which he had emerged as a public figure between 1900 and 1908.

Chesterton's influence on English politics on the whole has been Conservative, his poetry and personality having been absorbed, alongside Kipling's, Eliot's and Belloc's, into the romantic patriotism of the anti-Socialist Liberal–Conservative consolidation of the 1940s and 1950s. This, though an established, was an unexpected development, however, since Chesterton's own understanding of politics assumed an antagonism between Liberalism and Conservatism of which he was the exponent throughout.

On his first substantial appearances as a writer in 1900, Chesterton wanted a reconstructed Liberalism which would stand up to the conditions of the twentieth century. He was a nationalist supporter of the Boers and an enemy of the Jewish international Imperialism which was making war upon them. He was also a democrat and an optimist, by which he meant a way of thinking established by the French Revolution that had nothing to do with the scepticism, pessimism and 'diseased pride' of the Aesthetes and decadents of the 1880s and 1890s who had 'not even been conscious' of the existence of a 'public interest', 'whispering', as they did, 'in a million ears that things were not worth improving'.

From *The Defendant* onwards, Chesterton expressed a systematic distaste for the sexual perversity, separation of meaning from art and mandarin dislike of the people which he supposed the Aesthetes and decadents to have embodied. The 'hour of absinthe' and the 'ecstatic isolation' of the artistic and religious sense were over, he argued, and in Victorian literature he found a subject-matter on which to display the proper relationship between them.

Between 1900 and 1914, in addition to producing a great deal of journalism, Chesterton produced three volumes of poetry, five sets of collected essays and eight works of fiction. He also wrote books entitled *Charles Dickens, Robert Browning, G. F. Watts, George Bernard Shaw, William Blake, Heretics, Orthodoxy, What's Wrong with the World, Appreciations and Criticisms of the Work of Charles Dickens* and *The Victorian Age in Literature*. Of these, the most important was *The Victorian Age in Literature*, which was published as an early volume in the Home University Library to the accompaniment of an editorial disclaimer from J. A. Thomson, Murray and H. A. L. Fisher.

Chesterton wrote often about the strangeness that separated him from the earnestness of the High Victorians. On the other hand, he admired High Victorianism and in using the stylistic tricks of aestheticism and decadence used them in its service. He was embarrassed by earnestness and did his best to avoid it, his preference for paradox being not just an imitation of Shaw or Wilde but a concealment of embarrassment arising from the fact that he did not wish to seem as earnest as the Victorians had seemed, while meaning what he meant as earnestly as they had.

Of the Victorian authors whom Chesterton considered in detail, Browning was easy to admire, not only because of the obscurity of his style. Browning was neither an Aesthete nor a decadent, but neither was he the 'grim moralist and metaphysician' of the Browning Society and University Extension Lectures. He was married and a democrat, and his 'whole view of existence' professed the 'central liberal doctrine' which *The Ring and the Book* had made into the 'great epic of the age' – the 'epic of free speech' whose painful characters taught the 'hardest lesson that humanity had been set to learn', that 'no man ever lived upon this earth without possessing a point of view.'

In *Robert Browning*, Chesterton made the points that he wished to make about Victorian earnestness, making them chiefly by contrast and bringing them to a head in the claim that Browning had 'made the world stand on its head that people might look at it'. In *G. F. Watts*, he described another 'great Englishman', a mirror of his age 'more accurate' than 'politicians who thundered on platforms or financiers who captured continents' and who painted in the way in which religious painters painted – 'on his knees', moved by an 'intense conviction' that there was within any person that he painted 'a great reality' which had to 'give up its secret before ... the model ... left ... the throne'.

Chesterton rejected the scepticism, stoicism and quasi-Puritanism that he found in Watts's public personality, along with the timeless symbolic Art which Watts had hoped would outlive the Cross. But though he liked neither Watts's message nor the manner of its delivery, he admired Watts's sense of the 'priesthood of art' and the vision that his art had conveyed of the 'public idea'.

In literature, as in politics, Chesterton was a Democrat, arguing that the 'indecency' which the educated classes thought they found in popular literature was to be found chiefly in their own literature, and that the 'heroic truisms' which dominated popular literature were sounder and embodied mankind's historic soundness of which the educated had lost sight. This view was summarized, somewhat slickly, in the adage that philosophy and theology, so far from being the exclusive concern of 'those who passed through Divinity and Greats', were the concern of 'those who passed through birth and death'.

Chesterton's concern for mankind was expressed initially as a concern for the poor. On the one hand, he anathemized Protectionist Imperialism as a rich man's racket which the poor should avoid. On the other hand, he admired 'plebeian pungency' and the moral vigour which Dickens had associated with it.

Chesterton's admiration for Dickens began from the fact that Dickens had been 'in love ... with the universe' and had shown his love by loving 'the man in the street'. Dickens was said to have been a 'citizen of the street', to have had the 'key of the street' and to have 'walked in darkness' and been 'crucified' in the street. He was described as believing that there were 'no pleasures like the pleasures of the poor' and as suffering with 'the secret anger of the humble'. It had been a 'grotesque' democracy that he had called out, consisting not only of 'free men' but also of 'funny' ones who were dealt with not as they were in the manner of the literature of the educated but 'greater than they were' in the manner of a mythology. Dickens's life-work was a 'sacrifice to the ordinary man', an outpouring of 'riches and blood ... in front of the people' and had created out of the 'large heart and narrow mind of the inspired cockney radical that he was as universal a statement as Shakespeare had made about the human condition'.

Charles Dickens was Chesterton's antidote to aesthetic perversion. It was also his antidote to the 'softness' of the aristocracy – a continuation of the Orwellian Conservatism of traditional literature which had been written by 'men of the people' from the Robin Hood ballads of the Middle Ages to the 'penny dreadfuls' in the local paper shop.

In criticizing, as in writing, literature, Chesterton gave religious twists to his arguments. These were not all Christian, some of them praising merely the 'spiritual view of things' that he found, for example, in Lear and Lewis Carroll. The effect, nevertheless, was to suggest that Puritanism was a form of 'rationalistic aggression against the chaotic ... part of human nature', that Shakespeare, Scott, Stevenson, Sterne, St Francis and Rostand all gave joyful testimonies to the individuality of the soul and that literature and criticism both had a part to play in destroying the 'Victorian compromise'.

The 'Victorian compromise' involved on the one side Tractarianism and romantic Protestantism, and on the other the 'simple ...

rationalism' represented by Macaulay who 'never talked about his religion' and by Huxley who was 'always talking about the religion he hadn't got'. It was in reaction against the 'dull' accommodation that went with it, the dominance it had enabled religious people to establish over religion and the cynicism and paganism of the consequent anarchy that Chesterton wrote *The Napoleon of Notting Hill, The Club of Queer Trades, The Man Who Was Thursday, The Ball and the Cross, Man Alive, The Flying Inn*, and both *The Innocence* and *The Wisdom of Father Brown*.

The *Napoleon of Notting Hill, The Club of Queer Trades, The Man Who Was Thursday, Man Alive* and *The Flying Inn* were fictional fantasies and soaked in the idea that Rationalism was inadequate. *The Ball and The Cross* and *The Innocence* and *The Wisdom of Father Brown* alone made the point in a Christian fashion.

Brown personified the view that reason was simpler and deeper than the Rationalism of Flambeau. Brown's decency and unassumingness, his bumbling and blinking, and his umbrella, were all meant to be sympathetic. What gave him significance for religion was his penetration of mystery, his ability to look beneath the surface and the numinous and impalpable reality which he was supposed to perceive when he did so.

Like Greene's priest in *The Power and the Glory*, Brown was an ordinary man, not a sinner in the Greene sense, but not pompous or high-minded either, and bringing a touch of the eternal into ordinary life. Brown was supposed to be a better detective for being a Roman Catholic and his investigative intelligence to be an aspect of his Catholicism. In *The Ball and the Cross*, too, the hero was a hero because he was a living embodiment of Christianity.

The Ball and the Cross was a fantasy in the manner of *The Flying Inn* and *The Club of Queer Trades*. Its central theme, like the central theme of the Brown stories, was the tension and sympathy between a Roman Catholic – the Jacobite MacIain – and Turnbull, the Rationalist atheist. MacIain was noisier, more belligerent, more vigorous than Brown but also as natural. Turnbull was as completely the incarnation of a type as Flambeau and was shown up in the same way. Flies were cast over many modern phenomena, including the Aesthete, the Tolstoyean, the modern woman, the average philistine, the newspaper as a 'minister of modern anarchy' and the 'bloodless mentalities' of Evolutionary Science as the cause of the 'ruthlessness' of civilization. Poetry was praised by comparison; religion was praised for its sense of

paradox, for imposing the duty to 'quarrel about a word' and for the
intensity with which it demanded that the atheist and the Christian
should either kill each other or convert each other. It was made clear
that the conflict between MacIain and Turnbull, and the fate of Professor Lucifer, addressed the central religious problems of the age.

In his fiction, Chesterton confined himself to implying the existence of
an area of 'magic' which 'the age' had given him 'no encouragement' to
experience. In discussing Ibsen, Gorky, Nietzsche, Tolstoy and Shaw
he came closer to saying what he meant.

In Ibsen and Gorky, Chesterton found a Gissing-like morbidity
combined with 'so much faith' that they 'really believed in scepticism'.
In Nietzsche, he found a rebellion against the 'half-baked impudence'
of the Utilitarians and Spencerians. Tolstoy's plea for the 'simple life'
was blamed as 'blasphemous' and 'puritanical' since it was not only
'more humble but also more human to be content to be complex'.
Tolstoy's Christianity, on the other hand, was 'one of the most thrilling
and dramatic incidents in our modern civilization', a reassertion of the
'impossible ... common sense' which had characterized 'the most
extreme utterances of Christ' and, in spite of the touches of insanity
which had been caused by Tolstoy's neglect of mysticism, a proof that
there were still 'theories of life' and 'examples of faith' as 'insanely
reasonable' as the Athenian and as 'fierce and practical' as the Moham-
medan.

In Ibsen, Gorky, Nietzsche and Tolstoy, Chesterton found enemies
of some of the things he disliked. Shaw alone among contemporary
British writers attracted the regard that he felt for Dickens and Browning.

Chesterton admired Shaw for restoring to the theatre the 'stream of
fact and tendency' which it had had in the age of Shakespeare, and for
'obliterating' the 'mere cynic' by obliterating the sentimentalism
against which the cynic complained. He praised Shaw's 'innocence',
'chastity', even 'sanctity'; his 'fierce fastidiousness'; the 'cleanness of
the thought that lay behind the demand for sexual revolution' and his
urgent concern for progress in the public realm. Why, then, did he
claim, with the authority of 'the only person' who 'understood' Shaw,
that he 'did not agree with him'?

The defects that Chesterton discerned in Shaw were numerous – a
want of terror and frivolity and the traces Shaw retained of the 'noise

and narrowness' of the secularism of the 1880s; Shaw's fear of the passions, the difficulty this created in understanding women and sex and the inability it induced to give an 'emotional' or 'sentimental' account of anything; the 'severe, explanatory' manner in which Shaw attempted to do good, the self-deception that he suffered in the process and the damage done by his 'ungraciousness' to the good he was trying to do; his Calvinistic superiority about the 'charity and gentleness' which the Roman Church had inserted into the Irish character; above all, the deficiency in Dickensian and Catholic humour and humanity which had permitted him to attack Shakespeare and to prefer the stud farms of *Superman* to the 'beer-drinking, creed-making, fighting, failing, sensual, respectable men' who were to be found 'in the street' and among the peasantry.

In the course of creating a public *persona* for himself between 1900 and 1908, Chesterton had picked up two religious ideas – the Mallockian idea that 'men elect their gods even if they cannot elect their kings', and the philosophical idea that in the election of gods, Christ's 'impossibilities' were no more 'fantastic' than the Rationalism, materialism, atheism and secularism which were threatening to replace them. This was why Carlyle was praised as the 'founder of modern irrationalism', why the Age of Reason was said to have disturbed the proper relationship between 'choosing an assumption' and 'arguing upon it' and why the 'great mass of logicians' were to be criticized not for the reasoning that they did within the framework of their assumptions but for refusing to accord to the choice of assumptions the principal rôle in the decision to believe.

About Chesterton's Christian polemic, there was no despair. There was, however, contortion, and the question we have to ask is, given that he could not assume the truth of Christianity, did not feel it appropriate to make plain statements and wished to avoid the seriousness of the High Victorians, in what ways did he justify it?

He justified it principally in these years as a form of public activity. Public religion, ritual and superstition, a public morality, even public martyrdom, were said to be 'natural', and far more natural than the modern identification of 'sanctity' with 'secrecy'. Christ had to be crucified 'upon a hill' and St Paul to 'publish' his ethical diary before he could 'found a civilization', and so much was this the case that Christianity was not only the 'only coherent ethic' that Europe had known but had also made itself known at all social levels, incorporating the gay virtues which the 'joy of Christ' had created. This was why Christianity was the 'religion of the mob', why it was to be found on that 'queer, common ground' where 'the Cross was a sublime gibbet and the gibbet a caricature of the Cross' and why Christ was able to look for the 'honest man inside the thief' and say that 'any man could be a saint if he chose' exactly as 'democracy' looked for the 'wise man inside the fool' and said that 'any man could be a citizen if he chose'.

Until *Orthodoxy* was published in 1908, Chesterton's justification of Christianity even in such deliberate books as *Heretics* had been casual and incidental. In *Orthodoxy* he provided the first constructive statement of the problem.

Orthodoxy was a record of the process by which Chesterton had become a Christian and a statement of what he took it that Christianity meant. Not all parts were equally impressive. The first four or so chapters in places were painful while the autobiography was fragmentary and unsatisfactory, and did not describe the difference between being 'ten minutes in advance of the truth' and being 'eighteen hundred years behind it'.

In *Orthodoxy*, Chesterton's chief tactical point was that the main Christian dogmas were more liberal in their implications than the self-consciously liberal dogmas by which they were being assaulted. It was judged significant, for example, that Christianity was the only religion to have made its God a 'rebel' and 'for a moment ... an atheist', and that the Christian God alone had 'broken the universe into ... pieces', separated it into 'souls' and made a 'sacred' and 'eternal' division between Himself and mankind. It was judged equally significant that this was the basis for the Christian doctrine of the free personality which supplied a more demanding stimulus to 'pull down oppressors ... and lift up lost populations' than modern secularism which either laid the world waste or provided spurious reasons for being apathetically contented with it. Most glaringly of all, Christianity was connected with Chestertonian fantasies about men 'not being made mad by dreaming', about 'mysticism keeping them sane' and about 'ordinary men' always having remained sane because they 'had one foot in fairyland'.

This was not put very well. But it was connected with a harder idea – the idea of Christianity as the 'slash of a sword' which would destroy natural religion, the Arnoldian compromise, and the Inner Light, and establish that the world was a good deal less 'regular' than it looked. It was to a world where 'life' was 'unreasonable' and superstition abounding, and where 'earthquakes of emotion' could be unloosed about a word that Christian vigilance was presented as the response.

However feeble some of the things that Chesterton was trying to establish in *Orthodoxy*, he was also trying to establish two difficult paradoxes. On the one hand, that Christian vigilance about sin and the Christian doctrine of original sin supplied a more persuasive basis than secularism could supply for the 'perpetual revolution' that was needed against the rigidity and self-satisfaction of established systems. On the other hand, that the 'complexity' of the modern world and the varie-gated nature of the evils which free thinkers discerned in Christianity proved Christianity's truth by showing that it consisted of 'insane positions' which 'somehow amounted to sanity' – 'duplex' positions which mixed 'fierceness' with 'meekness', 'haughtiness' with 'humility', 'anger' with 'tenderness', 'pride' with 'prostration', 'love' with 'wrath' and 'pleasure' with 'pain', all of them 'burning at the top of their energy', Christ himself being 'both things at once and both things thoroughly, very man and very God'.

Chesterton wanted to establish that God was neither despotic like the pagan Gods nor deadly like the Fates, and could supply men with the assurance that the universe would survive them. Christianity indeed dissipated despair and gave the universe a meaning. It alone made possible the pathos and pity that were available to those who accepted it, Christ himself being an 'extraordinary' and 'often angry' being whose 'diction' was 'gigantic', whose 'tears' were open and whose 'shattering personality' concealed the 'one thing' that was 'too great for Him to show when He walked the earth' – a thing which may or may not seem persuasive to readers of this work but which Chesterton undoubtedly wrote of as his 'mirth'.

It is difficult to be fair to *Orthodoxy*, or to know whether its glibness or its whimsy was the more offensive. Yet, though both were present, and were offensive, *Orthodoxy* had two signal merits. It provided a libera-tion from agnostic, secular, rationalistic and materialistic solemnity, and it offered a tonic against intemperate attempts to ignore sin, evil, humour, wit and limitation in considering human life and religion.

After *Orthodoxy* Chesterton continued to defend Christianity against its enemies, attacking Eugenics as part of an illiberal materialistic conspiracy and divorce as part of the 'plutocratic' conspiracy through which the 'modern rich' insulted the 'modern poor'. There were sneers at American 'creedlessness', at the narrow-mindedness of 'modern scepticism' and at the illusion that it was the Church rather than the 'modern world' which was on its death-bed. An introduction to a work about Modernism stated that Modernism was no longer modern; *The Catholic Church and Conversion* explained that only Roman Catholicism was really modern since it alone was as new a religion as it had been in the second century. *Chaucer, St Francis of Assisi, St Thomas Aquinas, The Well and the Shallows, The Thing* and *The Everlasting Man* all explained why Roman Catholicism was to be the religion of the future.

Chesterton had little talent for philosophical, theological or theoretical statement. All he had – though he had this to the point of genius – was a talent for compressing long arguments into short paradoxes which left the reader to suggest applications for himself. This talent was remarkable, and was obvious throughout his writing. It was at its best in *The Thing*. Its limitations were most obvious in *The Everlasting Man* where the attempt at a philosophy failed because it was beyond his capability.

In certain respects *The Everlasting Man* succeeded. The attacks on Evolutionism and Comparative Religion as denials of the 'uniqueness' of Christianity were not without weight, and neither was the view that 'paganism' was Christianity's 'only real rival'. Part II included powerful passages about the political implications of an 'outcast ... deity', about the 'democratic' and 'dramatic' instincts which separated Catholicism from other philosophies and religions and about the extent to which the Catholic Church was to be admired for the challenge it offered to the 'sexually diseased imagination'. Even the 'dazzling ... super-human mysticism' with which the section on 'The Riddles of the Gospel' rescued Christ from the 'platitudes' of the 'agnostic moralist' did not stop the structure of the book cracking under the strain of its own weightlessness.

The variety of Chesterton's writing between 1920 and 1936 did not prevent it being repetitive, the mass-production of a brand name as readers and publishers required it; successful in its satire, persuasive as an agent of general culture against the specialized culture of the universities, but irritating by its prolixity and failing by and large to be compelling about the positive fantasies it invented.

II

Chesterton's prose was disconcerting, but Chesterton himself was harmless and amiable. Belloc[1] was less harmless and less amiable, more pugnacious, harder-minded, and much less prone to whimsy – a don manqué who complained ceaselessly about his fate as a writer who needed to write in order to live.

Belloc was older than Chesterton, was half-French, and after school in England had been conscripted into the French army. He was born a Roman Catholic and despite backslidings in his fifties never ceased to be one. On his mother's side he had a Nonconformist and Unitarian, and on his father's side a Huguenot and a Napoleonic, background. He was an undergraduate at Balliol where he read History, was a contemporary of Birkenhead and Simon at the Oxford Union and in the Liberal landslide of 1906 became a Liberal M.P. After retiring from parliament in 1910, writing was his only occupation.

[1] Joseph Hilaire Pierre René Belloc (1870–1953). Educ. Oratory School and Balliol College, Oxford. Liberal M.P. 1906–10. Author of *Verses and Sonnets* 1896, *The Bad Child's Book of Beasts* 1896, *More Beasts for Worse Children* 1897, *The Modern Traveller* 1898, *A Moral Alphabet* 1899, *Danton* 1899, *Paris* 1900, *Robespierre* 1901, *The Path to Rome* 1902, *Caliban's Guide to Letters* 1903, *Emmanuel Burden* 1904, *The Old Road* 1904, *Esto perpetua* 1906, *An Open Letter on the Decay of Faith* 1906, *Hills and the Sea* 1906, *On Nothing* 1908, *Mr Clutterbuck's Election* 1908, *A Change in the Cabinet* 1909, *Marie Antoinette* 1909, *On Everything* 1909, *Pongo and the Bull* 1910, *Verses* 1910, with Cecil Chesterton *The Party System* 1911, *The French Revolution* 1911, *British Battles* 6 vols. 1911–13, *The Servile State* 1912, *The Green Overcoat* 1912, *Warfare in England* 1912, *Three Essays* 1914, with J. Lingard *The History of England* 1915 vol. xi, *A General Sketch of the European War* 2 vols. 1915, *The Last Days of the French Monarchy* 1916, *The Second Year of the War* 1916, *The Free Press* 1918, *The House of Commons and Monarchy* 1920, *Europe and the Faith* 1920, *Pascal's Provincial Letters* 1921, *Catholic Social Reform versus Socialism* 1922, *The Jews* 1922, *The Road* 1923, *Mr Petre* 1925, *The Cruise of the Nona* 1925, *A History of England* 4 vols. 1925–31, *A Companion to Mr Wells's Outline of History* 1926, *Mr Belloc Still Objects* 1926, *The Catholic Church and History* 1927, *Oliver Cromwell* 1927, *James the Second* 1928, *How the Reformation Happened* 1928, *Joan of Arc* 1929, *Richelieu* 1929, *Wolsey* 1930, *Cranmer* 1931, *Essays of a Catholic Layman in England* 1931, *The Praise of Wine* 1931, *Napoleon* 1932, *The Question and the Answer* 1932, *William the Conqueror* 1933, *Becket* 1933, *Charles the First* 1933, *A Shorter History of England* 1934, *Milton* 1935, *An Essay on the Nature of Contemporary England* 1937, *The Crusade* 1937, *The Crisis of Our Civilization* 1937, *The Case of Dr Coulton* 1938, *The Great Heresies* 1938, *The Catholic and the War* 1940, *On the Place of Gilbert Chesterton in English Letters* 1940, *Elizabethan Commentary* 1942.

In comparing Chesterton with Belloc, it is necessary to remember that almost all the opinions which Chesterton expressed about the 1914 war, Italian Fascism and Jewish internationalism were also expressed by Belloc, that Chesterton's *William Cobbett* and *A Short History of England* gave Chesterton's version of their common view of English history, and that *Irish Impressions* showered the same praise on the Irish peasantry and drew the same contrast between Catholic 'uncertainty' and Calvinistic 'certainty' about salvation as Belloc did.

Belloc was an educated man for whom public utterance was a natural activity and who, from his earliest years, was an exuberant controversialist with pen and tongue. On paper he was less startling than Chesterton and less capable of paradox, and he lacked the lightness and sharpness of Chesterton's controversial manner. He was, however, as good a poet and a more plausible novelist. In historical writing his superiority was incontestable from *Danton* and *Robespierre* onwards.

In *Danton* and *Robespierre*, the argument was that the French Revolution has been a revolution of 'conviction' and that Danton was superior to Robespierre by reason of the 'energy' with which he organized the army of 1792 and the 'contempt' he felt for the 'theorists' who killed him. It was Danton who had wanted a 'united republic', Danton who had embodied the 'real France on the Sambre and ... the plains of Valenciennes', Danton who had 'loved ... the Revolutionary Thing' in so practical a way that 'whatever crises western civilization was to pass ... through ... in the future and whatever form its edifice would take when the noise of the building was over', its corner-stone would be such as had not only been 'planned by the philosophy', but also 'hewn by the force' of the revolution.

In accounting for the normalization of the revolution after 1794, Belloc stressed the part played by the peasantry. It was the peasantry which had 'toned down the crudities of political formulae', the peasantry which had put flesh on the 'dry bones' of revolutionary principle, the peasantry which had constructed the *modus vivendi* between the Church and the Republic as it was described in Belloc's Home University Library volume, *The French Revolution*, in 1911.

The French Revolution was written in the shadow of Dreyfus at the end of a decade of intense conflict between the Republic and the Church. It was the work of one who, as both a Roman Catholic and an admirer of the revolution, wished it to be understood that the 'political theory of the Revolution' and the 'theology of the Church' were compatible and complementary and that there had been no philosophical reason why the Church should have come into conflict with the revolutionary tradition in France or the democratic tradition anywhere else.

Belloc did not blur the deliberateness of the 'de-Christianization' which occurred during the Terror or the 'martyrdoms' which were suffered in the process. But he explained them as the result of a misunderstanding arising from the fact that the revolutionary leaders, like the rest of the educated classes, had been infected by Huguenotism, Rationalism and Erastianism, had been unable to understand either the strength of the Church or the popularity of the clergy and would have avoided entanglement if they had realized that the popular determination to remain Catholic between 1572 and 1610 would be matched by an equal determination to remain Catholic during the crisis of the 1790s.

The crisis of the 1790s was presented as establishing a new political system and new political dogmas, including the 'transcendant dogma' of the 'equality of man'. This was what the French had become soldiers for and had succeeded even in defeat in imposing on the governments of Europe, and Belloc praised it not only because it was 'true' but also, as Rousseau had understood, because it could not have been achieved without a religion.

Belloc rejected the civic religion which Rousseau described in *The Social Contract*. But he admired Rousseau's sense of the *need* for religion and in *The French Revolution* and his works about British politics subsequently explained why the *political* principles of *The Social Contract* were compatible with Catholicism.

In British politics Belloc was a Radical. He differed, however, from many Radicals in despising the House of Commons and denying that 'representative government' was a desirable concomitant of a democratic polity. In the books that he wrote in the decade after he left parliament, his chief argument was that Christianity and Democracy were both threatened by an 'economic conspiracy'.

In *The Party System* and *The Free Press*, Belloc attacked the control of news which the ownership of newspapers gave to capitalists and the control of parliament which collusion gave to front-bench politicians. In *The House of Commons and Monarchy*, parliaments were described as being essentially 'aristocratic' and the English parliament as being incapable of 'representing the mass', protecting the Courts and preventing the 'precarious and ephemeral acquisition of wealth' now that its aristocratic basis had disappeared. These, nevertheless, were things that Democracy required, and it was in the name of egalitarian, as against representative, Democracy, that monarchy was designated the sole guarantor of the nation's 'greatness and homogeneity' in the future.

Belloc did not know whether the restoration of monarchy would come about through 'elective machinery', the 'accidental popularity of one man' or a 'return to power of the Hereditary House'. All he knew was that aristocracy was an unusual form of polity, that 'much the greater part of states in history had been egalitarian' and that monarchy alone could control the corrupt judges, venial politicians and secret financiers whom he had been attacking from *The Servile State* onwards.

The Party System, The Free Press and *The House of Commons and Monarchy* were essays about the breakdown of aristocracy. In *The Servile State*, Belloc had supplied reasons for believing that this would lead to a re-invigoration of Christianity.

The Servile State contained both a warning and an analysis. The warning was that the slavery which Christianity had abolished in the Dark Ages was returning, and that both Christianity and Democracy needed to be rescued from it. The analysis suggested that Christian Democracy could only be achieved when capitalism and Socialism had been demolished.

As *The Servile State* explained it, the 'slavery' to which Europe was returning was the outcome of the capitalistic methods which the English aristocracy had applied to land, especially monastic land, at the Reformation, and had extended to all property and labour by the time of the Industrial Revolution. This analysis was neither new nor peculiar to Belloc. What distinguished his version was the view that the conflict between the Protestant oligarchy and the Christian monarchy had been a conflict about capitalism, that the 'slavery' which had been imposed by the oligarchy was incompatible with Christianity and that the only compatible polity was a 'Distributist State'.

The Distributist State differed from capitalist and socialistic states in resting on the 'free mind' and in looking back to the 'economically free' society which England had been before the 'seizure of the monastic lands'. It assumed that the concentration of land ownership which had distinguished England from France and Ireland could be reversed, that proletarianization could be diminished and that it was politically possible to resolve the 'contradiction' between the 'free man' needed by the 'Christian tradition of our civilization' and the 'unfree' man that capitalism needed in order to rob him of his labour. The argument of *The Servile State* was that these objectives should be approached by keeping land and capital out of the hands of the 'political officers of the community', by restoring co-operative guilds and a 'more even distribution of property' and by a 'Conservative or Traditionalist' effort to re-establish the ancient forms of Christian life.

Belloc's analysis was nostalgic and pessimistic. It assumed that the propertyless man could not be a free man, that the products of popular education in England lacked that 'instinct for property' on which freedom depended and that the 'servility' which he associated with the 'decay of faith' was being increased by brutal intrusion from an alien force of which the Jewish financier was the symbol.

In a pamphlet that he wrote in 1940 in support of the war against Hitler, Belloc gave an unequivocal denunciation of the Nazi treatment of the Jews. In *The Jews* eighteen years earlier, he had advocated segregation as the only way of appeasing the antagonism of which the Nazi attitude was to be the outcome.

The Jews was written cautiously and carefully, and discussed antiSemitism in sorrow rather than in anger. But it predicted that, unless the 'rising tide of antagonism' could be dealt with, there would be persecutions more appalling than any that European Jews had suffered in the past.

For Belloc, as for the Chestertons, the pre-war Jewish problem had been the part which Jews had played in creating the corrupt capitalism of the Panama scandal in France and the Marconi scandal in England. In 1922, the problem was Bolshevism.

The Jews discussed the proletarianization of western Jewry since the 1880s, the Jewish invasions of European and American cities and the Jewish ancestry which it attributed to Kingsley, Matthew Arnold, Mazzini, Browning and General Booth. It emphasized the prominence which Jews had achieved in government, the infiltration they had effected into freemasonry, universities and journalism and the leadership they were supplying to the socialist movement. Jewish secrecy and superiority and Gentile disingenuousness and uncharitableness were touched on, as were the Jewish rôle in the South African war, the part played by Jews in attacking the temporal power of the Pope and the profits which Jews were alleged to have made by selling arms and raw materials to both sides during the 1914 war. So far as France and Britain were concerned, Jewish service during the 1914 war was held to have balanced the account but it was made clear that the Russian Revolution had unbalanced it again.

The Jews included an extended attack on assimilation, especially in Palestine and Eastern Europe, and on the liberal stupidity which had failed to understand that the Jewish problem in the past had been about national loyalty and the capitalist Jew's inability to understand the 'European sense of property'. Only the Catholic Church was credited with understanding that Bolshevism was a 'Jewish movement' in 'half-alliance' with international Jewish finance, that the Bolshevik Jew had much the same attitude to property as the capitalist Jew and that the immediate problem was to protect both the 'European sense of property' and the homogeneity of the Christian nations, abandonment of which – though Belloc did not say so – had turned Newman away from Tory Anglicanism in the first place.

Belloc's Catholicism had many personal peculiarities, including the often exasperated devoutness and verbal license about Christianity's Jewish origin that made obedience to the Church the only ground for accepting it. Here we shall discuss his view of Catholicism's history, and the Catholicizing propaganda which he conducted with increasing intensity after his wife's death in 1914.

In the *Open Letter on the Decay of Faith* which he wrote to Masterman in 1906 and in the introduction to Lowell's *Poems* which he published two years later, Belloc rejected the idea that Christianity was dying or that the 'silent enemy' of Masterman's imagination had 'conquered' for ever. Drawing on De Maistre and praising him at the expense of the pessimists and the Hegelians, he drew attention to 'the faith ... of the Irish' and the proof they had given 'over all the ends of the earth' that a dawn was breaking in which the future would not belong to the English middle classes, the Puritan states of New England or the University of Oxford.

This sort of resentful optimism had disappeared by the time of *The Servile State* six years later. Though Belloc continued to assume that Catholicism was what free men wanted and what Catholic apologetic was increasingly arguing for, he assumed that prevailing conditions would make it difficult for anyone to get it. Even the Polish resurgence of 1919 left him as pessimistic as the 'literary pessimists' he had criticized Masterman for absorbing.

Between the wars Belloc's position was not only that the 'Faith was
... Europe' and 'Europe ... the Faith' but also that 'the Church was
Europe ... and Europe the Church'. It was not the barbarians but the
Church that had saved civilization and provided the 'cohesive political
principle of the great majority of human beings' in the fourth century.
It was the Church which had defeated the Arian, Islamic and Scandinavian threats and been at the centre of Christendom's revival from the
eleventh century onwards, the Church which had resisted the 'isolation' into which 'the soul' had been plunged by the Reformation, the
Church which had defended 'peasant society' against industrial capitalism and as author of its 'philosophy of life' was Europe's only defender
in the crisis of civilization which threatened. In rejecting Communist as
he had rejected socialist remedies, Belloc agreed that capitalism was
odious and destructive, and that the Distributist State would not work
unless the Reformation was undone, Protestantism submerged and
Europe 'reconverted' to Catholicism.

Before 1914, Belloc had feared the 'atheist theory' and Protestant a-
morality which he identified as the cause of Prussian expansionism
from Frederick the Great onwards. Between the wars he feared not
only the Communist but also the Masonic threat, the threat from the
'atheist individualism of the great towns', and the threat from Hitler
against whom, though a 'screaming Eunuch', it was necessary to fight a
'religious' war in 1940. He was comforted by the belief that Prussian
Protestantism had been resisted by Kaunitz's Catholic alliance in the
eighteenth century and destroyed by the Anglo-French alliance in the
twentieth, and that 'in England, Scotland, the Dominions and the
United States' Protestantism was in 'dissolution'.

The 'Europe' that Belloc defended was a Europe of nations governed
by a 'public law' which had survived from Christendom. Its essence
was defined by the battle lines that he drew in *The Great Heresies,
Essays of a Catholic Layman* and *The Crisis of Our Civilization*.

The battle Belloc envisaged was not a battle between paganism and
Christianity, far less was it a battle between paganism and religion. The
battle was a battle between paganism and Catholicism to which the
'vague Christianity' of recent generations would be irrelevant. The
battle was to be a battle of ideas between Catholic life and doctrine on
the one hand and the fatalism, satanism, determinism, monism, materialism, atheism and superstition which challenged it on the other. The
challenge went deeper than any of the challenges which the Church had
faced in the past and, being no longer confined as in the nineteenth

century to a 'comparatively small number of intellectuals', was acting as a social force which had brought with it a cruelty and irrationality unprecedented in Christian history.

Once its foundations had been laid, Belloc's apologetic was unsubtle, occasionally even childish. There was something to be said for blowing on Pascal and Milton and for mounting an attack in the year of *The Whig Interpretation of History* on the anti-Catholic Protestantism of the academic and governing classes in England. But Belloc's attack was inferior to Newman's attack in *The Present Position of Catholics in England*, and even his criticisms of Inge, Coulton, Haldane, Frazer and Wells, justified as they were, were, except in the case of Wells, too broad and typecast to be persuasive.

Belloc deserves to be remembered for his poetry, travel-books and novels, for his skill as a military historian and for the historical imagination he displayed not only in *The French Revolution* but also in *Oliver Cromwell*.

Oliver Cromwell was only one of more than a dozen books that Belloc wrote about sixteenth- and seventeenth-century England. But it put more succinctly and expressed more powerfully the essence of his view of the problem and provided the best statement that the Tractarian tradition has produced about the Reformation and the English Civil War as episodes in a class struggle to preserve the political and financial power of the new millionaires who had as certainly 'staked all' on the extirpation of Catholicism and the confiscation of Church property as the Joels and Barnatos had 'staked all' on the South African diamond boom of the 1880s.

Belloc admired Cromwell as a military commander and praised the sincerity of his religion. He emphasized the nervous tension in Cromwell's personality, his capacity for dissimulation and intrigue and the average nature of his Puritanism when compared with the excesses of his contemporaries. But, though descended on one side from a family of Cromwellian Puritans, he attacked the evils of which Cromwell was the outcome – not only the evils which had arisen when Cecilian Erastianism had conspired to stop Elizabeth and her people returning to the Catholicism that they had wanted, but also the evils which the Tractarians had imputed to Calvinism – its hatred of Catholicism, its rejection of good works, its denunciation of pleasure, its emphasis on the priesthood of the laity, its 'doomful and avengeful God', its doctrine of the predestined sanctification of the few and the predestined damnation of the many and its unbearable conviction of the superiority of the few who had, over the many who had not, been elected to glory.

Oliver Cromwell, whether right or wrong historically, was a brilliant display of Belloc's imagination. Passages from two other works may serve further to illustrate his doctrine.

It was imagined at ... Robespierre's ... death [went a passage from *Robespierre* in 1901] that the West would abandon or attempt with an ever-diminishing energy the solution of that awful problem of political freedom whose complexity he had himself so little seized. A relief ran through the kings; the rich began to draw breath carelessly. It was thought that the Republic, which had certainly suffered madness, would leave no more effect than attaches to the memory of evil dreams. Whatever instinct or demand had surged up from the blind depths and origins of mankind, that primal appetite had, it was thought, sunk back into its antique repose. But it is not so likely, nor in so immediate a fashion that change can be provoked in the development of a civilization. The universal reaction which men awaited could find no stuff, the theories counter to democracy no new philosophy in the mere falling of a sharp steel. Today, through the wide perplexities of a world ten-fold his own, the central thought, to which this man was registrar and whose propagation he imagined to be his mission, has reappeared to lead us through unknown dangers to unknown destinies; for we are certainly on the threshold of the Republic.

The second passage comes from *A Companion to Mr Wells's Outline of History* in 1926.

The lesson to be learnt from the immense sale of such a second-rate popular book as Mr Wells's *Outline of History* is that the old doctrines, for the great mass of our modern English-speaking non-Catholic population, have gone. Mr Wells ridicules the Resurrection; the Incarnation he could, of course, not grasp, but *also* – and here is the significant point – he does not think that others really entertain it. He does not admit any part of the Christian scheme. On the intellectual side he proposes as true things of which we know nothing; and as obviously untrue things on which the best minds of Europe have long been assured ...

In all this he is not an innovator. He challenges no one. He risks nothing. He follows the sheep. Mr Wells makes no attempt to be a leader. He merely puts, in a nice, clear, simple fashion, that which the myriads to whom he addresses himself already believe – that there is no Creator, no Saviour, no Resurrection, no Immortality, no Communion of Saints ...

It is not true that the modern world as a whole has suffered such a revolution. The Catholic culture in the continent of Europe not only stands strong, but is rapidly increasing in strength. The two branches of reaction against it (the German Protestant reaction of which Prussian atheism was the climax, and the more respectable anti-clericalism of French and Italian tradition) are both manifestly weakening. The doctrines that would dissolve society have been exposed and are now counter-attacked with an increasing vigour. Europe – the Soul of the world – is hesitating whether it will not return to the Faith: without which it cannot live.

But is that so in the world to which we belong, or at least of which we Catholics are exceptional inhabitants? Is it true of that English-speaking culture which was founded upon the Bible and whose peculiar virtues and weaknesses, advantages and disadvantages (many of them alien to us Catholics, but all well comprehended by us), were the texture of life in England and Scotland, in the English Dominions, and in the United States?

I think not. Men hesitate to say it; they are afraid of facing the truth in the matter, but truth it is: the foundations have gone. I do not mean that in their place other foundations may not be discovered. I do not predict chaos, though chaos is a very possible result of it all. What I do say is, that Christian morals and doctrine, and all that they meant, are, in our English-speaking world much more than in any other part of contemporary white civilization, in dissolution.

Though there had been random English, and also an Irish, Catholic Radicalism before Belloc, Belloc's was the first systematic English attempt to show that the principles of 1789 and the attack on capitalism were compatible with Roman Catholicism. Belloc and Chesterton both jibbed at 1917. It was left to Greene to imply that the principles of 1917 might also be compatible.

III

Graham Greene[1] was brought up to a half-hearted pedagogic Anglicanism. He was converted to Roman Catholicism when young in anticipation of marriage to a Roman Catholic wife and, after a period of uncertainty, began to use literature to demonstrate Roman Catholicism's meaning and possibilities. Greene had beliefs and it is likely that

---

[1] Graham Greene (1904–). Educ. Berkhamsted School and Balliol College, Oxford. Subeditor on *The Times* 1926–30, Foreign Office 1941–4. Author of *The Man Within* 1929, *Stamboul Train* 1932, *It's a Battlefield* 1934, ed. *The Old School* 1934, *England Made Me* 1935, *The Basement Room* 1935, *A Gun for Sale* 1936, *Journey without Maps* 1936, *Brighton Rock* 1938, *The Confidential Agent* 1939, *The Lawless Roads* 1939, *The Power and the Glory* 1940, *British Dramatists* 1942, *The Ministry of Fear* 1943, contributor to *Why Do I Write?* 1948, *The Heart of the Matter* 1948, *The Third Man* 1950, *The Lost Childhood* 1951, *The End of the Affair* 1951, *The Quiet American* 1955, *Loser Takes All* 1955, *Our Man in Havana* 1958, *A Burnt-Out Case* 1960, *The Comedians* 1966, *Collected Essays* 1969, *Travels with My Aunt* 1969, *A Sort of Life* 1971, *The Honorary Consul* 1973, *The Human Factor* 1978, *Dr Fischer of Geneva* 1980, *Monsignor Quixote* 1982.

finding out what he believed, or needed to say about belief, followed from a considered conception of the rôle of literature in public thought. His reasons for writing in the first place and for writing at the length at which he has written for over half a century, however, had nothing to do with religion. His first five books, including his one volume of poetry, dealt therapeutically with personalities in tension but gave no indication either that the tension was religious or that Greene knew that he was going to write about religion later. It is likely that he wrote about religion as he wrote about espionage because there was a public waiting to hear about it.

Greene's mentors included T. S. Eliot, Chesterton and Herbert Read, who were all highly didactic. But others, like Stevenson, Buchan, Ford Madox Ford and Conrad were not didactic, and the attempt to extract a message from Greene's writing is likely to be frustrated by a mode of expression which has avoided theory and been oblique about doctrine, even in the literary criticism, travel-books and handful of novels in which he was most explicit.

In considering Greene's early criticism, it would be misleading to exaggerate the importance of religion. It would be equally misleading to ignore the animadversions on Ellis's 'invincible ignorance', on Virginia Woolf's 'provincial understanding' of Christianity and on the disagreeable tone of Samuel Butler's rejection of immortality. In criticizing the harshness of Belloc's, the bitterness of Noyes's and the eccentricity of Gill's Catholicism, and in expressing the 'embarrassment' that he felt at the Conservative disposition of English Roman Catholicism and the 'parochial' nature of English Roman Catholic writing, Greene made important disconnections. Through the 'serious, even grim ... vices' that had preceded Rochester's conversion and the 'memories of ... Catholicism' that 'worked like poetry through ... Conrad's ... agnostic prose', he found passing evidences of permanent preferences. In discussing Rolfe he did something more.

In writing about *Hadrian VII* in 1934, Greene discussed the 'angelic conflict' between 'heavenly virtue' and 'satanic vice' which had occurred when the 'spoilt priest' who had been expelled from the Scots College in Rome became a 'swindler and pander' because he 'would be a priest or nothing'. Rolfe was not exactly held up for admiration, as Campion and Chesterton were. But he was praised for wanting 'desperately' to serve the Church and for having a 'genuine piety', perhaps even a 'sanctity', behind his viciousness. Rolfe, indeed, had been obsessed with 'damnation' and, in 'choosing to go about sheathed in flame in the hey-day of the Entente Cordiale, Sir Ernest Cassell and Lily Langtry', had been no more eccentric than Henry James who, during a life-time 'listening at the chamber of the soul', had created a world of 'treachery and deceit', put the 'flush of the flames' on the 'faces' of his 'malefactors' and raised problems about the blackness and mercilessness of human nature which only Catholicism could resolve.

In discussing James, Greene emphasized the 'private universe' which James had spread upon the world as literature. In Greene, too, there is a private universe which has, and also has not, been exposed in his autobiographical writings. This has included suicide, espionage, psycho-analysis, mutilation and sexual gloom, and an acute sense of the burdensome weight that the soul experiences in exercising its freedom. In Greene, far more than in James, however, religion is central – or was thirty years ago when it was in an ambivalent relationship with modern political establishments.

Religion was disconnected from modern political establishments because Greene's primary interest was in the soul and its relation to God; it could not be disconnected because the Church was the agent by which the soul knew God, and both the Church and the soul were threatened by the world. Greene's anxiety to protect the soul's freedom on the one hand and the writer's autonomy on the other made him critical of Marxist establishmentarianism when he encountred it in Mexico in 1938 and helped him to see in Marxism's strenuousness as great a threat to literature and religion as he saw in the Utilitarian 'sense of social responsibility'. On the other hand, Greene was critical of capitalism when he encountered it in Africa in the 1930s, and, in condemning capitalistic régimes thereafter, lined himself up behind Castro, Ho Chi Minh and Allende both as improvements on *The Quiet American*'s innocence and corruption and as up-to-date versions of the charismatic hope with which Priestley and Churchill were supposed to have expelled hypocrisy and cynicism from Britain after the fall of France in 1940.

Like Hampshire's, which they much resemble, Greene's politics have been selective, and have not entered very fully into the 'murky intricacies of political thought'. Greene assumes that, though Catholicism is democratic and revolutionary, politics should be instrumental and unobtrusive, because the distinctively human characteristics are to be found in private matters rather than in public ones, and because Christianity is as vulnerable to the bland threat from Liberal Democracy as to the brutal threat from totalitarianism.

In his main phase as a Christian novelist, Greene claimed to be conscious of a tension between the 'personal moral' which the novelist could offer and the 'edification' which Church leaders required. He assumed that 'disloyalty' was essential if literature was to do its work and adduced Newman's authority to suggest that a 'Christian literature' which avoided sin would lead to the elimination of everything that made literature a possibility. Certainly sin and salvation formed the central theme of his treatment of Christianity between *Journey without Maps* and *The End of the Affair*.

In describing the visit that he had made to Monrovia, Liberia and Sierra Leone in 1935, Greene drew a crucial contrast between the westernized Africans of the Coast and the 'purer terror and gentleness' that he found among the 'witches and ... secret dancers' of the interior. In this respect, *Journey without Maps* registered merely nostalgia and regret at the false turnings which had led to the evils of Western civilization. It was not until *The Lawless Roads* and *The Power and the Glory* that Greene's regret became Christian.

The Lawless Roads drew a running contrast between the 'ugly indifference' that was to be found in Trollope's Barchester novels, which Greene had been reading while travelling in Mexico, and the faith and devotion which had been stimulated by the Mexican government's persecution of the Mexican Church. The reality of religion was found in Christianity's 'supernatural promise', in suffering under persecution and in the difference between the 'chromium' life of Mexico City where the poor were being deprived of religion and 'hate' was giving way to 'love' in the school curriculum, and the Catholic life of Chiapas and San Luis Potosi where churches were the theatres of the poor and the poor got the religion that they wanted.

In *The Lawless Roads*, Greene was concerned primarily with the external conditions that were necessary to the realization of Christianity. An important theme from the Wisconsin Police Chief there to the chief character in *The Quiet American*, however, was the 'ease' of the soul that Greene associated with liberal self-congratulation, and the spiritual 'emptiness' with which Anglo-Saxons on both sides of the Atlantic were described as priding themselves on the rectitude and incontrovertibility of their liberalism.

In *The Power and the Glory*, Greene achieved his first systematic statement about the soul, inventing a central character whose piety under persecution was more real than his conventional piety before persecution and in whom, as in Rolfe, there was only the narrowest dividing line between sanctity and sin. *The Power and the Glory* was against the sentimentality of social Catholicism. But it was also against the totalitarian attack upon it, and the 'plump hands' and 'glossy stares' of the schoolmasters who were replacing it. The Christianity it celebrated was the Christianity of the catacombs with the priest being a Christian hunted by lions and the story of his martyrdom a blow-by-blow criticism of the conception of martyrdom as pious Catholics understood it.

If the priest in *The Power and the Glory* is compared with Father Brown, Greene's intellectual experience will be seen to have been more adult than Chesterton's. In *The Power and the Glory* there was no whimsy and no pretence that fantasy was indispensable. To the main question, was Brown a more credible antidote to 'rationalism' than the whisky-priest, the answer is that catacomb heroism treated realistically in a modern setting and a fallen world was infinitely superior to the faery world of Chesterton's imagination.

The Christianity described in *The Power and the Glory* was a Christianity which had been stripped to the bone. It was neither hampered by social respectability nor sustained by political power. It was the Christianity of the trenches, out of touch with ecclesiastical headquarters and well aware of the precariousness of its expectations. It assumed that Christianity had to fight its way back, that martyrs would be needed if it was to do so and that the only ground for optimism was the hint that the supply of martyrs would be inexhaustible. In no work published in England since 1833 has there been so sure a sense of the nature of Christianity as the Tractarians wished it to be understood, and would have understood it once the polite threat from the Whigs had given way to the modern threat from Marx and the merciless desert of Evangelicalism been reclaimed by the tolerance with which sin is treated in almost all of Greene's writings.

Greene appears to suppose that modern readers need to be brought slowly to the Christian truths. He moves cautiously and assumes that only 'modern' Catholics can make sin edifying. He treats suicide and adultery in the way in which Ibsen treated them – as sins which should not be subjected to rancorous condemnation by those who have not been tempted to commit them. The priest's adultery in *The Power and the Glory*, Scobie's adultery in *The Heart of the Matter* and the woman's adultery in *The End of the Affair* seem to be less important than the disposition of their souls and it seems to be suggested that allowances should be made for those whose sins arise from the integrity of their hearts. There is so much that suggests this – so much that makes it doubtful whether God's rules can be observed – that the antinomian atheism which is bawled at the silent God in *The End of the Affair* is obviously designed to reflect a very modern anxiety about His existence.

The End of the Affair was a cunning book. Though also about love and sex, it was principally about conversion. There was much manoeuvring and scene-setting and a narrative taste which was flawed only by the introduction of the heroine's mother. But it was the journal and the priest's truths which supplied the meaning, and this was conveyed the more naturally and effectively because, in her promiscuity, the heroine was superficially as unworthy as the priest in *The Power and the Glory* or Scobie in *The Heart of the Matter* and could be used, as *A Burnt-Out Case* was to be used later, to emphasize the fallen nature of the only heroism that is possible on earth.

If it were not for the oddness and quirkiness, the dryness and diseased irritability of Greene's distaste for human accomplishments, and his Luddite contempt for the 'petty social fulfilment, tiny pension and machine-made furniture' of the modern world, one would think of praising him for insisting on the fallen nature of all human activity. He certainly deserves praise for the resistance he points at the intellectual pharisaism of the schools and the moral pharisaism of the Christian devout, and, however hard he has to work at avoiding it, for his success in avoiding edification and the didactic. Whether his theology is coherent with his gloom, however, whether his hatred of uplift is not a hatred of virtue and whether his mentality is ultimately more Christian than Ibsen's, are questions to which the answer is obscure.

Greene's Christianity included an element of counter-attack but was concerned principally with the difficulty involved in living a Christian life in the modern world. Greene on the whole has avoided theory. In the last two thinkers we are to discuss, theory has been predominant.

IV

Dawson[1] was born in 1889, became a Roman Catholic in 1914 and died in 1970; Copleston was born in 1907, became a Roman Catholic in 1925 and was still writing in 1984. Dawson's public career spanned the period from the middle 1920s to the middle 1950s, Copleston's from the early 1940s to the middle 1980s. In Dawson, historical arguments and modes of expression merged into a Christian sociology. In Copleston, they have merged into a Christian philosophy.

In the 1950s there was an American attempt to present Dawson as a Christian Toynbee. This was unconvincing and did not in any case begin until Dawson had ceased to matter in England. It was for English audiences, nevertheless, that he had written principally and first; his mental engagements even in the 1950s and 1960s were the essentially Tractarian engagements that he had displayed in *The Spirit of the Oxford Movement* in 1933.

In the 1950s Dawson saw in the secular nationalism which was destroying the European empires and the traditional structures of Asia and Africa a major opportunity for Christian expansion provided the Reformation was reversed, cultural Eurocentricism abandoned and a 'free market in ideas' permitted to produce Christian leaders from the 'lower middle-class population' of contemporary Asian cities in the way in which the 'free market in ideas' had produced them from the Asian cities of the Roman Empire.

About Asia and Africa, Dawson knew nothing of consequence. His reflections about their future were applications of the assumption that

---

[1] Christopher Henry Dawson (1889–1970). Educ. Winchester and Trinity College, Oxford. Converted to Roman Catholicism 1914. Author of *The Age of the Gods* 1928, *Progress and Religion* 1929, *Christianity and Sex* 1930, *Christianity and the New Age* 1931, *The Modern Dilemma* 1931, *The Making of Europe* 1932, *Enquiries into Religion and Culture* 1933, *The Spirit of the Oxford Movement* 1933, *Medieval Religion* 1934, *Religion and the Modern State* 1935, *Beyond Politics* 1939, *The Judgement of the Nations* 1942, *Europe – A Society of Peoples* 1946, *Religion and Culture* 1948, *Religion and the Rise of Western Culture* 1950, *Medieval Essays* 1953, *The Mongol Mission* 1955, *The Movement of World Revolution* 1959, *The Historical Reality of Christian Culture* 1960, *The Crisis of Western Education* 1961, *The Dividing of Christendom* 1965.

the problem of the age was the secular intolerance which accompanied Western education, and that Christianity had an advantage in dealing with it by reason of the fact that it had had greater experience of it than any other religion except Judaism.

These were Dawson's leading ideas, and he stated them in three different ways – as an historical account of the Middle Ages, as a polemical account of the history of European thought since the Renaissance and as an anthropological account of culture's dependence on religion. In all three respects the argument was about the central rôle which Christianity had played in creating mediaeval culture, about the erosion it had suffered from Liberalism since the Renaissance and about the erosion which Liberalism had suffered in the twentieth century. The erosion of Christianity was symbolized by Deism, Robespierre and the Terror and the erosion of Liberalism by Marx, Nietzsche, Sorel, Spengler, Lawrence, William James, Freud and Jung. It was made clear that a serious study of psychology would show that religious 'images and ... experiences' were 'invulnerable in their own field' and that the 'disintegration of modern civilization' into a 'world of reason ... which was ... spiritually void' and a 'world of the soul' which had lost the 'consecrated ways' of expressing itself through culture, had left civilization at the mercy of the 'negative ... and destructive ... forces of the Unconscious'. Most of all, in *Progress and Religion*, the Christian counter-revolution was a necessary response to the new type of civilization which had emerged in the twentieth century – a 'mechanical', 'mass' and 'materialistic' civilization which, even when 'checked' by an 'ancient body of social and political teaching', had imposed so heavy a burden that it was doubtful whether anyone who experienced it could stand up to it psychologically without a 'Catholic ideal of culture' and that Christian concern for the 'world to come' which the Roman Catholic Church had been propagating since Leo XIII.

The obstacles to re-Christianization as they were specified in the course of the 1930s included not only the intellectual fences which had been erected since the Renaissance, but also the breakdown of traditional, including traditional sexual, morality and the advance of totalitarianism. Dawson did not mince words about Marxism and Nazism which were setting free the 'dark forces that had been chained by a thousand years of Christian civilization'. He used both, however, and especially Marxism, to expose the defects he discerned in bourgeois and democratic religion, and, in playing Newman, Maritain, Berdyaev,

Mauriac and Babbitt against them, argued that Europe would have to 'return to the foundations' which existed at the 'deeper levels of consciousness' in all the great religions of the world if it was to achieve that 'higher process of spiritual integration' which was the 'true goal of progress'.

In *The Age of the Gods* in the 1920s and in *Religion and Culture* in the 1940s, Dawson affirmed religion's naturalness and ubiquity and the inability of Frazerianism and Marxism to understand it. Mankind was said to have been 'spiritually creative' before it was 'economically productive', to have invented art and religion before it had invented agriculture and industry and to have conceived of an 'order of nature' being known by 'initiation into divine mysteries' before it had conceived of it as being known by 'observation and logical thought'. It was ritual and sacrifice not secular science to which were attributed the 'earliest ... forms of knowledge', and it was the conception of a 'sacred science' rooted in the 'underworld of magic' which were described as leading not only to Copernicus and Kepler but also to the idea of the world as a 'true cosmos which was intelligible to scientific reason because it was the work of the Divine reason'.

Dawson emphasized that 'in all the great civilizations of the world' except modern Europe, religion and intellectual culture had been 'inseparable', and that every fully developed culture had depended on an 'interior discipline' and 'spiritual organisation' which had preserved the sacred literature, philosophy and ritual, and 'defined and canonised' the ideals of ... excellence' admired within it. This was the sense in which 'spiritual order' was 'indispensable' to progress, and it was only when the disintegrative criticism of the post-Renaissance intelligentsia was replaced by modern variants of the Comtean control which the priesthood had exercised over the 'non-moral ... and irrational' enemies of civilization in the Middle Ages that Europe would get the 'integrated system of principles and values' which it needed.

Dawson was a learned, though a glib, thinker, and, despite the 'timeless quality' which Knowles claimed for him, lacked a sense of difficulty and concentration. His accounts of the ubiquity and naturalness of religion were serious and significant, as were his statements of the connection between prophecy and progress and of the modern world's inability to understand the contemplative negativity which was to be found in Orphism, Shamanism and hermit-Taoism. In many ways, however, his view of religion was merely a Catholic inversion of Murray's inversion of Catholicism and failed as signally as Murray's did to sustain the points that it was designed to make. Even if it is true that it was the Church which had created European civilization, it is difficult to see why this should have been thought important once Europe had ceased to be Christian. Certainly, if this sort of mediaevalism had been going to survive as a creative doctrine, it would have needed the critical strengthening which Copleston was trying to effect from the early 1940s onwards.

V

Copleston[1] was converted to Roman Catholicism at the age of eighteen, and, after a period as an undergraduate at St John's College, Oxford, joined the Society of Jesus at the age of twenty-three. Apart from periods in Rome and the United States, he has been a priest and teacher in England ever since.

Copleston is a solid thinker and a prolific writer. In his seventies he has published a set of Gifford Lectures and a book about the non-Christian religions after spending the previous forty years mounting the critical counter-attack on Christianity's intellectual enemies which is to be found in *Friedrich Nietzsche, Arthur Schopenhauer, Aquinas, Contemporary British Philosophy, Philosophers and Philosophies* and the nine volumes of *A History of Philosophy*. His achievements have been a modern statement of political scholasticism and an historical account of the truth and sanity of the rational Thomism which he began to point at Nietzsche and Schopenhauer openly and at their English followers by implication in books which were published in his first phase of public utterance during the 1939 war.

---

[1] Rev Frederick Charles Copleston (1907–). Educ. Marlborough College and St John's College, Oxford. Converted to Roman Catholicism 1925, entered Society of Jesus 1930, ordained 1937, Professor of History of Philosophy Heythrop College 1939–70, Professor of Philosophy at University of London 1972–4, and at the Gregorian University Rome 1952–68. Author of *Friedrich Nietzsche, Philosopher of Culture* 1942, *Arthur Schopenhauer, Philosopher of Pessimism* 1946, *St. Thomas and Nietzsche* 1946, *A History of Philosophy* vols. i–ix 1946–75, *Existentialism and Modern Man* 1948, *Medieval Philosophy* 1952, *Aquinas* 1955, *Contemporary Philosophy* 1956, *A History of Medieval Philosophy* 1972, *Religion and Philosophy* 1974, *Philosophers and Philosophies* 1976, *Philosophies and Cultures* 1980, *Religion and the One* 1982.

When *Nietzsche* was published in 1942 it distanced itself from Nazism and anti-Semitism, and described its subject as a 'searching and earnest soul' who still presented a challenge to Christians fifty years after his death. It also argued, however, that, in spite of the 'religious' character of his thought and the 'tragic' quality of his 'prophecy', Nietzsche had been 'intellectually wicked' because he had 'propagated atheism' from the point in 1865 at which, like many of the thinkers discussed in this volume, he had begun to absent himself from Communion.

Copleston approved of Nietzsche's revolt against scholarship and his belief that knowledge had to be 'lived'. He expressed a Tractarian distaste for intellectual specialization and, while questioning the Nietzschean identification of culture with aristocracy, agreed that specialization had left culture at the mercy of journalism.

Copleston had no illusions about Liberal Democracy, bourgeois complacency or the dangers which were presented by the deracinated Jew, and he had an intellectual waste-paper basket to which he consigned Utilitarianism, secular individualism and the Rights of Man. On the other hand, he denied that Nietzsche shared Shaw's 'stud-farm' view of human nature and interpreted Superman and the 'will to power' as merely Goethean affirmations in regard to mind and body.

Copleston admired the subversion of Freudianism which he saw implicit in the will to power and the exposure which Nietzsche had made of conventional Christianity's whittling down of the Christian message. But he saw no benefit in the will to power itself. He rejected the Nietzschean distinction between Christ and St Paul and insisted that the lives of the saints were essential developments of Christianity. In denying that the 'saint' was a 'eunuch', that culture required an aristocratic morality or that Christianity embodied the 'slave morality' through which 'the herd' fed on the 'higher race of men', he asserted simply that Christians should be shocked by Nietzsche's selective contempt, that culture was a manifestation of 'the divine perfection' in which 'all men and women' were involved and that Christian humility was the remedy for the hubris which accompanied neurotic rebellion against 'finite individuality'.

To Schopenhauer, Copleston was as sympathetic as he had been to Nietzsche, discerning in his work an 'ethical' debt to Christianity and a justifiable reaction against Kantian and Hegelian optimism. But Schopenhauer's 'joy' was criticized for being 'negative joy' – the joy of the artist or the Indian ascetic, not the joy of St Francis of Assisi. The Schopenhauerian metaphysic was said to have affirmed the meaninglessness of life, the 'irrational blindness' of the impulse which lay behind the 'inner nature of the world' and the inseparability of individual wills from the single Will which constituted existence.

Copleston praised Schopenhauer's emphasis on evil and suffering. But he questioned his reaction to them, and in five crucial chapters dismissed his chief remedies for them – on the one hand the conception of art making men 'impersonal spectators ... of the eternal idea', on the other hand the conception of 'ethical renunciation' quietening the 'striving' with which the Will pursued goals that were unattainable.

In *Schopenhauer* Copleston's exposition was closer and denser than in *Nietzsche*. But its conclusion was as definite – that phenomenological voluntarism was self-contradictory and, if the world really was as illusionary as Schopenhauer had believed, that Schopenhauer's philosophy, like the world it had created, must have been 'illusionary' also.

In *Nietzsche* and *Schopenhauer*, Copleston set up targets which he then proceeded to knock down – in *Nietzsche* because Nietzsche's abandonment of Christ made him an enemy of the culture he professed to defend, in *Schopenhauer* because Schopenhauer's rejection of dualism entailed a hatred of ordinary existence, a perversion of holiness and a preference for Maya and Nirvana over Christian asceticism; in both cases because culture could not be sustained without a belief in the external reality of nature, the value and purposefulness of individuality and a Christian understanding of God.

In both works Copleston's scrutiny was strong and searching, appreciative of deviations from liberal optimism, but sensitive to diminutions of Christianity and committed to the belief that a cutting-edge could be obtained by writing the history of philosophy from a Thomist standpoint. His main tactic since has been to use Thomism as a standpoint from which to explore the 'blind alleys' down which philosophy has wandered from the pre-Socratics onwards.

Copleston's judgment of Greek philosophy, though respectful of 'one of the greatest treasures of our European heritage', was that it had failed to discover the 'true solutions' which it was reserved for Christianity to discover and at some point before the thirteenth century had been demoted from being a 'way of salvation' into being a 'praeparatio evangelica' and the preoccupation of universities. He treated modern philosophy's detachment from theology as a defect, emphasized the inseparability of philosophy from theology before Aquinas and the difficulty as well as the importance of the separation which Aquinas had effected, and insisted on the superiority of a 'theologically-minded metaphysician' like St Bonaventura, for whom 'the material world' was a 'shadow ... or revelation of its divine original' to the modern scientist's interest in the 'dynamic process' of the 'quantitatively determined immanent structure'.

In volumes iv–ix of *A History of Philosophy*, Copleston detailed the inroads made by philosophy on theology, and by mathematics, physics and history on philosophy, between the sixteenth and the nineteenth centuries, along with the process by which ethics and history had become autonomous in relation to theology – in the thought of the atheists and materialists in France, and in England and Germany in the thought of Bolingbroke, Gibbon, Frederick the Great, Reimarus, Mendelssohn, Lessing and the Deists. This was a cautionary tale in which Suarez was a crucial thinker and Renaissance Scholasticism of central importance, and in which political Liberalism was rooted in the Hobbesian emasculation of Natural Law. It showed Bacon, Descartes and Leibniz failing to combine 'mechanical causality' with proof of God's existence, Kant alone asking why 'scientific conceptions' had been allowed to 'monopolise man's view of reality', and the Kantian solution being to expel freedom and God from science in order to locate them within the moral order. Though Copleston rejected Kant's Copernican revolution and his bifurcation of reality, he used them to prove that deductive Rationalism was as powerless as empiricism to account for human knowledge.

Copleston dismissed Hume's dismissal of metaphysics, his atomization of experience and his theory of ideas, and described Kant's 'agnosticism in regard to the object of metaphysics' as opening the way to 'agnosticism in regard to any objective ... value in human existence'. He showed idealism turning the Kantian categories into 'categories of reality' and teleology into the 'purposiveness' of 'Nature', welcoming it in so far as it had revived interest in the religious consciousness but accepting Kierkegaard's rejection in so far as it had turned God into the Absolute. In the critical account of Romanticism that he gave in the closing pages of the introduction to Volume VII, he concluded that idealism lacked a 'theory of absolute moral values', 'interpreted the process of reality ... according to the pattern of human consciousness', and had made man's knowledge alone the determiner of the universe's 'goal' and 'significance'.

Copleston has been concerned not just with the past but with its relevance to the present. Since *A History of Philosophy* took nearly thirty years to write, it reflected changes in the philosophical situation, the restoration of English philosophical culture in the 1970s in particular depriving its accounts of Sartre, Merleau-Ponty and French Thomism in Volume IX of the polemical edge which had been prominent earlier. It was only in the first eight volumes that Copleston was able properly to object to the narrowness and a-morality which he had disliked in analytical philosophy as it was conducted in English universities in the 1940s and 1950s.

Copleston's objection to analytical philosophy was that it ignored metaphysics and renounced the attempt to give moral guidance. In discussing Existentialism, he discussed the situation to which it was alleged to be a response – philosophy's expulsion from the mind by psychology, from Society by collectivism and totalitarianism, and from Nature by the natural sciences, and the need to react by discussing the 'human problems' which surrounded the individual person. Existentialism was a search for the 'authentic freedom' of the individual person, and it was for this reason that Copleston focussed sympathetically on the ramifications of choice and the concept of the 'responsible agent who ... stood out against the ... world' in Kirkegaard, Marcel, Sartre, Jaspers, Camus, Heidegger and Mousnier.

Copleston criticized Existentialism's subjectivity and '*fin de siècle*' rejection of metaphysics, and in some glib pages accepted the Marxist view that it was the 'last convulsive effort on the part of the dying bourgeoisie to avoid submergence in the inhuman force of collectivity'. Though a useful contribution to the 'reawakening of metaphysics' and a modern 'way of salvation', Existentialism was also, moreover, a 'philosophy of crisis' where what Europe needed was rational discourse, a 'dogmatic philosophy' and a scholastic conception of the connections between the 'God of the philosophers' and the 'God of religion'.

Part III of *Religion and Philosophy* rejected the idea that philosophy and theology were separable activities. It argued against the Positivist, Occamist and Barthian separations and in favour of the view that metaphysical philosophy had a 'religious' value. A 'religiously orientated philosophy' could express a 'religious ... quest even when disconnected from organised religion', and religion was necessarily at odds with a philosophy which offered 'ideal values' with an 'overriding claim on human wills'. Having contrasted the absence of tension by reason of the absence of Churches in Greek and Hindu philosophy with the tension which had arisen between pagan philosophy and the early Church in the Roman Empire, it gave a constructive account of relations as they had been established in the thirteenth century.

In providing a Thomist account of the value of a theological philosophy, Copleston used the agnostic strategy which Mansel had used in a Kantian idiom a century earlier, emphasizing the 'veil' which separated the human mind from the 'transcendent', the obstacles this put in the way of mastering 'reality as a whole' and the testimony supplied by the dialectical succession of philosophical systems to philosophy's inability to transcend the 'conceptual web of human reason'. It was because metaphysics had tried to take reality 'by storm', he argued, that it was an extension of the religious impulse, but it was because it could not take reality by storm that Christian theology had something to say to it.

The argument of *Religion and Philosophy* was that religious experience could not be ignored, that prayer and worship had ontological implications and that the gap which divided men from God was bridgeable by love. In these circumstances, Copleston concluded, theology had nothing to fear from analytical philosophy which had no monopoly of reflection on religious language and, for all its refusal to presuppose God's existence, discussed God in ways which would not have been possible in Islam, Zoroastrianism or early Buddhism.

Like Ward, Copleston is both a convert to Roman Catholicism and a Thomist. But the one aspect of Ward's thought that Copleston has avoided is its emphasis on authority. Whatever obedience he has given as a priest, Copleston's emphasis as a thinker is on the *de facto* nature of the connection between Thomism and Catholicism, on argument as the proper mode of philosophical procedure and on Leo XIII's Encyclical *Aeterni Patris* as an encouragement to philosophical argument among Catholics. Aquinas has been presented as an innovator in the thirteenth century and one philosopher among many subsequently, and it has been emphasized that since Thomism is 'not part of the Catholic faith' any judgment of its 'philosophical merits' must be made by philosophers.

In *Aquinas*, Copleston's tactic was cautious. He did not 'defend' Aquinas and found it unreasonable to expect a thirteenth-century philosopher to give a definitive account of relations between philosophy and the 'particular sciences'. On the other hand Thomism was not a 'museum piece', had a social doctrine and was vigorously alive in France, Belgium and Germany, as volume ix of *A History of Philosophy* and innumerable references to Maritain and Gilson were to show. It was a 'balanced' and 'perennial' philosophy, avoiding materialism and dualism, juxtaposing rationalist and empiricist elements and refusing to make 'once-for-all' statements about the 'abiding pattern' which it attributed to the universe.

Thomism, moreover, was as sensitive to language as modern linguistic analysis, had stood up to Kant far better than other philosophies and had a conception of the 'spiritual side of the human personality' which was as far removed from Hobbesian pessimism as it was from Rousseauvian optimism. So far was the discovery of sense-perception from being the work of the British empiricists that Aquinas had not only seen man as a 'union of soul and body' in which the mind in knowing effected an 'active synthesis' of what it got from the senses but had also combined an unshakeable belief in the importance of philosophy with a denial that philosophy enjoyed private access to a sphere of reality from which ordinary people were excluded. Aquinas had started, indeed, 'where everyone else started', had not implied that philosophy could transcend human experience', and, in seeing 'material things' as dependent on a 'transcendent being', had relied on the mind's 'natural drive towards transcendance' and the cognitive agent's capacity to 'know God implicitly in everything he did'.

Copleston emphasized Aquinas's respect for the ordinary man's certainty about truth, and for the intimacy of the connections between metaphysics and 'common experience'. Like Mansel, however, he also emphasized the negative nature of metaphysical knowledge, and the difficulty which metaphysics encountered in acquiring and retaining theological truth. While professing a 'profounder confidence' in reason than Mansel had professed, he professed the same 'vivid consciousness' of its 'limitations'. As in almost all the thinkers discussed in Part I, his most significant claim was that grace gave the will the power to 'love God' even when the intellect could not know Him.

Copleston's writing is repetitive and at times crude. But it has strength, structure and a strategy, a suggestive sense of the relationship between Thomism and philosophical error and an almost infinite capacity to turn other philosophies to its advantage. Copleston professes as strong a desire to understand as to emasculate philosophers who differ from him, and in many parts of his writing has been successful. We may leave him certain, notwithstanding, that a Gladstonian openness conceals a more deliberately calculated assault on the enemies of Christianity than any narrow polemicism could have conceived of by itself.

Conclusion: Assaults and Accommodations

'It is only in so far as he succeeds, through hermeneutics, in transmuting his materials into spiritual messages that the historian of religion will fulfil his role in contemporary culture.' Mircea Eliade *The Quest* 1969 p. 36.

'The question concerning the essence of truth touches a profound crisis not only of theology but also of the Christian churches and Christian faith generally in the present age. Since the Enlightenment, the question of the truth of their faith has been put to Christians with constantly increasing poignancy ... The question ... is not about ... a particular truth of one kind or another but with truth itself ... with whether Christianity can still disclose to us today the unity of the reality in which we live, as it once did in the ancient world.' Wolfhart Pannenberg *What is Truth* (1962) in *Basic Questions in Theology* 1971 edn vol. ii p. 1.

'And after all what is a lie? 'Tis but
   The truth in masquerade, and I defy
Historians, heroes, lawyers, priests to put
   A fact without some leaven of a lie.
The very shadow of true truth would shut
   Up annals, revelations, poesy,
And prophecy, except it should be dated
Some years before the incidents related.' Byron, *Don Juan*, Canto XI 1823.

The discussion in which we are engaged began with the destruction of the confessional state and the ancien régime and has surveyed the most coherent attempts to provide arguments in favour of a successor-régime. It has been concerned with arguments rather than with actions – with the fears and hopes entertained by the thinkers with whom it has dealt, not with the successes and failures which have followed. The purpose has been hermeneutic as well as historical, to descry omens as well as to tell a tale, and it has given due weight to the view that the fantasy which the Tractarians projected upon the world in the 1830s has not only come true but is of high consequence for the future.

For the thinkers discussed in this volume the future has been of first significance; their prognostications have been conducted with piety and passion, and with a deep sense of the duties which intelligentsias owe to themselves, to the nation, to truth and to religion, however imperfectly most of them have understood the vanity of intelligentsia activity and the complicated nature of the connections between principle and hope on the one hand and the fleshly temporalities which disappoint principle and hope on the other.

This has not been a very fleshly history but that is because there is not a very fleshly history to relate. If Salisbury, T. S. Eliot, Knowles and Waugh are included from Volume I, as intellectually they should be, we shall have discussed nearly forty thinkers. Only one was a woman; apart from Wells, none resembled Casanova. Some were celibate, some bachelor, some homosexual, a few were sexually deranged, a number were divorced, in law or in fact, nearly half were childless. About one in four had been ordained (initially, with two exceptions, into the Church of England); about one in four had been converted in one direction or another. A few had experience of family bankruptcy; a few were seriously rich, but among most of these marriage and inheritance were as important as the work of their own brains. None died a violent death, unless the accidental poisoning of Tyndall counts as a violent death; only Russell suffered imprisonment. Greene and Maugham were involved for a time in espionage; Reade and Waugh were war correspondents, and Waugh served with fighting units of the British army. No one else came within sight of appearing as a participant on a battlefield, and no one, so far as can be discovered, killed anyone. Most would have been improved by injections of Byronic flippancy.

All these thinkers were educated up to the age of sixteen; about half were educated at universities. Most published half a million words; some published so many words that the number cannot be counted. Many published fifty books, some more than a hundred. Almost all had something to say, not just about politics and religion but also about everything else. In this, however, they were far from being unique. Books have been crucial instruments of modern thought and the proliferation of books a central feature of modern life, and, since proliferation in the nineteenth and twentieth centuries has been overwhelming, it may be desirable by way of conclusion to re-state the connection between the principles which have been used in selecting authors for consideration and the tensions which it has been the object of this volume to display.

In this volume there has been no systematic discussion of publishers, newspapers, the cinema, wireless and television, of the content of education, legislation, the legal system and public policy, of the influence of financial and commercial institutions, of foreign thinkers, of English thinkers whose writing lives ended before the 1830s, or of agencies of propaganda like the South Place Ethical Society, the Rationalist Press Association, the Left Book Club and Penguin and Virago Books. Some thinkers who have been excluded have been excluded by reason of intellectual inadequacy or want of range, or because they said nothing that others did not say better. Others have been excluded because they were concerned not with assault or counter-attack but with the preservation of entrenched types of Anglicanism, Roman Catholicism and dissent, the establishment of Unitarianism or a creedless Christianity, or the confirmation of a post-Christian normality.

Anglican, main-line Roman Catholic, dissenting and creedless Christianity will be discussed at the beginning of Volume III. This discussion will be followed by discussion both of thinkers whose contribution to post-Christian normality has been explicit and of thinkers whose contribution has been a silent one. In some cases it will be difficult to separate the two or to distinguish thinkers who belong to the first category from thinkers who have been discussed in Parts II and III of the present volume. The distinction is nevertheless a real one, depending to some extent on tone and to some extent on the deliberateness of the undertaking. In discussing the category of silent contributor the critical challenge will be to unearth assumptions which thinkers for one reason or another have been reluctant to expose.

The category of silent contributor is large and distinguished. Gissing's pessimism, Galsworthy's Radicalism, Macdonald's Socialism, Schiller's pragmatism, Bowra's paganism, A. C. Bradley's Mazzinianism and F. H. Bradley's idealism, the gloomy Goetheanism of Gooch and the religious Goetheanism of J. G. Robertson, all belong to it. So does Darwinian Evolution, however little Darwin may have intended this. So do Gosse, Parry, Bosanquet, Keynes, Kidd, Wallas, Hobhouse, Ogden, Richards, Jeans, Eddington, Waddington, Leavis, Maitland, Pollock, Moore, Meredith, S. R. Gardiner, F. W. H. Myers, G. M. Trevelyan and F. York Powell. Austin and Ryle, Annan and Kermode, Ricks and Crick, Orwell and Joyce Cary, Murdoch and Compton-Burnett, also belong to it, as do Wain and Amis, Leach and Goody, Skinner and Dunn, Hindess and Hirst, and Raymond and Bernard Williams. Flew – atheistic, Thatcherite libertarian – has been far from silent, but there has been much silent erosion in Ayer after *Language, Truth and Logic*, in Trevor-Roper's Gibbonian Erasmianism, and in the atheist (or Catholic–atheist) marriage which Scruton is proposing between Eliot, Kant, Hegel, Leavis, Wittgenstein and *The Meaning of Conservatism*. Bloomsbury's erosions will be seen to have been silent once Russell and Lowes Dickinson have been excluded and Strachey's *Eminent Victorians* and Forster's over-rated ramblings forgotten. So will the erosions effected by Laski, Ginsberg, Bronowski, Koestler, Hobsbawm, Pevsner and Postan, whose lapsed-Jewish mentalities would have depressed the Tractarians if they had been able to anticipate them more even than they were depressed by anticipations of an unlapsed Jewish mentality. And there is, as there has been for so long, that continuation of Murray's aims by other means – the mind of Sir Isaiah Berlin which treats Christianity as a facet of Romanticism and by omission obscures the features which divide successor-religions from it.

In making the centre of attention in Volume III the relationship between Anglican, main-line Roman Catholic, dissenting and creedless Christianity on the one hand and a consensual disregard for Christianity on the other, no doubt will be cast on the sincerity of belief on either side, whatever doubt may be cast on the intelligence with which belief has been developed. It will be recognized that Thomas Arnold, Maurice, Jowett, Dean Stanley, T. H. Green, Edward Caird and even Mrs Humphrey Ward, to say nothing of less latitudinarian thinkers, intended to be as Christian as the Tractarians, and that the silence embodied in 'The Post-Christian Consensus' has been no less hostile to Christianity because hostilities seem to have ended. The point is, nevertheless, that many of the thinkers who are to be discussed in Volume III displayed a mentality which was very different from the mentalities discussed in this volume, and very much more prone to avoid the difficulties which arise when questions about religion are brought into the open.

In almost all the cases discussed in this volume conflict has involved a call to coherence and a dismissal of those who have refused it. Those who have refused it have been more numerous than those who have responded, and more successful in insinuating themselves into the fabric of public thought. Why this has been so is an interesting problem raising fundamental questions about the relationship between conduct and aspiration and practice and theory, and about the hypocrisies which are necessary in practice, however antipathetic to truth or inconvenient to sincerity.

Truth and sincerity are problematical conceptions requiring an ambivalent tendentiousness towards the ideals that they hold up for admiration and a cynical sense of the inadequacy of coherence as a basis for action. In Volumes IV and V the inadequacy of coherence will be given further consideration, and it may be that further consideration will produce a different conclusion. For the moment we conclude with the thought that in modern England blurred aims and a reluctance to draw lines have been endemic, and that the Dickensian or Tennysonian fog through which the English conduct life has been no less pervasive in religion than anywhere else.

Notes

Where a work is mentioned in these endnotes without the name of its author, it is the work of the subject of the section in which the endnote occurs.

Introduction (pp. xiii–xxvii)
For the review by the Provost of King's of *Religion and Public Doctrine in Modern England* Vol. I see *London Review of Books* vol. 3. no. 6 April 1981; for the author's reply see *London Review of Books* vol. 3 no. 7 May 1981. For W. MacNeile Dixon, see *The Human Situation* 1937 pp. 14–15. For 'Jacobitism of the mind' see *Religion and Public Doctrine in Modern England* 1980 pp. 453–4. For Geoffrey Faber on the Tractarians see *Oxford Apostles* 1936 (Penguin edn) pp. 10–11. For 'the criticism and philosophy of the nineteenth century' (George Eliot's phrase) see above p. 121. For a transposition backwards of some of the ideas sketched in this volume see J. C. D. Clark *English Society 1688–1832* 1985. For a judicious discussion of related matters, see Charles Covell *The Redefinition of Conservatism* 1985 and Peter Fuller *Images of God* 1985.

pp. 6–8 (Rose)
J. W. Burgon *The Lives of Twelve Good Men* (5th edn) 1889 vol. i pp. 130, 139–43, 149, 201–3, 207–8, 214–21 and 229. For Rose generally see *The State of the Protestant Religion in Germany* 1825 esp. pp. 38–42 and 45–51; *An Appendix to the State of the Protestant Religion in Germany* 1828; *A Letter to the Lord Bishop of London in reply to Mr Pusey's Work on the Causes of Rationalism in Germany* 1829; *Brief Remarks on the Disposition Towards Christianity Generated by Prevailing Opinions and Pursuits* 1830 esp. pp. 7–13, 21–4, 27–33, 36–43, 77–8 and 82–3; *The Gospel: An Abiding System* 1832 esp. pp. x–xxxi, xxxvii, lii–lxi and 29–37; *Eight Sermons Preached Before the University of Cambridge* 1831 pp. 204–6. For William Palmer's attack on Liberal Anglicanism see *On Tendencies Towards the Subversion of Faith* in *English Review* vol. 10 1848 pp. 399ff.

pp. 8–11 (Froude)
J. Keble, J. H. Newman and J. B. Mozley (ed.) *Remains of the late Reverend Richard Hurrell Froude* 1838 Part I vol. ii esp. pp. 44–57, 82–93, 172–83, 244, 250–5, 308, 322–3, 336–40, 363–5, 379–80, 389, 395 and 433–4; *Remains* 1839 Part II vol. i for *Remarks on State Interference in Matters Spiritual* (1833), *Essay on Rationalism* (1834), *Remarks upon the Principles to be Observed in Interpreting Scripture* (1835) and *Remarks on the Grounds of Orthodox Belief* (1836) esp. pp. 2–15, 27–8, 38–40, 72–3, 187–95, 229–30, 272–3, 344–51 and 358–75. For Froude on Becket see *Remains* 1839 Part II vol. ii.

pp. 11–13 (Ward)
The Ideal of a Christian Church Considered in Comparison with Existing Practice 1844 esp. pp. 31–2, 34–5, 42–3, 50 and 587. Among Ward's articles in *The British Critic and Quarterly Theological Review* see esp. *Mill's Logic* (October 1843) pp. 352–4, 364, 404–8, 412 and 417, *Athanasius against the Arians* (October 1842) pp. 395–6, 415, 417, 418 and 420, *Church Authority* (January 1843) pp. 209–11, *Arnold's Sermons* (October 1841) pp. 302, 345 and 355, *Goode's Divine Rule of Faith and Practice* (July 1842) pp. 36, 50 and 76 and *Whately's Essays* (April 1842) pp. 255–9 and 278–9.

pp. 14–26 (Newman)
For Newman's opinions in the early 1830s see I. Ker and T. Gornall *The Letters and Diaries of John Henry Newman* 1979 vol. ii pp. 15–16, 90–1, 122–33, 160, 185, 267–71, 277–8, 281–3, 299, 309 and 316–19, 1979 vol. iii pp. 14–45, 70, 119, 127ff, 193–8, 223–5, 231–5, 246ff, 258–65, 275–81 and 287–300, 1980 vol. iv pp. 63–5, 76–7, 87–9, 208–11 and 339–43. For Newman up to 1842 see *Fifteen Sermons Preached Before the University of Oxford 1826–43* (1872 edn) pp. 7, 38–43, 210–13, 231–3, 239 and 250; *The Arians of the Fourth Century* 1833 pp. 4–5, 22, 25, 37–8, 97, 110–46, 218–53, 262–3, 286–8, 292–327, 349–50, 355 and 358–97; *Lectures on the Prophetical Office of the Church* 1837 pp. 5, 11–12, 81, 101–5, 121, 156, 225 and 267; *A Letter to the Rev. Godfrey Faussett* 1838 pp. 28–9 and 98; *Lectures on Justification* 1838 esp. pp. 95–7, 103–4, 109–13, 134–42, 160, 179, 196–207, 260–3, 270–6, 364–73 and 384–5; *Selina, Countess of Huntingdon* (1840) pp. 263–6, 269–73, 280–1 and 294–5, *Private Judgement* (1841) pp. 108–22, *Palmer's Treatise on the Church of Christ* (1838) pp. 357–9, *Todd's Discourses on the Prophecies relating to Anti-Christ* (1840) pp. 437–8, *The Life of Augustus Herman Franké* (1837) esp. pp. 94–113, *State of Religious Parties* (1839) pp. 409–10, 418–19 and 423–5, *The Catholicity of the English Church* (1840) pp. 63–87, *Affairs of Rome* (1837) *passim* and esp. pp. 270 and 274–8 and *Wiseman* (1836) pp. 374–9 and 393, all in *The British Critic and Quarterly Theological Review*. See also *The Brothers Controversy* (1836), *Exeter Hall* (1838), *Burton's History of the Christian Church* (1836), *Jacobson's Apostolic Fathers* (1839), *Dr Hampden and the University of Oxford* (1836), *Geraldine: A Tale of Conscience* (1838), *The Works of the Late J. W. Davison* (1842), *Le Bas' Life of Archbishop Laud* (1836) and *Milman's History of Christianity* (1841), all also in *The British Critic and Quarterly Theological Review*. *Tracts for the Times* 1833–41 esp. Tract 3 (1833) pp. 1–3, Tract 73 (1836) pp. 2–9 and 18–22, Tract 85 (1838), pp. 9–14, 19–23, 25, 30–3 and 73–99, Tract 83 (1838) pp. 1–20 and 33–52, Tract 41 (1834) pp. 7–12, Tract 78 (1837) and Tract 90 (1840), *passim*. For *Poetry With Reference to Aristotle's Poetics* and *The Tamworth Reading-Room Addressed to the Editor of the Times by Catholicus* February 1841 see C. F. Harrold (ed.) J. H. Newman *Essays and Sketches* 1948 vol. i pp. 70–3, vol. ii pp. 174–88, 191 and 196. See also L. Allen (ed.) *J. H. Newman and the Abbé Jager* 1975 esp. pp. 34–51, 75–105 and 118–44. Brougham's *Inaugural Discourse on Being Installed Lord Rector of the University of Glasgow* is in *Works of Henry, Lord Brougham* 1872 vol. vii pp. 117–41.

pp. 29–51 (Ruskin)

For Ruskin's early opinions see *A Reply to Blackwoods' Criticism of Turner* 1836 in E. T. Cook and A. Wedderburn *The Works of John Ruskin* 1903–11 vol. iii pp. 635–40; *Essay on Literature* 1836 in Cook and Wedderburn vo. i pp. 357–75; *The Poetry of Architecture* 1837 in Cook and Wedderburn vol. i pp. 5–264; *Essay on the Relative Dignity of the Studies of Painting and Music* 1838 in Cook and Wedderburn vol. i pp. 267 and 285; see also *Letters to a College Friend 1840–1845* in Cook and Wedderburn vol. i esp. pp. 397–8, 440–1, 465, 480–6 and 493. For Ruskin on Lord Lindsay see *A Review of Lord Lindsay's Sketches of the History of Christian Art* 1847 in Cook and Wedderburn vol. xii pp. 169–248. For Ruskin's opinions from 1843 onwards see *Modern Painters* 1843 vol. i (Cook and Wedderburn vol. iii) pp. 81–8, 92, 109, 133–7, 142–5, 254 and 629–38, 1846 vol. ii (Cook and Wedderburn vol. iv) pp. 16–17, 27–31, 35–8, 46–50, 53–5, 59–61, 76–141, 146–7, 151, 176–7, 209–11, 217–18, 224, 236, 239, 248, 250–1, 287–91, and 'An Additional Chapter being Notes on a Painter's Profession as ending Irreligiously' pp. 384–89, 1856 vol. iii (Cook and Wedderburn vol. v) pp. 50–9, 145–9, 153–4, 162, 193, 224–5, 232, 255–63, 285–7, 297–30 and 305–13, 1860 vol. v (Cook and Wedderburn vol. vii) pp. 5, 202–3 and 349–53. See also *Modern Painters* (2nd edn) 1844 vol. i pp. 7–52 and (3rd edn) 1846 vol. i pp. 52–3 in Cook and Wedderburn vol. iii. *The Stones of Venice* 1851 vol. i pp. 1, 4–10, 13–17, 24–5, 30–1 and 120, 1853 vol. ii pp. 19, 154, 167–70, 180–1, 191, 198, 206 and 268, 1853 vol. iii pp. 10–12, 14–15, 51–3, 59–61, 63–6, 104–5, 107–11, 132–4, 166, 174–5 and 181–2. *Notes on the Construction of Sheepfolds* 1851 in Cook and Wedderburn vol. xii pp. 528–58. *The Seven Lamps of Architecture* 1849 pp. vii, 7–9, 13, 17ff, 153, 182–9, 193–7 and 200–2. *Lectures on Architecture and Painting* (Edinburgh 1853) in Cook and Wedderburn vol. xii pp. 18–22, 55, 64–5 and 147. *Giotto and His work in Padua* 1854 in Cook and Wedderburn vol. xxiv esp. pp. 17–45. *Pre-Raphaelitism* 1851 in Cook and Wedderburn vol. xii pp. 342 and 358. *Lectures on Politics* 1852 in Cook and Wedderburn vol. xii pp. 595–9. For Ruskin's poetry see *Poems* 1850 in Cook and Wedderburn vol. ii. See also D. Leon *Ruskin* 1949 pp. 156–61, 288–95, 308–11 and 562–9; Ruskin to his father, 21 June and 10 July 1845 in H. I. Shapiro *Ruskin in Italy* 1972 pp. 123 and 143–4; Ruskin to his father 5 October 1851, 4 February 1852, 4 January 1852, 25 January 1852 and 9–19 April 1852 in J. L. Bradley *Ruskin's Letters from Venice 1851–2* 1955 pp. 30–2, 123–4, 148–53, 162–3 and 243–54; Ruskin to Rev. G. Osborne 10 March 1844 in Cook and Wedderburn vol. iii p. 665; Ruskin to Dr J. Brown 27 June 1846, to W. J. Stilman c.1851 and to Henry Acland 24 May 1851 all in Cook and Wedderburn vol. xxxvi pp. 60–2, 114–15, and 123–5; Ruskin to Rev. H. G. Liddell 12 and 15 October 1844 in Cook and Wedderburn vol. iii pp. 667–74.

pp. 53–6 (Keble)

For Keble generally see *Sacred Poetry* (1825) and *Copleston's Praelectiones* (1814) both in *Occasional Papers and Reviews* 1877 pp. 49–50, 81, 91–4, 98ff and 152–5; *Favour Shown to Implicit Faith* (1822), *Implicit Faith Recognised by Reason* (1823), *Implicit Faith Reconciled with Free Enquiry* (1822 or 1823), *Danger of Sympathising with Rebellion* (1831) and *National Apostasy* (1833), all in *Sermons Academical and Occasional* 1848 esp. pp. 4–7, 24, 107–9, 135 and 146; *Oxford Lectures on Poetry* 1912 (a translation of *A Johanni Kebli Praelectiones Poeticae Oxonii Habitae* 1844) pp. 13–14, 15–18, 25–30, 33–7, 465–6, 471–3 and 477–84; Tract 89 *On the Mysticism Attributed to the Fathers of the Early Church* (1840) 1868 edn pp. 1–4, 10, 39–42, 107–48, 152, 166–83 and 189–90. For Keble as a preacher, in addition to *Sermons Academical and Occasional* 1848, see esp. the eleven volumes of *Sermons for the Christian Year* 1875–1880.

pp. 57–64 (Pusey)
For Pusey's opinions before 1845 see *An Historical Enquiry into the Probable Causes of the Rationalist Character Lately Predominant in the Theology of Germany* Parts I and II (including *Explanation of the Views Misconceived by Mr Rose)* 1828–30 vol. i *pp. 3, 8–10, 15, 25–31, 41, 49–50, 52, 102–3, 108, 111, 115–23, 151, 156, 162, 168–9 and 171–5,* vol. ii *pp. 412–16; Remarks on the Prospective and Past Benefits of Cathedral Institutions* 1833, pp. 12, 89 and 96; *Letter to Richard Lord Bishop of Oxford* 1839 pp. 12–13, 182, 184 and 212; *A Letter to His Grace the Archbishop of Canterbury* 1842 pp. 6–9, 16–19, 31–4, 50–9, 64–5, 70–4, 93, 99 and 103–4; *Patience and Confidence … a Sermon preached on the Fifth of November 1837* 1837 pp. v–vi and *Appendix* 1838 pp. 34–42; *The Articles treated of in Tract 90* 1841 pp. 10, 37, 141 and 152; *The Holy Eucharist, a Comfort to the Penitent* 1843; preface to F. Swain *The Foundations of the Spiritual Life* 1844; *Churches in London* 1837 pp. 2–4; *Dr Hampden's Theological Statements and the Thirty-Nine Articles Compared By A Resident Member of Convocation* 1836 pp. vi–viii and xxii; *Dr Hampden's Past and Present Statements Compared* 1836 pp. 3–4; *A Sermon at St Paul's Church Bristol* 1841 pp. 5, 6–10 and 14; *The Church the Converter of the Heathen* 1838 p. 30. For Pusey after 1845 see *Collegiate and Professorial Lectures and Discipline* 1854 pp. 6–8, 43 and 50ff; *An Eirenicon in a Letter to the Author of the Christian Year* 1865 vol. i pp. 5–12, 15–17, 53, 58–9, 98, 121–81 and 279–85, 1870 vol. iii pp.3–7, 30ff, 286ff and 338–43; *Sermons Preached Before the University of Oxford 1859–72* 1872 esp. p. 29; *A Letter on the Essays and Reviews reprinted from The Guardian* 1861 pp. 2–4; *The Councils of the Church* 1857 p. 3 *Daniel the Prophet* 1864 pp. iv–vi, xi–xii, xiv–xxxii and 565–8; *The Royal Supremacy* 1850 pp. 3, 9–11, 14–15, 194–5 and 206–12. See also *A Letter to The Bishop of London* 1851; *Renewed Explanation in Consequence of the Rev. W. Dodsworth's Comments on Dr Pusey's Letter to the Bishop of London* 1851; *The Proposed Ecclesiastical Legislation,* 1874; *Habitual Confession* 1878; *A Letter to The Rev. W. V. Richards* 1850; *Postscript to the Letter to Rev. W. V. Richards* 1850; *Unlaw in Judgements of the Judicial Committee of the Privy Council* 1881; *Summary of Objections Against the Proposed Theological Statute* 1854; *A Correspondence on the Practice of Confession* 1854; preface to the Abbé Gaume's *Manual for Confessors* 1878; preface to Lawrence Scupoli *The Spiritual Combat* 1846; *Correction of Some Criticisms of the Manual for Confessors* 1879; *On the Clause And the Son in Regard to the Eastern Church and the Bonn Conference* 1876; *Case as to the Legal Force of the Judgment of the Privy Council in re Fendall v. Wilson* 1864; H. P. Liddon, *Life of Edward Bouverie Pusey* 1893 vol. i pp. 173–4, 214–19, 304ff and 359–60, 1897 vol. iv pp. 199–200.

pp. 65–70 (Liddon)
The Divinity of Our Lord and Saviour Jesus Christ (Bampton Lectures for 1866)
1867 esp. pp. viii, 6–9, 17–20, 22–7, 54–5, 62, 182–3, 190–7, 203–5, 220–30,
242–3, 660–3, 680, 708, 715, 733 and 740–6. *Some Elements of Religion* 1872
(1881 edn) pp. xxii, 7, 9, 15, 17–19, 21, 27, 37, 42–3, 49–50, 66–7, 80–1, 84,
122–3, 135, 150–3, 157–8, 167 and 171–4. See also *Life of W. K. Hamilton,
Bishop of Salisbury* 1869; *A Funeral Sermon on the Death of the Very Rev.
Dr Mansel August 6 1871* 1871; *Some Words for God Being Sermons Preached
Before the University of Oxford Chiefly During the Years 1863–5* 1865; and
J. O. Johnston, *Life and Letters of Henry Parry Liddon* 1904 pp. 98–9.

pp. 71–7 (Mansel)
For Mansel as a poet see *The Demon of the Winds* 1838. For his philosophical
opinions generally see *Psychology The Test of Moral and Metaphysical Philosophy* (1855), *The Philosophy of Kant* (1856), *Modern German Philosophy*
(1859), *Free Thinking, Its History and Tendencies* (1864) and *Philosophy and
Theology* (1866) all in H. W. Chandler (ed.) *Letters, Lectures and Reviews* 1873
pp. 140–7, 171, 192–201, 205–11, 293ff, 334–6 and 341–51; *Metaphysics* 1860
(originally in *Encyclopaedia Britannica*) pp. 283–8 and 320–98. Earl of Carnar-
von introd. to J. B. Lightfoot (ed.) *The Gnostic Heresies of the First and Second
Centuries by H. L. Mansel* 1875 pp. vi and xiii. For Mansel's account of religion see *The Limits of Religious Thought Examined in Eight Lectures* (Bampton
Lectures of 1858) 1858 (4th edn) esp. pp. 22, 60, 112–13, 127–8, 130, 134–6,
151–2, 161–2 and also Notes 4, 22, 23 and 30. For Mansel's defence of the
Lectures see esp. his preface to the 4th edn, *An Examination of Rev. F. D.
Maurice's Strictures on the Bampton Lectures of 1858* 1859 pp. 8–10 and *A
Letter to Professor Goldwin Smith Concerning the Postscript to His Lectures on
the Study of History* 1861 along with *A Second Letter to Professor Goldwin
Smith* 1862 pp. 52 and 66–7. See also *The Philosophy of the Conditioned* in
Contemporary Review 1866 p. 46; Mansel's letter in *Contemporary Review* 1867
pp. 18–31; and *Prolegomena Logica* 1851.

pp. 78–85 (Gladstone)
D. C. Lathbury, *Correspondence on Church and Religion of W. E. Gladstone*
1910 vol. i pp. 2–5, 77–8, 82, 88–90, 95–7, 114–17, 222–8, 348 and 350–9,
vol. ii pp. 3, 82–4, 90, 98–9, 148. *Catholic Interests in the Nineteenth Century* in
Quarterly Review December 1852 pp. 139, 142, 146 and 149–56. For Gladstone
on marriage see *The Bill for Divorce* (1857) in *Gleanings of Past Years* 1879
vol. vi pp. 102–06 and *The Question of Divorce* (1889) in Lathbury 1910 vol. ii
pp. 358–63. For Gladstone on papal infallibility see *The Vatican Decrees in
their Bearing on Civil Allegiance* (1874), *The Speeches of Pius IX* and
Vaticanism An Answer to Reproofs in *Rome and the Newest Fashion in Religion*
1875. For Gladstone's Anglicanism see *The State in Its Relations with the
Church* 1838 esp. chs. v and vi; *Church Principles* 1840 pp. 40, 42–5, 52–3, 71–8
and esp. ch. 2; *Financial Statement of 1860* in *Financial Statements of 1853,
1860 and 1863* 1863. On *'Ecce Homo'* 1868 pp. 4, 12, and 34–6; *Studies in
Homer and the Homeric Age* 1858 vol. i pp. 5–14, vol. ii pp. 3–5, 8 and 26.
Rectoral Address to the Students of Glasgow 1879 pp. 4–33. *Inaugural Address*

Delivered Before the University of Edinburgh 1860 pp. 6–10, 13–15, 18 and 21. Gladstone to Stubbs 27 December 1875 in W. H. Hutton (ed.) *Letters of William Stubbs* 1904 p. 148. *The Impregnable Rock of Holy Scripture* 1890 pp. 215 and 221–8. *Studies Subsidiary to the Works of Bishop Butler* 1896 pp. 8–12, 31–2, 78–80, 84–5, 100, 108, 116–32, 138, 334–5 and 340–2. For Gladstone generally see *Farini's State Romano* (1852) vol. iv pp. 152–3, *Tennyson* (1859) vol. ii pp. 176–7, *Wedgwood* (1863) vol. ii p. 187, *Giacomo Leopardi* (1850) vol. ii p. 120, *The Sixteenth Century and the Nineteenth* (1878) vol. iii pp. 240–5 and *Is the Church of England Worth Preserving?* (1875) vol. vi p. 175, all in *Gleanings of Past Years* 1879. See also *The Present Aspect of the Church* (1843) vol. v, *Ward's Ideal of the Christian Church* (1844) vol. v, *Blanco White* (1845) vol. ii, and *A Chapter of Autobiography* (1868) vol. vii, all in *Gleanings of Past Years* 1879. *Robert Elsmere: The Battle of Belief* (1888) vol. viii p. 98, and *True and False Conceptions of the Atonement* (1894) vol. viii p. 312, both in *Later Gleanings* 1897. See also *Dawn of Creation and Worship* (1885), *Proem to Genesis* (1885) and *Professor Huxley and the Swine Miracle* (1891) all in *Later Gleanings* 1897 vol. viii.

pp. 87–93 (Newman)

Lectures on the History of the Turks in its Relation to Christianity 1854 pp. 197–211, 233–4, 243, 258–9 and 280. For Newman on literature, see esp. *Catholic Literature in the English Tongue, Christianity and Letters* and *Literature* in *Lectures and Essays on University Subjects* 1859 pp. 1–186. For Newman on Science, see *Christianity and Physical Science* (1855), *Christianity and Scientific Investigation* (1855) and *Christianity and Medical Science* (1858) in *Lectures and Essays on University Subjects* 1859. C. S. Dessain, *Collected Sermons of Cardinal Newman* 1957 pp. 122–3 and 133. For Discourse V of *Discourses on the Scope and Nature of University Education* 1852 see C. F. Harrold Appendix to J. H. Newman *The Idea of a University* 1947 pp. 389ff. See also Discourse IX 1852 pp. 289–295, 298–312, 317–324 and 327–331; *The Office and Work of Universities* 1856 esp. pp. 3–25; and *Lectures and Essays on University Subjects* 1859 pp. 1–5, 37–39, 41–6, 63ff, 69–72, 82ff, 224–8, 238–41 and 245–8. *An Essay in Aid of A Grammar of Assent* 1870 (edn 1924) pp. 104–8, 118–23, 126, 138, 140–4, 341, 347, 350–2, 354–6, 359–61, 364–77, 385–90, 392, 396–400, 403–5, 413–17, 423, 444–5, 456 and 483. *Apologia pro Vita Sua* 1864 (Everyman edn n.d.) esp. pp. 216, 219–22 and 225–6.

pp. 93–5 (Ward)

For Ward's confutation of Mill see esp. *Essays on the Philosophy of Theism* 2 vols. 1884. For Ward's systematic theology see *Nature and Grace* Book 1 1860. For Ward on Pusey see *Historical Argument for the Church's Claims* (1866) and *Projects of Corporate Reunion* (1866) reprinted in *Essays on the Church's Doctrinal Authority, mostly reprinted from the Dublin Review* 1880 pp. 109–226. For Ultramontanism generally see *On the Theological Errors Below Heresy* (July 1864), *Rome and the Munich Conference* (July 1865), *The Pope's Declaration on His Civil Princedom* (July 1864), *The Church Infallible in Her Magisterium* (July 1865), *Doctrinal Decrees of a Pontifical Congregation* (October 1865), *Infallibility Claimed for the Encyclical Mirari Vos* (January 1865) and *Infallibil-*

ity Claimed for the Recent Encyclical and Syllabus (April 1865), all in *Authority of Doctrinal Decisions* 1866 pp. vii, xii–xiii, xvi–xxiii, 13–15, 19–20, 22–6, 30, 35–42, 48–9, 66–7, 70–5, 80–3, 97–8, 136–7 and 168. *Authority of the Scholastic Philosophy* (July 1869) and *Liberalism Religious and Ecclesiastical* (January 1872) in *Essays on the Church's Doctrinal Authority* 1880 pp. 82, 88–98, 517–20, 523–5 and 541–2. *The Relation of Intellectual Power to Man's True Perfection* 1862 pp. 4, 6, 10–11, 26–8, 54ff and 59, and *The Relation of Intellectual Power to Man's True Perfection Further Considered* 1862 pp. 1–3, 11–14, 18, 24, 28–30, 39–40 and 45–8.

pp. 95–100 (Manning)
For Manning's reflections on his Anglican life, see *Sermons on Ecclesiastical Subjects* 1863, pp. 1–9. For Manning on the Vatican Council of 1870 see *The True Story of the Vatican Council* 1877 esp. pp. 170–206 and *The Independence of the Holy See* 1877 pp. 78–81. For Manning's opinion generally see *Sermons on Ecclesiastical Subjects* 1863 pp. 14–15, 25–33, 48–51, 56, 62–5, 69–76, 138–45, 199 and 276; *Miscellanies* 1877 vol. i pp. 77, 87–92 and 132, vol. ii pp. 83, 97, 208, 238, 247 and esp. *Caesarism and Ultramontanism* (1873) pp. 129–59, *Ultramontanism and Christianity* (1873/4) pp. 165–99 and *The Dignity or Rights of Labour* (1874) pp. 67–99; *The Four Great Evils of the Day* 1871 pp. 39, 42–4, 47–53, 67–9, 72–82, 86–9, 93–5, 97–9, 101, 113, 122, 125–6 and 133–4; *The Fourfold Sovereignty of God* 1871 pp. 21–3, 60–1, 73, 85 and 135–7; *Religio Viatoris* 1887 pp. 1–20 and 29–55; and *England and Christendom* 1867 pp. vii–ix, xv–xxiv, xxx, xxxiii–xxxviii, lxx, lxxviii and lxxxiii, xcv–xcix, 48, 151–2 and 155ff. See also *Christ and Antichrist, A Sermon* 1867 pp. 4, 6–8 and 14, *The Workings of the Holy Spirit in the Church of England* (1864) pp. 81–136, *The Convocation and The Crown in Council* (1864) pp. 35–79, *The Crown in Council on the Essays and Reviews* (1864) pp. 3–32, all in *England and Christendom*. See also *Rome and the Revolution* 1867; *The Vatican Decrees in Their Bearing on Civil Allegiance* 1875; *The Eternal Priesthood* 1883; *The Catholic Church and Modern Society* 1881; and *The Office of the Church in Higher Catholic Education* 1885.

pp. 105–8 (Mill)
For the author's account of Mill's religion see M. Cowling, *Mill and Liberalism* 1963 pp. 77–96.

pp. 109–12 (Buckle)
History of Civilization in England 1857–61 (3rd edn 1903–4) vol. i pp. 8, 17–18, 113–19, 133, 140, 181–6, 194, 204–8, 218–31, 232 and 238.

pp. 112–17 (Lewes)
A Biographical History of Philosophy 1846 vol. iv pp. 233–7 and 245–62. *Comte's Philosophy of the Sciences* 1853 pp. 1–2, 8–13, 18–20, 55, 233–6, 239, 251–7, 288, 327–38 and 342–3. *Problems of Life and Mind* 1874 vol. i pp. v–ix, 1–4, 7–13, 16–19, 27–30, 40–5, 53–7, 63–4 and 85. *The Principles of Success in Literature* 1865 G. Tillotson (ed.) 1969, pp. 1–2, 6–7, 11 and *passim*. For Lewes's doctrine about drama see *The Spanish Drama* 1846 pp. 11–15, 16–19, 21–22 and 109–10; also *On Actors and the Art of Acting* 1875 and William

Archer and Robert W. Lowe (ed.) *John Forster and G. H. Lewes, Dramatic Essays* 1896. For the French Revolution see *The Life of Maximilien Robespierre* 1849 and for Goethe see *The Life and Works of Goethe* 2 vols. 1855.

pp. 117–26 (George Eliot)

Gordon S. Haight *George Eliot. A Biography* 1968 pp. 19–39. For George Eliot's friendship with the Hennells and for the comparison she drew with W. R. Greg see J. Wiesenfarth *George Eliot. A Writer's Notebook 1854–1879* 1981, pp. 229–37 and Haight 1968 pp. 83, 89, 93 and 96. For George Eliot's opinions in the 1850s see T. Pinney *Essays of George Eliot* 1963 pp. 18–20, 28–9, 30, 35–6, 51, 56, 80–4, 103–4, 135, 144–7, 154–6, 162, 174, 179, 183–91, 200ff, 257–8, 337, 341, 345, 367, 374–5 and 380. The quotation in the *Westminster Review* January 1851 (Pinney 1963 p. 45) from R. W. Mackay, is in *The Progress of the Intellect* 1850 vol. ii p. 173. *Address to Working Men by Felix Holt* in *Blackwood's Magazine* January 1868 pp. 3–5. See also Gordon S. Haight, *The George Eliot Letters* 1954 vol. ii pp. 213–15, Wiesenfarth 1981 for *Art and Belles Lettres* from *Westminster Review* 1856 p. 273. For George Eliot on women see esp. *Women in France* in *Westminster Review* October 1854 in Pinney 1963 pp. 46ff. For Francis Newman's view of the needs of the poor see esp. *The Soul* 1849 pp. 239–40 and 335.

pp. 126–40 (Spencer)

The Nonconformist 1842 pp. 410–11, 427, 474–5, 506–7, 603, 635, 700, 712–15, 775–9 and 827, 1843 p. 457 and 1856 p. 63. *Social Statics* 1851 pp. 3–5, 12–20, 24–30, 38, 41, 50–1, 65, 70–1, 76–8, 106, 250, 269, 279, 409 and 413–76. *The Man versus the State* 1884 (1969 edn) esp. p. 183. *Representative Government – What Is It Good For?* 1857 (1969 edn) esp. p. 243. *The Principles of Psychology* 1855 pp. 5, 11–12, 15 and 31. *The Study of Sociology* 1873 (1884 edn) pp. 18, 49–53, 58, 117, 159, 313, 345–6, 359–67, 370–83 and ch. xiii *passim*. *Ecclesiastical Institutions being Part VI of The Principles of Sociology* 1885 pp. 671, 689, 704, 722ff, 774, 785, 801–17, 823–5 and 834–43. Letter to *The Athenaeum* 22 November 1862 p. 663. For the *Prospectus* of 1860 see *A System of Philosophy* reprinted in *Autobiography* 1904 vol. ii pp. 479–83. *First Principles* 1862 pp. 8–9, 15, 27, 30–6, 45–6, 54, 66, 100–12, 118–20, 143, 148–9, 162, 176ff, 215ff, 432–6, 466–83, 486, 496, 502–3 and ch. ii *passim*. *First Principles* 2nd edn 1867 pp. xv, 127–57, 278ff and 539ff. Of the four essays which make up the work that is now known as *Herbert Spencer on Education* (F. A. Cavenagh (ed.) 1932) only one was published in the early 1850s. This was *Intellectual Education* which, when it was published in the *North British Review* in May 1854, was called *The Art of Education* for which see Cavenagh, 1932 pp. 61–3, 66–7, 71 and 79–84. For Spencer's views about education in the later 1850s see esp. Cavenagh 1932 pp. 39–53. For Spencer generally see also *Over-Legislation* in *Westminster Review* July 1853 pp. 51ff; *The Universal Postulate* in *Westminster Review* October 1853 pp. 513ff; *Reasons for Dissenting from the Philosophy of M. Comte* (1864) reprinted in *Essays Scientific Political and Speculative* 1874 vol. iii pp. 59ff; *Railway Morals and Railway Policy* (1854) reprinted in *Essays* 1858 pp. 55ff; and *Parliamentary Reform The Dangers and the Safeguards* (1860) reprinted in *Essays* 1863 pp. 228ff.

pp. 142–3 and 148 (Huxley)
Science and Culture 1880 pp. 139–40, 148 and 158. *On the Educational Value of the Natural History Sciences* (1854) p. 45, *A Technical Education* (1877) pp. 406–9 and 412, *A Liberal Education* (1868) pp. 81–9, 93 and 106–7, *Joseph Priestley* (1874) pp. 32–6, *Scientific Education* (1869) p. 133, *Universities Actual and Ideal* (1874) pp. 203–8, *Address on University Education* (1876) pp. 237–9, *Emancipation Black and White* (1865) pp. 66–75 and *The School Boards: What they can do and what they may do* (1870) pp. 374–403, all in *Science and Education* 1893 (1895 edn). *Evolution and Ethics* (1893) pp. 45–50, 78 and 82, *Social Diseases and Worse Remedies* (1891) pp. 188 and 200–27, *Evolution and Ethics: Prolegomena* (1894) pp. 4, 10–11, 20, 23, 31, 33–4 and 43–5, *Preface to Evolution and Ethics* p. ix and *Science and Morals* (1886) pp. 128–145, all in *Evolution and Ethics* 1894. *Scientific and Pseudo-Scientific Realism* (1887), pp. 74–6, *Science and Pseudo-Science* (1887) pp. 110–16, *Agnosticism and Christianity* (1889) pp. 311–18 and 344–7, *The Keepers of the Herd of Swine* (1890) pp. 367–8, *Agnosticism: A Rejoinder* (1889) pp. 265–8, 271–86 and 306, *An Episcopal Trilogy* (1887) pp. 128–42, *Agnosticism* (1889) pp. 252–61 and *Preface* and *Prologue* pp. vi–xi, 31 and 58, all in *Science and Christian Tradition* 1894 (1895 edn). *Administrative Nihilism* (1871) pp. 254–62, 270–5 and 284, *Natural Rights and Political Rights* (1890) pp. 340–50, *On the Natural Inequality of Man* (1890) pp. 308–12, 321 and 334, *On the Advisableness of Improving Natural Knowledge; A Lay Sermon* (1866) pp. 25–38, *Government: Anarchy or Regimentation* (1890) pp. 386–8, *On Descartes' 'Discourse touching the method of using one's reason rightly and of seeking scientific truth'* (1870) pp. 166–70 and 179–83, all in *Method and Results* 1893 (1894 edn). *The Origin of Species* (1860) pp. 52–7 in *Darwiniana* 1893 (1894 edn). *A Lobster or the Study of Zoology* (1861) pp. 218–19, 222–3 and 226–7 in *Discourses Biological and Geological* 1894. *The Evolution of Theology* (1886) pp. 365 and 371, *Preface* pp. x–xi and *The Evolution of Theology: An Anthropological Study* (1886) p. 371, all in *Science and Hebrew Tradition* 1893 (1895 edn). *Hume with Helps to the Study of Berkeley* 1894 p. xii and esp. pp. 58–71. See also *The Interpreters of Genesis and the Interpreters of Nature* (1885), *Mr Gladstone and Genesis* (1886) and *The Lights of the Church and the Light of Science* (1890), all in *Science and Hebrew Tradition* 1893 (1895 edn); and *The Value of Witness to the Miraculous* (1889) and *Illustrations of Mr Gladstone's Controversial Methods* (1891), both in *Science and Christian Tradition* 1894 (1895 edn).

pp. 143–8 (Tyndall)
For Tyndall's politics see *Professor Tyndall on Party Politics* 1885 pp. 2 and 4–6, and *Mr Gladstone on Home Rule* 1887 pp. 1, 6, 8 and 10–11. *Address Delivered before the British Association Assembled at Belfast* 1874 pp. xiii, 2–3, 27–31, 41, 52–5 and 62–5 (2nd edn) 1874 pp. vi–vii, and *Preface to the Seventh Thousand* 1874 esp. pp. xxii–xxiv. *Fragments of Science for Unscientific People* 1871 vol. i Preface, pp. 3–5, 17, 26–9, 41ff, 282, 295–302, 427ff and 436, 1874 vol. ii (1899 edn) pp. 96–9, 139, 239 and 248–9. *Mountaineering in 1861* 1862 reprinted in *Fragments of Science* 1871 vol. i pp. 34, 37 and 40; *Natural Philosophy in Easy Lessons* 1869 pp. 1–9. *Essays on the Use and Limits of the Imagination in Science* 1870 pp. 14–15, 17, 43, 51 and 66ff. *The Glaciers of the Alps*

1860 esp. preface. For Goethe and Carlyle see *Goethe's Farbenlehre* (1880) in *New Fragments* 1892 pp. 47ff and *Personal Recollections of Thomas Carlyle* (1890) in *New Fragments* 1892 pp. 347ff. See also *New Fragments* 1892 p. 237 and *Faraday As A Discoverer* 1869 pp. 118–47.

pp. 163–7 (Stephen)
Essays on Free Thinking and Plain Speaking 1873 pp. 6–21, 31–4, 44, 49–59, 117–18, 122–5, 135–41, 149, 321, 326–9, 340–8 and ch. 2 *passim*. *History of English Thought in the Eighteenth Century* 1876 vol. i pp. 2–8, 72, 79, 83–105, 149, 151, 158ff, 183–4, 270–1, 420–1, 426–7 and 452–64, vol. ii p. 2. *An Agnostic's Apology* 1893 pp. 351–2 and 377. *The Science of Ethics* 1882 pp. vii, 5, 31, 96, 101, 127–8, 132–4, 137, 144–8, 249, 351, 371–80, 444, 461 and ch. iv *passim*.

pp. 167–8 and 171–6 (Morley)
Modern Characteristicks 1865 pp. 135ff. *England and the Annexation of Mysore* (September 1866) p. 257, *Young England and the Political Future* (April 1867) p. 491, *The Liberal Programme* (September 1867) p. 359, *The Chamber of Mediocrity* (December 1868) *passim*, all in *Fortnightly Review*. *The Struggle for National Education* 1873 esp. pp. 2 and 47–113. *France in the Seventeenth Century* in *Fortnightly Review* January 1867 pp. 2 and 9–12. *Edmund Burke* 1867 pp. 227–9, 235, 240–3, 249 and 301. *Rousseau* 1873 vol. i pp. 3–5, 268ff and 313, and vol. ii pp. 198, 206–8, 217, 230–3 and 246–7. *Diderot and the Encyclopaedists* 1878 (1903 edn) vol. i esp. pp. 3–9, 55–6, 72ff, 172ff, 218 and 232. *The Life of Richard Cobden* 1879 (1903 edn) esp. p. 948. *George Eliot's Novels* in *Macmillan's Magazine* 1866 p. 272; see also *The Life of George Eliot* (1885) in *Critical Miscellanies* 1886 pp. 93ff. *Voltaire* 1872 (1909 edn) pp. 8, 12, 41, 69, 218, 247 and 277–80. *On Compromise* 1874 (1903 edn) pp. 8, 19, 21, 37, 40, 45, 56, 110, 114–18, 134, 135, 153–63, 197–8, 200 and 261. *Mr Lecky's First Chapter* (1869) pp. 519ff and *Mr Froude on the Science of History* (1867) pp. 226ff both in *Fortnightly Review*. *Condorcet* (1870), pp. 50–1, 77–83 and 109, *Byron* (1870), pp. 254–6 and 276–9, *Some Greek Conceptions of Social Growth* (1871) p. 296, *Carlyle* (1870) pp. 224–39, *Joseph de Maistre* (1868) pp. 115, 185 and 189–93, all in *Critical Miscellanies* 1871. *Macaulay* (1876), pp. 371ff, *Robespierre* (1876) pp. 27ff, *The Death of Mr Mill* (1873), *Mr Mill's Autobiography* (1874) and *Mr Mill on Religion* (1874) pp. 240ff, all in *Critical Miscellanies* 1877. *Auguste Comte* (1876) in *Critical Miscellanies* 1886 pp. 337ff. See also D. A. Hamer, *John Morley* 1968 esp. ch. viii and F. W. Hirst *Early Life and Letters of John Morley* 1927 vol. i pp. 7 and 15–40.

pp. 168–70 (Harrison)
Order and Progress 1875 pp. 382–5. *Septem contra Fidem* in *Westminster Review* October 1860 reprinted in *The Creed of a Layman* 1907 pp. 95ff. See also *The Creed of a Layman* 1907 pp. 33 and 35 and *The Choice of Books* in *Fortnightly Review* April 1879 reprinted and expanded in *The Choice of Books* 1886. For Harrison's addresses in Positivist Churches, see *The Creed of a Layman* 1907 pp. 270–347.

pp. 176–81 (Reade)

For Reade's fiction see *Charlotte and Myra* 1859; *Liberty Hall Oxon* 1860; and *See-Saw* 1865. For the Druids see *The Veil of Isis* 1861. For the Ashanti campaign see *The Story of the Ashanti Campaign* 1874. For Reade's religion see *The Outcast* 1875 (1933 edn) pp. 22, 47–8, 72–3, 96, 110–11, and 118–19 and *The Martyrdom of Man* 1872 (1924 edn) pp. 133–47, 151–9, 172–85, 193–201, 216–19, 242–3, 287, 328–31, 336, 356–9, 422–35 and 441–2.

pp. 187–91 and 204–11 (Murray)

The Herd Instinct and the War 1915 pp. 23–4 and 41; *The Exploitation of Inferior Races in Ancient and Modern Times* in F. W. Hirst, J. L. Hammond and G. Murray (ed.) *Liberalism and the Empire* 1900 p. 118. *The Future of the British Empire in Relation to the League of Nations* 1928 pp. 17 and 26–7; *Problems of Foreign Policy* 1921 esp. pp. 5–6; *The Evil and the Good of the War* (1915), *First Thoughts on the War* (1914) and *How Can War ever be Right?* (1914), all in *Faith, War and Policy* 1917 (1918 edn) pp. 6, 15, and 71–220. *The Ordeal of This Generation* 1929 pp. 15, 21, 24–7, 39, 44–8, 52–6 and 191–7. For the political writings of Murray's old age see esp. *Hellenism* 1941; *Myths and Ethics* (n.d.) in *Humanism and the World's Needs* 1944; *The Anchor of Civilization* (1942) in *From the League to the United Nations* 1948; and *The Need for Liberalism* in H. Samuel and Others *Spires of Liberty* 1948. *National Ideals* (1900) pp. 161–82, *Religio Grammatici* (1918) pp. 12, 15, 24–7 and 30, *Satanism and the World Order* (1919) pp. 202–21, *Poesis and Mimesis* (n.d.) pp. 107–124, *The Soul As It Is* (1918) pp. 148–51, *The Bacchae in Relation to Certain Currents of Thought in the Fifth Century* (1902) pp. 56–87, *Literature as Revelation* (1917) pp. 125–41, all in *Essays and Addresses* 1921. *Liberality and Civilization* 1938 pp. 15–28, 37–46, 60, 65–7, 70 and 87–90. *The Interpretation of Ancient Greek Literature* 1909 pp. 5–19; *The Rise of the Greek Epic* 1907 pp. 8–17, 35–40, 57–9, 82–7, 116–28, 134–5, 153, 173–5, 201 and 234. *Theopompus or the Cynic as Historian* (1928) in *Greek Studies* 1946 pp. 166–70. *A History of Ancient Greek Literature* 1897 pp. 1, 370–1 and 404–5. *The Value of Greece to the Future of the World* in *The Legacy of Greece* 1921 p. 18. *Four Stages of Greek Religion* 1912 (1935 edn) pp. 7–8, 59, 123–4, 153, 165 and *Five Stages of Greek Religion* 1925 (1935 edn) pp. 88 and 177. *Euripides and His Age* 1913 pp. 14, 48, 57–8, 63, 117 and 193. *The Classical Tradition in Poetry* 1927 pp. 78–9 and 260. *Aeschylus the Creator of Tragedy* 1940 pp. 1–3, 7–9, 72–7, 126–8, 160, 171, 179 and 184–7. *Pagan Religion and Philosophy at the Time of Christ* (1929), *What Is Permanent in Positivism* (1939), *The Conception of Another Life* (1914) and *The Stoic Philosophy* (1915), all in *Stoic, christian and Humanist* 1940 pp. 32, 74, 127ff, 156 and 175–9. *The Place of Greek in Education* 1889 p. 5. See also *Aristophanes. A Study* 1933. *Hellenism and the Modern World* (1953) *Prolegomena to the Study of Greek History* (1932), *Prolegomena to the Study of Ancient Philosophy* (1934), *Prolegomena to the Study of Greek Literature* (1933) and *Humane Letters and Civilization* (1937), all in *Greek Studies* 1946. For Murray's life see J. A. K. Thomson, *Gilbert Murray 1866–1957* in *Proceedings of the British Academy* 1957 vol. 43 and Francis West *Gilbert Murray. A Life* 1984.

pp. 191–2 and 196–202 (Frazer)
The Belief in Immortality (Gifford Lectures of 1911–12) 1913 vol. i pp. 1–25.
Creation and Evolution in Primitive Cosmogonies 1935 pp. 121–3. *Totemism*
(1887) pp. 5–21 and 83–7, *The Beginnings of Religion and Totemism among the*
Australian Aborigines (1905) pp. 141–2 and 150–70, *The Origin of Totemism*
(1899) pp. 91–5 and 116–18, all in *Totemism and Exogamy* 1910 vol. i. (See
also *Totemism and Exogamy* 1910 vol. i pp. xiii–xv and 1–3 and vol. iv pp. 4–7
and 166–9.) *William Robertson Smith* (1894) pp. 282–9, *French and English*
Chivalry (1919) pp. 404–5 *My Old Study* (1898), *A Dream of Cambridge* (1916)
pp. 443–6, *Pax Occidentis: A League of the West* (1906) pp. 393ff, *Our Debt to*
France (1 July 1925) pp. 401–3, all in *The Gorgon's Head* 1927. *Condorcet on*
the Progress of the Human Mind (1933) pp. 4–23, *Taboo* (1888) pp. 80–1 and
86–7, *Some Popular Superstitions of the Ancients* (1890) pp. 128–30 and 146,
The Cursing of Venizelos (1917) pp. 205–7 and 211 and *The Scope and Method*
of Mental Anthropology (1921) pp. 231–43, all in *Garnered Sheaves* 1931. *The*
Letters of William Cowper 1912 vol. i p. vi. *The Scope of Social Anthropology*
1908 pp. 4–6, 12–17 and 22. *Psyche's Task* 1909 pp. vii, 1–3 and 80–3. *Lectures*
on the Early History of Kingship 1905 pp. 1–9. *The Golden Bough* 1890 vol. i
pp. 8–32, and *The Golden Bough* 1900 vol. i pp. xv–xxiii and 1–232. *The Magic*
Art and the Evolution of Kings 1911 (1932 edn) vol. i pp. 44–243 and 423–5 and
vol. ii pp. 1–10, 24, 97–8, 116–29 and 266–375; *Taboo and the Perils of the Soul*
1911 (1936 edn) pp. v–viii, 1–7, 29–77, 100–16 and 418–21; *The Dying God*
1911 (1930 edn) pp. 1–5, 134–47, 174–95 and 226–71; *Adonis, Attis, Osiris*
1914 (1936 edn) vol. i pp. i–v, 1–12, 14–55 and 179–305 and vol. ii pp.217–18;
Spirits of the Corn and of the Wild 1912 (1933 edn) vol. i pp. i–ix, 1–34, 82–91,
168–70 and 304–5 and vol. ii pp. 1–3, 36–41, 48–9, 109, 138–9, 156ff, 166–8,
202–5, 261–3 and 298–309; *The Scapegoat* 1913 (1933 edn) pp. v–vi, 1–2,
46–7, 72–3, 221–8 and 411–23; *Balder the Beautiful* 1913 (1930 edn) vol. i
pp. v–xii, 2–7, 95–133 and 329ff and vol. ii pp. 20–44, 90–6, 153 and 277–306.
See also *Questions on the Customs, Beliefs and Language of Savages* 1884–1907;
Passages of the Bible Chosen for their Literary Beauty 1895; and *Plato's Ideal*
Theory 1879 (published 1930).

pp. 193–6 (Tylor)
Researches into the Early History of Mankind 1865 pp. 1–13, 117–18, 136–7,
148–9, 160–3, 272ff, 325ff and 361ff. *Primitive Culture* 1871 vol. i Preface,
pp. 1–62, 100–30, 142–4, 213–17, 247–87, 331–3, 377–88 and esp. chs. ii and
xi. See also preface to the second edition 1903 vol. i pp. vii–viii and vol. ii see
esp. chs. xii–xvi and pp. 401–10. See also *The Religion of Savages* in *Fort-*
nightly Review 1866 and *Anthropology* 1881.

pp. 213–22 (Wells)
Anticipations 1901. p. 8; *New Worlds for Old* 1908 (1914 edn) pp. 17, 23, 56, 58,
59 and 178. *Mankind in the Making* 1903 (2nd edn) pp. 8, 30–3, 92, 108, 125,
127, 159–64, 168, 234–5, 245–6, 256–7, 264, 270, 285–8, 300–11, 341, 356–67
and 388–90. *The Great State* (n.d.) pp. 99–105, 117 and 128, *The Labour*
Unrest (1912) p. 89, *Of the New Reign* (n.d.) p. 32, *The Disease of Parliaments*
(n.d.) p. 254, *About Chesterton and Belloc* (n.d.) pp. 180–1, all in *An English-*

man Looks at the World 1914. *In the Fourth Year* 1918 pp. vi–vii and 1–7. *The World Set Free* 1914 p. 10. For Wells's self-importance see esp. *The Open Conspiracy* 1928; *The Shape of Things to Come* 1933; and *The Anatomy of Frustration* 1936. For his frustration see *The Fate of Homo Sapiens* 1939; *The Rights of Man* 1940; *The Common Sense of War and Peace* 1940; and *Mind at the End of Its Tether* 1945. *A Modern Utopia* 1905 (Nelson Popular Editions of Notable Books n.d.) pp. 33, 47–9, 70–2 and esp. ch. ix. *The Discovery of the Future* 1902 (1913 edn) pp. 12–16 and 22–3. *First and Last Things* 1908 pp. 32–3, 36–43, 50, 64–86, 90–1, 95, 113–14 and 151 and *First and Last Things* 1917 pp. 150–61 and 169–71. *The New Machiavelli* 1911 (4th edn n.d.) esp. pp. 290–422. *War and the Future* pp. 117, 177 and 239, *Europe and Socialism* pp. 116, 130 and 275–95, *What the War Is Doing for Women* pp. 162–3, *How Far Will Europe Go Toward Socialism?* pp. 90 and 112, *The Outlook for the Germans* pp. 265 and 274, *Forecasting the Future* p. 11, *Braintree, Bocking and the Future of the World* p. 90 and *The New Education* pp. 149–53 and 159, all in *What is Coming* 1916. *The Schooling of the World* pp. 139–165, *College, Newspaper and Book* pp. 166–92 and *Envoy,* pp. 193–8, all in *The Salvaging of Civilization* 1921. *The Soul of a Bishop* 1917 esp. p. 285 and *God the Invisible King* 1917 (Odhams Press edn n.d.) pp. 283–98, 305–10 and 375. *The Religious Revival* pp. 209–24 and *The Yielding Pacifist and the Conscientious Objector* pp. 193–208, both in *War and the Future* 1916. See also *The Island of Dr Moreau* 1896; *What Are We to Do with Our Lives?* 1931; *The Work Wealth and Happiness of Mankind* 1932; and P. Parrinder and R. M. Philmns (ed.) *H. G. Wells's Literary Criticism* 1980.

pp. 221–36 (Shaw)
Bureaucracy and Jobbery (1890) pp. 111 and 120 and *Socialism and Human Nature* (1890) pp. 91–7 and 101–2, both in L. Crompton (ed.) *Bernard Shaw: The Road to Equality … 1884–1918* 1971. *The Transition to Social Democracy* (1888) reprinted in *Fabian Essays* 1889 in *The Works of Bernard Shaw* 1932 vol. xxx pp. 34–6, 39–40 and 50–4. *Major Barbara* (1905) pp. 117–18 and 126–8, *Back to Methuselah* (1921) pp. 480–99 and 500–21, *Mrs Warren's Profession* (1894) pp. 219–35, *Getting Married* (1908) pp. 1–2, *Three Plays for Puritans* (1901) pp. 704–21 and *Widowers' Houses* (1893) pp. 669–81, all in *Prefaces by Bernard Shaw* 1934. *Our Lost Honesty* 1884 pp. 1, 4–6 and 13; *Freedom and the State* 1888 pp. 37–53. *Socialism and Culture* (1918) pp. 296 and 317–19, *The New Politics From Lassalle to the Fabians* (1889) pp. 58–88, *The New Radicalism* (1887) p. 23 and *Capital and Wages* (1891) pp. 123 and 131–43, all in Crompton 1971. Andrew Boyle, *The Climate of Treason* 1980 p. 411. *The Perfect Wagnerite* 1898 (1913 edn) pp. 1–4, 13, 19, 31–3, 64–8, 76, 101–3 and 132–5 (see also pp. 99–108 for an insertion written in 1907). *The Sanity of Art* 1895 (1908 edn) pp. 17, 46–7 and 68–70. *The Economic Basis of Socialism* (1889) in *Fabian Essays* 1889 in *The Works of Bernard Shaw* 1932 vol. xxx pp. 4, 12 and 29–30. *Dramatic Opinions and Essays* vol. i 1907 pp. xxii–xxiii. *Plays Pleasant* 1898 (1931 edn) pp. viii, x and xiv. *Man and Superman* 1903 (1946 edn) pp. xxiii–xxvi, 233 and 264–8. *St Joan* 1924 pp. xl–xlv. *The Intelligent Woman's Guide to Socialism, Capitalism Sovietism and Fascism* 1937 vol. ii pp. 430, 432, 435, 438, 442, 447 and 454. H. M. Geduld

(ed.) *The Rationalisation of Russia* 1932 (1964 edn) pp. 37–8 and 102. *What about the Middle Class* (1912) p. 109 and *Socialism and the Artistic Professions* (1906) pp. 23–31 both in L. J. Hubenka (ed.) *B. Shaw Practical Politics* 1976. *The Quintessence of Ibsenism* 1891 (1926 edn) pp. 12–17, 42–7, 53–8, 81, 87, 120, 135–6, 150, 159, 160–7, 171–2, 202 and 207–9. *Proprietors and Slaves* (1885) pp. 6–11, *Modern Religion* (1919) pp. 110–12 and 118, *Literature and Art* (1908) pp. 41–9, *What Socialism Will Be Like* (1896) pp. 23–9 and *The Ideal of Citizenship* (1909) pp. 74–82 all in D. H. Laurence *Pulpit and Platform: Bernard Shaw* 1962. Preface to *Androcles and the Lion* 1916 (1946 edn) pp. 12–38, 45, 53–6, 68, 82–5 and 100–1 and to *The Doctor's Dilemma* 1906 (1946 edn) pp. 7–56 and 131–4. *A Catechism on My Creed* in W. S. Smith (ed.) *Shaw on Religion* 1967 pp. 128–31. *Ruskin's Politics* 1921 pp. 6–32. See also R. W. Ellis (ed.). *Shaw and Karl Marx: A Symposium 1884–1889* 1930. *Fabianism and the Empire* (1900), *Socialism and Superior Brains* (1894), *The Common Sense of Municipal Trading* (1904), *Socialism for Millionaires* (1896) and *The Impossibilities of Anarchism* (1891), all in *The Works of Bernard Shaw* 1932 vol. xxx.

pp. 236–46 (Ellis)
Whitman, Ibsen and *Tolstoy* in *The New Spirit* 1890 (Modern Library edn) and esp. pp. 106–8, 114, 117–19, 124–7, 146–50, 152–3, 169–74, 181, 189, 191, 195–7 and 214–16. See also *The New Spirit* 1890 pp. 272–292. *The Criminal* 1890 p. 297. *The Task of Social Hygiene* 1912 pp. ix, 7, 24, 32–3 and 43–5. For Ellis as theological reviewer, see *Westminster Review* 1886 vol. 70 pp. 231ff and 1887 vol. 71 pp. 191ff. *Man and Woman* 1894 pp. 11, 13–17, 19–44, 164–74, 185–94, 318–27 and 384–97 and esp. chs. 11–13 and 16. *Little Essays of Love and Virtue* 1922 esp. pp. 24, 36, 44–5, 51–5, 85 and 131–3. *The Dance of Life* 1923 (1926 edn), pp. xiii, 17–32, 75–6, 106–8, 116, 143, 194–211, 225–40, 251–80 and 290–1. *Nietzsche, Casanova, Zola, Huysmans* and *St Francis and Others* in *Affirmations* 1898 (1926 edn) esp. pp. iv, 2, 17, 35, 44, 51, 55, 58–9, 62–5, 70–96, 99, 134–46, 151–5, 205–15, 227–9 and 243. *Sexual Inversion* 1897 pp. v–ix, 10, 141–58 and esp. chs. I and V; *Studies in the Psychology of Sex* vol. i *The Evolution of Modesty* 1899 (1924 edn) esp. pp. 1–84 and 161–283; *Studies in the Psychology of Sex* vol. iii *Analysis of the Sexual Impulse* 1903 (1924 edn) pp. vi–vii, 66ff and 189ff, vol. iv *Sexual Selection in Man* 1904 (1924 edn) pp. 5–6 and 214, vol. v *Erotic Symbolism* 1906 (1923 edn) pp. v–vi and *passim*, vol. vi *Sex in Relation to Society* 1910 (1924 edn) pp. v–vi; *Sex in Relation to Society* 1937 pp. v–vi, 78, 221–2, 283–90, 293–5, 298–305, 321–4 and chs. V, VII and IX–XII. See also *Thomas Hardy* (1883) in *From Marlowe to Shaw* 1950 pp. 230–67 and *Women and Socialism* (1884) and *The Present Position of English Criticism* (1885) in *Views and Reviews* First Series 1932 pp. 1–37; *The Nineteenth Century* (1900), *The Genius of Russia* (1917), *The Genius of Germany* (1925) and *My Credo* (1939), all in *The Genius of Europe* 1939. For Ellis's life see his *My Life* 1940 and P. Grosskurth *Havelock Ellis: A Biography* 1980.

pp. 248–56 (Maugham)
For Maugham on espionage, see esp. *Ashenden* 1928. For homosexuality and Maugham's concealment of it, see T. Morgan, *Somerset Maugham* 1980 *pas-*

sim; *Theatre* 1937 (for Dolly's lesbianism); *Don Fernando* 1935 (for El Greco); and *Ten Novels and their Authors* 1954 (1969 edn) for Melville. *Strictly Personal* 1942 esp. p. 187. *A Writer's Notebook* 1949 (1951 edn) pp. 11, 16–19, 30, 49–56, 61, 123–5, 222–5, 241, 292–3, 294–7. *Great Novelists and their Novels* 1948 reprinted as *Ten Novels and their Authors* 1954 (1969 edn) pp. 12–13. T. Morgan, *Somerset Maugham* 1980 pp. 87–8 and 104. *The Land of the Blessed Virgin* 1905 pp. 263–5, 292 and 353–66. *The Gentleman in the Parlour* 1930 pp. 160–2. *The Saint* in *Points of View* 1958 pp. 58ff, 66ff, 74ff and 90ff. *The Painted Veil* 1925 (1952 edn) esp. p. 238. *Zurbaran* in *The Vagrant Mood* 1952 pp. 83–4. For Maugham's early religious opinions see *The Bishop's Apron* 1906; *The Making of a Saint* 1898; *The Land of the Blessed Virgin* 1905; and *Faith* and *The Punctiliousness of Don Sebastian* both in *Orientations* 1899. *The Hero* 1901 pp. 13–17, 37, 48, 52–3, 62–6, 81, 106–9, 174–5, 189–94, 206–8, 216, 245–8, 295–6, 298, 319 and 336–9. *The Summing-Up* 1938 (1976 edn) pp. 119–23, 155ff, 167–8 and 176–81. *The Razor's Edge* 1944 (1963 edn) esp. pp. 104–7, 151–77, 188–220, 238, 242–86 and 296. *The Narrow Corner* 1932 (1976 edn) pp. 48, 68–71, 76–7, 80–1, 94–101, 116–25, 134–8 and 190–4.

pp. 256–66 (Lawrence)
For Lawrence's opinions up to 1914 see J. T. Boulton (ed.) *The Letters of D. H. Lawrence* 1979 vol. i esp. pp. 24, 62–6, 117–19, 122–3, 187, 195, 229, 339 and 503 and G. J. Zytaruk and J. T. Boulton (ed.) *The Letters of D. H. Lawrence* 1981 vol. ii pp. 46–7, 74, 90, 94, 101–2, 110, 146, 165, 211–23 and 238–41. For Lawrence's opinions from 1914 onwards see Zytaruk and Boulton 1981 vol. ii pp. 254, 265–9, 273, 281–4, 291, 319–21, 343–59, 364–70, 380, 385–6, 392–3, 415, 420–5, 432–3, 449–52, 459, 470–5, 486–90, 497–9, 509–10, 528–9, 546–7, 604–5 and 618–24. For Middleton Murry's Christianity in the early 1920s see esp. *The Evolution of an Intellectual* 1920 and *To the Unknown God* 1924. *The Plumed Serpent* 1926 (1948 edn) pp. 331–2, 365, 368, 379, 415–16 and 450. *Movements in European History* 1921 (1981 edn) pp. 26–7, 97, 125–7, 181, 187, 216–18, 291 and 306. *Sea and Sardinia* 1923 (1979 edn) pp. 13–17, 64, 97–102 and 130–1. *Studies in Classic American Literature* 1923 (1978 edn) pp. 7–61, 70–82 and 89–93. *Apocalypse* 1931 (1980 edn) pp. 3–56, 70–1, 83–9 and 114–26. *Etruscan Places* 1927/8 and 1932 (1956 edn) pp. 4, 12–17, 19–20, 32–3, 48–57 and 68–73. *Mornings in Mexico* 1927 pp. 46–54, 60–8 and 70–80. *Fantasia of the Unconscious* 1922 (1977 edn) pp. 11–16, 17–23 and 25–31. *Psychoanalysis and the Unconscious* 1922 (1977 edn) pp. 202, 207, 210–14, 216, 218–19, 234 and 245. *Twilight in Italy* 1916 (1977 edn) pp. 9–21 and 40–46. H. T. Moore (ed.) *The Collected Letters of D. H. Lawrence* 1962 vols. i and ii pp. 481–543, 562–3, 576–7, 614–21, 639–41, 681, 686–7, 699–709, 722–3, 740, 760–1, 800–1, 828–9, 851–65, 886–99, 912–13, 1030–1, 1042–7, 1096–9, 1110–11, 1164–7. *The Reality of Peace* (1917) pp. 669–93, *On Being Religious* (1924) pp. 724–30, *The Proper Study* (1923) pp. 719–23, *Why The Novel Matters* (n.d.) pp. 533–8, *Christs in the Tirol* (1913) pp. 82–6, *Introduction to Pictures* (n.d.) pp. 765–71, *The Novel and the Feelings* (n.d.) pp. 755–60, *Resurrection* (n.d.) pp. 737–9, *The Real Thing* (1930) pp. 196–203, *Georgian Poetry* (1913) pp. 304–7, *Education of the People* (n.d.) esp. pp. 607–29, *Morality and*

the Novel (1925) pp. 527–32, *Life* (n.d.) pp. 695–8, *Study of Thomas Hardy* (1913–15) esp. pp. 403, 420, 426–7, 445–8 and 514–15, all in E. D. McDonald (ed.) *Phoenix* 1936. *The Risen Lord* (1929) pp. 571–7, *Hymns in a Man's Life* (1928) pp. 597–601, *The Two Principles* (1919) pp. 227–37, *Autobiographical Sketch* (1929) pp. 592–6, *À Propos of Lady Chatterley's Lover* (1930) pp. 487–515, *Pornography and Obscenity* (1929) pp. 178–81, *Reflections on the Death of A Porcupine* (1925) pp. 460–74, *Aristocracy* (1925) pp. 475–84, *Blessed are the Powerful* (1925) pp. 436–43, *The Crown* (1915) pp. 365–415, *Introduction to Memoirs of the Foreign Legion by Maurice Magnus* (1924) pp. 345–61, all in F. W. Roberts and H. T. Moore, *Phoenix II* 1968.

pp. 266–83 (Russell)
Mathematics and the Metaphysicians (1901) pp. 75–9 and 95, *The Place of Science in a Liberal Education* (1913) pp. 59–60, *Mysticism and Logic* (1914) pp. 20, 25–9, 31 and 41–9, *On Scientific Method in Philosophy* (1914), pp. 108–9 and 120, all in *Mysticism and Logic* 1918 and reprinted as *A Free Man's Worship* 1976; see also *The Free Man's Worship* 1903 reprinted as *A Free Man's Worship* in *A Free Man's Worship* 1976. *Seems Madam? Nay, It Is* (1899) in *Why I Am Not a Christian* 1957, pp. 74–5 and 80; see also *What I Believe* (1925) and *Why I Am Not A Christian* (1927) 'in *Why I Am Not A Christian* 1957 pp. 21–6, 45–7 and 65. *The Conquest of Happiness* 1930 (1979 edn) pp. 78ff and 176–9. *On Education* 1926 (1927 edn) pp. 4–27, 48–53, 62–6, 118–29, 190–2, 218–22, 225–6, 238, 243–4 and 248–9. *Has Religion Made A Useful Contribution to Civilization?* 1930 pp. 10, 17, 24, 25 and 26. *German Social Democracy* 1896 pp. v–vi, 1–40 and 130–66. *Roads to Freedom* 1918 (1977 edn) pp. 15–21, 25–6, 79–100, 109–30, 139 and 143–54. *Principles of Social Reconstruction* 1916 pp. 5–6, 12, 18, 23, 25, 37–40, 96, 113–19, 131, 133, 138–42, 147, 155–7, 177–8, 184–5, 188–90, 203–23 and 245–8. *Our Knowledge of the External World* 1914 pp. v–50 and 236–7. *The Problems of Philosophy* 1912 pp. 9, 24–6 and 220–50. *Marriage and Morals* 1929 (1976 edn) pp. 34–8, 66–7, 80, 87, 103 and 194–8. *The Essence of Religion* in *Hibbert Journal* 1912–13, esp. pp. 49–50, 54–8 and 61. *Human Society in Ethics and Politics* 1954 pp. 196–7 and 221. *War and Non-Resistance* (August 1915) p. 42 and *An Appeal to the Intellectuals of Europe* (April 1915) pp. 1–16, both in *Justice in Wartime* 1915. *Political Ideals* 1917 (1963 edn) pp. 43–4, 63 and 70. *The Practice and Theory of Bolshevism* 1920 pp. 5–7, 15–22, 34–7, 42, 72, 80, 100–9, 115 and 170. *The Problem of China* 1922 (1966 edn) pp. 11–17, 42, 65, 70, 76, 79, 84, 166, 169, 176, 190, 195, 204 and 250. In collaboration with Dora Russell, *The Prospects of Industrial Civilization* 1923 esp. pp. 8, 117–18, 155 and 246–8. *Religion and Science* 1935 (1978 edn) pp. 246–52. See also *Authority and the Individual* 1949 and *The Impact of Science on Society* 1952; *Our Sexual Ethics* (1936) in *Why I Am Not A Christian* 1957 pp. 115–122; *The Scientific Outlook* 1931 *passim*; *Icarus or the Future of Science* 1924 pp. 12–17; *A Critical Exposition of the Philosophy of Leibnitz* 1900 pp. 1–8, 173–201; *Introduction to Mathematical Philosophy* 1919; *Pragmatism* (1909) in *Philosophical Essays* 1910 pp. 87ff; *Freedom and Organisation 1814–1914* 1934; and *Free Thought and Official Propaganda* 1922 pp. 9–39.

p. 288

For Mark Rutherford see *Autobiography* (14th edn) pp. 138–9; for Karl Pearson see *The Ethics of Free Thought* 1887 (1901 edn) p. ix; for Julian Huxley see *The Humanist Frame* 1961 pp. 38–45.

pp. 290–7 (Patmore)

E. Gosse *Coventry Patmore* 1905 pp. 20, 176, 181–2, 195, 205–7, 217–18, 234–6, 238 and 249–58. B. Champneys *Memoirs and Correspondence of Coventry Patmore* 2 vols. 1900: vol. i pp. 72–3, 106–9 and 171–2 and esp. chs. v, vi, xi, xiii, xiv and xv, vol. ii pp. 6, 22–8, 80–6, 105, 107, 111, 143–9 and esp. chs. i–iii. *Lowe's Edinburgh Magazine* 1846 pp. 169–77, 417–19, 425 and 497–503. *Swedenborgiana* April 1858 pp. 356–9 and de Biran's *Pensées* July 1860 pp. 146–7, both in *National Review*. *Emmanuel Swedenborg* in *Fraser's Magazine* February 1857 pp. 174–82. *The Ethics of Art* in *British Quarterly Review* 1849 pp. 445–8 and 462. For Tennyson see *The Palladian* July 1850 pp. 94–100; *North British Review* 1848 pp. 43ff and 1859 pp. 148ff; and *Edinburgh Review* 1855 pp. 498ff. For some of Patmore's contributions to the *North British Review* see *North British Review* 1848 pp. 43–72, 1849 pp. 115–16 and 135, 1850 pp. 532–6 and 551–5, 1852 pp. 394–5 and 418–20, 1853–4 pp. 81–8 and 105, 1858 vol. ii pp. 124–49 and 512–16 and 1859 pp. 340–1; see also *Edinburgh Review* 1851 pp. 365–70 and 1856 pp. 339–46 and *Architects and Architecture* in *Fraser's Magazine* December 1852 pp. 653–5. *The Rod, The Root and The Flower* 1895 pp. 17, 49ff, 60, 149, 193 and 201. *Courage in Politics and Other Essays 1885–1896* 1921 pp. 9–18, 20–7, 46–50, 54–64, 70–83, 101–9, 110–14, 120, 129–30, 132–6 and 144–73. *Principle in Art* 1889 (1890 edn) pp. 3–5, 7–8, 11, 17, 31–66, 80–2, 92, 100–1, 110, 120–1, 134–5, 151–2 and 210. *Religio Poetae* 1893 pp. 19–21, 27–44, 58–61, 63–70, 102–3, 121–31, 138–53, 160, 213–29 and ch. xxiii. Hopkins to Patmore 4 June 1886 and Patmore to Hopkins 5 January 1884, 26 July 1884 and 17 June 1886, all in C. C. Abbott (ed.) *Further Letters of Gerard Manley Hopkins including his Correspondence with Coventry Patmore* 1956 pp. 350–1, 356 and 366–9. For Patmore's autobiography see Champneys 1900 vol. ii pp. 40ff.

pp. 297–303 (Mallock)

Social Equality 1882 pp. 3–7, 9–10, 13–19, 48–99, 102ff, 113ff, 133–4, 153, 166, 174–83, 213, 248, 250–62 and 269–74. *The Philosophy of Conservatism* in *Nineteenth Century* November 1880 pp. 726–7; *Radicalism and the Working Classes* September 1883 p. 129 and *The Radicalism of the Market Place* June 1883 pp. 509–15 and 522–3, both in *National Review*. For Mallock's politics between 1880 and 1885 see also *Radicalism: A Familiar Colloquy* in *Nineteenth Century* March 1881; and *Progress and Poverty* January 1883, *Socialism in England* October 1883, *The Statistics of Agitation* January 1884, *Radicalism and the People* March 1883, *Conservatism and Socialism* January 1884, *The Landlords and the National Income* February 1884 and *How to Popularise Unpopular Political Truths* October 1885, all in *National Review; The Functions of Wealth* February 1882 and *Civilization and Equality: A Familiar Colloquy* October 1881, both in *Contemporary Review*. *Studies of Contemporary Superstition* 1895 pp. 22, 96–108, 111, 114–16, 122, 127, 128–36, 183 and 196–8.

Aristocracy and Evolution 1898 pp. v–vi, 5, 7–8, 122–4, 131, 149–50, 153, 209, 224, 227, 260–2, 341–2 and Book IV ch. iii. For Mallock's view of the rôle of literature in public thought see *Lucretius* 1878 ch. v; *Mr John Morley and 'Progressive Radicalism'* in *Quarterly Review* 1889 pp. 249ff; *Lord Lytton and Poetry* in *Fortnightly Review* 1892 pp. 795ff; and *The Conditions of Great Poetry* in *Quarterly Review* 1900 pp. 156ff. For Mallock on Positivism see *Atheism and the Value of Life* 1884 pp. 74–94, 212–13, 227, 240–58, 264, 288 and 303 and *Is Life Worth Living?* 1879 pp. 6, 59, 62–5, 73–9, 94, 111, 135–8, 142–9, 150–7 and ch. III. *Religion as a Credible Doctrine* 1903 pp. 14, 19–21, 184, 217, 223–9, 235–6, 242, 249, 250–1, 259, 260–2, 271 and chs. III–X *passim*. For Mallock on Tennyson see *Atheism and the Value of Life* 1884 pp. 86, 96–100, 112, 114, 119, 130, 135 and 141. *Doctrine and Doctrinal Disruption* 1900 (1908 edn) pp. 13, 16–17, 51, 56–8, 109, 140, 161–2, 165–72, 174, 191–2, 199 and 241. *Lucretius* 1878 pp. 5–6 and 152–72. *Memoirs of Life and Literature* 1920 p. 144. See also *The New Republic* 1877, *The New Paul and Virginia* 1878, *The Veil of the Temple* 1904. See also *General Gordon's Message* in *Fortnightly Review* July 1884 pp. 57ff.

pp. 311–21 (Chesterton)
St George for England (1906) in D. Collins (ed.) *The Glass Walking Stick and Other Essays* 1955 pp. 65–9. *The Ball and the Cross* 1909 (1910 edn) pp. 16, 44, 64, 177 and 335. *The Defendant* 1901 pp. 8, 13, 16, 25–6, 34–5, 54, 58–9, 70 and 159. *G. F. Watts* 1904 pp. 2, 3–7, 13–18, 22–3, 30, 34, 53, 60, 65–6, 82, 143 and 153. *Robert Browning* 1903 pp. 16–17, 73, 86, 89–90, 100, 110–11, 114, 130, 151, 156, 165 and 171. *George Bernard Shaw* 1909 pp. 17–24, 57, 72–86, 91, 106–7, 174, 203–6, 246, 251 and 255. *Heretics* 1905 (1914 edn) pp. 12–14, 47–49, 59, 66–70, 74, 97, 107, 113, 180–6, 190–1, 228 and 299. *The Voice of Shelley* (1905) and *Eulogy of Robin Hood* (1903) in D. Collins (ed.) *The Apostle and the Wild Duck* 1975 pp. 131ff and 138–40. *The Patriotic Idea* 1904 pp. 3–5, and 40–2. *Twelve Types* 1902 pp. 63, 68–70, 80–3, 93–101, 117, 121–2, 125, 127, 139, 141, 145, 151–2, 156, 168, 172–6 and 185. *Professor Bradley on Shakespearian Tragedy* (1904) and *Milton v. Shakespeare* (1907) in D. Collins (ed.) *Chesterton and Shakespeare* 1971 pp. 139–42 and 159–69. *The Victorian Age in Literature* 1913 *passim* but esp. pp. 204–6. *Tolstoy* 1903 pp. 1–5. Introduction to M. Gorky, *Creatures That Once Were Men* 1905 pp. vi, vii and xiii. *Sentimental Literature* (1901) pp. 11ff and *The Philosophy of Islands* (1903) pp. 119–24 in D. Collins (ed.) *The Spice of Life* 1964. *The Everlasting Man* 1925 (1936 edn) pp. 97, 200, 208, 220–21, 223–7, 242, 285 and 296–303. For Chesterton on the 1914 war see *The Barbarism of Berlin* 1914; *Letters to an Old Garibaldian* 1915; and *The Crimes of England* 1915. For Chesterton on eugenics see *Eugenics and Other Evils* 1922. *Orthodoxy* 1908 (1961 edn) pp. 17–29, 60, 63–4, 70–6, 83–93, 99, 101, 113–15, 118–20, 126, 136–7, 139–40, 145–6, 148–51, 156 and 158–9. *Charles Dickens* 1906 (1913 edn) pp. 17–18, 33, 39–41, 52, 58, 68–72, 84, 99, 119, 122, 133, 166, 173, 186–7, 190–1 and 220. *Divorce versus Democracy* 1916 pp. 6–7, 10–11 and 13–14. *What I Saw in America* 1922 pp. 270–308. *The Superstitions of the Sceptic* 1925 pp. 16–18. Contr. to C. Gore (ed.) *The Return of Christendom* 1922 pp. 250–1. Contr. to F. Woodlock, *Modernism in the Christian Church* 1925 p. 111. *The Resurrection of Rome*

1930 pp. 248–58. *The New Jerusalem* 1920 pp. 226–53. For Chesterton on Ireland see *inter alia Irish Impressions* 1919 pp. 5, 30–5, 64–5 and 224. See also *The Thing* 1929 esp. pp. 7–19; *The Well and the Shallows* 1935; *What's Wrong with the World* 1910 (1912 edn) pp. 16–48; introduction to *John Ruskin Poems* 1908 pp. vi–xvi; introduction to *Book of Job* 1907 pp. v–xxiii; introduction to *Carlyle Past and Present* 1909 pp. v–xii; *A Sermon Against Pride* in *If I Were a Preacher* 1929 pp. 9–23; *William Blake* 1910; *W. M. Thackeray* 1903 pp. 1–11; *Charles Dickens* 1903 pp. 1–17; with R. Garnett, *Tennyson as an Intellectual Force* 1906 pp. xxix–xliii; and Maisie Ward, *Gilbert Keith Chesterton* 1944 pp. 56–69 and 70–6.

pp. 321–30 (Belloc)
Danton 1899 pp. ix, 18, 34, 39, 282–307 and 315–17. *The French Revolution* 1911 pp. vii–viii, 13–17, 23–9, 34–7, 217–31 and 250–3. For Belloc's view of contemporary English politics see *The Free Press* 1918 *passim*; (with Cecil Chesterton) *The Party System* 1911 pp. 8–9; *The House of Commons and Monarchy* 1920 pp. 46, 178–9, 182, 187–8 and esp. chs. iv and vii; and *The Servile State* 1912 pp. 49, 53–4, 57, 61, 66–7, 76–7, 83, 91, 99, 106 and 183. *The Catholic and the War* 1940 pp. 10, 17 and 30. *The Jews* 1922 pp. 3–13, 22, 44–51, 53–9, 93, 101, 105, 112, 126–33, 138 and 174 and ch. xii generally. Robert Speight, *The Life of Hilaire Belloc* 1957 esp. ch. 17; see also Robert Speight, *Letters from Hilaire Belloc* 1958 p. 28. Preface to J. R. Lowell, *Poems* 1908 in J. A. de Chantigny, *Hilaire Belloc's Prefaces* 1971 pp. 124–6. *Open Letter on the Decay of Faith* 1906 pp. 3–13. *The Great Heresies* 1938 pp. 3–22 and 240–74. *Catholic Social Reform versus Socialism* 1922 p. 7. *Europe and the Faith* 1920 pp. 5–6, 9–14, 94, 154, 227–30, 257, 317 and 329. *The Crisis of Our Civilization* 1937 pp. 3–6 and 230ff. *The Crusade* 1937 p. 305. *Pascal's Provincial Letters* 1921 *passim*. *Milton* 1935 esp. pp. 287–309. *The Case of Dr Coulton* 1938 *passim*. *A General Sketch of the European War* 1915 vol. i pp. 32–3. *On the Place of Gilbert Chesterton in English Letters* 1940 *passim*. *Essays of a Catholic Layman in England* 1931 esp. pp. 15–17, 20, 80–1, 195–236, 267–83, 301–5 and 317–19. *Robespierre* 1901 pp. x–21 and 366. *Marie Antoinette* 1909 pp. 8–10. *A Companion to Mr Wells's Outline of History* 1926 pp. 1, 8, 43–6, 113–14 and *passim* and *Mr Belloc Still Objects* 1926 pp. vii–viii. *The Catholic Church and History* 1927 pp. 102–5. *Oliver Cromwell* 1927 pp. 9–17, 39–40 and 70. *How the Reformation Happened* 1928 pp. 11–15. J. Lingard and H. Belloc *The History of England* vol. xi 1915 pp. vii, xii and 455–7.

pp. 330–6 (Greene)
With Elizabeth Bowen and V. S. Pritchett, *Why Do I Write?* 1948 pp. 30–2 and 46–51. *Journey Without Maps* 1936 (1980 edn) pp. 116, 128, 147–50, 224, 243–4 and 248. *The Power and the Glory* 1940 (1971 edn) *passim*. *The Lawless Roads* 1939 (1947 edn) pp. 21, 28–9, 34, 36–7, 43, 49, 62, 121, 133, 137, 175 and 184. *The End of the Affair* 1951 (1975 edn) *passim*. *The Heart of the Matter* 1948 (1951 edn) *passim*. *A Burnt-Out Case* 1960 *passim*. *A Sort of Life* 1971 (1972 edn) pp. 20–38, 49–68, 81–7, 92–7, 117–22 and 134–8. *Collected Essays* 1969 (Penguin edn) pp. 135–40, 372–5, 376–401, 402–4, 405–13 and 413–19. For Greene's opinions as a reviewer in the 1930s see the accounts of Leonard

Barnes 7 June 1935, Rochester, 9 August 1935, Douai 1 November 1935, Virginia Woolf 17 June 1938, Naomi Mitchison 6 October 1939, Ford Madox Ford 17 November 1939, Alfred Noyes 24 November 1939 and J. B. Priestley 13 December 1940, all in *The Spectator*. See also Greene's accounts of Conrad (1935 and 1937) pp. 111–15, Henry James (1933 and 1936) pp. 19–40 and *The Spectator* 26 April 1935, Rolfe (1934 and 1935) pp. 102–9, Samuel Butler (1934) pp. 134–47 and Ford Madox Ford (1939) pp. 98–100, all in *The Lost Childhood* 1951 (Penguin edn). For Greene on Havelock Ellis (1940), pp. 154–6, Buchan (1941) pp. 119–21, Eric Gill (1941) pp. 151–3 and Herbert Read (1941) pp. 157–63, see *The Lost Childhood* 1951 (Penguin edn).

pp. 336–9 (Dawson)

For Dawson as a prophet see J. J. Malloy ed. *The Dynamics of World History* 1957 and J. J. Malloy *Specific Programmes for the Study of Western Culture* in C. Dawson *The Crisis of Western Education* 1961 pp. 205–24. *The Spirit of the Oxford Movement* 1933 (1945 edn) pp. 7–11 and 116–26. *The Chesterton Review* May 1983 p. 113. *The Dividing of Christendom* 1965 (1971 edn) pp. 3–17. *The Historical Reality of Christian Culture* 1960 (1965 edn) pp. 20–3, 34–43, 78–87 and 112–20. For Dawson's view of mediaeval history see *The Making of Europe* 1932 pp. xv–xxiv; *Mediaeval Religion* 1934 pp. 3–7, 31–3, 118–20, 124–5 and 154; *Religion and the Rise of Western Culture* 1950 pp. 3–19: *Progress and Religion* 1929 pp. 191–2, 196, 198–202, 205–9, 212, 243, 249 and esp. chs. iv and vii. *Beyond Politics* 1939 (1941 edn) pp. 5–11, 26–31, 57 and 119–34. *Religion and the Modern State* 1935 (1938 edn) pp. vii–xxii, 113–25 and 128–53. *The Sword of the Spirit* 1939 pp. 10–11. *The Modern Dilemma* 1931 pp. 92–3 and 100–13. *Europe – A Society of Peoples* 1946 pp. 4–16. *Religion and Culture* (Gifford Lectures of 1947) 1948 pp. 8–9, 15–21, 27–34, 44, 49–50, 59, 66–8, 106, 110–11, 126, 132, 135, 144, 149–50, 167, 176, 179–81, 193, 206–9 and 214–18. *The Movement of World Revolution* 1959 pp. 144, 155–8 and 174–9. *The Judgement of the Nations* 1942 pp. 4–5. *Christianity and the New Age* 1931 pp. 14–22, 48–9 and 95–101. *Enquiries into Religion and Culture* 1933 pp. 3–17, 47–63, 139–56 and 261. *The Age of the Gods* 1928 pp. xii–xx.

pp. 339–45 (Copleston)

The History of Philosophy: Relativism and Recurrence in *Philosophers and Philosophies* 1976 pp. 17–27. For the religions of the world see *Religion and the One* 1982 and *Philosophies and Cultures* 1980. *Friedrich Nietzsche, Philosopher of Culture* 1942 pp. vii–xii, 58–62, 75–87, 93–100, 107–16, 130–5, 140–9, 152–5, 160–2, 177, 184, 201–3 and esp. chs. vii and ix. *Arthur Schopenhauer, Philosopher of Pessimism* 1946 pp. 5–6, 16, 75–95, 107–9, 145–7, 178–80 and 209–11. *A History of Philosophy* 1946 vol. i pp. v–vii, 1–11, 486–91 and 497–506, 1950 vol. ii pp. 1–12 and 552–65, 1953 vol. iii pp. 1–4, 11, 415–16 and 422–5, 1960 vol. iv pp. ix–xi, 1–11, 34, 41–3 and 60–2, 1960 vol. vi pp. ix, 393, 397–415, 434 and 436, 1963 vol. vii pp. 1–15, 18–31 and 422–41, 1966 vol. viii pp. ix–xi and 494–519 and 1975 vol. ix pp. ix–xvii and 250–71. *St. Thomas and Nietzsche* 1946 pp. 1–18. *Existentialism and Modern Man* 1948 pp. 6–7, 10, 20, 24, 27 and 28. *Religion and Philosophy* 1974 pp. vii–ix (1974) pp. 2–16, 20–5, 31–3, 39, 43–5, 48, 53, 56–7 and 91 (1969) and pp. 95–111 (1960–1). *Aquinas* 1955 pp. 15–69 and 235–55. *Contemporary British Philosophy* (1953) pp. 1–25, *Some Reflections on Logical Positivism* (1950) pp. 26–44, *Existentialism; Introductory* (1955) pp. 125–32 and 212–27, all in *Contemporary Philosophy* 1956.

Index of main names

DATE DUE
